The True Wallace Reid Story

by David W. Menefee

Foreword by Robert Osborne

WALLY: THE TRUE WALLACE REID STORY
©2011 DAVID W. MENEFEE

ALL RIGHTS RESERVED.

All rights reserved. No part of this book may be reproduced or distributed, in print, recorded, live or digital form, without express written permission of the copyright holder. However, excerpts of up to 500 words may be reproduced online if they include the following information, "This is an excerpt from Wally: The True Wallace Reid Story by David W. Menefee."

Published in the USA by:

BEARMANOR MEDIA
P.O. BOX 71426
ALBANY, GEORGIA 31708
www.BearManorMedia.com

All photographs and illustrations are from the personal collection of David W. Menefee, unless otherwise noted.

All program titles and program descriptions are used in editorial fashion with no intention of infringement of intellectual property rights.

ISBN-10: 1-59393-623-0 (alk. paper)
)ISBN-13: 978-1-59393-623-5 (alk. paper)

COPY EDITOR: DAVID W. MENEFEE

DESIGN AND LAYOUT: VALERIE THOMPSON

TABLE OF CONTENTS

ACKNOWLEDGMENTS . . . 1

FOREWORD . . . 2

INTRODUCTION . . . 6

BIOGRAPHY . . . 11

CHAPTER 1: HIS ONLY SON . . . 14

CHAPTER 2: THE WAYS OF FATE . . . 22

CHAPTER 3: MAKING GOOD . . . 31

CHAPTER 4: THE HEART O' THE HILLS . . . 44

CHAPTER 5: THE KISS . . . 59

CHAPTER 6: HEARTS AND HORSES . . . 78

CHAPTER 7: WHEN LUCK CHANGES . . . 92

CHAPTER 8: WOMEN AND ROSES . . . 110

CHAPTER 9: THE WALL OF MONEY . . . 130

CHAPTER 10: THE MAN WITHIN . . . 151

CHAPTER 11: WHO SO DIGGETH A PIT . . . 168

CHAPTER 12: A MODERN SNARE . . . 193

CHAPTER 13: OVER THE LEDGE . . . 205

CHAPTER 14: THE WHEEL OF LIFE . . . 226

CHAPTER 15: THE HOUSE OF SILENCE . . . 242

EPILOGUE . . . 272

PORTRAIT GALLERY ... 283

FILMOGRAPHY ... 317

BIBLIOGRAPHY ... 476

INDEX ... 500

ACKNOWLEDGMENTS

I want to thank my parents, Eunice and Doyle Menefee, for teaching me to have faith in Jesus. He led me to the kind assistance of the following contributors in the order in which they assisted. Without them, this book would have been impossible:

Lois Welborn Peyton

The staff of the Dallas Public Central Library
Fine Arts Department

Richard J. Maturi

Phil Alberton

Mike Hawks

Ronald Raburn

The staff of the Margaret Herrick Library
at the Academy of Motion Picture Arts and Sciences

Alice and Peter Gowland

Christopher J. Davis

Ben Ohmart

Valerie Thompson

Chris Macaulay

Foreword
by Robert Osborne

At last, a book about Wallace Reid!

For as long as I have been aware of movies and sprocket holes, I've been aware of Wallace Reid, but only in headline type quantities: Silent screen movie star! Clean-cut all-American idol! Career ruined by drugs! Dead by age 31! Bereaved-widow movie star Dorothy Davenport begins radio show defiantly declaring "This is Mrs. Wallace Reid!," a moment from life (or so it's always been said) borrowed by screenwriter William A. Wellman for his 1937 "A Star is Born" (and later also the final line in George Cukor's 1954 version).

But beyond those few word and images, so little has ever been written about Wallace Reid that for the past 80-plus years he's remained one of the great mystery figures of Hollywood's past. Volumes have been written about others within the film industry arc who've shown brightly and had exceedingly complicated lives and tragic histories—Harlow, Lombard, Dean, and Monroe high on the list, but also many from Wallace Reid's era, including, of course, Valentino, Fatty Arbuckle, Mack Sennett, and Mabel Normand, who have become such cultural icons they've either been the basis for movie bio-pics (such as Valentino and Arbuckle) or Broadway musicals (Arbuckle, Sennett, and Normand). Yet to my knowledge, this is the first book which really covers in detail the story of the sadly-fated Reid, who was one of the biggest, brightest stars of them all.

One reason, of course, that Reid's work has been so overlooked is because so many of his films have been lost to us. This gap was partially filled and Reid's name was briefly back in the news in late 2010 when ten digitally-preserved copies of previously lost or unavailable American silent films were presented to the Library of

Congress by Russian film archive Gosfilmofond, where they had been stored for more than eighty years since their initial release. They represent the first of a batch of some 200 silent films long thought to be lost forever, but which now will eventually be repatriated by the Russian archive. Two of those among the first ten star Wallace Reid: *You're Fired* (1919) and *Valley of the Giants* (1919), and with their rediscovery new light is able to be shed on his work.

As this book explains, *Valley of the Giants* is of particular interest because when the cast and crew were filming exterior scenes for that film in the wilds of the Sierra Mountains, a devastating train wreck severely wounded many on board. Unlike today, when a production would immediately be shut down in such a chaotic situation and the injured actors hospitalized, in 1919 Wallace Reid was expected to, and did, go on working as soon as his head wounds were bandaged. To keep the cuts on his face from interfering, he was instructed to turn away from the cameras. It was that day that this strong, stalwart, able, healthy man began being administered the morphine treatments which eventually destroyed his life and led to his untimely and tragic death only a few years later.

Unfortunately for people like me who've always been fascinated by Wallace Reid's story and eager to see his work, only a few of his many films survive, making any reliable judgment of his acting, writing, and directorial talent virtually impossible. Many writers have touched on his life, but the true measure of his appeal has, unfortunately, remained a deep, dark mystery.

Certainly, those who knew him well and worked alongside Reid have had only positive things to say about him. It's also a mark of his stature that the most celebrated directors of the silent screen era cast him in their films, most not just once but many times. The legendary D. W. Griffith was the first to feature him in a film and continued featuring Reid in numerous movies which Griffith either directed or supervised including *The Birth of a Nation, Intolerance, The Avenging Conscience, Old Heidelberg,* and *Enoch Arden.* Reid also appeared in films by directors of high stature such as Cecil B. De Mille, William DeMille, Allan Dwan, Donald Crisp, and James Cruze. Reid's leading ladies also included many of the greats: Lillian Gish, Dorothy Gish, Mae Marsh, Geraldine Farrar, Blanche Sweet, and Gloria Swanson.

Conclusion: this fellow with the tarnished reputation must have been delivering the goods or people of that caliber wouldn't have worked with him to the extent that they did.

Hopefully in the coming years, more Wallace Reid films will be rediscovered, and we'll be able to see first-hand and finally understand why audiences around the world clamored for Wallace Reid as enthusiastically as they greeted any new film in which they could see Mary Pickford, Charlie Chaplin, Doug Fairbanks, and/or Rudolph Valentino. Until then, we have this book, which enthusiastically covers Reid's life and career in detail, accompanied by many photos which further bring the storybook life of Wallace Reid into sharp focus.

For that, thank you, Dave Menefee.

ROBERT OSBORNE
PRIMETIME HOST
TURNER CLASSIC MOVIES

Introduction

Wallace Reid was a talented musician, singer, writer, film director, and painter, but the world made a "matinee idol" out of him. The public demanded stardom from him because of his rare combination of good looks, hard work, and intelligence. God ironically bestowed a handsome face and a strapping figure in the cards he handed Wally, but a marked card was in the deck, and he did not realize the consequences of playing that card.

Many people believed that he was the handsomest man in the movies, handsome in a thoroughly masculine way. With regular features, broad shoulders, and long legs, he was the athletic type. Had he only been spared intelligence, he might have been content to be nothing more than a "matinee idol" with fame dogging his every step, but he was not a Narcissus. He was grounded enough to realize that fame based on good looks was little more than a fleeting phenomenon.

". . . I'm in the same class with a Follies girl," he once said to his friend, Herb Howe. "When I lose my face and figure, I'm gone."

His life was crowded. At various times, he earned a living as a cowboy, civil engineer, reporter, assistant editor of an automobile magazine, motion picture cameraman, motion picture director, scenario writer, stunt man, stage actor, and a movie star. The son of Hal Reid, a noted and prolific playwright, he was favored with the heritage of genius and personal charm that won him hosts of friends. Likeable, versatile, and intensely human, he flashed into public favor in an astonishingly short period of time during an era when people first went to the movies. As the motion picture art emerged from infancy, Wally crowded more life experiences into his few years than those reflected in any of the characters he portrayed so engagingly before the camera.

A movie star by the time he was twenty-one years old, Wally possessed the traits that fit into productions abounding in wholesome situations and clean humor. He captivated the public's fancy until he became one of the best-known and most affectionately thought-of actors in Hollywood. He was also among the first-born of motion pictures. For many people, their first experience seeing a motion picture was a film featuring him.

Wally was a famous star, who rose in majestic splendor during the filming of *The Birth of a Nation*, grew in brightness with the making of *Across the Continent*, and reached the crowded zenith of the motion picture sky with *The Affairs of Anatol*. It might be more fitting to compare his career to a meteor flaring up in the early evening sky and streaking across the heavens until burning out before dawn.

On Thursday, January 18, 1923, the last reel in Wally's life story turned on its spindle, and the last few yards of celluloid flickered onto the screen the words, "The End." The final few frames clicked through the gate and then flung wildly around the twirling reel. Wallace Reid, idol of millions of male and female screen fans, had died. The spectacular career of a gifted man who caused millions to laugh and cry ended. His end came in a secluded room following almost unmentionable suffering.

For about a dozen years, millions of movie devotees applauded Wallace Reid's acting. In 1923 at the time of his death, popularity polls proved that he had a larger personal following than any actor in Hollywood, with the exception of the phenomenal Mary Pickford and Charlie Chaplin. Wally's millions of admirers were powerless to help him when the icy fingers of the drug demon reached out and clutched hold of him.

It must be said to his everlasting credit that once he faced up to his predicament, he began a noble fight against his enemy. He determined to free himself, or die. So far as it is known, while he remained conscious, he refused even a diminished dose of the drug that would have eased the racking pain in his body. Wally could have gradually tapered off the drug until he reduced his daily consumption to a minimum, but he preferred to rise up against the monster that had him in its grasp and tear from it in one desperate effort, or die trying. He lost his life, but there are many who believe that he saved his soul. Wally's best friend other than Dorothy, his wife, and his mother and father, was Charles "Buddy" Post, who was by his side when he died.

"Wally was just a big mischievous kid," Buddy frankly admitted. "This line has been spoken and written of Wally many, many times before his tragic death and after. I may say that from all outward appearances, Wally appeared to everyone as just a big, wholesome, kind-hearted boy. Everyone liked him, a few spoke of him as a loved friend, and a very few worshipped him. In the latter group were his parents, his young son, Billy, his daughter Betty, and his devoted wife, Dorothy . . . ."

To the rest of us, Wally's statistics are amazing:
- He wrote at least twenty known films between 1912 and 1916.
- He directed at least fifty-four known films between 1912 and 1917.
- He appeared in more than 204 accredited roles in motion pictures.
- All his films were silent; he never made a talking picture.
- He never made a sound recording, even though he was said to be a wonderful singer and once fronted his own band.
- He was prominently featured in D. W. Griffith's *The Birth of a Nation*, which many consider to be of the best silent films, and certainly, the most famous and controversial.
- He loved to paint, an inherited ability that ran in his family; J. Wilson MacDonald, the renowned sculptor, was his great-uncle.
- He played every musical instrument in an orchestra.
- He only married once.
- In a 1923 poll at the time of his death, he was voted The Most Popular Leading Man in motion pictures.

Today, it is difficult to understand how a superstar can be at the top of the movie business and then become virtually forgotten within a few decades. In Wally's case, part of the reason is because his films were all silent. When many forgotten movie stars of the 1930s and 1940s found new popularity in the 1950s with the emergence of television, silent pictures were largely left in their cans and seldom broadcast to a generation fascinated with the sight *and sound* that was possible with broadcast technology. The parade passed by most of those men and women who were only in silent pictures, and it did not return until decades later when a newfound appreciation and respect for the art of the silent cinema emerged. By that time, most of Wally's early films had been irrevocably damaged by neglect, destroyed by the very studios that made them, or accidentally lost to nitrate film decomposition.

He was not the only popular silent movie star that found their work destroyed by the ravages of time, the deterioration of nitrate film stock, or the deliberate obliteration of prints and negatives by shortsighted studios. The list of stars that have suffered scrapped and largely forgotten careers includes Florence Lawrence, Gene Gautier, Francis X. Bushman, Alla Nazimova, Dorothy Gish, and Theda Bara, to name but a few. Wally's personal self-destruction was horrible, but the greatest misfortune that he suffered was that most of his life's work has been lost.

Wally's life was much more than those last two years. This author has taken careful steps to chronicle the intimate, personal story of a brave man's fight against drug abuse, but this book also attempts to reveal Wally, the man, and rediscover Wallace Reid, the movie star. I have also tried to explain why he was such an important figure to movie audiences during the first two decades of the twentieth century.

This book is in three parts: a Biography, a Portrait Gallery, and a Filmography. The Biography draws from a variety of sources to reassemble a jigsaw puzzle portrait of the man as he was perceived in his time by those who knew him. The Portrait Gallery shows how photographers captured Wally's essence with the art of portraiture. The Filmography details each known film, and then examines the feature-length films from the perspective of contemporary, national, and local critics to show how they considered them at the time of their original release.

"Wallace Reid had inherited his father's gift for storytelling, had a keen sense of humor, a good singing voice, played the saxophone and piano, and was altogether the most magnetic, charming, personable, handsome young man I've ever met. And the most co-operative," wrote Jesse Lasky in his book, *I Blow My Own Horn.*

This is Wally's story.

BIOGRAPHY

James Halleck "Hal" Reid, Wally's father, and one of America's most prolific playwrights.

Four portraits of James Halleck "Hal" Reid, Wally's father.

Chapter 1
HIS ONLY SON

During the Revolutionary War, Lieutenant Colonel James Reid and his son, John Reid, founded a homestead on lush land situated in Ohio between the towns of Cedarville and Zenia. Hugh M. Reid, a Professor of Dentistry in the Ohio Dental College, fathered James Halleck Reid. People called him "Hal."

As a boy, Hal showed talent as a writer. As a young man, he found working a reporter's beat at the *Cincinnati Times Star* very much to his liking. His editor was Charles P. Taft, one of the brothers of William Howard Taft, a former United States President. Through his association with the newspaper, Hal met and became friends with several notables, including John Hay and Theodore Roosevelt.

From 1882 to 1887, Hal was married to Mae Withers, a short, five-year relationship about which little is known other than that there was one child.

Newspapers could not contain Hal's imagination. He accepted assignments whether they were of interest to him or not, and he always turned in appropriate columns with no byline, but the dramatic stage with its seemingly limitless opportunities for excitement and emotion held Hal fascinated. When he was away from newspaper assignments, he wrote many plays, including *At the Old Cross Roads, The Knobs of Tennessee, The Street Singer, Human Hearts, The Night Before Christmas, The Confession, The Peddler, The Little Red Schoolhouse,* and *Prince of the World.*

Bertha Bell Westbrook, a St. Louis socialite and aspiring actress, met Hal, and in 1889, two years after Hal's divorce from his first wife, he and Bertha were married in Kansas City at the home of a Southern Methodist Episcopal minister. From there, the young couple moved to Chicago, and then from there, to Cincinnati. The young Reids followed their dream and made small dents in various northern cities with Hal's successfully produced plays in various productions. He was considered one of Broadway's most promising young playwrights.

Bertha appeared together with him in various roles, sometimes billed as Bertha Belle Westbrook. In *The Two Orphans*, he played the rascal, Jacques Frochard, and she impersonated the pathetic, blind girl, Louise. She was so good in the role that Hal wrote a play especially for her, *A Daughter of the Confederacy*, in which she again showed her talent portraying another blind girl. That play ran for many years under various producers and gave many other budding actresses an opportunity to wring tears from an audience. Success gave the young couple the clout to form their own company, and from that time on, they never played in any works other than those written by Hal, and every one of them found favor with audiences.

A little over two years into their marriage, Bertha became pregnant. She used the occasion to rally her creative powers and merge them with her strong belief in Christian Science. Bertha gave herself over to what she believed was the immeasurable power of pre-natal influence. She conscientiously surrounded herself with pictures of beautiful children and studied them intently to imprint their fair countenances onto her baby. She organized her thoughts by reading good literature in an effort to force her baby to absorb their attributes. She imprinted faith in God and soulful contemplation into the child's psyche by spending hours in deep religious meditation. To instill musical talent into her child, she practiced classical music. She exercised her talent for drawing and painting in a determined effort to instill the baby with talent. For nine months, she encircled her growing newborn with as many positive influences as she could find. The result of her efforts finally paid off.

On April 15, 1892, William Wallace Reid was "born in a trunk" in St. Louis, Missouri. He weighed eleven and three-quarter pounds, and he first saw the world through large, bright blue eyes. If Bertha's prenatal efforts were true to form, she expected the boy to be attuned to fine literature, have deep religious convictions, be

Broadway at 42nd Street in New York in 1898, when Bertha and Hal were enjoying their first blush with theatrical success.

blessed with a profound musical talent, have the ability to draw and paint, and earn a reputation for being positive-minded. He was her only child, and she expected great things from him.

When he was seven months old, Wally could speak the words "Mamma," "Papa," and "Cotton-top," the nickname his parents gave him for his flaxen hair. His first years were spent with his parents on trains rolling from town to town across America. The up-and-coming playwright and his actress-wife found work wherever it could be obtained in small towns and big cities. They were thrilled when a job came to appear in New York, the epicenter of the theatrical world.

In the 1890s, New York theaters were filled with glamorously dressed men and women. Women wore gowns with bell-shaped skirts and long sleeves that were narrow at the bottom and puffed with leg-of-mutton tops. Gaslights were giving way to the incandescent glow of Edison's new and remarkable electric light. New York was a far different place compared to what it is today. There were no means of transportation around the city other than noisy, smelly trains, stagecoaches, horse-drawn trolleys and carriages, and bicycles. The principal residences were in Washington Square and its vicinity. Delmonico's had attained wide popularity as the place to go after an opera was given at the Academy of Music, and aristocrats flocked there after seeing a show. Any entertainment was given without the use of microphones, and actors had to project to the upper rows of a balcony by the sheer volume of their voices.

In New York in the late 1800s, there were no skyscrapers. Trees still stood on both sides of Broadway. The main avenue through the East Side was the Bowery, on which many popular theaters were situated. 14th Street was considered uptown. Brownstone houses mushroomed everywhere, and to own one was considered a mark of moderate wealth. A new play was often trotted out to unsophisticated audiences along the east coast for years before it made its way into New York. When a play found favor with audiences, it was performed by any number of traveling troupes once it had left the big city. Sarah Bernhardt, Eleonora Duse, and Helena Modjeska were the three great actresses of the "Gay Nineties." Musical farces and extravaganzas were beginning to grow in prominence, while old-time melodramas were giving way to modern problem plays. Swashbuckling adventure stories with their romantic matinee idol heroes were popular. New York boasted thirty-nine legitimate theaters, and they were filled at most performances. William Gillette scored a run of 216 performances in *Too Much Johnson*, and Fanny Davenport introduced her *Gismonda* to great success.

In New York, Hal and Bertha found roles together in a revival of *The Phoenix*. While they were on stage each evening and during matinees, four-year-old Wally had to be quietly kept in a seat just beyond the footlights where, unknown to audiences, Bertha could see him from the corner of her eye. He knew no difference between what his parents did on stage or off.

"When I came upon the stage as the little flower girl," Bertha recalled in 1923, "much to the delight of the audience, Wally shouted gleefully, 'Oh, there's my mamma!'" It was difficult for her to keep a straight face and maintain character while her son affectionately called to her from the front rows.

For Hal, life as a playwright had dry spells and triumphs. Edmund Collier, a famous actor in that time, approached him to write *Human Hearts*, a new play tailored to his talents, but Collier died before the play could be produced.

"I carried the manuscript of *Human Hearts* up and down Broadway for three years looking for a producer," Hal remembered. "From office to office, I trudged with no success. Finally, one rainy day, I found the Harms Brothers, D. W. Truss, Gus Williams, and John T. Kelly seated in a room in Truss' office. I went in and asked them if they would listen to a play."

Rather than hear his work, they brushed him away, declining to listen to a word of it. Hal was desperate. His room and board were long overdue, and there was nothing to do but make a last-ditch appeal to their sympathy.

"I'll tell you what I will do," he argued. "Let me read it, and if I don't make you all cry real tears, you don't have to consider the play. If I do make you cry, you produce it."

They laughed, but they agreed to his proposition. Before he had finished reading the third act, he caught them all crying and reminded them of the agreement. They took on the fledgling playwright's work. The Harms Brothers and Truss made the production a big success. *Human Hearts* continued to run for the next twenty-seven years. Its success, along with Hal's other popular productions, sent lucrative royalties pouring in, and the Reids enjoyed a level of prosperity that had been unknown to them.

Wally had every advantage, but his playrooms were often the darkened wings behind brightly lit theater stages, and his nurseries were swaying train cars. He learned to read in his early youth, and he had favorite books at an age when most children were struggling to understand the captions on newspaper cartoons.

Sometimes, while Bertha and Hal were away on a particularly long road tour of a play, Wally was kept with his grandmother at her home in St. Louis, Missouri. On the afternoon of May 27, 1896 during one of those visits, his grandmother felt the air become stifling and unusually humid. A strange breeze stirred noticeably, yet the uncomfortable temperature seemed oddly pressured and heavy for early afternoon. She went to one of her two bay windows and gazed out only to discover that an ominous darkness had fallen over the city. A glance at the clock showed the time was 4:30 p.m.

As she continued to study the menacing and portentous clouds, they took on a greenish cast and were accompanied by rising winds forcing their onrushing current against the house. Within minutes, the blustery weather became an air stream roaring at thirty-seven miles an hour and escorted by vivid lightning flashes. Clearly, a major storm was about to erupt. She took another look back at Wally and saw that he was playing quietly on the floor, oblivious to her worries. She clutched her hands with dread when her fears over the first rumble of violent weather could no longer be disguised.

Wally glanced up from his playing, but his grandmother distracted him with soothing words and a practiced smile. Behind her forced grin, tension drew her face into troubled lines that she could barely hide. Each rumble of the impending storm brought wind gusts that sped to sixty, then seventy, and finally to more than eighty miles an hour. The window shutters vibrated wildly in response to the onslaught, and as they clattered, the anxious woman stood rigid in a nervous vigil at the bay window. Outside, vivid forks of lightning could be seen bolting from the churning, low-hanging ceiling of dismal, gray clouds where there had been sunshine minutes before.

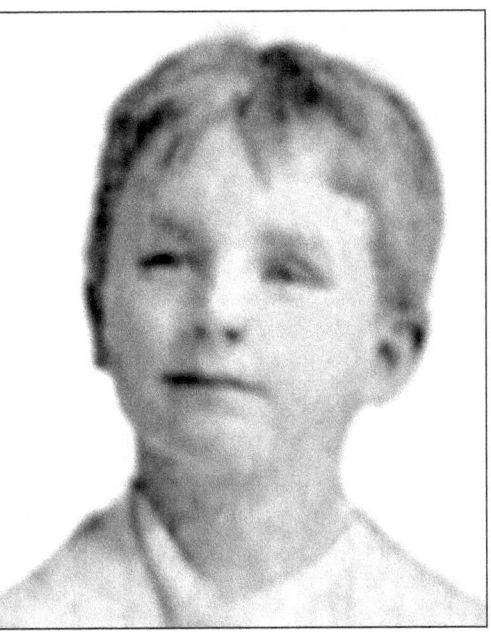
Wally at age four.

Minutes dragged by in what seemed like hours. The temperature fell rapidly, and as the clock inched nearer to 5:00 p.m., gray sheets of rain painted the western horizon in a thick, appalling wall of water that seemed to be encroaching nearer. Just outside, neighborhood trees were bending midway at their trunks, and scattered debris flew madly in all directions up the street. Time seemed to stand still, and then the tempest suddenly reached out and shook the house with a violence she had never felt. In the next moment, she gasped, as a terrifying roar accompanied the sight of a roof lifting like a box top from a home across the street. It caught in the wind and blew away like a leaf. In seconds, the rest of the house shattered like it had been made of paper. To her horror, the torrent swept the cluttered remains of the structure completely from sight. The sound of what seemed like a hundred cannons shook the atmosphere, a noisy, appalling reverberation she had never heard before. The world was falling apart right before her eyes, and the woman and child were directly in the path of an unprecedented rage of nature.

Wally's grandmother could not see past the maelstrom of devastation beyond her bay window. Had she been able to view over nearby rooftops to the rest of St. Louis, she would have witnessed a cyclone of epic proportions entering the town from the southwest. It had just torn through Compton Heights, one of the city's most elevated terrains, a desirable and highly regarded residential section. Over an expanse of more than ten blocks from north to south, and six blocks from east to west, more than 300 homes were splintering into the wind or undergoing haphazard tears to their weakest parts. The sound of what seemed like hundreds of cannons continued to resound throughout the city, born from the angry wallop of roofs, pianos, trees, and whole buildings as they struck the ground and exploded into shards. Thousands more homes were ruined in the cyclone's demolition course, and the flimsy frame houses offered no resistance to the cyclone's fury.

The roof over Wally and his grandmother held tight during the beginning moments of nature's attack, but their safety was short-lived. Overhead, a crash shook the walls of the structure under which they cowered. In the next moment, two chimneys tore from their flashing and fell with terrifying thuds against the housetop. Bricks broke free, slung riotously in the swirling current, and flung wildly against the house.

Beyond their street, the devil was in the cyclone. It spun its angry torrent and wind-whipped water spray over unsuspecting homeowners until it carved a path across Mill Creek Valley to the Mississippi River. It scooted steamboats and small craft across the water and dashed them against the opposite shore like toy boats. Even the Eads Bridge swayed wildly in the cyclone's path. Trains balancing precariously on the bridge toppled from their tracks with ear-splitting crashes. The city power plant buildings at the Union Depot Railway system exploded in a brilliant spray of electric sparks as if bombs had detonated from within, and then its huge smokestack fell to the ground. In one saloon, the proprietor was in front of the bar playing cards with two of his customers when the whirlwind struck the tavern with the impact of a dozen freight trains, demolishing the structure and burying the gamblers.

Lafayette Park, conspicuous for its elegant, century-old shade trees, had become an incomprehensible swirl of maniacal annihilation. The handsome iron fence skirting the grassy walkways bent, twisted, and snapped asunder, landing in unrecognizable tangles of iron across the grass. In the midst of the chaos, the stubborn, venerable statue of Thomas H. Benton stood valiant and unmoving as if it were anchored to the core of the earth, while destruction billowed around the artwork.

Wally's grandmother sensed a vibration in the glass panes of the bay window she faced, and as she took steps backward in growing fright, she stared flabbergasted at the thin, rain-splattered panels. Her jaw dropped when one, then two, and then whole rows of the windowpanes shattered in consecutive bursts and spewed razor-sharp fragments with wind-whipped ferocity. She instinctively turned from the flying shards and threw her body over Wally, as he trembled in bewilderment. All about them, dangerous chips of splintered glass shot uncontrollably past their cowering figures like tiny knives. In the next moment, she saw a second bay window explode and fling shattered remnants over the floor in a carpet of wood, water, and glass. A roar like a freight train bore down on the home, and the full force of the St. Louis cyclone closed in upon them.

Chapter 2
THE WAYS OF FATE

Wally and his grandmother were helpless in the face of the St. Louis cyclone as it packed winds of nearly 100 miles an hour and bore into their home with devastating muscle. The terrified woman scooped up the frightened boy and ran straightway through the door to a stairwell that led down to their underground basement. All electric power was suddenly lost, and the unexpectedly darkened steps had to be taken cautiously one at a time. With the boy in her arms, she inched her way into the dank and musty cellar, while the roar of the wind tore mercilessly at the house.

While they hid, widespread ruin held the rest of the town in a vice-like grip. For the next ten minutes, the cyclone ripped through one street after another until havoc took hold of the terrified citizens. Then, as unexpectedly as it began, the cyclone stopped. Blinding rain lashed down in the storm's wake, and fires erupted in many structures. Flames leapt high in the sky and met the torrential downpour with angry hisses. The streets were inundated with more than three inches of floodwater, swamping torn buildings and drenching upturned furniture piles. The majority of businesses had closed, but they hid panicked employees caught between work and home. They struggled to withstand the heavy showers, and the bravest among them emerged soaked and shaken to face the carnage left by the cyclone.

Wally fell to his knees on the scuffed basement floor and he prayed aloud for the Lord to spare his grandmother and him. Over his heartfelt plea, the scourge of pounding rain whipped against the tiny basement windows. His answer was a crack of thunder and flashing bursts of lightning.

Wally and his grandmother were among the blessed survivors of the St. Louis cyclone that tore through Missouri with unprecedented destruction. Wally emerged with his outlook on life permanently altered.

Outside, tens of thousands of people were in agony. Whole sections of the city had been blotted out, and wreckage was strewn as far as their eyes could see. People huddled together in groups, while the city's ruined power system left them stranded in an eerie darkness, which seemed like the end of the world had come.

When the wind and rain gradually subsided, the shadowy landscape became dotted with men and women crawling from their hiding places to face houses demolished down to their foundations, upturned cars, destroyed businesses, and bodies of the dead and dying. The city hospital had been partially destroyed, and when the cyclone's victims began to stream in, the staff was unprepared to handle the awakening reality of unprecedented numbers of wounded and maimed survivors.

That night, a special edition of the local newspaper was published with headlines boldly announcing the sudden appearance of the cyclone and the carnage it wrecked. Boys hawked the edition in the streets because streetcars were immobilized by the city's downed power supply.

By morning, nothing but wall fragments remained where homes once stood. Where there had been a three-story building, only two floors remained with exposed rafters and open-air tops. Telephone poles were strewn around like trampled cornstalks in a field. At the river, steamboats were broken in half and their wreckage lay on the opposite banks where they had been hurled. People rushed to fire alarms and telephones, but they found that those devices were powerless.

Wally's grandmother's cautiously emerged from her basement only to discover that her neighborhood was lined with destroyed houses.

"A little child's prayer was answered, for not one of our family was hurt," Bertha later said, grateful that her mother and son were spared.

In all, at least 185 people were later reported missing, and their bodies were never recovered. 8,800 buildings were either destroyed or damaged. Property was recovered from as far away as Vandalia, Illinois. The St. Louis cyclone had left, but its carnage remained for years.

Musician Lonnie Johnson was inspired to write "St. Louis Cyclone Blues," musically chronicling the tragedy in a song. For years, it was a standard for musicians and instrumentalists. The 1896 St. Louis Cyclone was the single most deadly event to hit the city in its recorded history.

For Wally, the event left an indelible impression on his mind. In the aftermath of the devastation, he saw things no child should

AMUSEMENTS.

MACDONOUGH THEATRE
CHAS. P. COOK..........Manager.

ONE NIGHT ONLY. | **NEXT TUESDAY**

ADA REHAN DALY and the COMPANY
Presenting "SCHOOL FOR SCANDAL."

Choice seats now on sale. Prices, 50c to $2. Gallery, reserved, 50c.

OAKLAND THEATER.
Twelfth and Webster Streets.
FRANK BACON - - - - Manager
Telephone 56.

TO-NIGHT | **AND EVERY NIGHT THIS WEEK**

THE HODGES COMPANY, Headed by

WALTER HODGES and ESSIE TITTEL

In the Sensational Comedy Drama in 5 acts

LA BELLE MARIE

A sparkling Comedy, interspersed with numerous Specialties

Popular Prices—Evenings, 10c, 20c, 30c; Tickets on sale at Reilly's Drug Store, 1067 Bd'wy
☞ Next week—Milton Nobles in "FROM SIRE TO SON."

RESERVED SEATS

Hal Reid's first play, *La Belle Marie*, ran for decades across America. This advertisement, appearing in the *Oakland Tribune* on June 5, 1896, was from one of its earliest California presentations at the Oakland Theater in California.

see. The sights, sounds, and smells of the ruined city fired his imagination and may have given a push to the creative expression he later sought with music and writing.

"About this time," his mother thought back, "his imagination, the fabric from which authors build, grew so vivid that he would get up in the small hours of the night and sit by the window watching what he thought were real people disporting themselves in the moonlight out upon the lawn and among the trees and shrubbery. Whoever of the family discovered him would listen to what he saw. Then, he would be perfectly satisfied to go back to bed and to sleep. Children of his own age did not understand him, so he preferred mostly the companionship of grown-ups, especially in my father's home where reading aloud was the nightly custom. He was kaleidoscopic . . . as the clock went round and round . . . the design and coloring constantly changed. Consequently, many people had no conception whatever of the fineness of the real man down in the calms beneath the restless ebb and flow of the surface."

Wally had that aspect of his character in common with his father. Hal's earliest beginnings as an actor gave him the material to become an appreciated playwright. "I started in at the bottom," he told writer Arabella Boone, when looking back years later. "My object was to study audiences from the stage, to see what they would applaud, what they would laugh at, and what would make them cry. I went to Robinson's Opera House in Cincinnati, Ohio, and applied for a job as an extra—only they called them supernumeraries in those days before the movies came. Kiralfy Brothers had on their *Around the World in 80 Days*, and in it was a water scene, which represented the ocean. It was necessary to give the semblance of waves, and with others I got under a sea cloth—a very dusty green baize—and bobbed up and down to make one of the waves. It was rather dusty, that water."

Hal kept at the hard work, and then after eight years, he advanced to appearing on stage carrying spears, or offering his arm to leading ladies. He graduated from supernumerary to actor, and as a playwright, he finally struck gold with *La Belle Marie*. The play ran for more than a decade and was performed all over the country in many theaters with many other actors. One of the earliest performances was at a theater in Newark, New Jersey. An item in the *Newark*

The majestic Reid family home on the Shrewsbury River where Wally spent much of his boyhood years.

Daily Advocate on February 20, 1895, praised "the Waynes," a husband and wife acting team, saying, "The Waynes were greeted with another large audience last night to see *La Belle Marie*. This magnificent drama gives plenty of scope for Mr. and Mrs. Wayne to show their artistic work, especially Mrs. Wayne, whose dialect in broken French is the best ever heard in this theater." At the same time on the other side of the country, another one of the earliest productions of *La Belle Marie* was playing in Oakland, California, with Walter Hodges and Essie Tittel in the leading roles.

That month in 1895, *La Belle Marie* had competition in Newark. At the local Baptist church, Mr. Byron W. Rice of New York State gave music demonstrations using Thomas Edison's new and fantastic invention, the phonograph. He had one specially fitted with a bell for magnifying the sound so that an entire group of people could witness the mechanical marvel at one time. A notice in the Oakland newspaper said, "No ear tubes will be used, but all will hear the music as it comes from a large trumpet attached to the instrument. Solos, quartets, and concerts will be rendered. Admission is twenty-five cents."

Wally in a formal portrait taken at age thirteen.

In 1895, Hal did not realize how those early recordings would ultimately influence his life and the life of his young son. The old-world way of theatrical presentation was evolving, and for Wally, developments were converging that began to pave the way for his future.

In 1896, Wally's first genuine experience as an actor took place in St. Louis. He played the part of a little girl in *Slaves of Gold*, a melodrama written by his father. From that time on, he appeared with his parents in various plays when a handy child was needed.

The wind of fate was brushing against him before he had even started school, and he was unknowingly heading toward a destiny that was being shaped by a fairy princess and a man known around the world as "The Wizard of East Orange."

Portrait of Wallace Reid at age eighteen with his mother, Bertha.

Chapter 3
MAKING GOOD

In 1896, Wally was taking his first steps in front of American audiences, and Thomas Edison was simultaneously working out the major theme of motion picture destiny by establishing the manufacture of his new invention, the Vitascope, for the projection of photographed views upon a screen or canvas. Newspapers were giving much attention to this new invention, and many writers were already calling him "The Wizard of East Orange."

Jimmy Blackton, a freelance reporter for the *New York World* newspaper, was gifted in the art of sketching with ink or chalk. This talent was useful in the rough and ready world of newspapers because he could quickly produce a line drawing for the illustration of news events. He was so good with his chalk drawings that he had worked his talent into an amusing act for clubs, and he frequently performed on a bill with two of his friends, Albert E. Smith, a spirit-cabinet performer, and Ronald Reader, a prestidigitator. In 1896, Blackton was assigned by his newspaper to investigate Edison's work, and he went to interview "The Wizard of East Orange" about his new marvel, the Vitascope.

Edison took an instant liking to the deft sketches Jimmy demonstrated, and he especially found his caricatures of Grover Cleveland and William McKinley hilarious. Responding in seconds to Edison's laughter, Jimmy drew Edison, who was so taken with the aggressive youngster's talent that he led him into the little building where he photographed his motion pictures. The structure was called the "Black Maria" because it was wrapped in black tar paper and it swung like a bridge on a pivot to follow sunlight. It took its name from the somber vehicles police used to carry drunks to jail. Edison stood Jimmy in the full glare of the little sunlit stage against a background as black as night, and he filmed Jimmy's chalk-talk act. When they were finished, Jimmy interviewed Edison, and it was then that he first learned of the Vitascope machine that could project short motion picture films onto a screen or wall so that any number of people could view them at the same time. Jimmy was intensely intrigued.

Edison sent Jimmy's film out as *Blackton, the Evening World Cartoonist*. When Jimmy told Albert Smith, his stage cohort, about the apparatus and his appearance in the short film, they joined a list of waiting buyers for one of the machines. As soon as the Edison manufacturers could produce it, Blackton and Smith received Edison projector No. 13, and in November 1896, they began giving exhibitions to audiences.

Smith had built his spirit-cabinet act on mechanical contrivances born out of his ingenuity with machinery, and after he examined the new projection device supplied by Edison, he engineered housing for the intermittent mechanism that could convert the machine into a camera. He and Blackton induced the building's janitress and their office boy to perform a little story on the rooftop of the Morse Building at 140 Nassau Street, just above their office. Titled *The Burglar on the Roof*, it was the first motion picture they produced. Blackton and Smith needed a name for their fledgling company. They thought up a word that played off the word for the Vitascope: Vitagraph. This tiny beginning gradually rose to become a major player in film production and distribution.

Over the next five years, Wally grew as the early film industry evolved, and his parents become more prominent in the legitimate theater. In 1901, Hal and Bertha were making great strides. In an article in the June 1901 *New York Times*, a theater critic wrote:

> "The Donnelly Stock Company presented to a good sized audience in the Murray Hill Theater last evening Hal Reid's Christian play, *The Prince of the World*, which is to be continued during the remainder of this week. The play is a robust drama with plenty of spirited situations. Written on a background similar in many ways to *Quo Vadis*, the cast includes Miss Bertha Bell Westbrook, one of the authors."

When Wally was ten years old, the Reid family moved back to New York, the hub of the theater world, and he attended public schools. The Reid's lived in a leased apartment on West End Avenue, but they also leased another flat on 116th Street near Columbia University overlooking Morningside Park where the view in all directions was of an unspoiled, wide-open terrain. When Bertha and Hal saved enough money to buy a country home, they purchased a charming residence perched on a hillside at Highlands, New Jersey, which overlooked the picturesque Shrewsbury River and the rolling expanse of the Atlantic Ocean. They returned there when they were not on the road touring in stage plays.

Like many boys, Wally learned to swim in the Hudson River. His inaugural sink-or-swim rite of passage took place there when his friends threw him into the water. He survived, later learned to swim well, and then became a champion swimmer. He took long swims far out into the Atlantic Ocean, and he won accolades for his diving skills. "He did some effective rescue work, both in aid of the regular life savers, and alone, for he was a swift and powerful swimmer and was possessed of unusual endurance," his mother later recalled. "He also enjoyed swimming unimaginable lengths of space under water."

Reverend Hadley, the son of the President of Yale University, officiated at Wally's confirmation. Wally was deeply religious, and he surprised many with his logical questions about theological matters. Always introspective with his thoughts, he sought out reasonable answers to questions of Faith, and he often pondered the concept of eternity. This meditative tendency also manifested itself during many hours when he haunted the Metropolitan Museum of Fine Arts and other renowned New York museums.

During one childhood scrape, he was seriously injured with a wound that required hospitalization and surgery. While he was under the numbing effect of ether, his mind dredged up long speeches that he had memorized, and he amazed the nurses when they overheard him murmuring the lofty scripts. This habit of committing to heart whole passages from poems and novels stayed with him his entire life.

In his schooldays, he liked sports more than Latin or algebra. He also spent time learning verse, drama, and short-story writing. Some of his compositions appeared in a school magazine.

Following in his father's steps, Wally starting writing at an early age. In 1922, he confessed to a writer for *Pantomime*. "I always had a secret ambition to write." He was just twelve years old when he wrote poems to his mother and father on Christmas 1904, and dedicated "with all the love of her son, Wallace Reid. Dedicated to my mother, she who has stood by her two erring boys with the patience of Job and the forgiveness of the Savior:

MOTHER LOVE

"As I sit by the rain-lashed window
Looking out on the dreary day,
Thy vision comes before me,
And drives the rain away,
To leave but the glorious sunshine
Of a love so pure and good,
I deserve not, tho' it is mine
The love of motherhood."
"That love so great and glorious,
That the waters as they swirled—
Sand, "The Hand that rocks the cradle,
Is the hand that rules the world."
The poets sing of heroes
And martyrs great and good,
But none so pure as thou dear,
With thy love of motherhood."
And when thou diest, thou wilt leave
Below thee, here on earth,
Two rusty links of a broken chain,
That wither at thy birth.
Then thou wilt wait to greet us,
As we travel the darksome wood
Waiting the while to meet us
With thy love of motherhood."

A SIMILE

'Tis dull and gloomy—
the pall of the mountain mist
Hangs low upon the land.
No sound except the curdling shriek
Of a fast receding train,
The dismal clang of bells—
Indeed the world is dull and bare
And the trees with naked branches in the mist,
Can send a shudder to your very soul."
"But lo! The sun bursts forth Driving the mists
Like a flock of frightened sheep
That have been ravaged by the killer.
Away! To seek a refuge
In the mist-clad mountain-top
And see the trees, that 'fore
Had seemed so bare and naked,
Now unfold the gorgeous colorings of the Autumn leaves,
Which had been hidden in the
All enshrouding mists—
The whole arth takes on
A cheerful aspect—then—
"So like thy life, oh father, just
The mist of misery and unrest, and then
The glorious sunshine of the re-enlightened soul."
"So be it always—to which, Amen."

Wally had big shoes to fill. His father was prolific with his playwriting. Between 1901 and 1905, Hal wrote many plays that were produced in New York on Broadway, including *The Prince of the World* (1901), *At the Old Cross Roads* (1902), *The Peddler* (1902), *A Mother's Love* (1903), *A Working Girl's Wrongs* (1903), *At Cripple Creek* (1904), and *A Crown of Thorns* (1905). All told, he wrote more than 126 plays in his career.

As boys often do, Wally planned to run away from home with two of his friends to explore the world. To stop him, his mother had to resort to an inspired bit of wisdom.

"Now dear, if you and Johnnie want to run away, it is not necessary for you to go secretly," she told him. "I will give you the railroad fare up to the city and enough money to give you a bed and food for two days. But after that you must look to your earnings, as you are now such big men. But for a little boy like you not to appreciate your home and family, horses and dogs any better than I see you do, then I shall immediately get another boy to take your place and he shall have your room and place at the table and there will be no further room for you; so you must not come back again. I will kiss you goodbye, and you can write to me when you and Johnnie have conquered the world. I will pack your things and Hughie can drive you to the station."

After quickly considering the replacement of another boy, Wally suddenly decided the trip was better off left to fantasy. Just what prompted him to consider making a dramatic break from home life is unknown. It could have been the general upheaval in his parent's life that was taking place along with the boy becoming a young man. In 1901 when Wally was eleven years old, Bertha and Hal divorced. The shattering of their relationship had been long in arriving, and when the two went their separate ways, they spared Wally the worst of their bickering. They arranged for him to go to the Freehold Military School in New Jersey. Not only was the experience good for him, but it also temporarily removed him from daily contact with them while they worked out the details of their divorce.

Before he left for military school, his parents bought him a sterling silver napkin ring, one of the required items of equipment, along with tailored uniforms. Inside the ring, they inscribed the words "On Guard," which Wally secretly thought of as a constant reminder to beware of instructors who kept putting him "on guard."

There was one particular scuffle with a hotheaded Latin youth while he was at the military school. During the fight, Wally took a knife cut deep in his leg, which resulted in his being hospitalized in the school's ward.

After military school, Wally went to the Perkiomen Seminary in Pennsylvania, and then he passed his exams for Princeton. It was at prep school where he first fell in love with automobiles. One of his cohorts had a car, and with him, Wally learned driving and engine mechanics. The two boys spent so much time cruising around that their grades suffered. He persuaded his parents to buy him a car, and he named the machine "Long Distance." He drove the three-mile span of space from their home to the drawbridge at Highlands, and he took delight in testing the speed limits of the machine. Once, he tried to jump the drawbridge, but crashed into the iron structure, totally wrecking his car, which had to be towed on a boat to New York where it met a final resting place in a junkyard.

At home for the holidays, Wally enjoyed the comfort of his entire family. One dark night while his father and a friend were staying over, the three men decided to dress themselves in various coats, cloaks, hats, and veils from his mother's closet. With much suppressed laughter and whispering, they disappeared and were gone for some minutes. Then, the doorbell rang.

The family's Negro maid dutifully answered the ringing bell, and when she opened the door, there stood three huge, heavily-veiled women who spoke in falsetto voices, and called for "The Madame" They told her that they had heard she wanted a cook, parlor maid, and laundress. The maid stood wide-eyed and speechless in the semi-darkness, failing to recognize them. She curtly replied that none were needed. The three persistent females disputed her claim so vehemently that the maid slammed the door in their faces. Trembling and shaking, she went straightway to Bertha. Thoroughly frightened, she told her there were three lunatics at the door and urged her to telephone for the police at once. Bertha, who was overly suspicious and suspected the truth of the matter, opened the door to find the three men rolling on the porch, holding their sides with laughter.

On another night, he came into his mother's boudoir, sat in a rocker in front of her big cheval mirror, and practiced flexing his arm muscles while she engaged in her nightly beauty routine.

"Don't you have a better use to make of your time?" she asked as she worked.

"I'm just teaching them to play a tune," he told her.

The Reids were a two-car family, and Wally borrowed his mother's car for frequent excursions with his friends to a popular shore restaurant. On Saturday nights, the young men enjoyed their first brushes with dating, cocktails, and meeting young women. Those youthful jaunts occupied their free time throughout the summer, but when vacation was over, Wally went back to college.

At prep school, Wally planned on becoming a surgeon. He attended medical lectures that were above and beyond the curriculum, and he was a model student. His grades were high, he was captain of the football team, and he was the editor of the college paper. While at the school, he encountered his first romance with a young lady attending the co-education school. She was pretty as a picture with dimpled cheeks, a rose leaf complexion, and laughing blue eyes. She was dainty as a fairy, and his mother later described her as "brilliantly intelligent, intellectual, and with perfect poise." Wally proposed marriage, but the girl declined. She also refused to kiss him.

In that first decade of the twentieth century, motion pictures were a suddenly popular fad. The primitive theaters were usually located in a vacant store rented cheaply by an enterprising businessman. Front windows were often painted black to make the interior dark and keep outsiders from peeping in. For one nickel, patrons sat on a folding chair and watched pictures projected on a sheet or a white wall, while a woman played musical accompaniment on a piano. The music came close to matching the tempo of the action on the screen and was often as entertaining as the pictures. Those tiny theaters were called "nickelodeons" and they were springing up everywhere. Poor people could afford the 5¢ admission price, and the rows of seats were filled with scruffy mobs. The better classes of people did not want to be in their company and they feared being in a dark building surrounded by imagined pickpockets and riff-raff. They stayed away and left the cheap amusement for the consumption of the lower classes, and those people attended in unheard-of masses. Going to the movies became a national pastime, and by 1908, they were firmly established as part of popular culture.

Around that time, David Wark Griffith, a tall, hawk-faced Kentuckian, was out of work. He was a writer of sorts with some stories and poems that had been published in magazines. In 1907, he had received $1,000 from James K. Hackett for his play called *A Fool and a Girl*, which Hackett produced in Washington. It closed after one week. Undaunted, Griffith made a living as a reporter and stock actor under the pseudonym Lawrence Griffith. He toured in various stock companies, and by early 1908, he was married to a girl named Linda Arvidson. They needed money, and in her later autobiography, Linda recalled their first opportunity to consider working in the lowly motion pictures:

"You've heard of moving pictures, haven't you?" asked Max Davidson.

Griffith looked blankly at the actor, who had been his friend since his youthful days in a Louisville stock company. "Why, I don't know; suppose I have, but I've never seen one. Why?"

"I work in them during the summer and make $5 some days when I play a leading part, but usually it's $3. Keeps you going, and you have time to call on managers, too. Now, you could write the little stories for the pictures. They pay $15 sometimes for good ones. Don't feel offended at the suggestion. It's not half bad, really. We spend lots of days working out in the country. Lately we've been doing pictures where they use horses, and it's just like getting paid for enjoying a nice horseback ride. Anybody can ride well enough for the pictures. Just manage to stay on the horse, that's all."

"Ye Gods," exclaimed Griffith, even though he was tempted. "Some of my friends might see me. Then, I would be done for. Where do they show these pictures? I'll go see one first."

"Oh, nobody will ever see you—don't worry about that."

After investigating the movies, Griffith was sufficiently interested to apply for work at The Edison studio with a motion picture synopsis he had adapted from the play, *La Tosca*. They turned down his scenario, but offered him a part in a film Edwin S. Porter was about to make, a one-reel story about a woodsman who rescues a baby from certain death. *Rescued from an Eagle's Nest* allowed Griffith to climb a cliff and save a child from the clutches of a soaring eagle. The film was shot on the Palisades of the Hudson River and inside the Edison studio. The exterior scenes looked realistic enough, but the interior scenes were played against painted backdrops where wires artificially suspended the stuffed eagle. The baby was real, and so was the pay he received.

Griffith also worked at the American Mutoscope and Biograph Company. On his first day, he earned $5 and a request to return the following day. A few days later, Linda dressed up and also applied for work with them. Together, they appeared in a short film, *When Knighthood Was in Flower*, and individually, they appeared in a number of one-reel pictures. They were very attracted to the excitement and the money they made in the strange, new business, but they kept their sights set on theater work. When an offer came to appear in Peake's Island, Maine, and play villains in a summer stock company for $40 a week, Griffith had to weigh the two options and go one way or another. When the Biograph managers invited him to direct films, he decided to gamble on the money and the movies.

Griffith directed a one-reel picture called *The Adventures of Dolly*, and he found that the Biograph owners liked it enough to offer him a one-year contract for $45 per week with a royalty of a mill a foot on all film sold. They made so much money that Linda had to open bank accounts in a number of different banks.

During those years, Wally saw many Biograph movies. They were extremely popular with children, and his parent's saw that he had enough spending money to enjoy the entertainments he wanted.

Wally's love for his mother was profound, and when an occasion arose to bring her a present paid for with his own money, nothing but the best would do. To him, bigger was better, and he commissioned a local milliner to create one of those peach-basket hats, a huge, black velvet monstrosity adorned with so many pieces of artificial fruit that it took genuine dexterity to balance the eyesore on one's head.

"When he came home, I saw him coming down the driveway carrying a pasteboard trunk," Bertha recalled. "Poor lad, his small earnings . . . how sorry I felt . . . ."

For Wally's sake, Bertha rallied her considerable skills as an actress, put on a heroic front, balanced the atrocity with the help of several strategically positioned hatpins, and wore the hat when he was home. She was relieved when, some time later, he commented that the hat did not exactly fit her particular style.

As a lark during vacation from school, his parents arranged for Wally to take a role in a try-out production of a new play starring Robert Edeson. *Unto the Fourth Generation* brought Wally unexpected attention from many influential family friends when they came to see the play. He was a twenty-year-old, blonde, blue-eyed, six-foot-three, slim-waisted, broad-shouldered giant of young manhood, and in that play, he appeared in a tailor-made role as a college boy. He noticeably stirred hearts from the girls gazing at him from over the footlights.

In that era, young women came to matinees in droves and they made stars out of their matinee idols. Hundreds of fluttering, starry-eyed females came to the theater's backstage door and cornered the handsome young actors like wolves surrounding a stag. When their idols emerged after a play, they showed no hesitation at reaching out to touch his coat or ask for an autograph. "Rush seats" were those located in the center front rows. There, young women glimpsed their favorite celebrity from a close-up view. Those matinee girls were often adorably in their early twenties, and many were annoyingly in their middle teens, usually in bunches, and invariably talkative both in the theater and outside. They loved Wally.

Caryl Frohman, sister of Daniel Frohman, the Broadway impresario, was so impressed with Wally in *Unto the Fourth Generation* that she sought his parent's permission to bring him to the attention of her brother for a contract she was certain he could obtain. The eager reactions from people in the professional theater came as a complete shock to Bertha and Hal, who had spent the past two decades trudging across the country in one play after another. They wanted him to have a life free from the drudgery of greasepaint and one-night-stands. They knew first hand the pitfalls waiting for a young man lost in the chaotic world of actresses and acclaim, as well as the uncertainty of a performer's finances. The life of an actor was unstable, at best. To their surprise and dismay, others thought that their strapping son had star potential and they attempted to lure him with job offers. Hal and Bertha intimately knew all the sweat and grime associated with the life of an actor, and that turn of events alarmed them terribly.

The Reid's had other plans for their son. Bertha wanted him to pursue a career as a "man of letters," and she did her utmost to discourage him from taking advantage of that early opportunity to work in the theater. Instead, she and Hal conspired to spirit him as far away from the ranks of theatrical enterprises as they could get him. Quickly, they thought through their long list of contacts, and then they came up with the brilliant idea of sending Wally out into the Wild West. There was only one living person who epitomized

William "Buffalo Bill" Cody, famous scout, at the time of his popular Wild West show.

all that was noble about the idealized American West, a culture that had already passed and become the stuff of folklore. His name was William Cody, but he was known to audiences as "Buffalo Bill."

Hal Reid knew "Buffalo Bill" Cody well, having crossed paths with him during their simultaneous theatrical careers. Cody had just been in New York in search of a new play, and together with

Hal, he worked out the details of a new play that they hoped would give the living symbol of the Wild West a proper vehicle to further foster public fascination with his self-erected myth. Wally spent many hours listening to the banter between the two showmen, and he was enthralled with the Western adventure his father concocted. After Cody left, the Reid's quietly contacted him at his home on the Hudson River, and in a matter of days, arrangements were made to send Wally as far away from the New York stage and footlights as they could get him.

Cody had been a frontier scout, Pony Express rider, Indian fighter, rancher, husband, and father. From 1868 to 1872, he was a scout for the United States Army, and he received the Medal of Honor for gallantry in action while scouting for the Third Cavalry. He was also a consummate showman. Cody toured the United States in a string of plays based on his various alleged adventures in the West, and his renowned *Buffalo Bill Wild West* show had become a popular, circus-like attraction that swept audiences away with exciting reenactments of Indian raids, rifle exhibitions by Annie Oakley, and rough-riding demonstrations. In 1887, the show had toured Europe, performed before Queen Victoria in her Jubilee year, and then when they returned to America, it was a stock feature of the Chicago World's Fair. In 1895-1896, *Buffalo Bill's Wild West* show played in more than 130 towns across America. In 1897, the show played in Canada for the first time since Sitting Bull, a legendary Indian, had joined as a headliner. For Cody, the West was both folklore and grand theater, and it had proven to be a goldmine.

It was into this man's care the Reid's sought to place Wally in order to rid him of any further thoughts of stage acting or show business, a plan which, in retrospect, seems difficult to comprehend. They certainly had not thought of Wally ever being in the lowly motion pictures, which Cody had already done. Despite those who were trying to draw Wally onto the stage as a fledgling actor, Bertha and Hal sent him out West with a letter to Cody's sister. So he would forget about show business, they hoped joining him up with the one man who was the self-avowed P. T. Barnum of sawdust showmanship would affect a cure.

Chapter 4
THE HEART O' THE HILLS

As Wally was traveling to Wyoming to meet up with "Buffalo Bill" Cody's sister, *Buffalo Bill's Wild West* motion pictures were playing all over New York and in many other cities around the world. Among the earliest of movies, they were still being shown in the hundreds of nickelodeons springing up around America and across Europe.

In the fall of 1894, when Wally was only two-years old, those early films were made with "Buffalo Bill" Cody, Annie Oakley, and a handful of Indians, who traveled from Ambrose Park in Brooklyn to appear before Edison's motion picture camera. His Black Maria studio was situated in front of the inventor's laboratory near Orange Mountain in New Jersey. Edison was enchanted that his kinetoscope machine could replicate the sight of gun smoke belching from a cowboy's gun and Oakley's rifle shots shattering glass balls. Those modest films were initially shown only in peep-show machines. The public went into a kinetoscope parlor, shoved a nickel into a machine, and then viewed the films through a slot in the cabinet. To their astonishment, wondrous images in full, lifelike movement appeared right before their eyes. Viewers were enthralled with the novelty.

Sioux Ghost Dance, filmed by W. K. L. Dickson and William Heise on September 24, 1894, featured Buffalo Bill Cody and members of his *Buffalo Bill's Wild West* show. The Sioux Indians performed in full war paint and war costumes, according to Edison catalogs.

Buffalo Dance, filmed the same day by W. K. L. Dickson and William Heise, featured Last Horse, Parts His Hair, Hair Coat, and Sioux Indians from *Buffalo Bill's Wild West* show in a dance filmed in Edison's Black Maria motion picture studio.

Hadj Cheriff Arab Knife Juggler, also filmed the same day, featured Hadj Cheriff and his small troupe executing dances and feats of strength.

Bucking Bronco, filmed the same day, featured cowboy star, Lee Martin, riding the bronco, "Sunfish," in a small corral built outside the Black Maria studio.

Annie Oakley, filmed inside the confinement of the Black Maria studio, pictured the female sharpshooter giving a rifle exhibition and shooting at glass balls.

As Wally headed West on a train, he realized he had made, with his parent's help, a momentous decision not to go back to prep school. Instead, he was striking out on an adventure that would have been the envy of any youth. On his own, with his parents left behind on the east coast, he expected to experience life in the wide-open spaces of the American West, a priceless chance that he viewed with the same zest he added to everything he did.

Back in New York, the little Edison kinetoscope machines caught the attention of Adolph Zukor, a New York furrier. Zukor visited a small penny arcade on 125th Street that was owned by a friend, Max Goldstein. Curious to have a look at the kinetoscope motion picture machines and phonographs filling the store, Zukor stood about observing the many customers with great interest. The parlor was making a lot of money, and after he realized the potential the innovative collection of machines could make, Zukor decided to raise $75,000, a huge sum at that time, and open a similar arcade. He leased a building on East 14th Street at Broadway and installed an assortment of the slot machines. In addition to phonographs and kinetoscope motion picture machines, the long room was outlaid with slot machines delivering peanuts and candy, athletic devices, and a shooting gallery. All were operated by inserting a copper penny in a slot. From its grand opening, the enterprise was a success, taking in $500 to $700 daily.

By the end of 1903, Zukor opened other penny arcades in several cities. His next step was to convert the upper floor over the 14th Street arcade to a motion picture theater utilizing the Vitascope projection apparatus. The theater was named the *Crystal Hall* because patrons reached the theater by way of ascending a glass staircase lit with colored lights and decorated with cascading water. For the cost

Adolph Zukor, whose long-standing dream of feature-length films came to fruition and became the industry standard.

of one dime, the attractive theater exhibited fifteen minutes of motion picture subjects. Edison's *The Great Train Robbery*, a nine-minute Western, proved to be a gold mine the following year. People today have difficulty understanding how extraordinary those moving images were to viewers a hundred years ago. The experience was so novel and the images seemed so lifelike that people reached out to lay a hand on them, tried to talk to them, screamed in terror when they saw a locomotive speeding in their direction, and flinched when they saw a cowboy aim a gun directly at the audience and fire the weapon.

"I was finding show business very much to my liking," Zukor recalled in his autobiography. "Those of us who became film producers hailed from all sorts of occupations—furriers, magicians, butchers, boilermakers—and for this reason, highbrows have sometimes poked fun at us. Yet one thing is certain—every man who succeeded was a born showman."

Zukor observed audiences closely at the *Crystal Hall*, and he noticed many patrons stayed to watch the show twice, sitting for thirty to forty minutes at a time. He began to think about longer movies that could be exhibited for a higher admission fee. At that time, most film producers were not making long films, and he continued to mull over the idea while exhibiting one-reel and two-reel pictures.

In the summer of 1909, while Zukor was dreaming of taking motion picture film exhibition to a larger dimension, Wally arrived by train at the town of Cody, Wyoming, which his dreamy, young thoughts had imbued with all the glamour of James Fennimore Cooper's *The Pathfinder* and *The Deerslayer* stories that he had savored for years. When he saw the forest-crowned hills and rich, woven tapestries of landscape, he broke into a radiant smile. He was no longer "Hal Reid's son," but a unique and vigorous young man liberated and out on his own for the first time in his life. Although his father had always indulged him in everything a youth could desire, he stepped from the train with only 15¢ in his pocket and a letter of introduction to "Buffalo Bill" Cody's sister.

Wally later recalled that the first person he met was a pretty waitress at a restaurant in the train station. He gallantly gave her his 15¢ as a tip and struck out without a penny to his name. Fending for himself was part of the fun. No one knew he had a letter of

Buffalo Bill Cody with his sister, "Aunt May" Cody Decker. She ran the Irma Hotel where Wally worked during his sojourn in Wyoming in 1908.

CHAPTER FOUR: THE HEART O' THE HILLS

The Irma Hotel in Cody, Wyoming where famed Western showman, Buffalo Bill Cody, found work for teenage Wallace Reid after his parents sent him away from New York to keep him from a life in the theater.

introduction to "Buffalo Bill" Cody's sister, "Aunt May." He kept it hidden, but went in search of the woman.

He did not find "Aunt May" at her home at 2932 Lafayette Street, but he later found her at the Irma Hotel, which her brother owned, and which she managed along with her husband, Lou Decker. Wally shyly presented his letter from her brother. After reading the note, "Aunt May" looked up at the tall youth standing before her and steeled a long, penetrating gaze at him.

"Well, now, we need a night clerk around here, and I reckon you'll do. I'll give you $30 a month and cakes," she told him, an old expression that meant a salary and meals. Wally accepted the position, and he began working the front desk that very night.

In 1901, "Buffalo Bill" Cody had begun construction on the hotel, and in 1902, it was completed. At that time, Cody, Wyoming had only a thousand inhabitants. People came from miles around to attend the grand opening. What attracted him to the area was the priceless oil in the vicinity, and he invested in 40,000 acres on Carter Mountain in the Big Horn Basin. The Irma Hotel became the town's gathering place for plainsmen, Indians, and cowboys. Nearly every night, lively and colorful old-timers lounged in the brown leather chairs and swapped stories about the old days, Wild Bill Hickok, Calamity Jane, and Billy the Kid. Wally was so fascinated by the banter of the hotel's striking clientele that he could barely keep an eye on patrons. Their thrilling tales of adventure filled him with a desire to experience first-hand the excitement of the West. He soon became frustrated by the stifling job behind the front desk, and with echoes of adventuresome tales filling his head, he told "Aunt May" that he wanted to go wander the West.

"I hate to lose you," she told him, "but I reckon it won't do you any harm. You're too young to stay put yet awhile."

For the next six months after he left the Irma Hotel, Wally roamed Wyoming earning a living as a ranch hand. Much of the talk around the Irma Hotel and among the cowboys with whom he lived out in the wild seemed to center on the ambitious Shoshone River dam project. Wally heard about the huge labor force recruited to build the long-dreamed-of dam that would irrigate the arid regions of northwest Wyoming. In 1897 after several false starts, Cody and Nate Salisbury finally received a permit to irrigate 120,000 acres of land with water from three canals diverted from the Shoshone River. The three-canal system proved unfeasible, so Cody and Salisbury were forced to wait until May 29, 1899, and then try again. They acquired water rights to irrigate 60,000 acres around Cody, Wyoming. The State of Wyoming segregated the land under the provisions of the Carey Act, and as soon as Ethan A. Hitchcock, the Secretary of the Interior, successfully arranged $2.25 million for construction, preliminary drilling began in July 1904. Because of the hard granite bedrock of the Shoshone River, the cold temperatures encountered, and the rough topography of Shoshone Canyon, drilling was not completed until ten months later.

Wally joined a team of surveyors on the Shoshone Dam project while it was in the middle of its dangerous construction journey, and he found the work interesting but tiring and hazardous.

"Some folks might call it engineering," he later told an interviewer for *Picturegoer*, "but actually it was hard work with a pick and shovel gang. At first, that is. Afterwards, I learned to ride and shoot, and box a bit, too. I guess I finished growing out there."

The Shoshone River Dam in Wyoming, which Wally helped build.

The hazardous work resulted in a premature explosion in the downstream portal of the diversion tunnel, and two men were killed. In the spring of 1908, the foundation pit flooded, and then crews were compelled to start over. In November 1908, freezing temperatures forced the work to halt. Their efforts continued through the coldest months, and on January 15, 1910, the dam was finally finished while the temperature at fifteen degrees below zero. At completion, the project cost $1.4 million, and the lives of seven men. The dam was 325 feet in height and stood as a monument to Cody's vision, the lives of the men who died during its construction, and the sheer will power of men to alter the course of nature.

Throughout that time, the labor, outdoor living, and cowboy experiences honed Wally's physique. He grew even taller, gained more muscle, and reveled in fishing and riding with the mountain men, who steered him through every hidden valley and secluded peak in the country.

One night, he and some cowboys ventured into the Big Horn basin to hunt. The thick woods and underbrush obscured any clear path, and on the third day, Wally shot an antelope. As darkness fell, he became lost among the wilds, and he hated to admit it to the cowboys by sending out distress signals with rifle shots. It had taken weeks for him to downplay their first impression of him as a "tenderfoot," and so he decided to stay the entire night alone in the wild country with the antelope laid out in front of him rather than call for help.

At dawn, Wally woke after a very sound sleep. To his astonishment, at his feet lay the mangled carcass of the antelope, reduced to nothing but bones and ragged sinews. Nearby, the tracks of a mountain lion were clearly imprinted in the forest floor, and they led away from the carcass at his feet where the feeding frenzy had taken place.

"I never knew why he didn't eat me too," Wally later told Adela Rogers St. Johns. "Guess he filled up on antelope and didn't want any dessert."

Wally was not discouraged. He was satisfied to live in the beautiful, half-tamed outdoors. It was a good, clean environment for a young man, and he found he was capable of standing on equal footing with the other cowboys despite his Eastern breeding and good looks. It was a world that bred inner peace and strength of character, but the adventure was short lived.

After many weeks had passed, Bertha and Hal grew homesick for Wally. They wrote to him imploring him to return, but their letters brought no reply because Wally was lost in the distant terrain of Wyoming. They knew he would not return home simply because they requested him to do so. Instead, they concocted an elaborate ruse to lure him back. They were able to track him down, and this time fired a missive that was calculated to spur the youth to respond. Hal sent a telegram to the bunk house where Wally was staying, telling him that Bertha was seriously ill and near death.

Once he heard the news and became distraught, Wally immediately started back on the long journey across the country. In those days, there were no airplanes, and the train ride from Wyoming to New York took many days.

When he finally arrived home, he was frantic with anxiety, but he soon discovered that Bertha had gone out for a ride in their car. He also learned that she had never been ill and certainly was not near death. She was out shopping. The joke was on him, but the Reid's had their son back. What they did not expect was that Wally had changed while he was away. He had grown up. He was no longer the only son of a successful playwright and his wife. He had come into his own.

In 1923, Bertha philosophically wrote, "When a young birdling once falls from its nest, he may be replaced a dozen times, but he will at once proceed to fall out again. So it was with Wallace. He had the taste of freedom, given by self-earned money, and Princeton had lost all charms for him."

Instead of the free environment of the great outdoors, where Wally developed cool judgment and a respect for nature, he was swiftly sent on a course that rushed him pell-mell into another world where exterior things alone were enough to lead him to accomplishment.

His friend, Adela Rogers St. Johns, later wrote that she believed the circumstances of his life always seemed to control him more than they did most people. "The versatility of his talents prevented any strong and definite urge that might have driven him on one straight course," she reflected. "He had loved the Western life, but not passionately enough to return to it now, in the face of his mother's plea, his father's opposition, and the joys and comforts of home. He had grown in that year beyond all possibility of going back to school, although his mother renewed her urging in that direction. Her farseeing love, her deep instinct, seemed to feel always the need of going slowly with this handsome, gifted son of hers. But it was useless. Wally loved speed. He was trying in those days to find himself. Sometimes, I think he never did."

Try as Bertha could to inspire him to return to college and pursue an academic course of study fitted for a sterling career as a surgeon or a man of letters, Wally had lost all desire to buckle down and pour over books. Instead, he went to work as a reporter for the *Newark Daily Star*, contributing a weekly column called, "As Told in Esex." He went into newspaper work with his eyes tainted by romantic tales his father had told him about his years as a newspaper man. To Wally, newspaper men assumed the proportions of demigods. His idealism soon came face to face with the harsh reality of the sweatshop grind of a daily newspaper.

"When I had finished prep school, I turned to a newspaper office much, I imagine, as a duck turns to water . . . I was a reporter," Wally thought back in a 1922 interview for *Pantomime*. "It was the tales I used to hand in to the editor in lieu of the absence of news that started me on the road to stardom in the silent drama. Newspapers are conducted on a 'strictly business' basis, and people buy them in order to find out what's going on in this world. My ideas of what constituted a news item and the editor's views on the same subject differed considerably. Consequently and eventually, I was soon doing other and more lucrative labor. My salary as a cub reporter, at that time, was $10 per week."

Few newspapermen were well-paid. Wally struggled to make his weekly pay envelope stretch to cover his expenses. He ate in restaurants patronized by common people, and he barely managed to make ends meet.

Wally was given assignments ranging from police and court reporting to following up on new arrivals at the city morgue. The daily drudgery of a cub reporter's route sank into an uninspiring routine of dull projects, obliged tasks, and mundane writing chores. Then, a telephone call to the newspaper alerted the managing editor to a breaking story of a fire at one of the biggest hotels in Newark. He sent Wally out to cover the catastrophe, and Wally ran the short distance to the site of the blaze in less than ten minutes. When he got there, he was startled by what he saw.

"I found the great conflagration was already a thing of the past," he later remarked, "a charred awning being the only evidence left. I was greatly disappointed, having pictured myself writing a huge, front-page yarn about the blaze. Unwilling to be cheated of my story, I went into the hotel office and asked to see the proprietor. When the hotel man learned that I was a newspaper reporter, he opened up like a shark's mouth. He filled me with more bull in a minute than a Coney Island barker could in a week. And I, like a boob, I swallowed it all . . . ."

Based on what the proprietor had told him, Wally raced back to the office and wrote a three-column report about how the blaze swept through the marble hotel halls and how the elegant and attractive female guests were forced to flee the inferno in scanty clothes. When he turned in his yarn, the hard-boiled newspaper editor read his composition and then looked up at Wally with nothing but a weary scowl on his face.

"Young man," he said, "you have too much imagination for this sheet. We got a report on this fire from the Fire Department, and the loss was just $25. All that burned was a measly awning. Here you go writing the whole front page about it!"

Wally had a strong desire to write, but he lacked the ruthlessness needed to be a newspaper reporter. Drama, pathos, unusual angles, and sentiment were what interested him, a point of view stimulated by his father's example. The ferret quality of diving down deep and bringing up what was hidden was not in him the way it was in other reporters.

Wally's tenure with the *Newark Daily Star* was short-lived. When the *New York Journal* offered him a job as their Atlantic Coast correspondent, he moved over to that publication and stuck with the newspaper game a little while longer.

Perriton Maxwell, a family friend and editor of *Cosmopolitan*, had known Wally since he was a boy. The Maxwell home was adjacent to the Reid home on the banks of the Hudson and was part of Wally's boyhood playground. Maxwell knew about his passion for automobiles, and he offered Wally a journalist job on *Motor Magazine* as an Assistant Editor. Wally later admitted that it "sounded very large and satisfying, and the salary, while not overly gratifying, especially in these days of fairly high wages, went its predecessor several points better."

Friends thought that the new assignment was ideal for him. They knew he adored automobiles. They had seen him sit on the curb and gaze at a new roadster for hours, pointing out its lines, emphasizing its beauties, and explaining its mechanical attributes. He was also a fine driver. His love for cars crystallized with that opportunity to work for *Motor Magazine*.

He went to work with the same romanticized zeal that had accompanied his entrance to newspaper journalism, but the job immediately took on more exciting proportions. First, the subject matter of the publication focused on the latest trends in automobiles and motorboats, a topic of keen interest to Wally since his days at the military school. Second, the title of Assistant Editor inferred a more esteemed position than that of a cub reporter. His boss was Julian Chase, who was a stickler for accuracy, detail, and speed. He kept Wally's nose to the grindstone.

"But I was doomed to disappointment," Wally admitted when he later looked back. "Hard work was substituted for romance and adventure; automobile shows took the place of death-defying races. I saw every conceivable motor and all of its nuts and bolts repeatedly in the course of the many exhibits which were held."

The part he liked best was reporting on motor races. He even spearheaded a special theme section highlighting garages. Special sections were a staple of nearly every newspaper and magazine because of the added revenue generated by participants corralled together within an editorial environment complimentary to their business. Wally approached all of his contacts. Advertising revenue increased, but he did not earn so much as $5 extra for the intense, additional labor the one-time project demanded. A low point came when he was compelled to render a special article titled "The Oiling Tendencies in Motor Boats." It put the cap on his continued interest in the fabulous world of motor boating and marked the close to his career as an Assistant Editor. "I would rather drive a car than write about one," he declared, "and I would rather read a newspaper with my breakfast than get out before breakfast and help to write one."

Despite his mother's protests, another set of circumstances blew up suddenly on his path. His father wrote a one-act play designed to be performed in vaudeville, which was then the rage throughout America. *The Girl and the Ranger* was an abridged version of one of Hal's full-length plays. It was cast and rehearsed, but just before the date scheduled to launch the little drama on its road tour, the actor playing the young husband had to drop out. A replacement was needed in a hurry because the departure date for the tour was imminent. Hal suggested Wally take the part, and the young man was very willing to take on the role for fun, adventure, and what money it would pay. The tour was a one-shot excursion onto the stage. It was not a lifelong career choice, but a brief interlude while he was between careers. Hal thought it would be a good experience for him and Wally liked the idea, but Bertha became enraged when she got wind of it.

"I was bitterly opposed," she remembered in her memoirs, and she fought with Hal about drafting Wally into the show. She was still determined that he should not be an actor. She was fearful that another experience in a play would only incite further, positive reactions from audiences, and she was certain that the experience would result in temptations that he would not be able to withstand. Bertha lobbied harshly against him taking part in the tour. She also was shocked at his interest in it. She could not remember at any time having heard him mention acting as a possible life's work. He was interested in inventing, engineering, medicine, ranching, writing, and music, but never acting. She threw those other interests up in a blinding array to attempt to thwart his involvement in the play, but during their debates, Hal kept coming back to the point that there was no time to get anyone else. He reasoned that Wally was handsome, could confidently speak the few lines the play offered, and that was all that would be required of him. Hal and Bertha fought a bitter battle over Wally going on the stage and it was the worst fight they ever had.

Bertha had known the disappointments of theater work. Their recent successes had not glossed over her memory of the ugly side of that kind of life, and she had a great fear of its inherent temptations. She also worried over what the wear and tear of traveling on one-night stands would do to someone with Wally's easy-going nature. She knew him so well that she was certain the world of show business would corrupt him. Her objections were based on a mother's intuition, and she was correct. Wally was unaware of his own masculine charms, but Bertha knew. With a mother's fighting temper, she objected with the full force of her convictions.

Hal also had a strong will and hot blood, an equal match to Bertha's, but he did not believe Wally's clean sweetness would suffer by intimate contact with the glittering, free, careless life of the stage. He felt that she was making more of the brief tour than it would ever amount to. Hal promised he would find another actor to take on the role for the duration of the tour if she would just step aside and allow him to take the role for the first few dates. He argued that he could simply remain with the short tour as an understudy after a replacement actor could be found.

To this plan of action, Bertha finally but reluctantly agreed. Wally memorized the small role and went on the road with his father, opening the sketch in New York and then taking it on the road to a series of cities.

"My part was so big you could hardly see it," Wally later said candidly.

The world of vaudeville was colorful and exciting, not unlike a three-ring circus. Wally drank it all in and enjoyed the experience immensely. The tour ended in Chicago.

Two momentous events that took place there were significant for Wally, and ultimately, meaningful for many other people. Without realizing it, he had come to a major crossroad in his life. Just over the horizon, a fairy princess and a machine were to change the entire course of his destiny.

Chapter 5
THE KISS

In the first decade of the twentieth century, hundreds of theatrical road shows of varying degrees of quality crisscrossed America, but the rising popularity of motion pictures brought a swift end to them.

"I had sixteen plays on the circuit drawing me satisfactory royalties, when, one by one, these heretofore prosperous plays began to come in and rattle into the store house," Hal told an interviewer in 1919. "I asked why—and the answer was, 'The Movies.' Managers told me theaters, which used to run my plays, were being turned into picture houses. But I only laughed—a long, sarcastic contemptuous laugh—I sat on my large, comfortable front porch looking out on the Atlantic and waited two years for the picture fad to pass. It did not, so I figured that the only way to get even with pictures was to get into them."

At that time, one of the hotbeds of motion picture creativity was at The American Mutoscope and Biograph Company in New York, called "Biograph." David Wark Griffith, the tall Kentuckian who had chosen film work to picking hops, had become the most-admired director in the business. He was refining and developing the art of the screen with each passing week. In 1909, *Pippa Passes,* his film based on a poem by Robert Browning, used light to show rising sunrays spilling through an open window, and it had never before been done. Everyone was skeptical of the effect until the results were projected. At first, watchers murmured hushed and awed comments one by one, and when the showing was over, the little experiment with a lighting effect won rousing enthusiasm. Released on October 4, 1909, *Pippa Passes* was even reviewed in the *New York Times* on October 10, 1909, which immensely startled the filmmakers.

"Browning Now Given in Moving Pictures," began the article's headline, which went on to describe the applause the little picture was generating wherever it was shown. The reviewer went on to note, "That this demand for the classics is genuine is indicated by the fact that the adventurous producers who inaugurated these expensive departures from cheap melodrama are being overwhelmed by offers from renting agents. Not only the nickelodeons of New York, but those of many less pretentious cities and towns are demanding Browning, and the other high-brow effects."

"There certainly was a decided change in the general attitude toward us after this wonderful publicity," recalled Griffith's wife, Linda Arvidson. "Directly, we had phone calls from friends saying they would like to go to the movies with us; and they would just love to come down to the studio and watch a picture being made . . . it was all too much—too much. The newspapers were writing about us. A conservative New York daily was taking us seriously. It seemed incredible, but there it was before our eyes. It looked wonderful! Oh, so wonderful we nearly wept. Suddenly, everything was changed. Now, we could begin to lift up our heads, and perhaps invite our literary friends to our movies . . . ."

All eyes were turned toward Griffith, the Biograph films, and the movies in general. At that same time, many stage actors found work increasingly difficult to obtain in the legitimate theater. Stage actors still held films with contempt; working in them was for those in need of cash paid daily. Actors who posed for them were anonymous to the public and most of them did not want their names to be known; they only appeared in them for the easy money the producers paid at the end of each day's work. It was a good way to earn money while they were between legitimate engagements. Many actors found work in those little motion pictures, and some of them went to great lengths to disguise their faces so no one would recognize them. Despite such attempts, certain actors began to emerge as favorites with nickelodeon audiences. The more often they appeared in pictures, the more familiar they became to the millions of common people across America, as well as others around the world. The masses came in unprecedented numbers. By 1910, there were

The Selig studios in Chicago, around the time when Wally and his father first explored making motion pictures.

David Wark Griffith, when he was working with Wally at Biograph.

The Star Theater, a typical nickelodeon, at the time when motion pictures sprang up by the tens of thousands around the world and all but ended the traveling live theater troupes.

9,480 movie theaters in the United States, and the demand for new films was tremendous.

When *The Girl and the Ranger* tour ended its vaudeville run in Chicago, Hal took the opportunity to investigate the motion picture phenomenon more as an act of self-defense than one of interest. He was no longer young, but he was smart enough to realize how times were changing. He decided to join the new film business rather than attempt to fight it. He and Wally visited the Selig Polyscope Company in Chicago, and it was the first time that either of them had seen the inside of a motion picture studio. Hal took a synopsis of one of his stories, *A Girl from Arizona*, to the studio. Selig-Polyscope had a great need for a capable writer with Hal's credentials. They bought his story, and he started his writing career all over again in their scenario department. They also hired him as an actor. Wally was also intrigued with the work that went on inside the studio. With characteristic zeal, he saw something new that was a combination of mechanics and art, two subjects that greatly interested him. Selig-Polyscope hired him as an assistant cameraman. At first, he merely turned the camera crank on the little black box that made the motion pictures while his father supplied the studio with stories and occasionally joined in as an actor. In a short time, Wally jumped into the work as a cameraman, writer, director, and on a few occasions, he also stepped in front of the camera to play little parts.

When asked in 1922 what prompted him to take a job in movie work, Wally replied, "Curiosity. And the chance of trying something new. I'm fond of variety, in some ways. You get it all right in the movies."

At that time, Bertha was injured severely in an automobile accident, and her recuperation forced Hal to return to New York. Wally came dutifully with him, but the desire to continue with motion picture work behind the camera remained ingrained in him. He and Hal began to look for other opportunities in the business.

Hal was a close friend of President Taft, and he was able to use his connections to bring the first motion pictures of the President signing a document in the White House to Vitagraph, the company originally founded by Jimmy Blackton and Albert Smith. In the decade that had passed since their first little film was made on the rooftop of a building, Vitagraph had become a leading contender in the growing motion picture business. Hal quickly became the head of the company's scenario department, and he personally wrote many of the melodramas produced by the pioneering film company. Within his first few weeks there, he brought Wally over. Wally's strapping good looks caught the eye of Milton Nobles, who was a writer/director preparing a short film called *The Phoenix*. The film was planned to star Nobles and his wife, Dolly. He asked Wally, who had worked in newspaper journalism, to play the part of a young reporter in the film.

"I landed my first job because I could swim . . . I saved the heroine from the icy waters of Lake Michigan, and then from a burning building in the same picture."

The Phoenix was a one-reel condensation of the same story of the play in which Bertha and Hal Reid had once appeared. Six-foot-three Wally moved with a naturally athletic gait and he projected as

The Vitagraph studio, ca. 1910 (TOP) **in the middle of shooting an interior scene with actor Tom Santschi seated at the table beneath the arc lamps. The scene as it was planned to appear in the finished film is illustrated** (BOTTOM).

strong a presence in the finished film as he had done in his brief fling at stage acting.

"During my first picture, I was very nervous. I never knew when, where, or how that camera was going to shoot. When I saw my first film, I was appalled. I had no idea I could be as awkward as I was," he wrote in *Motion Picture Magazine*.

John Bunny, comic actor appearing at Vitagraph at the time when Wally and his father first left stage work to venture into early motion pictures.

He soon found himself posing for several other films at the studio, but his real interest remained with the technical areas of writing, directing, and camera work. To his dismay, the studio wanted him *in front of the camera*, not in behind-the scenes work. Wally wanted to just run the camera and direct films, but he was easy going and cooperative. He needed the money so easily obtained with film work, so he went along with any request for his help in front of or behind the camera. "I was utility man, and always wore variegated whiskers, and learned how to write scenarios. At that time, I had no idea of sticking to the work," he later admitted.

Hal and Wally were just two of the many who were turning from the stage and its dwindling opportunities to the movies, which were picking up remarkably in popularity and supplanting the stage as the entertainment medium of choice for the average person. Rotund stage comedian, John Bunny, was another actor finding himself all too frequently unemployed and in need of quick cash. In the summer of 1910, he finished an engagement with Annie Russell in a stage production of *A Midsummer Night's Dream*, and then he decided to risk the contempt of those in the legitimate theater and try work in the movies.

Francis Agnew, in her book, *Motion Picture Acting*, asked him how he began his work on the screen at Vitagraph. Bunny recalled, "That's a long story. About three or four years ago, I was one of the foremost comedians on the stage. I have played good parts with the Shuberts, Charles Frohman's productions, and all the biggest managers. However, I awoke to the fact that the stage game was not what it had been and that the movies were the coming thing. So I decided I would rather be behind the guns than in front of them. I wanted to be with the 'shooters' rather than with the 'shot,' so I canceled my thirty weeks' contract with the Shuberts, threw aside all the years of experience and success I had, and decided to begin all over again."

Bunny went to the Vitagraph studios on East 15th Street and Locust Avenue in Brooklyn, New York, inquiring about work. Albert Smith, President of Vitagraph, recalled in his memoirs, *Two Reels and a Crank*, "His face was extraordinarily expressive despite small features almost lost in a head big and round as a billiard ball. He was short, dumpy, thick-chested, a sort of firm-bodied Sydney Greenstreet."

"Do I get the job?" asked Bunny, after the screening of his first performance in the picture. His eyes twinkled and teased, but his voice betrayed a serious overtone.

"There is a place for you here," Smith answered, "but we're facing a problem of price."

"Well, make me an offer," Bunny pressed.

"I'm afraid it would be useless," Smith replied.

Smith finally blurted out the amount of $40 dollars a week. Before he could finish the sentence, Bunny interrupted with a hearty laugh, and said, "I'll take it!"

(LEFT TO RIGHT) **William "Pop" Rock, J. Stuart Blackton, and Albert E. Smith, the three Vitagraph film pioneers.**

Wally's fifth appearance on the screen as an actor was with John Bunny in *Chumps*, a comedy about marital problems and a flying trapeze artist. Wally liked the work and found it was much easier than the experiences he had had in the theater. "I prefer it to the speaking stage," he told readers of *Motion Picture Magazine*, "because there's no running all over the United States to do the work. If there's a trip to be taken, there's always a home to come back to. And I can work fifty-two weeks in the year if I want to."

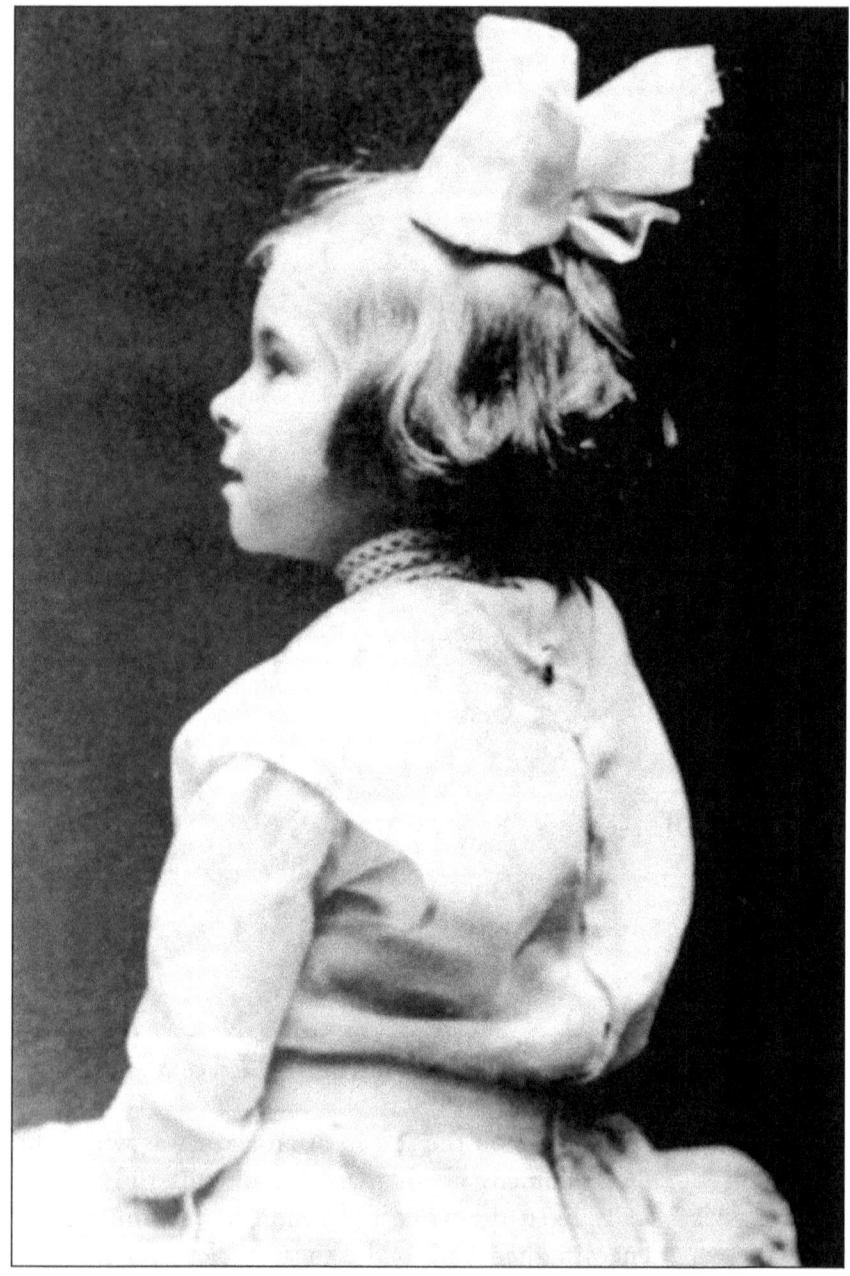

Child actress, Helen Hayes, at the time she and Wally were working in early films at Vitagraph.

One by one, even prominent stage stars were making movies. In 1910, Sarah Bernhardt was the most famous actress in the world, and she dared to make a short film of highlights from her popular stage play, *La Tosca*. A child actress, Helen Hayes, who years later would be known as the "First Lady of the American Theater," had appeared on the New York stage for several seasons, and she had barely settled into the routine of the theater when Fred Thompson, her director from the Columbia Players in Washington, approached her mother about bringing her to Vitagraph. He urged her to let Helen play in one of the films he was then directing, *Jean and the Calico Doll*.

Helen's mother quietly led her out to the Vitagraph. Both Helen and her mother were startled when they literally bumped into Bunny on their arrival. "We were stunned and then amused," Helen recollected.

"I won't tell on you," Mr. Bunny blustered, "if you won't tell on me!"

Helen's mother kept a pack with Bunny. Neither mentioned to any of their associates they were working in motion pictures. It was considered a disgrace. Mrs. Hayes even went to the extreme of trying to disguise young Helen by curling her hair for the first time and changing her mouth with makeup to keep her from being recognized in the film. "But when my first picture in support of a collie dog named Jean was shown, there I was, unmistakably me, but me looking very odd indeed. The silver screen was hardly the place to hide."

Helen remembered making pictures at the Vitagraph was a lark and a vagabond-like existence. The producers piled the cast and crew into a long line of automobiles, and drove until they spotted an estate that had the visual appeal needed for the film in production. They would jump from the cars with their tripods, cameras, and props, and hurriedly play a scene on the lawn of the estate before someone from the residence would spy them and send them packing. "We always ran faster than the owners or their servants, who sometimes came out to chase us off their property," Helen reminisced.

Wally made a big hit in Vitagraph's *Leather Stocking Tales*, a series of films directed by Laurence Trimble. He earned $25 a week playing in a number of those stories, but he still preferred operating cameras and occasionally writing scenarios during his nine-month experience at Vitagraph.

Vitagraph took full advantage of Wally's popularity, and a large part of it was his physique. Knowing that audiences would enjoy seeing the strapping youth practically stripped, they arranged roles that had him wearing very little clothes. "To be sure, I wore a string of beads and a leopard skin at Vitagraph when I made a series of Indian pictures, but it seemed all right," Wally mused. "Funny what a psychological effect a coat of tan makes. Brown like an Indian, the primitive costume seemed wholly appropriate, but with white skin you feel so darn undressed prancing about."

American maidens, who once flocked like birds to see him in matinee performances on the stage, came in long lines to reassemble in the darkness of those early nickelodeon theaters. They came by the millions. All Wally had to do was look at or near the camera and it seemed to the palpitating girls that he was looking directly at them. When he spoke by way of a subtitle, it was as if he was whispering in their ears. No stage actor, politician, or prominent person had ever been seen or admired by so many people in so many different places at one time. The producers of those films duly noted their reaction, and they concentrated on supplying appropriate films that would keep those girls and women returning several times a week. Wally quickly became one of the most popular men in the movies.

Mood music accompanying actors while they emoted in front of a camera is said to have come into use as a spur of the moment inspiration at the Vitagraph in 1910 while actress Florence Reid was finding the noisy studio atmosphere prevented her from feeling the right emotion for a scene. Another actor, Dick Rosson, picked up a violin and played music for her, inspiring her emotions so that she could play the scene with the needed feeling. While watching that moment, Wally became touched by the musical tone of the instrument. Before a few months passed, he had learned to play the violin and the viola, and when not engaged in front of the camera, he earned additional money as an off-camera mood musician, supplying atmosphere for the studio by playing his violin. He still had no desire to be an actor. Despite his ease before the camera, he had an ongoing interest in writing and directing, and his other interests were wide and varied. Cameras captured his spirit, and as his popularity grew, producers made it increasingly difficult for him to return to behind-the-scenes work. He began to lament the turn of events, but he continued to work in all areas of film production.

"I am looking forward to the time when the scenario departments will be systematized," he told readers of *Motion Picture Magazine*. "The stories are the weakest link in the chain now, and they, of course, are the foundation of the whole thing. Give us good stories, and we will show you good pictures," he promised.

In addition to the viola and violin, he also learned to play the saxophone. His mother later recalled, "He was a good violinist, to me a wonderful violinist, and he spent a good many hours of his scant leisure with his instrument."

"Movies were little more than flickering figures on a screen," related Miriam Cooper years later. "They lasted ten minutes, cost ten cents—or a nickel—and were shown in vacant stores. They did not have to understand the language to enjoy the show because, of course, all movies were silent then. That's who pictures were made for, and they looked it."

In 1910, fledgling movie producers plucked handsome young men and pretty girls from the ranks of every-day life whether they had any ability or experience. Miriam Cooper remembered that they were mostly poor girls with a family to support. "Few of us knew anything about acting . . . Mary Pickford, Blanche Sweet, and Lillian and Dorothy Gish had been on the stage for most of their lives, but Mae Marsh, Constance Talmadge, and I got in the movie on looks alone. And that was the look on our faces, not our bodies."

While Wally was working at Vitagraph, Adolph Zukor, who by then was the owner of several nickelodeons, persisted in his theory that audiences would like longer pictures. He decided to put his idea to a test and he purchased the right to show a three-reel, European version of the story of Jesus. His small theater in Newark was chosen for the experiment with the forty-five-minute film. An organ was installed, posters were created and hung on the storefront, and he began running the film one morning. The respectful, tremulous organ music drew some women inside, and the viewers gave Zukor one of the most remarkable experiences of his life: many watched the picture with religious awe, and some even fell to their knees struck with spiritual wonder. Called *Passion Play*, the

Actors on Broadway in Hal Reid's *The Confession*, one of his most popular stage plays.

picture had a good run at the Newark theater and at Zukor's other locations. The success set his mind jogging. He was attracted to the notion of longer pictures, and he wondered how much more people would enjoy seeing famous actors in motion picture versions of their famous plays. He believed that if he could only find some way to convince the producers of famous plays on Broadway to participate in the making of a motion picture for the masses, he could strike gold.

Hal continued to work in motion pictures, but he never lost his love for the stage. His play, *The Confession*, had its original production in Baltimore with the written approval of the late Cardinal Gibbons. *The Confession* opened on Broadway at the Bijou Theater, March 13, 1911. The original cast included Theodore Roberts and Orrin Johnson. Opening night brought a house crowded with many distinguished New Yorkers and a number of titled personages. Wally attended along with Bertha, and the event brought him into contact with many society people. He met a dazzling, brilliant, and talented beauty in the form of a highly cultured young American girl. He looked his dashing best in new formal clothes, and the girl was greatly attracted to the tall, blond, slim and handsome young man. She was among the throng milling about the theater lobby at intermission and after the first performance concluded. Wally first noticed her glowing dark eyes, and when her gaze met his, they gravitated toward each other and began a conversation. He learned that her name was Elizabeth Modini-Wood, and she was the daughter of Mr. and Mrs. Charles Modini-Wood of Los Angeles. Her family was full of California pioneers. She was of the Spanish type, dark and slim, dressed all in gauzy white, and was a popular debutante in Los Angeles society. She had masses of black hair and adored it with brilliant combs and lace mantillas to enhance the effect. She was beautiful of character and disposition, as much a powerful magnet to Wally as she was to everyone.

Then, Wally learned that she had a fascination for music, particularly the classics. She had made up her mind to leave behind the social whirl and study grand opera abroad. Wally learned of her plans to sail with her parent's permission to Italy that coming spring. In every way, Elizabeth seemed like a fairy princess. In fact, that is what he called her when he first told his parents about her.

Throughout the winter of 1911, Elizabeth and Wally went dining at New York's great hotels, driving through New York parks, and dancing. For two months, they were in love. They seemed eminently suited to each other, and when Wally proposed marriage, Elizabeth accepted. They were engaged, and had the official blessing of both Bertha and Hal. Then, a rude awakening slammed home with a force that Wally had never felt since the St. Louis cyclone. Elizabeth's parent's strongly objected.

The Woods did not object to Wally personally, and they did not feel negatively about his parents. Hal was, after all, a famous man, a celebrity of renown in the world of the theater. What they objected so strongly to was the idea of their daughter being married to *anyone*. They believed she was capable of a great career. At the age of nineteen, they reasoned that she had many years down the road to consider marriage. Then, there was the small matter of Wally's work—he was a motion picture actor. Neither of her parents actually knew just what that type of work was, and they did not fully understand how Elizabeth could survive on the kind of earnings he was making. She was used to the life of the rich, and there was the trip to Italy imminently on her horizon. They made all the appeals to her reason that parents could, and she reluctantly had to break the sad news to Wally that their engagement was off.

There was one last moonlight ride in Central Park. Under the stars, promises were made to renew their affection when she came back from Europe. There was a heartbroken farewell. There was a final kiss. The next day, the fairy princess was whisked away to Europe, away from the young motion picture actor and far from any chance of a rash elopement brought on by any sudden change of their minds.

After she was gone, New York became unendurable for Wally. The bright lights of Broadway were nothing but a blurry glow when he looked at them through a veil of tears. There was no excitement in going somewhere without his glamorous girl on his arm. He had suffered one of the great disappointments of his life, and it was a tremendous blow to his broken heart. Nothing could repair the damage or fill the aching void.

Wally struggled to work at Vitagraph where he directed several films and acted in many others. He was so good in front of the camera that Vitagraph wanted him to continue as an actor, but he had no intention of staying with the work. Since Elizabeth had gone to Italy, everything on the east coast had taken on a gloomy pall. He remained with them for only a few more months, and then he and his father went to Reliance, a competitor of Vitagraph's, where Hal directed several short films.

Hal sent Wally to Universal to close a contract with them for making a motion picture adaptation of one of his stories, and he

Pioneering film producer, Carl Laemmle, at Universal Studios, where Wally got his first opportunity to direct motion pictures.

succeeded in closing the deal. Hal worked at Universal for a while as an "idea man," contributing his writing skills to captions, consulting on story material, advising them on their acquisition of new talent, and writing scenarios for production.

The film business was a small world then, and nearly everyone was working without a contract and jumping from one production outfit to another, as opportunities came and went. In 1911, David and William Horsley, two Englishmen who owned the Centaur

(TOP) **Universal at the time Wally and Dorothy were working on early motion pictures. Behind rails and above the stage, visitors could observe films being photographed.** (BOTTOM) **The Nestor Company, an early film troupe, working on the west coast of California.** (STANDING LEFT TO RIGHT) **Harry Rattenbury, George French, Anton Nagy, Al Christie, Eddy Barry, Charles Christie, unidentified cameraman, director Horace Davis, unknown, Mr. Lyons.** (SEATED LEFT TO RIGHT) **Lee Moran, Ukulele Jane, Eddie Lyons, Betty Compson, Billie Rhodes, Ray Gallagher, Stella Adamas, and Neal Burns.** (ON FLOOR) **Joseph Janecke, Gus Alexander, and unknown.**

Film Company, opened a West Coast branch called Nestor Films, which was releasing pictures through Universal. Nestor was one of the first studios in Hollywood. Otis Turner, who had directed Wally in *Before the White Man Came* for Reliance, was directing pictures at Universal, and he invited Wally to go with him to Hollywood. Several companies were already out west taking advantage of the nearly yearlong sunshine to make motion pictures. It was summer, and Wally wanted to leave behind New York and the bittersweet memory of Elizabeth. Making a complete break from the recent past seemed like a good idea.

Bertha recalled in her memoirs the following dialogue between Wally and her when he telephoned to break the news that he was leaving his home on the east coast to move to the opposite side of the country in California. The call came unexpectedly, and she was unprepared to face the moment every mother knows will come, but dreads.

"Mother dear, please come up town and meet me at the Knickerbocker Hotel for luncheon. I will not have the time or opportunity to come down home, and I cannot go, sweetheart mother, without seeing you before I do."

"*Go?*" Bertha inquired, her heart chilled by the word. "*Go where, dear?*"

"The company very suddenly concluded to send me out to the coast, to their studio there."

There was a chilly silence on Bertha's end of the line.

"Did you hear me, mother dear?" Wally asked.

"Yes, dear boy, and I will take the first Sandy Hook boat going up, and wait for you at the hotel. Now, don't forget!" she admonished, as cheerily as she could muster.

By the time Bertha arrived, she was in knots about Wally moving far away again. She put on a buoyant front despite the leaden feeling in her heart over the long journey about to take him away from her. He told her that he had said yes to Turner, and in one hour, packed his bags, boarded a train, and started the journey westward. Unknown to him, already on the west coast was a teenage girl with a remarkable sense of humor and a will of iron. The train he rode was heading straight toward the land of his ultimate destiny and the woman of his dreams.

Chapter 6
HEARTS AND HORSES

In 1912, Hollywood was very different than today. Few people had ever heard of the town. Pasadena was known to be a resort where millionaires sojourned for two months to escape the freezing New York winters. The mission at San Gabriel was frequently shown in photographs, and of course, the beaches were justifiably famous. San Francisco and a few other major cities were on everyone's lips, but Hollywood was an unknown place, a little town laced with orange groves left over from when the Spaniards settled there many years before. The Hollywood Inn was the only exclusive winter resort between the city and the ocean.

Selig-Polyscope already had a studio in the vicinity of Hollywood and Los Angeles, not far from the City Hall. In the early days of 1908, they brought Frank Boggs out there to make some films. Since 1909, Bison had been making Westerns out there. Kalem had made some films in California, and even Biograph had sent D. W. Griffith there with a company to escape the gripping New York winter.

By that time, Hollywood was rapidly becoming the creative center of motion picture production, and for Wally, the invitation to work at Universal in California was the chance of a lifetime. When he arrived, he immediately understood why California was desired as a location for making motion pictures. There were quaint missions, a desert, the Sierra Mountain vistas with fascinating trails, canyons, and foothills, long expanses of ocean and beaches, somber cliffs, and flowers everywhere. It seemed like every known variety of plant life was in full blossom with gigantic, mature specimens that took one's breath away. Hollywood was still a small town with houses climbing only halfway up into the towering hills. There were big bungalows and minor mansions, and it was not unusual to see a gaggle of actors setting up a camera to photograph a film scene in front of any picturesque background they wished. Los Angeles was a remote and secluded spot in the California foothills, and Hollywood was a sweet little country village a few miles away with a small residential community nestled among the orange groves. Hollywood Boulevard, a quaint street lined with palm trees and profusions of geraniums, connected the two towns. Beverly Hills was a distant vista way out in the country, and beyond that, the wide expanse of the San Fernando Valley spread out for miles of open desert, wild flower fields, and unspoiled vistas.

Wally was assigned to work with Otis Turner making pictures for Universal. He was Turner's "general utility man," and assisted with writing stories, directing, turning the camera crank when the cameraman was missing, and acting when necessary.

Dorothy Davenport was a young actress who had arrived in California the previous summer along with her mother, Alice Shepard. Dorothy was a girl with a striking personality, red-brown hair, and big brown eyes. She was from one of the oldest and best American theatrical families. Names now forgotten but then renowned included her grandfather, a great actor in the late 1800s. E. L. Davenport was another family member prominent in the theater. Her aunt, Fanny Davenport, thrilled American audiences with her outstanding characterizations on the Broadway stage, and her father, Harry Davenport, was a multitalented actor.

Dorothy and Alice were working at Nestor with Tom Ricketts, a film director. Nestor released their films through Universal. Harold Lockwood was Dorothy's leading man, and Victoria Forde, later to become Mrs. Tom Mix, was playing ingénue roles with them. Alice worked with the unit as a character actress. Both actresses were getting $10 a week, and they worked on one or two short films each week.

Dorothy told William Parker in a Los Angeles Herald interview, "It was back in 1911 when I first met Wally Reid. I was then working for the Universal Film Co. While the pictures were restricted to one reel, 'Dorothy Davenport' was a star. I am, as many of the fans know, a niece of the famous Fanny Davenport. Wally Reid had come to the

Young Dorothy Davenport, at the time of her first work in early motion pictures.

coast with the late Otis 'Daddy' Turner—'The Governor' he was called—Wally worked as assistant director, scenario writer and general utility man. My director, Milton Fahrney, was ready to make a one-reel picture entitled *His Only Son*, a Western subject. We were without a leading man. Turner was not ready to start, and Wally, being on the company payroll at $40 a week, was assigned to us as leading man. At that time I was being paid $35 a week."

Dorothy Davenport (LEFT) **in an early Nestor film with Harold Lockwood, Donald MacDonald, and Eugenie Forde.**

Wally was not overjoyed at the prospect. He had come to California to write and direct pictures, not to act in them, but he did as he was asked. *His Only Son* followed an Easterner mistaken for an outlaw and saved by a ranch owner's daughter, who loves him and proves his innocence. *His Only Son* featured Wally's 19th film appearance and Dorothy's 27th film appearance.

"I was introduced to her this way," Wally recalled to an interviewer in *Picturegoer* in 1922. "Mr. Reid, meet Miss Davenport. Now, tell her how much you love her. Don't be so shy. Take her in your arms as though you meant it. Now, Dot, say 'Yes,' and smile at him."

"I was seventeen then," Dorothy interjected.

Wally was irritated because he was being forced in front of the cameras against his wishes. He openly moped.

Dorothy stepped aside and spoke to Jack Conway, the director. "My word, but he's a rotten actor! Where in the world did you get him?"

She was stuck with Wally. "My first definite impression of him, as a personality, was of a very good-looking, nice boy, terribly shy, and aggravatingly conscious of his height, his hands, and his feet. Though his hands proved useful, they *were* terribly big," Dorothy remembered when she looked back in 1926. "When occasionally there was nothing for him to do, he awkwardly tried to hide them behind his back, or in his pockets. After my first day's work with him, I decided that he was a very bad actor."

Dorothy was offended that she was forced her to work with someone who seemed like a big, overgrown youngster. It appeared to her that Wally did not know the first thing about acting. She went home angry after that first day spent working with him.

"At that time, I was at the very glorious age of a woman—seventeen," Dorothy thought back in a later interview, "and had been playing for some time with men of more mature years, such as Henry B. Walthall, James Kirkwood, and others. For them to give me a leading man who was only twenty-one, I considered the height of audacity. I didn't consider a man grown up until he was bordering on thirty."

The second day, her aversion to him took a remarkable turn. They were photographing a scene, and the cowboys working with them determined to put Wally in his place. Among them were Hoot Gibson, Curly Eagles, and Milt Brown, all of whom took delight in picking on dude actors who came from the East. They selected the most rambunctious horse in the corral and brought it out for him to ride in the scene. The cowboys nonchalantly lounged against the fence rails expecting to enjoy the rousing hilarity of watching the young man struggle with the rambunctious horse they knew would stop at nothing to unseat him. To everyone's surprise, Wally held on and rode like he was born in a saddle. His experience as a ranch hand in Wyoming paid off, and they were all stunned by the easy, cool, graceful way he took the tailspins in the corral. After that experience, they accepted him as "one of the boys," and Dorothy, even though she thought his profile was far too perfect to permit him to have any brains, did admire his pluck and skill. The glint of admiration and astonishment in her eyes was his reward, and Wally noticed.

"He had been playing G-string Indian roles," Dorothy explained to Grace Kingsley in 1921, "and he used to sail up past my dressing room on horseback, dolled up in a loin cloth and not much else. He used to kind of roll his eyes around to see if I was looking. Well, I will say he looked well in a G-string. He was only twenty, and straight as an arrow. Oh, yes, and I want to say right here, he had carried his family since he was thirteen years old, and this was the first time he had had a chance to get away from them and do something for himself."

Wally used to ride past my dressing room in his Indian regalia," she told a reporter for the *Los Angeles Herald*. "Mother used to rave over his handsome appearance. It was my almost daily practice to slam the door when he would appear because I knew that he knew that he was good looking, and I was not going to let him think that I had succumbed to his good looks. It sounds somewhat childish for me to relate it, but . . . I was very proud that I was a film star. Gradually, I don't know just how or why, we began going together. One night a week we went to a theater. Wally called this his 'Dorothy night.' It might appear that he had a girl for every night, but this was not true."

Dorothy was a popular young lady among the youthful players in Los Angeles in those days. At Levy's café, a round-up for picture players in the evenings, they came together on Tuesday nights. Wally asked her to go for a ride in his funny little roadster that had a top speed of twenty miles per hour. In the car beside him, she had plenty of time to study the profile that she thought was too good-looking.

Wally told her that he did not have a very good boarding place. At that time, she and her mother, Alice, were living in a little home on Alta Vista Street. Alice was as easily overexcited as Dorothy was aloof and austere. Some years before, she and Dorothy's father had divorced. There was a gruff but lovable way about Alice, and she understood young people. They frequently shared their predicaments and pleasures with her. When Wally complained about his accommodations, Alice had an idea: Wally, one of his friends, Dorothy, and she could share house expenses and she could manage the property while they handled their busy careers.

Dorothy asked Wally to come and board with them. He and Eugene Pallette moved into the house, and Alice managed it for them. With their own hands, Dorothy, Eugene, and Wally erected a set of

Two early films featuring Dorothy Davenport: (TOP) *The Best Man Wins*, a 1911 Nestor film with Dorothy at far left, Russell Bassett, and her mother, Alice Davenport, far right, with Gordon Sackville, and (BOTTOM) in a 1912 Thistle Film melodrama.

stables for three newly purchased horses, and he and Dorothy used to go out on Sunday rides in Griffith Park, up mountains among unspoiled vistas and down through the natural landscapes and free-flowing streams. The romantic atmosphere was alluring, and riding through the wilds of the virtually untrammeled countryside gave them a rare opportunity to be alone with each other and away from the hurly-burly atmosphere of making motion pictures. They also rode their horses to the studio and home at night. On Sundays, their single day off from picture work, they went riding alone through the Hollywood foothills.

In the following weeks, she was amazed at his varied abilities. "I used to wonder how many hands that boy had, that he could do so many things at once," she marveled years later in an article in *Picture-Play*. "He used to grind the camera with one, jot notes on the script with the other, and I give you my word, be putting up a set or doing something else at the same time. And he usually managed to be holding a ham

Dorothy Davenport with Wally around the time they were making *His Only Son* (1912), a Nestor-Universal film, their first appearance together on-screen.

sandwich *somehow*."

Dorothy and Wally drifted into a close friendship, and for several months while they each worked on pictures without the other, they reserved every Tuesday evening for a standing date. "It would probably have been a lot oftener, but $40 a week didn't buy many orchestra seats and fruit salads," Dorothy recalled.

"It was on one of those Sunday equestrian excursions that he first proposed to me," she thought back warmly. "We had ridden out to Griffith Park, and had brought our horses to a walk along the mountain road when he broached the question of matrimony."

"I guess it would be nice if we got married," Wally mentioned casually.

It may have been the lack of romance in the words, or her complete surprise, but Dorothy loftily informed him that they were too young to do anything of that kind, and then she spurred her horse and left him staring at her with a gaping jaw.

"But, do you know, I got the gravel from Dorothy's horse's hoofs right in the eye," Wally ruefully recounted. "She ran right away from me. No, I'm sure I never proposed again. I was awfully hard hit, I'll confess, but I was too proud for that."

Despite her rejection of marriage, Dorothy and Wally continued to date each other on Tuesdays. "He started proposing and got into the habit," she thought back fondly. "I took it for granted that the evening would always be topped off with a fervent, 'Dorothy, you're going to marry me *some* day, so you might as well say 'Yes' now, and then we won't have to argue about it any more.' I told him I thought we were both much too young to think of marriage. As a matter of fact, though I was only seventeen and he twenty-one, I meant that I thought *him* too young. For I always felt much older than Wally. My first feeling for him was maternal. His greatest charm, and he retained it to the very last, was a real boy spirit."

For the rest of the year, Wally made short one-reel and two-reel films for Reliance, Imp, Bison, and even Vitagraph where he made *Every Inch a Man* with his father. This eleven-minute film depicted Wally as the son of a farmer apprehending cattle rustlers with a clever fake robbery. In the picture, he strikes a strong, imposing figure with his height and strength, even carrying two men who are tied together.

In those months, Wally doggedly pursued Dorothy and repeatedly endured her rejections of his marriage proposals. Finally, he just decided to leave her alone. She clearly meant what she said about not getting married at such a young age, and by giving in to her wishes, he stoically suffered a second rejection from a girl he really loved. It was too much for him to endure. He decided to leave.

"He wanted me to go along as his bride," Dorothy told *Los Angeles Herald* writer William Parker. "He saw mother before he left. He said to her, 'I'll make her care for me. I've never been licked yet—and I'm not licked now.'"

1912 was the year of the *Titanic* disaster, the discovery of the South Pole, the election of Woodrow Wilson, the Becker-Rosenthal murder in New York, and the first eruptions of tango and ragtime music. People were going to the "movies" by the millions.

In 1912, Adolph Zukor was finally edging closer to making his dream of longer pictures a reality when he learned from Edwin S. Porter that Louis Mercanton, a French producer, wanted to make a four-reel film of Sarah Bernhardt in her play, *Queen Elizabeth*. The project needed funding. Zukor contacted Mercanton's American agent, and agreed to pay $40,000 in advance for the exclusive rights to the film. The gamble went forward, and *Queen Elizabeth* was filmed in Paris in May of 1912. When the finished film negative was shipped from France to New York, Zukor made arrangements to launch the film.

On July 12, 1912, *Queen Elizabeth* premiered at the Lyceum Theatre in New York for a promotional showing to the press and a distinguished audience. It was soon a huge hit in America and in Europe and vindicated Zukor's belief in longer length pictures. The film had wide distribution, a great impact on the industry, and far reaching consequences. It served to establish the effectiveness of multi-reel features in an era characterized almost exclusively by one and two reel shorts. Its success and Sarah's appearance in it raised the moving picture from its low reputation as a sideshow gimmick. It attracted huge audiences. Sarah earned 10 percent of the gross, and Zukor cleared over $80,000 by marketing it as a road show on a State's Rights basis.

Because of the success of this film, Zukor was able to finally launch his long-dreamed-of Famous Players company. By the end of 1912, Wally had been in more than twenty-five films. Nickelodeons all over the world were showing films featuring his handsome face, masculine walk, and strong personality. He directed many of those films, as well as played the leading roles. People were recognizing him on the street, and he gave himself over to the burgeoning industry whole-heartedly.

The future seemed limitless, and he was so sure of his prospects that he joined the American Film Company in Santa Barbara to act and direct films in a second production company. This firm was born from the defection of several executives and a talented team of players poached from Essanay, another pioneering film company. Those executives left Essanay, and then took up production in California with three different stock companies filming comedies, dramas, and Westerns. With them, actor Allan Dwan became a director, and he had no previous experience. When another director, Frank Beal, departed abruptly, he stepped into the job, initially relying on other more experienced actors to tell him what to do. He quickly picked up the tools of the trade. J. Warren Kerrigan and Pauline Bush were their leading players. Dwan made three pictures a week for American, mostly one-reel length, and later, they graduated to two-reel films. Dwan supervised the unit headed by Wally. As with many other directors, he watched David Wark Griffith's work at Biograph closely.

"I watched everything he did," Dwan recalled in an interview with Kevin Brownlow, "and then I'd do it, in some form or another. I'd try to do it in another way—I'd try to do it better. And I'd try to invent something that he'd see."

Griffith was the one to watch. Everyone in the industry had their eyes on him, including Wally. When Griffith started positioning actors with the sun haloed behind them, other directors started using the same technique. When Griffith lit their faces with light reflected by propping silver-painted cardboard sheets in front, others followed. He was known widely as a star maker, and Wally wanted to pair up with the best. For the time being, he worked with Allan Dwan at the American Film Company, and going to Santa Barbara meant putting distance between him and Dorothy.

She later recalled: "About a year after we met, he went to Santa Barbara with the American Film Company, where he stayed almost a year, writing and directing. I heard from him occasionally, and saw him a few times when he came to Los Angeles, but it was all very cool and casual . . . Wally came to Los Angeles occasionally to see me. He wanted me to play leads in Santa Barbara, but I did not want to break up housekeeping, and besides, I was not particularly anxious to be with him."

Allan Dwan directed the first company working at Santa Barbara, and Wally directed the second company. The two men lived with Dwan's mother.

While Wally was gone from her life, Dorothy joined the Kay Bee

Film Company, which was headed by Thomas Ince. She and Wally were separated by decision and kept apart by distance. For Dorothy, the disconnection offered time to step back from Wally's repeated and eager marriage proposals. Wally simply felt rebuffed. After the many times Dorothy had turned down his marriage proposals, he decided he was not going to offer himself again. That decision hurt Dorothy's pride, and she was surprised to find that she missed the attentive adoration he had lavished on her. Thinking his love would go on and on forever, she waited six months, and never heard from him. During that time, she starred in at least fifteen films. Then, Wally, Allan Dwan, and his leading lady, Pauline Bush, signed with Carl Laemmle at Universal.

In 1913, feature pictures received new momentum with the success of *Quo Vadis*, an eight-reel epic produced in Italy. It was presented in legitimate theaters and even ran for twenty-two weeks at the Astor Theater in New York.

Not to be outdone, in 1913, D. W. Griffith, as he then called himself, made his first spectacle, *Judith of Bethulia*, in four reels. It was the last film he made for the old Biograph Company. He signed with Mutual and was put in charge of the amalgamated Reliance-Majestic Companies. 1913 was also the year that Adolph Zukor put full steam behind his Famous Players company. His first American-made release was *The Prisoner of Zenda* with Broadway star James K. Hackett. Other pictures followed starring James O'Neill, Minnie Maddern Fiske, and Lily Langtry, and he even captured the most popular star of them all, Mary Pickford, who had left films and was appearing on the Broadway stage in David Belasco's *The Good Little Devil*. That qualified her as a "famous player," and with the best talent under his regime, Zukor was off and running to prove to the world that his idea of famous actors in famous plays would pack crowds into theaters.

There was increasing competition. In 1913, great popularity came to the Keystone Comedies when Mack Sennett, a former actor with D. W. Griffith, branched out on his own and gave full vent to his inclination for comedy with films featuring Mabel Normand, Ford Sterling, Roscoe "Fatty" Arbuckle, Mack Swain, and Hank Mann. Soon, a young Englishman named Charlie Chaplin joined them.

Universal scored an enormous success with *Traffic in Souls*, a story exposing the white slave traffic in America. Directed by George Loane Tucker, a former actor, it was made in four weeks, and ultimately grossed over $500,000. Universal also found favor with audiences with a new production of *Uncle Tom's Cabin*. The studio was doing well, and with Wally, one of the most popular male actors in the business, Carl Laemmle was ready to establish his company as a leader.

"In 1913, he came back to Los Angeles with Allan Dwan and went to Universal," Dorothy recalled to William Parker. "Wally played leads, Pauline Bush played the feminine leading roles, and Marshall 'Mickey' Neilan was the director with the company. Now here is an odd thing—Wally had returned with the determination to make me propose to him. It was a little drama in real life. Wally would come to our house for a social call. The telephone would ring. 'Is Wally Reid there?' a voice would ask. Wally would go to the telephone and say importantly, 'All right, I'll be right over.' I learned later he was having people call him up just to make me jealous."

"Once he said to me, 'You are going to marry me this fall!'"

"'Oh,' I replied, 'I suppose I have nothing to say about it?'"

"'No, you haven't,' he said. 'Your mother and I have decided it.'"

"A picture in which I was working called for location at Pine Crest, a scenic spot in California. Wally went to the railroad station with our company. He picked up a magazine on the cover of which was a picture of a girl wearing a bridal veil."

"'That's the way you are going to look this fall,' he declared. I said nothing—a fatal sign with any woman."

"At Pine Crest, I began to develop symptoms of being in love . . . I would not dance when the others danced, and I spent much time alone, thinking, thinking. Following my return to Los Angeles, Wally said one evening, 'You are going to marry me Saturday.' This time I did not say I would not marry him. I was not through protesting, however."

While Wally was in the Los Angeles area in mid-1913, he and Marshall Neilan alternated as directors, and he also wrote and acted in the films he produced. There was an incident just before he returned that made headlines, including the following report in *Motography* on January 18, 1913:

Wallace Reid, director of one of the "Flying A" companies, sustained severe injuries to his left leg when, on horseback, he was giving chase to a runaway on the boulevard one afternoon recently. His horse fell with the rider beneath it. Mr. Reid and Miss Lillian Christy, leading woman of the company, had been at the plaza and were about to return uptown. The two horses were untied when that of Miss Christy's dashed away. Mr. Reid was immediately astride his own and giving chase to the runaway. He was in a wild gallop about a block from the plaza when the animal lost its footing on the pavement and fell, carrying its rider with it. Mr. Reid's left leg was pinned beneath his mount and he suffered a severe sprain of the left ankle. The runaway stopped of its own accord upon overtaking other "Flying A" horses, which it had started to follow. Mr. Reid's injuries did not interfere with the direction of his company, although he will not be able to wear a shoe on the injured foot for several days."

The injury sustained while doing this stunt sent Wally into a hospital for treatment. He emerged seemingly in good shape, but the damage to his leg was deeper than doctors initially determined. The constant pain he felt was just the beginning of mounting agonies the leg would give him for the next ten years. When Dorothy heard about that accident, she experienced a surge of unexpected pity for him. She softened her coldness toward him and tried to think of a way to bring about their reconciliation. Perhaps she missed him more than she had realized. Those Sunday rides among the orange groves and eucalyptus were beginning to seem like distant, dreamy memories, and she realized that Wally was the perfect companion with his books, his dreams, his talent, and that smile he flashed when he had persistently proposed to her. Dorothy made up her mind that she was going to do something bold that would make him pay special attention to her again.

Chapter 7
WHEN LUCK CHANGES

Dorothy's first step to win back Wally's love was to go to work for Universal at the same time as him and make sure that they crossed paths. At first, they did not actually work together. Pauline Bush, a lovely young star at Universal, also found Wally very much to her liking, and he appeared exclusively with Pauline for many weeks in one film after another. Then, there was Cleo Madison, another beautiful and altogether enticing young woman making strides with her career at Universal. She, too, wanted Wally to play opposite her, and she made sure that she got him for several pictures. Despite those women, Dorothy saw to it that they occasionally cross paths, and she expressed a desire to work with him again. Her plot worked.

After Wally scored a big hit with *The Heart of a Cracksman*, he asked to have Dorothy play a role in the sequel, *The Cracksman's Reformation*. Wally wrote the original scenarios for both pictures, and he was careful to create the leading lady role just for Dorothy. He may not have realized it at the time, but he was falling for her all over again. He wanted her to be able to work closely with him day by day, week after week. She did not know it, but he had never lost his deep affection for her. As much as she wanted to be near him, he wanted to be with her, but first, there was Cleo Madison to consider. She obtained Wally for a picture called *Cross Purposes*, but by the very next week, Wally made sure that Dorothy was in place as his leading lady so that they could work together in a picture ironically titled *The Fires of Fate*. After that, they appeared together almost exclusively in pictures with each other. Wally still wanted to marry her, but he was also still stung by her previous refusals and held back from proposing marriage again.

Dorothy remembered the awkward situation. "He had decided that I must make the overtures, and that he would spurn me. Well, we started working together—writing, directing, and acting our one-reelers. In some way or another, we determined one day to get married. Wally always swore he never proposed to me again, and I think he was right . . . ."

Neither Dorothy nor Wally could later recall which of them was first to ask about marriage, but they both found the other adoring, attentive, and ready.

In August, Wally wrote his mother a letter announcing that they were to be married at Christmas. He told her that Dorothy was the only girl in the world for him. Bertha took the liberty of advising them not to be in too much haste, but the young lovers ignored her.

"I do not know yet whether I ever was quite forgiven for the awful offense," she later reported. "How could a mere mother . . . especially one dreaming alone to the music of the whispering, thundering, old Atlantic with nothing but the scent of the sea in her nostrils and only the light of the moon and the stars by which to read her thought-books. How could she understand the perfectly simple booking of passage on this much traveled sea?"

Dorothy and Wally surprised Bertha even more when they suddenly moved their marriage date from Christmas to October.

"If it is to be at all, it must be on the 13th," Dorothy told Wally. "Thirteen, I have always believed, is my lucky day, because of a series of three and thirteens in my life. I was born March 13, the third month of the year and the third day of the week. So I became the wife of Wally Reid, Oct. 13, 1913. We were married at 6:30 in the evening at the Church of the Holy Cross by the Rev. Baker P. Lee."

They were married quite casually and without any fuss or excitement. Actor Phil Dunham served as Best Man, and actress Ruth Roland stood as the bride's attendant. The only other persons present were Ed Brady, Isidore Bernstein, General Manager for Universal, and Dorothy's mother.

"After the ceremony, we went to the home of Mr. Bernstein in Morgan place," Dorothy recounted to William Parker. "Warren Kerrigan and Charles Worthington and Warren's mother dropped

Monday, October 14, 1913, the day after their wedding, newlyweds Dorothy and Wally were paraded down Sunset Boulevard in front of Universal Studio's building to cheering crowds of well wishers.

in. Mr. Bernstein proposed a toast to the newly married couple. It was drunk with lemonade, for that, and water, was the only liquid Mr. Bernstein ever had in his home. What a terribly place is Sinful Hollywood!"

There was no honeymoon. They were both making two pictures a week and did not have time to fuss over the usual post-wedding, romantic holiday. On the day after their wedding, they were both back at work at the Universal studio on Sunset Boulevard, the site of the present day CBS building. Together, they worked on *The Lightning Bolt*, a story with Wally as a Canadian Mountie in love with Dorothy and saving her from a conniving comrade.

The morning after their wedding, they arrived at the studio, and to their complete surprise, everyone on the lot rallied to celebrate their union and met them with a tremendous serenade of cheers and popping guns. They even forced the newlyweds to ride down the street in an open car while they followed and cheered them with

Alice Davenport, standing next to Charlie Chaplin in Mack Sennett's *Making a Living* (1913).

a noisy, impromptu ovation. To local residents, it looked like a revolution was in progress.

In a 1966 interview with Dewitt Bodeen, Dorothy remarked, "Months after our marriage, our own small unit went up into the Sierras to film several scripts, all of which had a mountain background. This location jaunt gave Wally and me a belated honeymoon—and for free, which was important then. Later on, it seemed that Wally always got jobs on pictures to be shot at the studio, while I got the sleeper-jump locations. That meant getting up at dawn, taking the red, electric car downtown, racing from Hill to Main on foot, and catching another Pacific Electric car out to Long Beach, or some place like that, where I had to be ready to start shooting by eight o'clock."

They worked on their honeymoon. The little trip to the Sierras was one in which they made an astounding quantity of five two-reel pictures in just ten days, an average of one finished film every other day. This tremendous output was not unusual for the penny-conscious Universal. They were grinding out popular short films as fast as they could be made to feed the ever-growing demand. Most movie theaters changed pictures daily, and the insatiable requirement for product put every manufacturer on full production. Speed often overtook quality, but few cared because no one thought the movies were going to last. In 1913, filmmakers believed they were riding the wave of a phenomenal fad and that it could pass just as quickly as it had mushroomed in popularity. People thought of films the same way they thought of daily newspapers, as disposable items to be seen once and then discarded. Despite the rapid working conditions, Wally wrote and directed each picture, and they were proving to be highly admired by both industry critics and the public.

Wally entered into his new arrangement at Universal with tremendous enthusiasm. He served as writer, director, and actor, and always regarded that period of his career as his happiest. His agreement with Laemmle gave full vent to his multiple talents, and he made certain that Dorothy was there to be a daily part of the newfound wonder and the creativity engaged with it.

His big hits at Universal were *The Heart of a Cracksman*, and its sequels, *The Cracksman's Reformation* and *A Cracksman Santa Claus*. Those films were establishing him and Dorothy as young lovers in the public's mind. Audiences loved seeing the two together as a gentleman-crook saving an heiress-heroine from villains. The couple also took liberal advantage of California scenery for staging many variations on stories with Wally as a woodsman entangled with a beautiful girl struggling to maintain control of a mine.

Newfound wealth, love, and devotion were the themes Wally frequently wrote about, which reflected the prosperity, adoration, and commitment he found with Dorothy. Week after week, he lovingly sharpened his pen to fashion film stories that showed Dorothy at her best, and he dotingly trained the cameras on the beautiful young woman enriching his life. It was dazzling for his friends to see his tender affection and fondness translated into brilliant, flickering shadows on a movie screen each week. His certainty that millions of people were sitting in darkened movie theaters around the world sharing his adulation kept him galvanized with inspiration. In the past, artists in love could only compose a song, write a poem, or in extreme cases, carve a statue or paint a portrait of their lover. The new power of the motion picture gave Wally a canvas on which to project his love for Dorothy in pictures the size of a roadside billboard. He reveled in the brand new liberty and creative outlet, and Universal allowed him to give full vent to his imagination.

In 1913, Wally and Dorothy played together in five movies, and the following year, they were in twenty-seven films. They were ballyhooed in magazines as an acting team, the same way Essanay was promoting Francis X. Bushman and Beverly Bayne.

In 1914, huge changes affected the old way of American life. Shortly after New Year's, Henry Ford raised the pay for his workers from $2.40 for a nine-hour day to $5.00 for an eight-hour day. Beyond Hollywood, flames of war leapt from country to country. Some of the European countries engaged in fighting were unheard of to many people in America. They had to go to their maps to look up Bosnia and some of the other geographical locations where the conflict was accelerating.

At that time, D. W. Griffith was attracting worldwide attention, and Wally was still very anxious to work with him. Griffith had finally shown a personal interest in him, but *as an actor*. Wally arranged to meet the director, and on the day of his appointment, he and Dorothy drove together to Griffith's studio. She waited in the car while he kept his appointment, and a short time later, she was shocked to see him return red-faced and fuming. Once he was in the car, Wally told her that he felt like Griffith had completely wasted his time. Instead of talking intimately with him about future work, the director joked and shadowboxed on the set, and he appeared to have barely noticed Wally at all. There was no interview, as such, and Wally felt that he had been treated discourteously.

"But Griffith did send for him again, and Wally started to work in a great many features supervised by Mr. Griffith," Dorothy recalled in her 1966 interview with Dewitt Bodeen.

In May 1914, Wally left Universal for Mutual, and his long awaited opportunity to work with D. W. Griffith. At that time, Mutual and their two subsidiaries, Majestic and Reliance, were producing some of the most outstanding pictures. Wally gave up the backbreaking schedule to which Universal had him strapped, writing, directing, and starring in two films a week. He gladly went to work for Griffith for less money, which was a significant bow to the great director's prowess. Salaries were not very big for actors at most studios, and the little house he and Dorothy owned just off Hollywood Boulevard was not yet paid-in-full. They did not feel that his earnings were the important issue; being in quality pictures made by the industry's foremost producer was the point of making the move. The prestige and creative excellence that came with having experience working for Griffith meant more than money. Wally also harbored a continual wish that he would get to write and direct exclusively. For him, being an actor was just a means to hopefully reach that goal, but he was so good in front of the camera that they kept him there. He lamented in more than one interview that his "face kept me from getting a chance to be a writer or a director." Nothing annoyed him more than the thought that he was just getting by on his looks, but despite his ambitions, that seemed to be the case.

One aspect of the Biograph tradition that carried over to Griffith's Mutual-Majestic work was his use of a complete rehearsal, a practice to which he held throughout most of his career, and a technique that Wally had not experienced in the rushed work with other companies. That was a method of pre-visualizing scenes, shots, characters, and the mood of a film, and rehearsing players to interpret the story with psychological truthfulness. Griffith emphasized the importance of thought, feeling, and characterization, and he urged his players to remember that "thought can be photographed." Wally's performances were greatly enriched by his association with Griffith and the other directors trained in his methods.

Writer George Blaisdell wrote about going to Griffith's Broadway studio to talk with Henry B. Walthall, an actor in a film then being produced with Mae Marsh. He observed the unusual atmosphere of a Griffith scene as it progressed from rehearsal to film.

> "Near the Broadway end of the building, Jim Kirkwood was seated in a comfortable chair, his long frame sunk into its depths as he meditatively watched and guided the rehearsal of the players under him. We wandered to the Sixteenth Street part of the studio. Under lights fiercer than any that ever beat on a throne stood Blanche Sweet and Mae Marsh rehearsing a scene in the forthcoming feature production of Paul Armstrong's *The Escape*. In the play, the two are sisters.

Miss Sweet uttered no word. Her lips did not move. She looked. You felt what she was thinking. Miss Marsh, a slip of a girl looking even younger than she actually is—and she is in the teens—indulged in pantomime. Her lips moved, but she spoke not. A slight cough indicated the tuberculosis taint of the character she was portraying. It was all very interesting. For a quarter of an hour, we stood by the camera just behind a tall man seated comfortably, a big brown fedora hat pulled over his eyes to serve as a shade from the lights. He was talking into a megaphone. It was a mild, conversational tone. At times, there would be a lull. Then again, there would be advice, but the voice was not raised. So this was the man who so thoroughly inspires his players that they, in turn, may penetrate and stir the hearts of their audiences; who by his magnetism binds to him with hoops of steel these same players. It is a rare trait, this secret of commanding unbounded loyalty . . . especially in one of pronounced artistic temperament. It is a cordial handshake Mr. Griffith has for a stranger."

Wally came into this environment of carefully rehearsed, seriously considered stories, and he was ready to grow as an artist. He was eager to learn and refine the skills he had been practicing offhandedly for the past four years. There was another reason for his determination to get into the middle of the Griffith goings on: rumors were spreading that the renowned director was about to produce the greatest picture ever made. No longer content to grind out short films on a twice-weekly basis, he had proven to the narrow-minded directors of Biograph that audiences wanted longer, better pictures, the very idea with which Adolph Zukor had been obsessed for the past half decade. Both men were correct. Griffith planned to go a step farther with his next film and recall with broad scope the most moving series of events from recent American history. Griffith intended to reopen emotional wounds from the Civil War between the North and South, wounds that had barely healed. He was going to write history with the lightning strokes of the motion picture techniques he had honed to perfection in the four years and hundreds of short films he had produced at

Biograph. He was going to fan the flame of race troubles that were festering in every city of the country by depicting situations that would inflame barely squelched sentiments. In short, he was going to use every power at his command to make the biggest and best feature-length film ever made.

Two of Griffith's prized actresses came with him to Mutual. Back in 1912, both Lillian and Dorothy Gish had initially come from the theater to work for him. Both girls had spent most of their young lives touring in one stage show after another. Like Mary Pickford, their childhoods were spent working in theater plays. Working in the close-knit film community was their first real chance to stay together in one place as a family. With their mother, they eagerly followed Griffith when he left Biograph, and they stayed with him during that time when he shifted to making longer pictures on a greatly increased schedule.

In 1914, Wally worked under Griffith's supervision at Mutual, appearing with Dorothy Gish in *Arms and the Gringo*, *The City Beautiful*, and *Down the Road to Creditville*. He was with Lillian Gish in *Enoch Arden*, and he was with Blanche Sweet in five pictures. He appeared with other stars in at least nine other productions supervised by Griffith. All the while, Griffith kept close watch on his progress, scrutinizing every new film as it came off the Mutual assembly line. Wally did not know that he was mentally earmarking him for a role in his upcoming epic drama about the Civil War.

Many of the Mutual films were directed by George Siegmann, George Beranger, Fred Kelsey, John B. "Jack" O'Brien, Christy Cabanne, and Donald Crisp, but they were supervised by Griffith. During 1914 and 1915, they directed Wally in nearly two dozen films of varying lengths.

In 1914, Griffith personally directed him in the critically acclaimed film, *The Avenging Conscience* Wally's role was small, but the film was widely admired. Wally was kept active making interesting pictures for the Griffith organization, Griffith was busy secretly preparing one of the two independent pictures his contract allowed him to produce each year. He deliberately set out to make the world's greatest motion picture on a scale without precedent in the short history of motion pictures. He was eager for credit and triumph, and chose for a story a scenario based on *The Leopard's*

Stripes and *The Clansman*, two novels by the Rev. Thomas F. Dixon, Jr. The merged stories were to be shaped into a single story called *The Clansmen*. In the Griffith Studios at 4500 Sunset Boulevard, Hollywood, California, Fred Booth Hamer was casting all the principal and small parts.

Miriam Cooper, a girl from New York, had been pestering those in the Griffith organization for work. Christy Cabanne had even filmed a test of her, but they never called her back. She went to the Kalem Company, was hired to appear in a number of pictures, but when the job ended she was again out of work. She joined the line of actors waiting on a bench for any work Griffith might have available. One day, she happened to run into Christy Cabanne.

"Where've you been? I've been looking for you. You're not in the phone book."

"I don't have a telephone," Miriam told him.

"Well, Mr. Griffith wants to see you. Come to the studio at nine o'clock in the morning."

Miriam was flabbergasted. Her previously filmed test had been forgotten until Griffith had run it along with some other old tests. She was invited back to again test for a short scene with Bobby Harron, a youth who had found work at the Biograph Studio as a general office boy before becoming one of their actors. He had big, expressive, brown eyes, and he was well-liked by everyone. Griffith rehearsed Miriam in a scene with Bobby, urging her to pretend that she was a girl in the Civil War. He seemed satisfied with the way she responded to his direction. Griffith invited her to come with them to California to be in the Civil War story he was about to make. There was no contract to sign, just an offer to earn $35 a week if she was willing to ride on the train to California when they were ready to leave. She went.

Griffith's choice for the leading role in his civil war film was Henry B. Walthall. However, Walthall did not feel he was physically right for the character of the "Little Colonel." Walthall became ill and was unable to undertake the role. Some even said he was not expected to live. Griffith believed Walthall's subtle yet powerful body language and expressive eyes would make the character of the "Little Colonel" the outstanding part in the picture, but with him sidelined and sick, six-foot three-inch Wally Reid was on call just in case his services as a not-so-little colonel were needed. Walthall remained sidelined just as the picture was about to begin principal photography, and Wally was told to get ready to step into *The Clansmen* in the role.

On a dreary, cold, January day, other actors in New York who were to be in *The Clansmen* left for California. By the time their train arrived in Los Angeles, Wally and the rest of the actors and crewmembers were already on the west coast. On February 14, 1914, Griffith arrived, ostensibly to finish making *The Escape*, while at the same time, he was making arrangements for the use of thousands of extras, uniforms, and horses that had nothing to do with *The Escape*. His Civil War project was undertaken at the same time, an incredible feat for one man.

In a rural area of Los Angeles that was dotted with several turn-of-the-century houses, there was an insignificant street called Sunset Boulevard. In that neighborhood, Griffith converted a dark gray, two-story frame house into his new Reliance-Majestic studio and office. There, the actors rehearsed, and behind the buildings, two outdoor stages were erected with muslin sheets strung overhead that could be pulled back and forth to diffuse the sunlight. A profusion of cardboard squares painted silver lay haphazardly at the side of those stages that could be maneuvered around and pointed in any direction to reflect sunlight where Griffith wanted additional light to fall.

Griffith rehearsed *The Clansmen* for six weeks, and then on July 4, 1914, on America's Independence Day, he began filming in the countryside outside Los Angeles.

"Wally's enthusiasm was unbounded!" remembered Dorothy. "Costumes were made up to fit him, and about five-hundred feet of film was made of Wally in a few scenes of the part." *The Clansman* told the tales of two families torn apart by the ravages of the Civil War and the following Reconstruction period. It was epic in scope, and Wally's role in it was a golden opportunity for any actor. Even though he only wanted to write and direct, he was thrilled to play such an important part in such a noteworthy effort.

After acting the role of the "Little Colonel" in about half a reel of photographed film, Wally was hit with a big shock: Henry Walthall's mysterious illness was rumored to be little more than repercussions from a malaria fever he suffered while in the Army. Others whispered that the illness was self-imposed. Walthall was an alcoholic, and sometimes disappeared from the studio for days at a time. In either case, he returned to work on the *The Clansman*. Wally and Dorothy were nearly killed with disappointment. "Wally was incensed to the point of mayhem," Dorothy remembered.

According to Lillian Gish in *The Movies, Mr. Griffith, and Me*, a bodyguard was assigned to trail Walthall and insure that he arrived at work on time and did not imbibe excessively. Walthall was such a big talent that Griffith occasionally had to put up with such anxieties in order to have him work for him. Despite Wally's proven ability to play the lead role, Griffith still wanted Walthall in the part, and Wally was replaced.

With the big role going to Walthall, Griffith lessened Wally's disappointment by then telling him that he had him in mind for the undersized but spectacular part of Jeff, the blacksmith, a typical, small Southern townsman.

In the story, Gus, a Negro, chases Mae Marsh as Flora to the edge of a cliff. In fear of being attacked, she flings herself over the precipice and lands mortally wounded at the foot of the cliff. Her brother, Ben, finds her, carries her lifeless body home, and enlists townsmen to search for Gus, who hides in "White-Arm" Joe's gin mill. Wally appears as Jeff the blacksmith, one of the white townsmen, and faces up to the group of Blacks, who are hiding Gus. Tension between Jeff and the Negroes erupts into a long, brawling fistfight with hurled chairs, bare fists, and smashed gin bottles. As Jeff emerges beaten and shirtless but victorious, he stumbles outside only to be shot twice, once at point-blank by Gus. Now guilty of overt murder, Gus flees for his life with more white townsmen in pursuit.

Griffith thought Wally embodied the quality and substance of a white man filled with fury that he needed to pit against Gus in the fight scene. He was to single-handedly fight off the entire gang of rum-crazed Negroes. Wally agreed to do the part. What he did not know was that Griffith had counted on his fuming anger over the loss of the "Little Colonel" role to infuse his role as Jeff with so much fury that it would melt the screen, a ruse Griffith had used many times before on other actors. It worked. The angry fight, as recorded on film, was spectacular and mostly real.

Mae Marsh, who played the "Little Sister" in D. W. Griffith's *The Birth of a Nation* (1915).

Henry B. Walthall, who Wally thought he was going to replace as "The Little Colonel" in D. W. Griffith's *The Birth of a Nation* (1915).

Elmo Lincoln played at least three roles in *The Clansmen*. In a 1948 interview with Seymour Stern, he told how Wally tore into the fight with unexpected abandon. "The fight was terribly realistic," he said. "Round tables were used; one table was smashed. The Negroes got badly banged up in the fracas. Several persons in all were injured and had to be hospitalized. The fight started in rehearsal with such ferocity that Griffith stopped it and said he would take the close-ups first. After the close-ups were taken, the fight resumed for the camera. All thought of further rehearsals was abandoned."

Lincoln went on to relate that Wally was in good shape in those days and packed a powerful punch. He knocked Lincoln almost senseless. Although resin bottles were used for the fight, the prop department made the mistake of filling the bottles with water to represent gin. As the players began swinging, the result was wild carnage on the set, and ultimately, a rousing, realistic fight in the finished film that was infused with Wally's deeply felt fury. For the rest of his career, even though he staged a number of other fight

CHAPTER SEVEN: WHEN LUCK CHANGES | 105

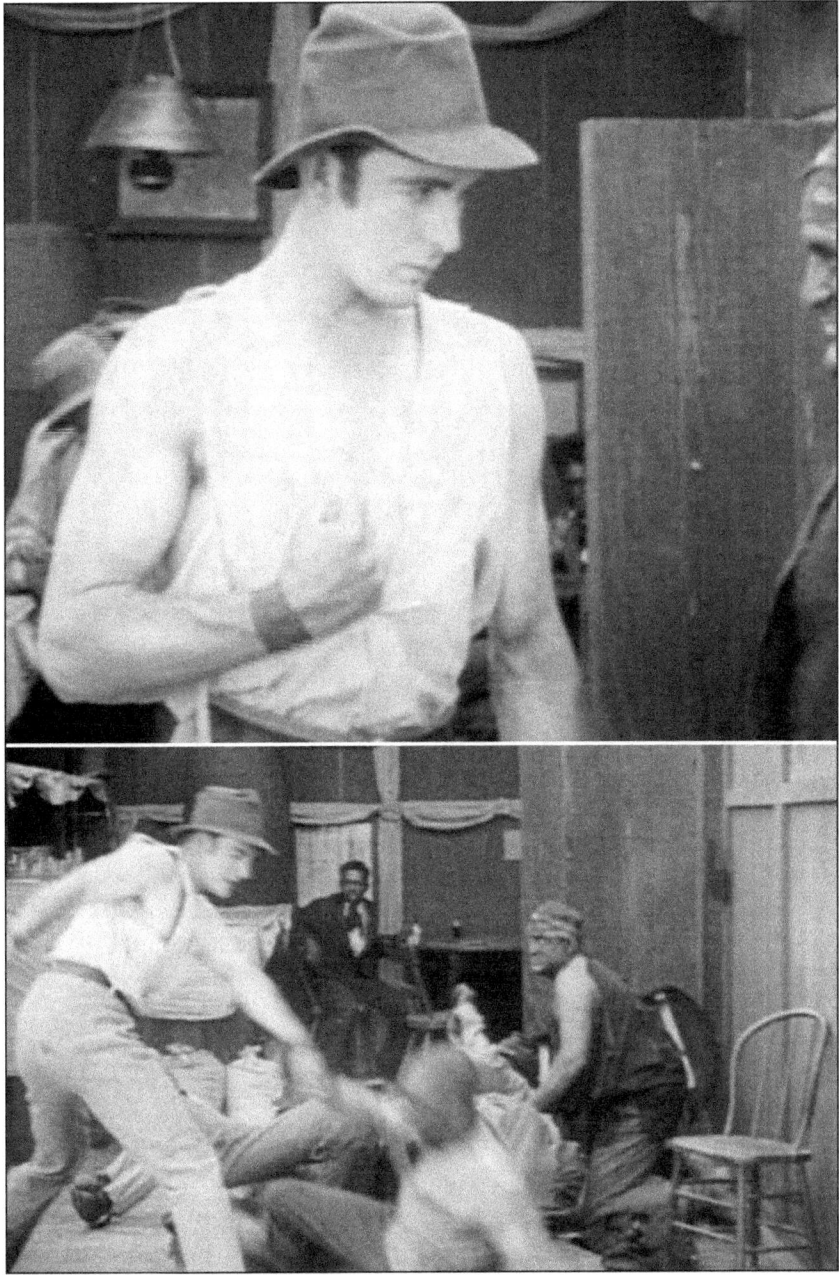

In D. W. Griffith's *The Birth of a Nation* (1915), Wally as Jeff, the blacksmith, faces off with (TOP) Walter Long as Gus. The confrontation quickly erupts into a fight between Jeff and (BOTTOM) an entire roomful of men with flying fists, smashed gin bottles, and broken chairs. In this three and one-half minute brawl inside a gin mill, Wally became an "overnight star."

Dorothy Davenport remembered Wally playing Jesus Christ in the allegorical ending to D. W. Griffith's *The Birth of a Nation*. In this frame enlargement, the face behind the beard and hair is either Wally's or someone looking remarkably similar to him.

scenes, none equaled the ferocious display Griffith managed to capture in this film.

Dorothy also claimed that Griffith used Wally as the Christ figure in the allegorical tableaux at the close of the film when an image of Jesus is double-exposed over figures of fighting men. Near the story's end, just before Ben and Elsie sit by the sea's edge, an allegorical Epilogue symbolizes the peaceful rejoining of the North and South after many battles and the painful Reconstruction Period. It is followed by a prophecy of the second coming of the Prince of Peace with this subtitle:

"Dare we dream of a golden day when the bestial War shall rule no more?

But instead—the gentle Prince in the Hall of Brotherly Love in the City of Peace."

Symbolic images of the demonic forces of war, throngs of suffering people, and piles of dead corpses are shown, and then they dissolve into a panorama of angels in flowing robes. A tableau with a benevolent Christ-like figure emerges from the background, signifying the vanquishing of the God of war and the reign of everlasting peace, unity, harmony, and brotherhood throughout the world. Ben and Elsie are shown again. Then, the film fades to its final subtitle:

"Liberty and union, one and inseparable, now and forever!"

No list of credits authenticates the name of the actor posing briefly as the Christ figure, but the face of the tall, white-robed actor looks remarkably like Wally.

On February 8, 1915, *The Clansman* premiered at Clune's Auditorium in Los Angeles. The film had everyone agog over the vastness of its theme and the emotional wallop it packed. It also met with immediate and tremendous controversy, exactly as Griffith hoped. In the second half of the film, Negroes were depicted as brutes lusting for white women. Audiences hissed, and when the picture was shown in Northern cities, riots broke out, and police were frequently called to shut down the screenings, or control the erupting violence. It became a must-see event, and for many viewers, it was the first motion picture they had ever seen. Wherever it was shown, people came from miles around to witness the remarkable epic. In Washington, the picture was shown at the White House to President Wilson and his family, and a special showing was staged for the Justices of the Supreme Court and members of the diplomatic corps. On February 20, 1915, another special showing was arranged in New York at the Rose Gardens on 53rd Street and Broadway. There, Rev. Thomas F. Dixon, Jr., the author of the original book, saw it for the first time. Stunned and enthusiastic, Dixon told Griffith that the name *The Clansman* was too tame. He suggested "*The Birth of a Nation.*" On March 3, 1915, under its new title, the motion picture went into wide distribution.

According to a report in the *New York Times*, *The Birth of a Nation*, as *The Clansmen* was then called, ran at the Liberty Theater in New York from March 3, 1915 to Jan 2, 1916, a total of forty-five weeks and 1,620 exhibitions. Simultaneously, outlying theaters showed the picture 6,266 times. In round numbers, an estimated 616,000 people saw the film at the Liberty, which when added to the other showings in outlying New York theaters, brought the figure up to approximately 872,000 people. That was about one-seventh of the city's population. Nationwide, more than 5 million people were estimated to have seen the film in the first year of its release. *The Birth of a Nation* was a phenomenon.

"They now say that movies are the art form of our time. If they are, it's because of Mr. Griffith," said Miriam Cooper in her 1973 autobiography.

The truth is that the multitude of smaller films that Wally had made over the last seven years had blanketed the world's film exhibition circuit with film prints containing his face and name. The instant his face appeared on a movie screen, he was recognized in the Orient, Europe, and Africa, as well as at home in America. By 1915, there were innumerable film prints trading through film exchanges containing an appearance by Wallace Reid, whether his name was on the film or not. He was as familiar as a favorite household product, and a murmur swept throughout a theater the moment his name or face shown was on the screen. The success of *The Birth of a Nation*, along with those many other films, brought him to a prominence shared only by Mary Pickford, Charlie Chaplin, and a few other actors, but some people still claimed that Wally became a star "overnight" with the unprecedented success of *The Birth of a Nation*.

The Birth of a Nation swept through the ranks of successful motion pictures like a whirlwind. It ran for twelve reels, a long film for that time, and quickly began to roll up record grosses. Each investor exhibiting the film in a State made millions of dollars. Everyone connected with the picture became famous. *The Birth of a Nation* was the single most successful motion picture produced up to that time.

"Wally Reid was now *Wallace* Reid, if you please, and a Big Name in his own right," recalled Karl Brown, Griffith's assistant cameraman, in his book, *Adventures with D. W. Griffith*.

Wally was attracting more than just a name change. In the East, one of the most brilliant figures among American women, a great talent, a famous beauty, a dazzling wit, a woman of dynamic force and wide experience, was literally waiting in the wings to blow full force into motion pictures and into his life. She was coming to California with all the pomp of a queen. With her, Wally had one, great, common love—music. Once again, Wally's destiny was about to change because of forces that were beyond his control.

Chapter 8
WOMEN AND ROSES

"Is Wallace Reid stuck on himself?" pondered H. C. Witwer in a *Picture-Play* article. "Does he upstage his little playmates on the lot? Just what kind of guy is he off the screen? Well, I think the following about answers the above questions: while he and I were waiting the pleasure of the cameraman, perhaps threescore and ten men, women, and children—passed before us. They were other stars, directors, extras, electricians, property men, press agents, stenographers, office boys, executives, painters, scenario writers, carpenters, visitors, et cetera. Not one of them went by without a wave of the hand and a grinning 'Hello, Wally!' and not one missed getting a smiling greeting back, with a comment on some subject of particular interest to the speaker." Witwer went on to describe how a grimy, overalled carpenter stopped to tell Wally about some new effect he had worked out, and Wally listened with great interest, promising to run down and see it.

Wally won many screen popularity contests. Those little incidents Witwer expressed, although trivial on the surface, told it all. He was "Wally" to the big directors, the money kings, and the stars, but to be hailed with an affectionate nickname by the hard-boiled and cynical mechanics, cameramen, and extras, case-hardened experts at reading character proved that he was just a regular guy who was unimpressed by the newfound fame thrust upon his life.

"Most of Hollywood's people had come from humble beginnings," noted Adolph Zukor in his memoirs. "They had never expected to have much money, yet here they were, rolling it in. Having struck it rich without knowing exactly how or why, they could not get it through their heads that the gold might peter out. Take for example a young actor or actress who a couple of years earlier had been making $25 or $35 a week as a clerk, or the same amount in stock. He or she might now be collecting $500 to $1,000 a week, more than the richest man in the old hometown, yet it was a rare performer who did not feel underpaid."

Celebrity status also came with a hidden price tag, as most of those young people were quickly learning. Movies were no longer a fad, a fact that became clear to everyone, but with success came scrutiny. With their leap in popularity came a loss of privacy. Wealth brought worries, and they either faced them squarely, or like Wally, pretended there was nothing to bother about.

He and Dorothy enjoyed frequent dancing at Baron Long's dance hall in the little town of Vernon. It was a gathering place for many movie stars, starlets, and hundreds of lesser lights. The hall boasted one of the best jazz bands in southern California. For many months, Wally won the weekly dance competition. Kenneth Harland was his only serious competition. Wally could play every instrument in the band, and he was not shy about taking the violin from the orchestra and playing perfectly the tune they were performing.

Making ends meet each month on $40 a week proved difficult. An inveterate smoker, Wally spent at least a quarter of this sum on expensive cigars and pipe tobaccos. Still, he swore to writer Kathlyn Hayden in an article in *Picture Show* that he had no trouble managing the household expenses despite his fancies.

"Well, of course, we are not counting the monthly payments on our new bungalow," he confessed. "And, of course, we are not counting the monthly payments on my ninety-horse-power automobile. Then, of course, there are my dues at the Los Angeles Athletic Club, they're outside the $40. And we don't count servants' wages either. But, outside of those details, we are keeping expenses strictly within $40 a week!"

Somehow, he did contribute a weekly amount to a brokerage firm, who managed a gilt-edged securities portfolio for him. With his newfound popularity came lucrative offers from other film producers. Nearly everyone involved with *The Birth of a Nation* found they were suddenly "in demand." Some, like Lillian Gish, stayed with Griffith for a number of years, but others lent an ear to increasingly frequent offers from competing motion picture producers.

"Eventually, I want to direct," Wally persisted in confiding to writer, Maude Cheatham. At that time, he was still hopeful that he could go back to working behind-the-scenes writing and directing as he had done so well at Universal. "I know well enough that my popularity will not always last, and though I intend to stay in motion pictures just as long as the public wants me, I shall leave them as soon as I feel myself slipping. Lord knows, when you have eaten a big dinner, no matter how enjoyable it may have been, it is terrible for the hostess to urge you to eat more. Well, I'm not going to force my pictures when the public feels they have had enough."

In 1915, one of the last pictures Wally made with D. W. Griffith's organization was *Old Heidelberg*, which was directed by John Emerson and supervised by Griffith. In the story of a student prince who falls in love with a tavern maid, played by Dorothy Gish, Wally faced perhaps the first and only time a leading lady refused to play a kissing scene with him. Lillian Gish recalled in *The Movies Mr. Griffith and Me*, "Mr. Griffith had almost a mania for cleanliness. He himself was always impeccably groomed, and he expected the young actresses on the lot to be equally immaculate. A female aspirant would lose out if she weren't scrupulously clean. One morning, Dorothy appeared at the studio wearing blue jeans, with her hair in kid curlers. He spoke to Mother about it, and Dorothy never repeated her mistake. Mr. Griffith's emphasis on hygiene once had an unexpected consequence. Dorothy had been assigned to play the role of Kathy in *Old Heidelberg*. Her leading man was Wally, who was much older than she . . . when they were about to film the first love scene, he told Wally to kiss Dorothy on the mouth."

"Oh, Mr. Emerson," she exclaimed. "We don't do such things in pictures."

"You're going to do it in this picture," Emerson said ominously. "How else are you going to play a love scene?"

"In films," she informed him, "we *pretend* to kiss. And with the camera at a distance, it seems that we do."

"Well, this time the camera is close, and I want you to kiss him."

Dorothy refused to argue in front of Emerson about his request. She ran to Frank Woods, the head of the story department, with

Dorothy Gish, who refused to kiss Wally on camera, is shown with the famous wig that she wore in so many films.

Emerson in hot pursuit at her heels. Kindly, white-haired Woods was also the judge in all studio disputes.

"You know Mr. Griffith told us we must never kiss actors—it isn't healthy," Dorothy complained to him, "but Mr. Emerson doesn't seem to understand."

"How can I do a love story without a love scene?" Emerson fumed.

Jesse Lasky, who partnered with Cecil B. DeMille and Samuel Goldwyn on Wally's Paramount films.

The dispute became the talk of the entire studio, and the controversy continued for several days with Dorothy and Emerson at a stalemate over the matter. Wally told his wife about the incident, and she took it upon herself to telephone Dorothy's mother. Indignantly, she informed Mary Gish that Wally was perfectly healthy and that it would certainly not hurt Dorothy to kiss him. In the end, Emerson won, and a weepy, defiant Dorothy Gish kissed Wallace Reid on the mouth while the camera cranked and filmed them in a tight close-up.

Griffith did not hold Wally back from professional growth. Having directed so many short films during the last seven years, Wally entertained offers from other companies, and he finally accepted an offer from the Lasky Feature Play Company. He hoped it would finally open the window of hope and lead to the fulfillment of his ambition to again write and direct films.

Jesse Lasky had first found work as a youth playing a cornet in a San Francisco theater, and for one brief period, he was the only white man in the Royal Hawaiian band. He did newspaper reporting for a few months, tried his luck at gold prospecting in Nome, Alaska, and bounded back to San Jose to join his sister, Blanche, in a juvenile act performing at benefits, clubs, and in vaudeville. He found he could make more money as a manager, and promoted several acts in partnership with B. A. Rolfe, another coronet player. As Lasky & Rolfe, they prospered, and Lasky quickly amassed several hundred thousand dollars, a fortune in those days. He invested everything in an idea to bring the Folies Bergére cabaret idea to New York. It failed, and Lasky was broke. He asked his young friend, Cecil B. DeMille, to write a libretto for an opera based on life in California, and the piece succeeded. One night, Lasky and DeMille were sharing a dinner and moaning about their financial woes.

"Perhaps," DeMille said, "we had better go down to Mexico and join a revolution."

"If it's excitement you want, let's make moving pictures," he said.

They sketched a plan for a new company on the back of a menu. Lasky warily approached his sister, Blanche, and her husband, Samuel Goldfish, and by pooling their resources into a $26,500 capital fund, they ventured into an arrangement named Lasky Feature Play Company. They spent $5,000 of that fund for the rights to a successful stage play, *The Squaw Man*.

Jesse Lasky and Cecil DeMille approached Dustin Farnum, a popular stage actor, as soon as they found him at the Lambs Club in New York. They asked him to play the lead in their first motion picture production of *The Squaw Man* for $1,000 and a percent of the earnings. Farnum agreed to appear in the picture, but he wanted $5,000 up front in cash. With a renowned actor on board, they went to Flagstaff, Arizona, and made their first film among the cactus trees. From there, they went to the wilds of California, rented an old barn at Vine and Selma Streets, and in a short time, they completed work on *The Squaw Man* and it went on to make the initial fortunes for their company. Jesse Lasky was President, Samuel Goldfish was Vice President, and DeMille was the director and partner.

By 1914, the movies had finally become respectable, and Lasky's busy studio stepped up their pace to thirty-six pictures in their second year of production. They needed a steady flow of new product and they were looking for other stars to further their success.

Cecil B. DeMille thought back in his autobiography to his first impression of Wally. "When Jesse Lasky and I had gone to see *The Birth of a Nation*, I had noticed in it a young man playing a very small part as a blacksmith. He stayed in my mind. He was handsome and clean-cut; he knew how to behave in front of a camera, making even his brief appearance memorable. His name, I made it my business to discover, was Wallace Reid. He had a few years' experience in films, but in parts so small that he welcomed the extra dollars he could make playing mood music for the big stars. I sent for him, and our conversation confirmed my belief that he was star material himself. I felt, as I have often felt since about stars and stories, that the public would like what I liked in Wally Reid; and I backed my judgment by giving him the lead in *Maria Rosa*, his first staring role."

Jesse Lasky also remembered seeing Wally in *The Birth of a Nation*. "A young man who played a bit part as a blacksmith had a perfect physique, large, expressive eyes, and flawless features," Lasky recalled in his memoirs. "He was about six feet tall and weighed in the neighborhood of 180 pounds. Seeing him was just like finding a 180-pound diamond, for within a year, we would be reaping gratifying profits from eight pictures featuring his brawn and irresistible appeal, and the tonnage of his fan mail would be making our distaff stars jealous."

Lasky signed Wally to a contract *as an actor*. With that agreement, his ambition to direct and write was forcibly ended. He may have thought the contract for his work as an actor would be temporary, and that once he was established, they would realize the full depth of his abilities and let him do the kind of capable directorial work he had already proven with many short films. For the time being, he swallowed his ambition, and put on grease paint.

In the films they proposed, there would be no female stars distraught about kissing him. In fact, they fully expected to depict in one screen romance after another. Jeanie Macpherson, an actress who abandoned her acting career to work as a writer for Jesse Lasky, delivered to the producers *The Golden Chance*, a splendid original story. Lasky thought the story was made to order for Wally. Wishing to establish their bright, new star on the roster of his new company, the story called for the finest production effort his people could give. That predestined the proposed film for their finest director, Cecil B. DeMille. There was only one problem: DeMille had already put into production on October 20, 1915, *The Cheat* with Sessue Hayakawa and Fannie Ward. The only way to get *The Golden Chance* made quickly was to accomplish the seemingly impossible task of simultaneously directing Wally in *The Golden Chance* and Sessue Hayakawa in *The Cheat*. According to records at The George Eastman House, production started on October 26, 1915, and then briefly halted. Production restarted on November 5, 1915 with a full crew and cast working on *The Cheat* from nine o'clock in the morning until five o'clock in the evening. After having dinner at his desk, DeMille slept until eight o'clock, a brief three-hour snooze, and then rose to meet the fresh-as-a-daisy cast and crew of *The Golden Chance*. DeMille worked the second picture's crew and cast until their quitting time around two o'clock the following morning. He slept another few hours, and after breakfast, he resumed the routine day after day until both pictures were concurrently completed on schedule. *The Golden Chance* was completed on November 26, 1915. DeMille endured that grueling schedule for the first and only time in his long career. The effort would have broken a lesser man, but he survived the ordeal, and both pictures turned out beautifully. DeMille then took a well deserved three-day vacation. *The Golden Chance* cost $18,710.81, and once released on six reels on January 31, 1916, the film grossed $83,504.03.

Having launched Wally firmly on his way to becoming a stellar attraction, Lasky continued to search far and wide for other talent. Morris Gest, David Belasco's son-in-law and prominent impresario, attended a dinner one Sunday night at the home of opera star,

Cleo Ridgely and Wally in Cecil B. DeMille's *The Golden Chance* (1915), which was filmed in eight-hour shifts at night while DeMille also filmed *The Cheat* during the day.

Geraldine Farrar, along with her father and mother, Mrs. David Belasco, and a few other friends. After dining, Geraldine reflected philosophically over coffee.

"How cruel it is," she exclaimed, "that riches, or at least comfort, come to most people when they are too old or too weary to enjoy life or the beauty of countries and peoples they have never seen!"

Geraldine led her guest to her library and pointed out portraits of various eminent Europeans. Among them was a portrait of the Emperor of Germany.

"How different he is now," she said, gazing at the portrait, and musing. "Really, to perpetuate one's youth one should have a photograph taken every day until age begins."

Morris seized the moment in conversation to hint about her considering an appearance in a motion picture. "The only way to really live forever,' he answered, "is on a picture screen. The chap who invented the movie camera found the eternal youth spring that Ponce de Leon missed."

Later, in a July interview, Morris recalled that Geraldine "laughed the suggestion away, but it occurred to me, in coincidence, that Mr. Belasco's *The Girl of the Golden West* was having its first picture showing that very evening at the Strand. Miss Farrar was very glad to attend, but in the limousine en route, she confessed to me that she had seen but one film in her life, and that was *Quo Vadis* at the Cinema Theater, Paris."

"I've been just too busy, resting or working, to go," she explained. "No prejudice, I assure you. I rather like them." Morris noticed how Geraldine referred to movies with the word "them," as if they were something quite distant from her.

Geraldine was amazed as she entered the Strand, a theater built exclusively for the exhibition of motion pictures.

"Why," she cried, "it is almost as big as the Metropolitan Opera House! I had no idea so many people went to see moving pictures, and such people! I really see opera-goers here!"

Morris hesitated, but put in, "Wouldn't it be a wonderful thing if . . . ."

"What?" asked Miss Farrar.

"I won't tell you now. I'm afraid you'd laugh."

Morris continued at intermission. "Look around . . . here are nearly four-thousand people in this enormous theater. There is a play, which was given by high-salaried artists in a high-priced theater to a very limited audience. Here we have four times Mr. Belasco's original audience, seeing a superb production of his play for a quarter of a dollar and perhaps thirty other audiences, in thirty widely separated cities, are seeing the same thing."

"Well?" the prima-donna interjected.

"Just this," Morris continued. "Wouldn't it be a wonderful thing for the thousands of people who may never see or hear you, through limitations of purse or geography, to see your image on the screen, in a great dramatic part?"

"Do you mean that, Morris?"

"I was never more serious in my life."

"I don't believe that the people would really have any interest in seeing me in pictures," she answered solemnly. "They come to the Metropolitan to hear me sing, but if I should lose my voice over night, do you think they would still come to see me? No! And they would make unkind remarks, too; I am afraid I should be an awful failure if I relied on acting alone."

Later, on another occasion, Geraldine confidentially confessed to Morris that she had been thinking very seriously of his suggestion. "I have seen some pictures, and I believe a new and very great art is being born. Let's make a real business appointment and talk this over."

Morris reasoned at length with Geraldine, pointing out what a wonderful thing it would be if her performance of *Carmen* could be immortalized with motion picture photography.

"There are nine million records of your voice to-day," he declared, "and everyone who owns Farrar records has a *Carmen* record. Every one of those people, as well as many others, would be more than glad of the opportunity to see you as an actress even as they now hear you as a singer. Your voice is heard in every American town and city of consequence, and yet you've been in comparatively few of these places. Do you think that your actual moving personality would have less appeal?"

Days later, Morris invited Jesse Lasky to attend a matinee of *Madame Butterfly*, which presented Geraldine Farrar in her farewell appearance of the season at the Metropolitan Opera House. Lasky attended, taking a position in the rear of the theater because the performance was sold out.

Geraldine Farrar was the most successful soprano in grand opera, and she enjoyed adulation of unheard-of proportions. Her idol-worshipers were called "Gerry-flappers," and her popularity was then at a frenzy. Lasky insisted on going backstage to meet Miss Farrar, and secretly, he intended to tempt the star with an invitation to appear in Lasky motion pictures.

Backstage, he came quickly to the point.

"Miss Farrar, I don't know whether you have ever seen a motion picture, but my company makes them, and I'd like to persuade you to do the story of *Carmen* for us. We have no trouble securing famous plays and engaging their stars, but they're always afraid acting in a movie will hurt their stage prestige. I could see by the ovation you got today that your prestige is such that whatever you do, your public will accept it as right."

"You think I could turn the tide?"

"I'm sure other stars would follow your lead, and I can see that you'd photograph beautifully. If you consent . . . ."

Lasky went on to offer Geraldine their best director, DeMille, a private railroad car to bear her to Hollywood, a furnished home with staff and servants, and a daily chauffeur at her private disposal. In addition, a private dressing room on the Lasky lot equipped with a grand piano. Lasky found Geraldine charming and gracious.

"I was enthusiastic," she told her admirers in her autobiography. "The opportunity of acting, the charm of summer in California, the vocal repose—all seemed to point to a happy adventure of interest and novelty."

For Geraldine, the respite of a summer in California was much needed balm for her overtaxed voice. Her career had been grueling, she was too thin, a victim of insomnia, and suffered from an ever-present fear of losing her voice. Her opera success rested entirely on her voice, and taking several months off to work in silent motion pictures seemed both fascinating and fortunate. For $20,000, she took the plunge.

The Farrar expedition from the east coast to the west coast was trumpeted in front-page newspaper headlines in city after city, as she journeyed the breadth of America in her private railroad car. The fanfare mounted while Lasky returned to the west coast to prepare her entrance with all the pomp of a visiting queen.

For weeks, she badgered Samuel Goldfish, who had suddenly changed his name to Goldwyn, about who was going to be her leading man in her first film. He kept dodging the question, knowing she had a reputation for being headstrong, and not wanting to alienate her with an improper choice.

"I was met at the Los Angeles station by a fanfare and crowd," Geraldine modestly recalled. In reality, Lasky spread a red carpet across the Santa Fe platform and depot from her private train car to her limousine. He had arranged for 5,000 school children to be given a holiday from studies, and they were brought out to line the regal pathway and toss roses at her feet as she alighted and took the first steps to newfound Hollywood fame. A welcoming committee consisting of the Mayor and other dignitaries heralded her landing, and the event was proclaimed in front-page headlines.

That first night, the Mayor of Los Angeles hosted a banquet in Geraldine's honor. Twenty-three-year-old Wally fixed his blue eyes on her from across the room, as Goldwyn led him to her side. He was nervous and fearful that she would not like him. As soon as they were introduced, she took an instant liking to him. A woman of dynamic force and wide experience as a musician and actresses, she swayed Wally as no other personality with whom he had come in contact in his life. It was her charm and his desire to work with her that persuaded him to continue acting, and for a time, forgo his desire to direct.

Production began on *Maria Rosa* at the extremely busy studio in an area of California overfilled with orange groves. Geraldine accomplished something in Wally that no one else had been able to do up to that time. She roused in him an awareness of acting as an art. She saw at once the potential within him, and set to work to bring out the best he had to give as a personality, as a man, and as an artist.

"Many orange trees had to be uprooted to make space for the studio stages and buildings," recalled cameraman Karl Brown. "The local people objected loudly. It had taken years to bring these trees to bearing, while in their view, the movies were a thing of the moment, soon to pass. This protest didn't change anything. The Lasky company owned the land, and down went the orange trees but not the peppers. They furnished welcome shade to the western side of the studio, shielding it from a sun that could get very hot indeed when it warmed up to work."

No sooner had Geraldine arrived in Hollywood than she met Lou-Tellegen, Sarah Bernhardt's leading man of the previous four years. Samuel Goldwyn engaged him for work in the new company

Geraldine Farrar, as she looked when she arrived in Hollywood in 1915, dressing like a queen in a fur coat that proved to be much to warm for the California climate.

Lou-Tellegen, leading man opposite Sarah Bernhardt during 1910-1914, was snapped up by Famous-Players Lasky to star in silent movies for many years.

and to be the star of a new series of exciting adventure films. There are differing recollections as to how Geraldine and Lou met, but Lou recalled it vividly in his memoirs. The day was May 7, 1915, and he claimed, "It was through my friend Ben Rimo, well-known in the theatrical world as a director, that I first met Miss Farrar. He gave a luncheon party in her honor just before she left for Hollywood. It was at the old Holland House on Fifth Avenue."

Shortly after their introduction at this party, one guest burst into the room screaming, "The *Lusitania* has been sunk!" Geraldine shot a frightened glance into Lou's eyes, and as the other guests began to murmur shock at the news of the world-shaking catastrophe, their individual friends pulled them away from each other and the party broke up.

The next day, the world learned the truth about the *Lusitania* disaster. The day before, Captain William Thomas Turner was at the helm of the RMS *Lusitania*, a luxurious and speedy British ocean liner. He encountered heavy fog and slowed the ship down as it traveled off the coast of Southern Ireland. Under the currents, the German U20 submarine had spotted the outline of the ship and targeted it for assault. At 1:40 p.m., the crew launched a single torpedo at the starboard side of the *Lusitania*. Although there had been sufficient lifeboats on board, the severe listing of the ship as it sank prevented many of them from being launched. In eighteen minutes, the craft disappeared beneath the Atlantic Ocean. 1,198 of the 1,959 people on board died. Americans were outraged to learn that 128 of those killed were from America, and the official government position was one of condemnation. Up to this time, America had been neutral in the raging war, but the sinking of the *Lusitania* heightened tensions between America and Germany, and the event swayed public opinion in favor of joining the war effort. President Woodrow Wilson declared a United States policy of absolute neutrality, but Germany's unrestricted submarine warfare posed a serious threat to American commercial shipping.

Dreadful war activities abroad came home to the United States in daily reports. Although America was officially neutral, public sentiments were in favor of the allies. Hoarse-voiced orators urged citizens to buy Liberty Bonds, and the constant din of "The Star Spangled Banner" pervaded every place of entertainment. War drums were pounding, and American patriots were cocking their ears to the call to arms. Bored society women took up charitable events for the war cause. Singers and actors appeared at fundraisers exhorting the business of supporting the efforts of the allies. The public eagerly devoured tales of atrocities and espionage, and it seemed that the whole country was on the verge of joining the international frenzy.

Despite the looming wartime conflagration and its effect on the film industry, work on Geraldine's debut in films began. She was so new to the peculiar form of silent film expression that DeMille smoothed the process of adapting her talents from the stage to film by first producing *Maria Rosa* and then filming *Carmen*, her well-known success from the opera stage.

"If we make *Carmen* first, he told his doleful colleagues, "we will have to throw half of it out. We have another property, *Maria Rosa*, a Spanish love story, not unlike *Carmen* in its setting. Let's let Miss Farrar cut her motion picture teeth on that, and then make *Carmen*, and she will give you a good performance in it. You can hold up the release of *Maria Rosa*."

They followed this course of action, and during the making of *Maria Rosa*, Lou-Tellegen met Geraldine again while she was in her Spanish costume. Samuel Goldwyn remembered in his autobiography:

"I want to meet Miss Farrar,' said Lou. "Won't you take me over?"

They were introduced again, and it was just as if a spark came from his eyes and was met by one from hers. They began speaking in French right away, and after that, they were seen together as soon as they could get away from the set.

"I rather liked this attractive Tellegen," Geraldine thought back. "He had come into our circle of friends, and was very sympathetic and charming in manner. His acting ability was limited, spectacular rather than of stable routine, while an unusual stature and exotic manners contributed to his early success on Broadway. His background gave him a romantic aura to which feminine hearts were very sympathetic."

Lou later recalled, "The fire of eagerness for life and the flame of genius gave the dazzling sparkle of youth to her eyes. Her brilliant personality and her youthful and *sogné* appearance were uncanny!"

Their social contact ripened into friendship in Hollywood where both stars were busy making individual photoplays for the Lasky firm. Within a few weeks, Geraldine was entrenched with her work under the direction of Cecil B. DeMille, but Lou fell in love with America's adored songbird.

Opera star Geraldine Farrar with stage and film legend, Lou-Tellegen, during their doomed romance.

Wally loved working with her, too. He found that he shared a deep love of music with Geraldine. The grand piano in her bungalow afforded her opportunities to sing while waiting to appear before the cameras. More than once, passersby gathered outside to experience her free, impromptu concerts. Wally spent many hours at her side with his violin. After work at her home or at the Reid's home, Wally played for Geraldine while she sang arias. They had a friendship

Cecil B. DeMille directing Geraldine Farrar and Wally in the vigorous fight scene between Carmen and a cigarette girl in *Carmen* (1915).

that motivated Wally in many ways. Her accomplishments in the world of opera, the few years she had over his age, and the association she had known with many members of the world's elite, and her affectionate attention and flattery lifted him up to a level he had not known before. She gave him a new self-confidence in his skill as an actor, and with that newfound facility, an untapped enthusiasm. He threw himself with concentration and passion into the roles he played opposite her. Geraldine's confidence in Wally lifted him to fulfill her assurance that he would bring to his work a performance complimentary to hers. He rose to the occasion, and his patience in establishing her with a measure of expertise in the medium with which he was so experienced brought the admiration of Zukor, De Mille, and Lasky.

On completion of *Maria Rosa* and *Carmen*, they filmed *Temptation*, the third and final film in the trilogy planned for Geraldine's first summer in Hollywood. Geraldine was so pleased with their results that she signed up for another season in Hollywood to begin once her opera duties were over. In October 1915, she prepared to leave, promising to return the following May 1916. Her work finished, Geraldine left to fulfill her commitments for the fall season of opera in New York.

Lou-Tellegen, by then hopelessly infatuated with her, came down to the train station to see her board the special train designed for her personal comfort, and as the huge machine began to rumble along the tracks in an enveloping cloud of steam, Lou ran along the platform beside the car, clinging to the hand Geraldine extended from the open window. He raced along for many yards, reluctantly parting only when the engine suddenly accelerated beyond the platform.

"When the train that took her away from California finally pulled out of the station at Los Angeles, I felt very lonely and weary," Lou later mused.

One evening in September 1915, Jesse Lasky and Cecil B. DeMille were returning from dinner and noticed the downtown New York sky glowing with one of the most spectacular fires in the city's history. Curious, they went down to 26th Street, and to their horror they found that the flames were consuming the Lasky studio and offices where their recently filmed productions were stored in cans. It seemed that all their work that summer was to be hopelessly lost.

Chapter 9
THE WALL OF MONEY

The disastrous fire tore through the Famous Player's plant at 213-227 West 26th Street, completely destroying the studio, offices, and many films. According to a report in the September 25, 1915 *Motion Picture News*, the conflagration was discovered at 6:55 p.m. on September 11 and had its origin in a factory that occupied the lower portion of the building. The upper stories served as the company studios, dressing rooms, property rooms, projection rooms, and executive offices. The laboratories, situated on the third floor, were the only rooms unaffected. Flames swept along an upward flight and ate their way through the roof itself. The blaze devoured the floors before laboratory manager Frank Meyer and two other men in the film plant were able to remove anything of value. So dense was the smoke that they barely succeeded in escaping with their lives by jumping to the roofs of adjoining buildings. New York firemen fought the flames for more than four hours before they were declared under control.

As they watched the fire with worry, DeMille and Lasky wondered if it was destroying their entire summer's work. They did not know if the negatives were safe, or if they had melted along with everything else in the conflagration.

Suddenly, DeMille noticed someone strange. "Look at that man," he whispered to Lasky, as they watched the horror unfolding. He pointed to a little man with his hands in the pockets of his overcoat, who was standing absolutely still among the milling, excited crowd. "He hasn't moved a muscle since we've been here. He has something to do with this fire. I don't know what, but I'm sure of it!"

Lasky agreed. "You're right," he said. "That's Adolph Zukor."

Adolph Zukor was Lasky's partner, and DeMille had not yet had an opportunity to meet him. They watched Zukor staring with fixed eyes on one spot on the wall of an upper story where a wall safe hung precariously in the charring structure. The safe contained the fragile negatives of all the company's unreleased films. Flames licked inches nearer to the safe. The future of their company rested on whether the safe was as fireproof as they had been led to believe.

Days later, once the smoldering ruins were cleared and the safe could be opened, they found a few of the films were completely destroyed, but most of them suffered only minor damage.

On Sunday, a temporary meeting place was established at the Hotel Astor so that their production activities could be resumed without further delay. Mary Pickford, Marguerite Clark, Hazel Dawn, Pauline Frederick, and John Barrymore were assembled along with other company officials, and they prepared at once to appear in a series of new productions to be substituted for those injured or destroyed in the fire. To prevent an interruption in their release schedule, printing of the first film on their newly arranged release schedule had already begun at another laboratory.

Zukor stated to the press that the work of the organization would go on uninterrupted. "We are undaunted by our tremendous loss, and will abate no effort to continue to hold our place as the foremost producing concern in the world," he declared from his temporary offices to a reporter for *Motion Picture News*.

Fortunately, the three pictures Wally and Geraldine had recently completed were confirmed to be safe. They were still in cans that had been shipped to California, but Mary Pickford lost the finished negative of one of her unreleased films and there were others that had been destroyed forever.

According to DeMille's plan, they first released *Carmen*, the second film made with Geraldine and Wally after she had experienced the full process of film work with *Maria Rosa*. *Carmen* immediately ran into difficulty with local censors when they previewed the picture before its release. An article in the *Lima Daily News*, October 1915, revealed the censor's concerns:

> "This is in spite of efforts of the state censors to save her life, and to save the life of her discarded lover, Jose. *Carmen*, the

opera, is about a gypsy girl who dupes an officer of the guards. He kills a fellow officer in her defense. She runs away with a bullfighter. The officer kills her himself at her side, while butterflies flutter about them in the sunlight. That's the story. Without this tragic ending, it wouldn't be *Carmen*. 'Cut out the suicide scene where man murders woman,' ordered the censors. 'Cut out suicide scene.' At the same time, Carmen was ordered not to smoke a cigarette, but she smokes it. She was ordered to cut short her hair-pulling encounter with another girl in the cigarette factory, but she fights it to a finish. Jose, the officer, had been ordered to cut short his saber duel with the other officer, but he fights it until the other lies dead across a table in the tavern. Geraldine Farrar said at the start that she wouldn't appear in a film-play of the opera that didn't present the story as it should be presented. The producers say the obligation to present the play as it was produced without cuts, or shot show it at all, was part of their contract . . . ."

Censors revised their requests, and once *Carmen* was trimmed and formatted to appease them, the film released on November 1, 1915. The picture became an instant hit and found worldwide popularity. The public first saw Wally in a starring role in *Carmen*, and it brought him to a new level of top-of-mind awareness, name recognition, and critical acclaim that seemed even greater than his initial brush with fame that followed his appearance in *The Birth of a Nation*.

Temptation, the last of Geraldine's first three films, was released on December 30, 1915. She and the picture earned uniformly good reviews, although the story was not as spectacular as *Carmen*. Soon after, Wally's *The Golden Chance* was released on January 13, 1916. The public again saw him in a starring role in a feature-length film, and *The Golden Chance* was his first with his name "above the title."

With his newfound status came confidence. Wally stepped outside of the film studios to appear on stage in a theatrical production for the first time since he had assisted his father in *The Girl and the Ranger*. For three weeks, he played the part of the Chauffeur in Harry Corson Clarke's English satirical play, *The Rotters*, at a Los

Angeles theater, and he received $1,000 a week for the run of the play. That endeavor involved leaving the studio after a long day filming, and then appearing live on-stage each evening in the play. He found the experience invigorating, and then soon went to work forming another live act that would give him an opportunity to help the war effort.

The Blue Bungalow Band featured Wally with his terrific singing voice and his ability to play many musical instruments. That outfit had its inspiration during the war when talent was needed to aid various war relief rallies.

"Had a great time up North," Wally said to Maude Cheatham, in an article in *Motion Picture Magazine*. "You know, I was appearing in a stage production, *The Rotters*, and it seemed mighty good to hear my own voice again, and to receive immediate response to my work. Believe me, it was just pure joy to hear them shout for an encore. You can't imagine how it spurs a fellow on to the highest tension. That is one of the things we miss in pictures." Once again, Wally proved that he was a dynamite performer in front of an audience.

Maria Rosa, the first of the three pictures Wally made with Geraldine, was the third to be released on May 8, 1916, and it was received as well as *Carmen* and *Temptation*. DeMille's strategy worked beautifully. No one sensed any naivety or inexperience in Geraldine's performance in *Maria Rosa*, and Wally was very visible as the co-star of the three major motion pictures he made with her, *Carmen*, *Temptation*, and *Maria Rosa*.

In the summer of 1916, Adolph Zukor merged his Famous Players Company with the Jesse L. Lasky Feature Play Company in a $12,500,000 consolidation. The officers of the new corporation were President Adolph Zukor, Vice President Jesse L. Lasky, and Chairman of the Board of Directors Samuel Goldwyn. Famous Players was releasing forty-eight pictures annually, and the Lasky Company was releasing thirty-six pictures annually. Their combined releases resulted in a major step forward in efficiency for both ventures, and the new company that emerged, Famous Players-Lasky, ultimately became the launching pad for Wally's epoch as one of the most popular stars in motion pictures, and eventually became what is now known as Paramount Pictures.

Also in 1916, nearly everyone in the film business took a hand in the making of D. W. Griffith's *Intolerance*. Although Wally was under an exclusive contract with Lasky, arrangements were made for him to appear in *Intolerance* as a soldier dying on a battlefield. On its release on September 5, 1916, many people proclaimed *Intolerance* to be the greatest motion picture ever made. It showed in legitimate theaters in all major cities in America and abroad and was inevitably a sensation and matter of significant wonder for its screen technique, unusual plot movement, emotional content, and its visualization of abstract thought. Unfortunately, the film required audiences to intellectualize the confusing screen algebra, and for the most part, audiences in 1916 could not digest it. Wherever it played, theaters were full for the first few days or weeks, and then attendance fell off sharply. Once the better-educated people had seen it, the general movie-going public found it bewildering. The rapid cutting between one historical era and another left some people confused, and some thought that they were watching Belshazzar in ancient Babylon run over by a modern automobile in America. *Intolerance* was ultimately a magnificent failure. Griffith bought the film back from its financiers, and went to work chopping it up into two individual features, *The Mother and the Law* and *The Fall of Babylon*, which were released separately to recoup some of *Intolerance's* enormous cost.

In October 1916, Dorothy told Wally that he was going to become a father. While they were waiting the birth of their first child, Wally bore the difficulties with a strength and sweetness that united him to Dorothy with everlasting ties. His attention was unfailing, and as each month passed, his excitement at the prospect of being a father grew.

In 1916, he appeared in an astounding *ten* feature-length motion pictures. His popularity with worldwide audiences was rivaled only by that of Charlie Chaplin and Mary Pickford. No other stars ever held the unique positions occupied by those three. In future years, the world would change, the entertainment arena would become too vast, and even fans would change from what they were in 1916. Mary, Wally, and Charlie occupied unique positions that would no longer exist. Never before in the history of show business had anyone risen so suddenly or to such a dizzying eminence. Their renown

Wally (LEFT) **watching D. W. Griffith direct *Intolerance* in 1916.**

surpassed that of the world's best-known kings and presidents. Once, when Mary arrived at a train station the same day as the President of the United States, she drew crowds that swamped those swarming around the President. Mary later said in her memoirs that she always thought her position was precarious, and she looked on the gathering with philosophical mistrust.

"I couldn't help but think that if a pink elephant came walking down the street it would draw a bigger crowd than either of us," she reflected soberly.

The unprecedented success bestowed on those three film stars came with the scrutiny once imparted only to royalty, and fame lifted them up to the dangerous position of demigods. At first, they did

Director, George Melford, Wally, and Cleo Ridgely taking a break while making *The House with Golden Shutters* (1916).

not realize the extent to which recognition had enveloped them, but they realized all too soon that they stood on extremely wobbly pedestals. They did not believe that their sudden fame would last, and they were all wary of a possible day when they would be as forgotten as they were then famous.

Despite having acclaim, applause, and glory, the desires of Wally's heart were humble. Thanks to his upbringing and Dorothy's influence, he remained, at least for a time, grounded. A letter he wrote to Dorothy while he was gone on location was later published in *Liberty* magazine, and it illustrates that he still held to the untarnished dreams of a high-minded youth:

> "There are only a few things worthwhile in this world—and they are so easy to get. An open fire, books, a little music, and a friend you can talk to or keep silence with. I think that everything you get beyond just that is in the end a burden and a temptation. The happy lives are the quiet lives, aren't they? And yet, it is so hard to be quiet! I think you know how I feel about most things. But sitting up here

alone at night thoughts come more clearly. Never to hurt anyone, to do good to others when you can, to keep your own code of honor unbroken, your soul unstained by lust or greed or pride, your mind unsullied by lies and pretense, your body strong and clean—those are the things you must do. You believe in God. Sometimes I do, too, though I can't always give Him a name. But always I do believe in good. I know there isn't any happiness possible for me without self-respect, and I could never respect myself if I fell below the standard I know to be right."

That letter, although idealistic, was rich with a boy's idealism and illustrates how Wally had no definite adult principles and no firm, mature philosophy of life. It is clear he was striving for spiritual good, but not with the careful steps of a wizened man. His love of beauty was that of a poet, not that of a realist.

In spite of his philosophical castles in the sky, Wally was more grounded than other young people finding such unlikely success in the movies. An example was one strange, young woman thrust into making a film with him. She was a fascinating, beautiful dancer, who was already famous. Her name was Mae Murray, and she was known as the "girl with the bee-stung lips."

Mae was born May 10, 1889, in Portsmouth, Virginia, as Marie Adrienne Koenig. Not much is known about her childhood, but by her teenage years, she was already working in New York making her professional debut singing "Comin' Through the Rye" as Vernon Castle's dancing partner in 1906 on Broadway in *About Town*.

Soon, Mae appeared in the 1908, 1909, and 1915 *Ziegfeld Follies* as a featured dancer. She amazed an audience at the 1915 *Ziegfeld Follies* with two specialty songs that stopped the show. In a single night, Mae made show business history. Her first number in a Persian harem setting gave her a chance to perform a sexy, tempting dance in front of a handsome prince lounging beside a moonlit pool. The second number had her enter the darkened theater from the rear of the house, come down the aisle, and then take a seat beside comedian Ed Wynn, excitedly telling him about her new "movie role." Then, a huge screen descended over the stage, and an actual motion picture was shown starring Mae as "Merry Pickum" in a satire of Mary Pickford. In the spoof, Mae wore Mary's trademark golden curls and swished around in an antebellum hoop skirt all too reminiscent of the Griffith girls in *The Birth of a Nation*. This skit created the impression that Mae was already working in films, and the impression was not lost on Adolph Zukor when he saw her in *The Ziegfeld Follies*. He quickly hired her, and then in 1916, paired her with Wally, a screen veteran, for her debut. She was hired to simply romp, dance, and freely express her lighter nature in a picture called *To Have and to Hold*. Zukor believed that pairing her with Wally would help her rise to her best, as he had helped Geraldine Farrar. Jane Ardmore described one of their first appearances together in front of the camera in her book, *The Self-Enchanted*:

"Kick it!" yelled the director, and hot lights jumped out from a dozen monstrous eyes. "O.K! Action . . . *Camera*!"

"She leaned against the door. That's all there was, two walls, a fireplace, and a door. She leaned against the door praying that he wouldn't try to beat it down. He was Wally Reid, playing Captain Ralph Percy, the dashing planter; and she was among the indentured maidens just arrived from England to be the planters' brides . . . ."
"You hear footsteps!" shouted director, George Melford. "You retreat to the corner. This may be a wild man; you may have to give yourself. Tremble . . . the door is opening . . . you're out of camera range!" He was bellowing like a bull. "Cut! Save it," he yelled. In a fury, he yanked off his coat, and threw it to the floor.
Wally helped lead Mae through her difficulty understanding why the combustible director roared instructions in front of the blinding klieg lights. During one frightening experience, Mae suffered the terror of temporary blindness that often accompanied those actors working directly in front of the horrible, white blaze of klieg spotlights. A doctor dropped cocaine on her scalded eyeballs and instructed her to never look directly into the lights. Wally was kind to her, and the end result was worth the trouble. Mae earned smashing notices for her debut film, and it started her on a fifteen-year career as one of Hollywood's biggest stars.

Mae Murray, who eventually became known as "The Girl with the Bee-Stung Lips," appeared with Wally in her first full-length motion picture, George Melford's *To Have and to Hold* (1916).

As the summer of 1916 neared, Geraldine Farrar ended her current concert tour, and she fretted about the stories Hollywood would have waiting for her when she returned to film studios in May. To her annoyance, no one from the film company consulted her about any script. The lack of anticipation became a major distraction for her because she was given to minute planning of every detail of her career in well-thought out steps. Although she was annoyed about the unnecessary waste of time, energy, and people strung along idly, she was eventually delighted when she learned that they planned for her to appear in a single film about Joan of Ark.

When the summer of 1916 came, Geraldine returned to Hollywood and prepared for the making of *Joan the Woman*. DeMille's favorite writer, Jeanie Macpherson, and William C. de

Mille, his brother, created a scenario that was a fanciful retelling of the Joan of Ark legend. Since the war in Europe was raging, the script featured a modern Prologue and Epilogue featuring Wally as Eric Trent, a World War One English officer inspired to fulfill his life's mission when he finds the decayed sword that once belonged to Joan of Arc. She appears to him in a vision, and then the story goes into a flashback and retells her leadership of the French Army and her tragic burning at the stake.

DeMille and Lasky spared no expense in that production. It was to feature marching crowds, prancing horses, courtiers, soldiers, cathedral scenes, and most thrilling of all, a spectacular burning at the stake scene, which the producers calculated would rival the epic quality of *The Birth of a Nation*. The film would be so complicated that it would take the entire summer to produce. Where the previous year she had made three pictures, this one epic would outdo them all. Wally joined the effort with great enthusiasm.

For Geraldine, the transition from courtier to peasant, and then from court lady to soldier, was thrilling, and she completed her cross-country train trip alive with anticipation. For Wally, it meant an appearance in a great epic of stupendous proportions. This time, he was not a substitute for Henry B. Walthall like he had been in *The Birth of a Nation*. Wally was DeMille's first and only choice to play Eric Trent in *Joan the Woman*.

Throughout the difficult making of the epic, Wally doted on Dorothy. In the early months of her first pregnancy, she was heavily involved in the making of a long string of pictures. Nineteen titles starring Dorothy Davenport were released in 1916. It was only in the later months of her pregnancy that she was able to remain quietly at home. By Christmas, she was beginning to show increased size, and she and Wally devoted the holidays to planning publicity appearances for the release of *Joan the Woman* and spending time alone together.

On completion of *Joan the Woman*, the cast and crew pooled their money and had a jeweler create a special gift for Geraldine, a hand mirror with a gold *fleur de lis* on a silver background where autographs of all the principal members of the company were etched. On the handle was a silver base-relief of Joan in armor arranged so that all the cast names are listed at her feet. When she was given the gift, Geraldine burst into tears of gratitude, and had to be consoled by Lou-Tellegen, who was by then her husband. Later, she wrote an emotional letter thanking them for their generosity, which was published in *Photoplay* magazine in a story called "Jerry on the Job":

> "My heart is too full to adequately express the sentiments that surge within me at the presentation of the beautiful gift this morning. My hearty thanks toward those valiant comrades who have followed the Maid from Domremy through the glorious triumphs of the battlefield and coronation to prison and martyrdom, whether it be in even through the merciless eye of the camera, or from the second story window of the costume department and the property room—I thank you one and all and my tears are of joy though they did leave me ashamed and silent. Thanks—thanks."

On December 25, 1916, *Joan the Woman* was released to worldwide acclaim and was circulated for years. It brought a great deal of prestige to Wally. Despite his newfound status as one of the most intense and likable stars in all of Hollywood, he never lost sight of his real ambition to write and direct. That aspiration became increasingly distant, as he became entrenched in a non-stop schedule of acting jobs, but he continued to predict that he would turn his attention to directing as soon as he was allowed. Dorothy, having worked under his direction in dozens of short films, was completely supportive of his desire.

"Wally's greatest ambition is to direct," she reiterated in an interview in *Pictures and Picturegoer*. "He often remarks that he is waiting in delightful anticipation of the day when his hair gets thin, and he can't act anymore, and can take up the work of directing and producing again."

Wally expressed those ambitions repeatedly to DeMille and Lasky, and they finally let him direct five short films in 1916 and 1917: *The Wrong Heart*, *The Wall of Flame*, *A Warrior's Bride*, *The Penalty of Silence*, and *Buried Alive*. Wally proved to Jesse Lasky how extremely capable he was as a director, and he hoped those efforts would open the door to further opportunities, but he could not have been more mistaken. Lasky had no intention of allowing his prized box office attraction to remain permanently behind the camera. Those were the last pictures Wally ever directed. What was more, Geraldine Farrar was coming back to Hollywood for a third summer season away from opera, and she wanted Wally to again star with her in the next Cecil B. DeMille extravaganzas he was planning to compose for the preeminent diva. What Geraldine expected, she got.

1917 began with the birth of an era of upheaval for Wally and the entire nation, and at the same time, it heralded the end of a bygone era. "Buffalo Bill" Cody, one of the final exponents of the nation's Western heritage, had lost money during the last several years on his *Wild West Show* when the movies took a hold of the public's imagination and diverted audiences to their more exciting and expressive displays of Western adventures. William S. Hart, Tom Mix, and other cowboys, both real and imaginary, had taken hold of the public's fancy. In 1917, "Buffalo Bill" Cody made one attempt at starring in a full-length film. As age caught up with him, heart problems sent him to his deathbed, and he passed away on January 10, 1917. His name and legend lived on in many later stories and motion pictures, and much of the town of Cody, Wyoming, stood in permanent tribute to the man and the myths surrounding him.

On January 2, 1917, President Woodrow Wilson made an historic speech that cut clean to the heart of America's looming involvement in the long drawn-out conflict in Europe. He stressed that there should be no peace without victory, and added, ". . . It is inconceivable that the people of the United States should play no part in that great enterprise. To take in such a service will be the opportunity for which they have sought to prepare themselves by the very principles and purposes of their polity and the approved practices of their government ever since the days when they set up a nation in the high and honorable hope that it might, in all that it was and did, show mankind the way to liberty."

A few weeks later on April 6, 1917, the United States finally declared war with Germany. American men rallied at recruiting stations by the tens of thousands, and many actors followed the call to arms. Popular songs reflected wartime sentiments, such as:

> It's a Long Way to Tipperary,
> It's a long way to go.
> It's a long way to Tipperary,
> To the sweetest girl I know.
> Goodbye Piccadilly,
> Farewell Leicester Square!
> It's a long, long way to Tipperary,
> But my heart's right there.

Music stores were flooded with sheet music of other songs about the glories of war and the soldiers who left their girls behind. They poured off the keyboards of hundreds of Tin Pan Alley songwriters. "Over There," "You'll Find Old Dixieland in France," "Come on Papa," "Uncle Sam's Ships," and "Three Wonderful Letters from Home" became popular hits and integrated the thrill of battle into American musical culture.

"Cecil was thirty-four years old, and I was thirty-five," Lasky contended in his memoirs. "Since we were both over draft age and had dependents, we didn't see service. But Cecil captained a Home Guard unit made up of studio personnel and, I have no doubt, prayed for an invasion. Our director-general drilled his 'army' with real Springfield rifles, up and down Vine Street with as much relish as though he were showing General Pershing how to do a scene."

The official news of the war declared against the Germans shattered the peaceful valley of Los Angeles like a canon. Citizens were urged to prepare for an invasion. DeMille earnestly offered the city his seventy-five men armed with machine gun rifles and ammunition. More members were recruited from several studios to protect the homeland as part of the Lasky Home Guard unit under his command. His brother, William, was positioned as the unit's top sergeant. Those civilians were drilled and carefully outfitted with real uniforms. When the troupe was sworn in to the California militia, the colors were ceremoniously presented by Mary Pickford, and proudly borne by Color Sergeant Wallace Reid.

The Lasky Home Guard ceremony was accompanied by a brass band composed of prop men, carpenters, grips, and actors, including Tully Marshall and Wally. Representatives from the major movie magazines were present to photograph their drills for publicity, and much ballyhoo was made over the Lasky Home Guard. The country was not invaded, and they never saw any live action, but it made for great publicity and helped explain why some able-bodied male members of the industry were not in line at the recruitment stations.

Among the men missing from real duty was Wally. He was only twenty-five years old, was more than six feet tall, weighed 190 pounds, was in great physical condition, a crack rifle shot, and had been in military school. Wally wanted to get into the thick of the war, and as he watched nearly every able-bodied man he knew give up his old life to join in the war effort, he wanted to follow them. All that was American in him responded to the thoughts and feelings then sweeping the nation.

"All that was boy in his heart heard the call of the great adventure—war," wrote Adela Rogers St. Johns in a *Liberty* article in 1928. "All that was dramatic in him reacted to uniforms, bands, battle tales, and the chance for service and heroism. All that was idealistic in him responded to Woodrow Wilson's call to make the 'world safe for democracy.'"

What followed was a repeat of what had occurred at nearly every turning point in his life: outside facts, circumstances, and *other people controlled his decisions to his undoing*. Another huge but wonderful roadblock to the course of his destiny came in the form of William Wallace Reid, Jr.

On the morning of June 10, 1917 when Dorothy began to feel labor pains, a sweltering California day greeted her. Throughout the day, the sun beat down on the landscape and house in simmering waves reflected by the white outside walls. Dorothy refused to go to a hospital, wishing to have an old-fashioned birth at home. The hours dragged on, and to keep her cool, Wally took her into their garden and sat fanning her in an attempt to dissipate the climbing temperature.

By evening, Dorothy was taken to bed. Wally stood by her every minute throughout the ordeal, training their one electric fan on her and placing towels soaked in perfume on her head. She was in labor for hours, and finally, she blacked out.

When she regained consciousness, Wally was playing a haunting, sweet melody on his violin, accompanying Billy, their son, into the

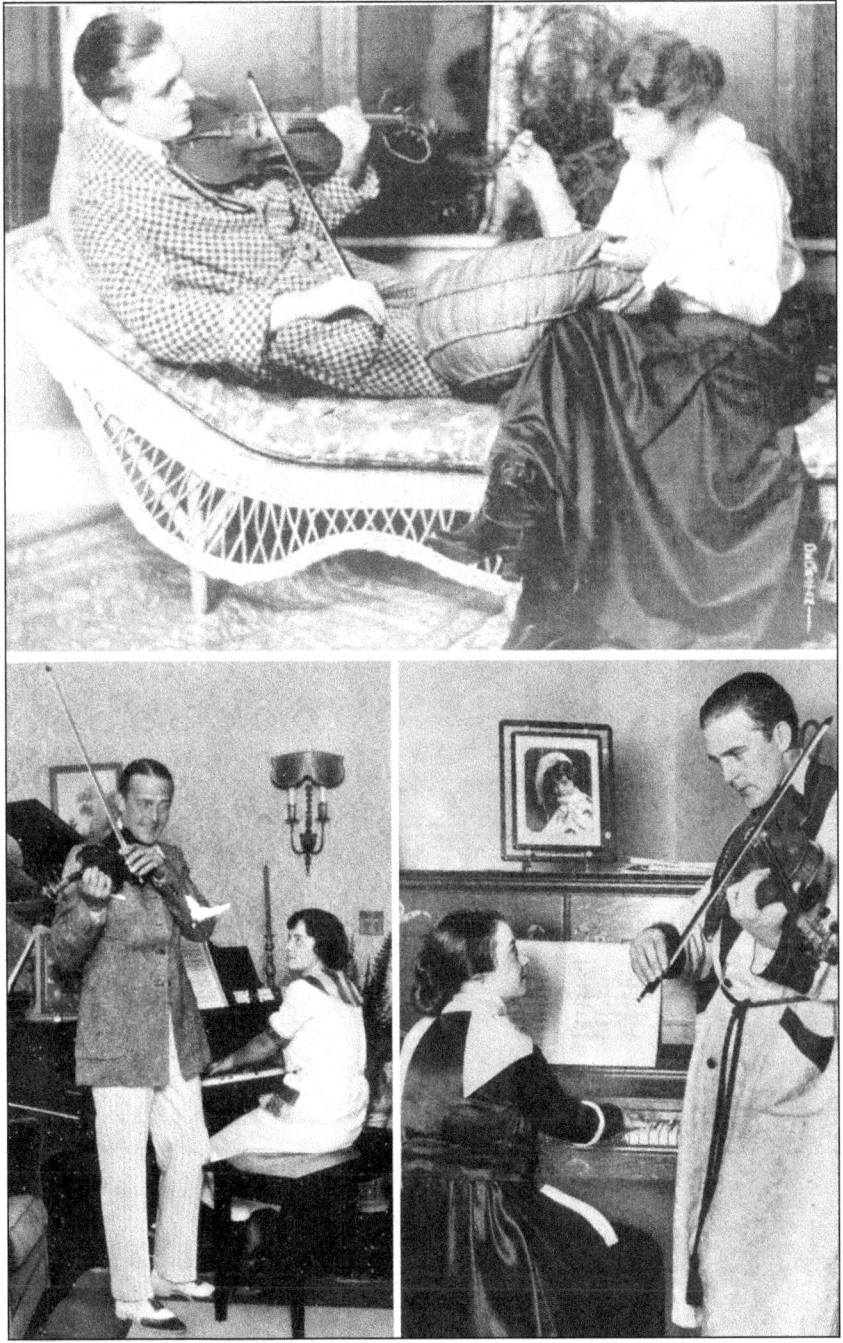

Wally and Dorothy both loved music, and frequently played together at their home. Photo ca. 1917.

Wally, Dorothy, and baby Wallace "Billy" Reid, Jr.

world to the melodic strains of his music.

"Dorothy! Look at his feet!" he cried with an astonished expression on his face. "Oh, my Lord, they're going to be as big as mine. Can't something be done about his feet?"

Wally wrote this poem about his new son:

LULLABY
By Wallace Reid

You cry for your daddy, Baby o'Mine –
Can't you see that I'm crying too?
You're asking me and I'm asking God,
For I'm just a baby like you.
You want to know when, O Baby o' Mine,
He'll be coming home to you.
And O how I'm longing and longing, dear,
To be able to tell you true.
I want to sob with you, Baby o' Mine,
But I must be brave for us three—
For you with your childish sorrow, dear,
For daddy, who's fighting—and me.
So come to my heart, dear baby o' Mine,
Let me comfort your baby woes.
And we'll trust in God to stay with the Flag
And with daddy, wherever he goes.

For Dorothy, the birth of her son brought no respite from her film work. In 1917, she appeared in eight motion pictures, but as soon as her contract ended, she voluntarily gave up her career to be a full-time wife and mother.

"Wally never expressed a desire that I give up my career—if you call it that," Dorothy revealed in a 1926 interview, "but I do think he liked to have his wife there, waiting for him when he came home. Most men do."

In the meantime, Wally urgently wanted to enlist in the military, but Dorothy was not well after the birth of their child. By that time, both his mother and father were financially dependent on him. Dorothy's mother, Alice, was another dependant, and Dorothy needed her help in order to manage the difficult and confusing first

Wally, cast, and crew in Big Bear country taking a pause while filming George Melford's *Nan of Music Mountain* (1917).

year of the child's life while she had to finish out her busy film contract. In addition, intense opposition came from all quarters of the Famous Players-Lasky studio.

The studio depended on his drawing power. He was the "whip" in their program, and with the loss of much of the European market due to the war, they relied more than ever on a steady output of Wallace Reid films. His pictures were guaranteed moneymakers, and the continued success of the studio was built largely on Mary Pickford and Wallace Reid pictures. They countered his burning desire to enlist by pointing out that if he joined the army he might be killed or disfigured, which would mean a loss of uncountable millions of dollars to them. They reasoned that he would be just another gunner in the army. They argued that there were plenty of other men younger than he, but without any family obligations, and they were more than willing and able to take up arms. They implored him to consider the wisdom of letting those younger men be the first to enlist, and if he was needed at a later time after the first wave of recruits met the nation's needs, the decision could then be discussed. They lobbied as strong of a fight as possible and bore into Wally with their arguments.

Wally beside Director Cecil B. DeMille, when he stepped in to supervise the blizzard sequence in George Melford's *Nan of Music Mountain* (1917).

Then, there was the matter of his personal income. Since marrying, he and Dorothy spent most of what they made as soon as money was earned, and they had never diligently saved for a rainy day. If he was to join the war, there was no guarantee that he would have a career when and if he returned. The studio heavily pressured him to remain way down on the list of men to be drafted. In a final appeal, they pointed out that the world needed amusement more than ever before and he could serve his country more powerfully by spearheading drives and benefits and using his talents to keep up the nation's morale.

Reluctantly, Wally gave in to their overpowering appeals, but the war created a soul problem of which few people knew. On the outward side, his war record never came under attack from any fervent patriot, but in his own eyes, he was stamped indelibly with the black "S" of "slacker." He felt that he had fallen short and failed to achieve the romantic ideal to which he had always reached. In his mind, his manhood was smirched.

He stoically kept his own dreams and desires to himself, never burdening those around him with the bitter disappointments that bothered his soul. The fact became painfully clear by that time that he was lost in an actor's world when all he wanted to do was write and direct. He was only in his mid-twenties, but he was saddled with a wife and child, and they would not sit idly by while he deserted them to trudge through the mud over in Château-Thierry or Vimy Ridge with the other young men his age who were risking their lives for their country. The things he wanted most to do were kept from his reach, and the occupations he least wished to do were consuming his every waking hour. For an idealist like Wally, fresh on the course of life and still brimming with deeply felt and equally elusive dreams, the shattering of his ambitions and personal goals came with a heavy thud.

The profound psychological rift then taking place within him was perhaps best illustrated by something so trivial that it went unnoticed by those around him. He had previously harbored an almost sacred love for the violin. The strings gave voice to his dreamy love of beauty and offered vent to his inner dreams. Jazz music was becoming a nationwide rage, and a profound transformation took place in his musical direction. As the merry-go-round of life increased in speed around him, Wally gradually put away the violin, which had been his instrument of choice and the object he most loved to use to express his deeply felt artistic sense. He sent his violin to his mother in New Jersey, which she kept like an artifact in the museum of his life. Then, he switched to the crass and brassy saxophone. Pressing in around him were success, money, and fast-paced, glittering excitement, all of which were swirling around him in an ever-increasing whirlpool.

Chapter 10
THE MAN WITHIN

Wally showed his innermost feelings when he gave to one friend a photo of himself pictured in *Joan the Woman* wearing the uniform of a British lieutenant. He had scrawled across it, "Just a so-and-so who never got into a uniform except when he put on his greasepaint."

If anyone had been able to predict the outcome of the inner tug-of-war taking place within Wally, they failed to give voice to their forecast. He felt that he was hopelessly stuck between aspiration and responsibility, and with the eyes of the world upon him, he was under a focused microscope that magnified his every move.

Nothing so fatally undermined Wally's self-respect as his failure to join the army. To make the matter worse, while newspapers were filled with daily accounts of the heroism displayed by other men on European battlefields, he was waking up each day to put on makeup like a woman and stand around posing in funny looking costumes for photographers, an occupation that seemed unmanly—especially in light of world events.

There was no escape for Wally in 1917. For the third consecutive summer, Geraldine Farrar returned to Hollywood. Jesse Lasky rallied the full studio around her as if her next film would be the year's outstanding event. *The Woman God Forgot* was the first film story chosen to showcase her talents, and once again, Wally was recruited to play her soldier-lover and Cecil B. DeMille was slated to direct.

"I cast Wallace Reid again as her leading man, and other veterans of *Joan the Woman* in supporting roles," DeMille remembered in his memoir. "Though I have never had the 'DeMille Stock Company' of my dreams on a permanent basis, I have, whenever possible, followed the practice of giving parts to actors and actresses who have worked competently and congenially with me in earlier pictures."

The story followed Geraldine as Tecza, the daughter of Montezuma, king of the Aztecs, and her passionate love of Captain Alvarado, played by Wally, a Spanish soldier in the army of Cortez. Tecza saves Alvarado from a certain death by opening the city gates to hoards of Spaniards who rescue him and storm Montezuma's castle. Because of her treason, the Aztec king prophesies that she will wander the earth deserted by the gods. Alvarado consoles her with his love and his Christian religion, and she faces the film's fadeout embracing both.

The big scene in *The Woman God Forgot* was a battle between the Aztecs and Spaniards. It was to be staged on the side of a temple pyramid. With no special effects department to create such an extravagant set, DeMille simply found a hill approximately the same size of a pyramid and covered it with the exterior walls and steps of the supposed pyramid. Warriors clambered up and tumbled down as the battle surged, and the momentous scene proved to be a rip-roaring climax to the opulent pageant that had preceded it.

"The gorgeous settings and costumes employed for the story of Aztec love and adventure made it a justifiable choice for my third season," Geraldine recounted. "No idea can be obtained, however, from the mere black and white photography, of the lavish splendor provided by Mr. DeMille's taste and imagination. It was the era preceding his golden beds, Swanson fantasia in dress and coiffures, and riotous effects of voluptuous and dazzling surroundings. For more and more opportunity was to be invited by the complicated sex urge in the screen dramas, as the basic of box office appeal."

While DeMille was filming Wally and Geraldine conquering Mexico, Mary Pickford was on a nearby set making the sugary *Rebecca of Sunnybrook Farm*.

"Though it was verboten to invade Mr. DeMille's territory," wrote Frances Marion, author of Mary's film, in her memoir, "he welcomed Mary, and one afternoon she took me on his resplendent set where hundreds of extras garbed as Aztec warriors stalked past us in brilliant plumage. Seated on a high platform, megaphone in hand, was the Grand Mogul surrounded by his satellites, who smiled when he smiled, frowned when he frowned, and rose and bowed when he rose and bowed. 'I wonder if they belch when he belches?' Frances whispered to Mary.

Wally was draped head to toe in heavy Spanish armor, and Geraldine wore a costume that outdid any costume ever seen on a human form. Frances observed that she looked weary and uncomfortable. DeMille worked diligently, often losing track of time while working out detailed effects for as long as twenty hours a day with only brief pauses for boxed lunches. He was an exacting taskmaster, but no one complained. The moment word came out that he was about to begin a new picture, casting offices were deluged with actors lining up to take parts.

In the second half of the summer of 1917, Geraldine's final picture for Lasky was *The Devil Stone*, and it was filmed entirely on the California coastline. It was Geraldine's last picture on her contract, and its critical reception was noticeably less than what was expected when it was released in December 1917.

Wally spent the last part of 1917 making *Nan of Music Mountain, Rimrock Jones*, and *The Thing We Love*. Lou-Tellegen, Geraldine's husband, directed *The Thing We Love*. Geraldine's marriage with Lou was already faltering by that time, and in an attempt to keep Lou near and rebuild their crumbling relationship on firmer ground, she persuaded the studio to allow him to direct Wally's picture.

When the film came out, it was a critical disaster. *Variety* reviewed the film a few months after its making, saying the end result was ". . . about as botched up an affair as has been placed on the market in a long, long time."

Plans for future Tellegen-directed pictures were cancelled

Cecil B. DeMille said, "He had already ruined one picture and we weren't about to allow him to direct another." Geraldine, motherly, protective, and enraged, fought back. Having completed her agreement with Lasky, she accepted an offer from Samuel Goldwyn, one of his competitors. After a power struggle with Adolph Zukor, Goldwyn decided to branch out on his own, and he eagerly invited Geraldine to continue her movie activities with him. That fit neatly into her plans, and from a commercial standpoint, the venture seemed to spell success.

Photo of Dorothy and Wally at the height of their fame, as they appeared in a 1918 movie magazine just after the end of World War One.

Moviegoers saw this ad for *Rimrock Jones* in the *Elvira Evening Telegram*, February 18, 1918.

It also spelled the end of Wally's association with Geraldine. Her pictures had lifted him from the ranks of the ordinary picture player and placed him among the stellar talents. The increased popularity brought him to a unique position among movie stars. Lasky sought only to capitalize on his fame by grinding out as many Wallace Reid pictures as could be manufactured. Quality, believability, and substance were sacrificed for sheer quantity, but no one complained as long as his face and personality shown brightly.

Dorothy, Billy, and Wally spent Christmas 1917 in New York. They went back to his old home and his mother, and he introduced his son to the family.

"I had not seen my over-sized 'baby' for about six years," Bertha recalled in her written account of this holiday. "Coming home! They would be East several months, and could spend four or five weeks with me—joyous news!" They arrived the day before Christmas Eve at Red Bank, New Jersey, and Bertha met them at the train station in her car. She pulled out all the stops for an old-fashioned Christmas dinner complete with all the trimmings.

After spending the Holidays with his family on the east coast, Wally took Dorothy and Billy back to California. They had outgrown their little home, and so they purchased a bungalow in Morgan Place, Hollywood. Then, plans were drawn up for a new home to be constructed on DeLongpre Avenue and facing Sunset Boulevard. It was to be a mansion on a scale equal to the palaces being built by other movie stars.

On January 21, 1918, *Rimrock Jones* was released, the first of *nine*, full-length Wallace Reid pictures to hit movie screens that year. His work kept him running full pace at the Lasky studio, but hardly a day passed that he did not come home with some gift for Dorothy. "He took delight in hiding it in the most ridiculous places," Dorothy recalled, laughing and giving me misleading tips while I searched for it. He was the most punctilious thing in the world about anniversaries and seized any excuse to make a celebration in memory of some inconsequential happening."

With Geraldine Farrar finally off the radar screen of Wally's career, and incidentally, making the worst mistake of her own film career by launching the series of Goldwyn pictures starring herself and Lou-Tellegen, Wally's producers finally courted his personality with a story custom made to play off his interest in automobiles.

Too Many Millions was the first picture of more than a dozen that James Cruze would direct with Wally starring as a devil-may-care youth. Most were lively and unpretentious comedies, and those films struck gold. At first, the success of *Too Many Millions* came as a surprise, and there were other films already scheduled to be made, but the studio went back to writer, Byron Morgan, to mine his cache of stories for more material with which to fashion additional auto-themed stories they could weave around Wally's smile and happy-go-lucky disposition. They had unwittingly arrived at a popular formula for him, and in those films, he found a new niche as a light comedian. Audiences responded with tremendous enthusiasm. Many of his pictures made at that time were crafted to provoke intense audience reactions. At some, audiences sat on their edge of their seats watching the thrills of racetrack action; at others, they rocked with loud laughter. In many towns, several Wallace Reid pictures were screening simultaneously.

At five o'clock in the morning on November 11, 1918, the official Armistice was signed that brought an end to the war in Europe. It also brought an end to the fearful, deep feeling haunting Wally that he had shirked his full responsibility in the effort. During that time, his life had taken on a fairy tale dimension: on one hand, he was working regularly and supporting his family, as a grown man should; on the other hand, he was still like Peter Pan, the boy who never grew up. Wally was a young man to whom life had always been kind, the proverbial boy born with a silver spoon in his mouth. Despite his wishes, it was his charm and good looks that opened every door for him and gave him a comparatively easy path to take in life. Those circumstances also brought around him other people who were too quick to forgive him anything and everything, including those things that should not be forgiven. He was regarded as an idol, something larger than life, but the acclaim undeniably bewildered him. He loved adulation in a boyish sort of way, but handled it in another way that was peculiar and dangerous. If a throng of adorers circled him, he immediately felt abashed by their admiration and tried to come down to their level to become comfortable again. He did not want anyone to think that he thought of himself as lofty or aloof.

"Why?" he asked one friend. "I haven't done anything. I haven't accomplished anything."

He was no hero returning from the war, had not beaten any enemy, nor conquered any great obstacle, and he felt that he had created nothing that benefited humanity. At first, laughing off his state of affairs with modesty belied emotions that festered just beneath the surface. Dropping any pretense of recognition of the value of his contributions to the world as a movie star, he exhibited a carefree attitude that invited problems of which he was unaware. He let the wrong kind of people come near when he should have kept them away. It was impossible for him to say no to anyone for fear that they would think he had grown conceited. Consequently, their home on Morgan Street became an "open house."

There were constant visitors. Wally had no privacy. People were always dropping in at their home because they were welcome and never turned away. Dorothy had a quiet dignity about her and a strong sense of values, and she encouraged him to keep some people at a distance, but her warnings fell on deaf ears. Wally felt that what he possessed should be shared with others who were less fortunate, and he was given to sacrificing their privacy to that end, whether the gesture was practical or not.

Adela Rogers St. Johns, one of their closest friends, considered that aspect of his personality when she wrote about him in 1928: "It was all but impossible for him to say no—almost impossible for him to shut his door upon anyone, refuse to see anyone, or to do anything that gave people even momentary unhappiness . . . He was never alone, never with time to rest and relax and read as he loved, and almost no time to think. More than that, it broke him away from the men and women who might have given him something worthwhile."

Wally did not work the way many others in the industry did, making two or three pictures a year, with some fun trips in-between. He appeared in eight or nine pictures annually. Many of those were made outdoors in hot climates and included physical labor, burning up a great deal of energy. After work, he played as hard as he worked. His life lacked balance. For a time, he managed to successfully juggle work and play, but it was like juggling while walking on a tightrope, and he had never been on the tightrope before. The balancing act was precarious.

On January 19, 1919, *The Dub* was released, the first of eight pictures Paramount ground out with Wally during that year. They quickly produced *The Roaring Road* (1919), another Byron Morgan racing story, and the success of that film helped cement his fan following, making him equally as popular with men as with women.

"Wallace Reid was the easiest actor to cast and work with in the whole of my experience," Lasky claimed. "He had a terrific vogue in automobile-racing pictures—the audiences couldn't get enough of him behind a steering wheel. We virtually turned these road-racing items out on an assembly line, and every one was a money-maker."

The whole country accelerated into what was later called "the jazz age," a post-war frenzy of growth, accumulation of wealth, and a falling away from old traditions, which was symbolized by the popularity of jazz music. The change in attitude also became apparent in women's fashions. Gone were the full-length gowns of the Victorian era. Shorter, tighter, more revealing dresses became the order of the day. For women, it became stylish to raise their skirts and bob their hair. Divorce no longer held the stigma of shame it once had, and the divorce rate skyrocketed.

Some film stars rocketed to unheard-of preeminence and wealth. An astute businesswoman, Mary Pickford was at the top of the field, earning with her new First National contract $750,000 a year with a $150,000 advance. She was to make just three pictures a year, and in 1919, along with Douglas Fairbanks, Charlie Chaplin, and D. W. Griffith, she formed United Artists in order to keep a major portion of the profits from their pictures for themselves. By comparison, Wally's contract with Lasky had no profit sharing clause, but he was still earning more in one week than most men made in an entire year.

"Wally was fairly launched on the high sea of popularity and monetary success," his mother recalled in her memoir. "Still, he remained the happy, carefree boy, thoroughly democratic and altogether a man's man, and yet a trusting, confiding boy to who intrigue was a sealed book, which he did not understand. Indeed, he but vaguely knew there was such a book, much less to know ought of its contents. His mind was as open as the sunlight and as carefree as the birds. He was the soul of hospitality, and his friends were legion . . . ."

Dorothy and Wally led an active social life. On Saturday, July 5, 1919, and Sunday, July 6, The Brentwood Country Club was the site of much festivity. The club was given over to the motion picture industry, and the members of the colony were invited to come and show their prowess on the club's golf course. Wally scored wonderfully in the game and grabbed a top prize. Samuel Goldwyn also shone in the morning's contest with Rex Taylor winning second prize. In the afternoon, Joe Morgan of Brentwood won a gorgeous loving cup. King Vidor did likewise, and on Saturday night, the club was invaded by the motion picture folk and their families, and a dinner dance was staged.

Among those who streamed into their home were many who were not as blessed as Wally and Dorothy, and as Wally's prosperity grew, so did their frequent requests for money loans. Hollywood became a Mecca for those who had confidence in their own talent and were willing to spend to the last penny their life savings only to find the colony of producers did not line up eagerly for what they offered. If they knew Wally and came to his house, they poured out their troubles to him. He was always willing to help them with the tender feelings that came so naturally for him. "Never in his life had he had any training in the handling of money," Adela Rogers St. Johns pointed out, "anything to teach him its value. If he got $30 a month and cakes, that was fine, and he was happy. If he got $2,500 a week, that was fine, too, and he was happy in a different way. I once saw a little black book in which Wally kept a sort of haphazard record of the money he had loaned to people. The names in it amazed me. But all you ever had to do was to ask, and Wally gave. He saw the other fellow's point of view only too well, and his sympathies were too easily stirred; he was too deeply tolerant of all kinds of faults and suffering."

"Gosh," he used to say, "I'm nobody to judge anyone!"

For Wally, there was a great deal of money to spend, and in the spring of 1920, they launched into action building their new home. For three months, he and Dorothy studied plans, rejected some, and added others. In June, they broke ground for their new home on a hill in Hollywood overlooking the great sweep of the city. It was a marvelous site on acreage between Sweetzer and DeLongpre, and the house was built to rival the resplendent mansions other movies stars were erecting in the Hollywood hills. When it was ready, they moved in. His salary increased, and so did his popularity. The new home reflected their status: it featured a 400-foot frontage facing Sunset Boulevard. The house was built overlooking a quaint winding road, and its back door looked right up at the eternal hills. William S. Hart's pretty New England house was on one side, and William Desmond Taylor's colonial home was across the street. Dustin Farnum's beautiful villa was right around the corner. Inside,

Wally carrying actress Eileen Percy (LEFT) **and writer Anita Loos** (RIGHT), ca. 1918

While acting in silent films, Wally emoted best to the soft strains of a violin played just out of camera range by a musician, while the director and cameraman looked on.

Wally stocked a library full of fine editions by the best authors and many rare editions of old volumes. He was fond of hunting, and he acquired an arsenal of fine guns and pistols for every sort of use. The house boasted a large swimming pool, which was filled with players nearly every night. The den was fitted with an upright piano, a pool table, and a large boulder fireplace. The basement boasted his own laboratory, remarkably equipped with all the tools and instruments for microscopic study as he wished.

His leanings toward musical expressions also went back to his earliest youth. He played the piano, saxophone, violin, guitar, and practically every musical instrument. If he found a freak instrument he could not master, he practiced it for hours until he could play it with aplomb. When guests came over, which was nightly, he would play endlessly, always obliging with any kind of selection requested. He owned enough instruments to fill an orchestra: a grand piano in the living room, a pipe organ, guitars, banjos, six saxophones, snare and bass drums, several fine violins, and a viola. They also had a 35mm movie projector. Each evening, Wally's chauffeur went to town, and then returned with a set of reels of the most current films. After watching the movies, Wally demonstrated magic tricks, with which he was astoundingly proficient.

The beautiful mansion built on the Hollywood hills by Wally and Dorothy.

The new house seemed to come with banks of ever-present people, from a dozen to twenty or thirty on any given evening. Some came alone; others came with their wives, or children, or in pairs. They had the general run of the mansion, and were as comfortable with the place as they were with their own homes. He was a great mixer, and a charming, amusing entertainer. During all this time, his genial companionship attracted many disguised losers and sycophants, who formed a court of flattering admirers cooing perfumed words and self-seeking adulation. What he needed was the friendship of men his equal, who could offer natural criticism and sympathy, honest male companionship with men of his own class and mental caliber, who wanted nothing but his friendship. What he got was a collection of the famous, the unknown, and the infamous, all surrounding him with their life-sapping tentacles.

Not to be satisfied with the studio's output, Jesse Lasky signed Fatty Arbuckle to a contract for feature length films. The comedian had become enormously popular during the preceding years in one-reel and two-reel comedies, many with Buster Keaton. High grossing successes, Arbuckle's hard work brought him a firm footing at the box office. Lasky rushed him into three films back-to-back and had them ready for release like a cache of gold.

A hurricane of temptations swept over Wally, the same temptations that were overtaking many other young men in the film industry. Popular directors such as Desmond, comedians such as Arbuckle, and leading men like Wally were all besieged by ambitious men and adoring women, particularly the latter. They invaded every part of their lives, and the marchers in the army of throbbing hearts came from the ranks of the poorest shop girls and the most-beautiful society women.

For one year, an exquisitely attractive woman, who was firmly set in the exclusive Los Angeles and Santa Barbara community, bombarded Wally with a continual stream of photographs of herself in intimate, revealing poses. When he did not respond to her temptations, she sent him the key to her apartment, a flat no one knew she discretely kept. That effort failed to arouse in Wally a desire to reach out to her, so she then rerouted her efforts and snuck into contact with one of those around him. She gave his valet a diamond ring valued at many thousands of dollars so that he would arrange for her to be admitted to Wally's dressing room at the studio. He took the offer and let her in to wait like a spider for his arrival. When Wally came in, little suspecting that she was ready and prepared to seduce him, he encountered the woman in the full bloom of her grace and splendor. He shied away from the proposition.

Dorothy had gone away for a brief vacation alone. While she was gone, Wally's boyhood friend and secretary had stepped in to handle his personal affairs. When Dorothy tried to contact Wally about her return, the secretary tried to prevent her return by intercepting messages and telephone calls, and by various other means. He disappeared shortly before she came back, leaving Wally's affairs in a tangled mess. Dorothy returned to find that the bookkeeping and general management of their home had been horribly muddled during her absence. Their efforts to locate the fair weather friend proved fruitless, and she resigned to the task of straightening out the mess he had made of managing Wally's business affairs.

Another aspect of his life that was out of control was the breach of their domain by fans. One day, Wally and Dorothy were leaving the studio to return home. While driving, Wally reached into the back of their car and found a person in the back seat hiding under a robe. Dorothy turned around, lifted the covering, and unveiled a pretty girl with bronze hair, great violet eyes, and the body of a wood nymph. Neither of them knew who she was. Wally washed his hands of her immediately and turned the problem child over to Dorothy. Later, she learned that the girl was nothing more than a breathless fan that had run away from home and left behind her parents, who were unaware of her whereabouts. The directors of a boarding school from which she had escaped were frantically searching for her and did not know that she had sold her jewelry in order to buy a one-way ticket to Hollywood. Dorothy deposited the girl on the street, and they left her behind.

To their shock, the girl did not go away. Next, she found her way into their home and hid beneath Wally's bed. She was discovered, and put out again. Undeterred, the girl haunted the studio, always dressed well, and eagerly waited for Wally to emerge. Finally, Dorothy confronted the child, demanded to know her circumstances, and found out the girl's identity. She discovered that the girl was the daughter of a high-ranking United States Army officer, and her mother was a prominent fixture in Washington. A wire was sent to her family to come get her. Her mother came from across the country to pick her up and take her back by train, but at a scheduled stop at San Bernardino, the girl escaped. She telephoned the Reid residence. Wally happened to answer the phone, and to his shock, the girl poured out a soulful gush of unchecked emotion, and then told him that she was going to kill herself if he did not pick her up. He did not come to her aid, and the girl eventually went home to stay.

Another star-crazy girl came to the studio to get a glimpse of him, trying in vain to meet him by pestering everyone with whom she came in contact. Her persistence got her as far as the outer perimeter of the Paramount studio where she waited at a vigil. Her big chance came when he drove off the lot. Not to let her opportunity pass, the hysterical girl threw herself in front of the car. Wally barely stopped before running her over. After getting out and discovering that her collapse was nothing but a madcap ruse to force a confrontation with him, Dorothy was summoned. While waiting for the frenzied, love-starved child to be claimed by her parents, Dorothy patiently counseled her about the stupidity of her obsession.

Wally and an unknown musician serenading actress Lila Lee during the making of James Cruze's *Hawthorne of the U.S.A* (1919).

Ex-Follies girls, screen hopefuls, and schoolgirls came to Hollywood in throngs hoping for film stardom. They also pursued Wally. He was still just in his twenties, but he was not the kind of man who sought out the companionship of other women. He had passed through one engaging, creditable, young love affair to a joyful and complete marriage with Dorothy. Those other women infesting his personal life were rebuffed with great annoyance, and separating them from every corner of his life became increasingly difficult. They attempted to undermine his moral fiber with flattery and persistence. Some offered favors that became increasingly difficult for him to pass.

On the Monday morning of March 2, 1919, while making the film, *The Valley of the Giants* (1919), director James Cruze took Wally, cast, and crew into the Korbel Mountains to photograph some exterior scenes just outside of Arcata, Oregon. The train bearing the company chugged along tracks heading north out of Los Angeles and toward the mountains where the single, most pivotal incident in Wally's life was about to take place. Disaster waited just ahead.

Director James Cruze shepherded Wally through many of his films.

Chapter 11
WHO SO DIGGETH A PIT

The train bound for a film location in the mountains of Oregon chugged resolutely on its path to where photography was to take place for *The Valley of the Giants*. The location had been used many times before, and the uneventful trip was lightened by the music and camaraderie Wally shared with his friends. In the middle of the smelly old caboose, Wally sat on a long, leather-padded seat to the right of the car, strumming his guitar and singing lustily. Speed Hanson sat nearby accompanying him on his banjo, and actress Grace Darmond, who was playing "Shirley Sumner" in the picture, swayed next to them in a fluffy dress, enjoying their duet. The creaking old caboose groaned, jerked, and bumped along the narrow-gauge mountain railway, moving almost in time with the song they were singing. Outside, signal flags rattled in their tin containers. The switchman dangled his leg from the open door. The monotonous atmosphere was it should have been, while the train rumbled along the tracks and the repetitive play of passing scenery whisked by the windows in an endless, boring panorama.

While passing over rickety tracks on the Noisy Creek Bridge, the caboose suddenly swayed perilously and then skipped the tracks, tipping over and falling off the bridge. The switchman leaned out just in time to watch in horror, as the rest of the cars jackknifed and fell from the little trestle. Before any alarm could be sounded, the rest of the cars careened in a mad plunge from the tracks with one sickening lurch after another. Miss Darmond's piercing scream reached to the tops of the solemn old pine trees, but her voice was immediately drowned out by the roar of crunching, snapping steel. No one in the caboose witnessed what happened next. One by one, each car toppled into space, and the entire train hurled down a fifteen-foot embankment, crashing in an appalling mangle of metal and hissing steam. In seconds, the short fall came to an abrupt end. The crash was over before anyone realized what had happened. Wally, Speed, and the others in the caboose looked up from where they lay in piles with their instruments smashed and flung about the debris. The train laid on its sides, panting and palpitating like a mortally wounded beast, a mass of twisted metal and spinning wheels lost among the stones and wild timber of the woodlands.

In shock, Wally crawled through the caboose door and dragged Miss Darmond with him. He could see that her once fluffy dress was now drenched with blood. His head spun dizzily. When he reached open air, he collapsed. Blood dripped down his gashed forehead into his eyes. He looked up to see the crumbled train cars overturned in a sickening pile and strewn about the crushed boulders in horrible confusion. His wonderful stamina roused and he came to his senses. Then, he felt something soft and warm ooze from the back of his skull, and a stabbing pain tore at his left arm. A piece of glass had sliced clean through his flesh to the bone. He stumbled to his feet, still strong enough to lurch among the other members of the party, as they scrambled for protection, rushing and calling for aid with a frenzy born from desperation.

Wally leapt to tend to their wounds, but he moved slowly. There was another pain wrenching at his back, an injury of the sciatic nerve. Despite the agony, he helped drag others from the wreckage. His training in medical science came to the fore and he diligently administered to their needs. Alone and in the middle of nowhere, they were without any outside help. There was no way to contact the outside world. For the next twelve hours, Wally used his medical skills to administer to those who were injured, and he even set four broken fingers for one of the prop boys.

Rescuers finally arrived, but only after the injured had languished in isolation for half of a day. Survivors were taken to a doctor in a nearby town. For the first time since the accident, Wally's wounds were dressed. He was among the very last to receive medical attention. The surgeon told him he had done a perfect job setting the broken bones on the prop boy and complimented him on the lifesaving effort he gave to others who were cut and scraped.

A bold article in the *New York Telegraph* brought wide attention to the accident:

> "Nearly every member of the Wallace Reid company was injured in an accident last Monday, March 2, 1919, in northern California, when a train caboose, carrying the Reid company of players, jumped the tracks on a trestle bridge near Arctas and turned over. Wallace Reid sustained a three-inch scalp wound, which required six stitches to close. Grace Darmond and others in the company suffered similar cuts and bruises...."

Today, every injured person in a tragedy such as that would be hospitalized, and the picture they were making would be postponed indefinitely until they made a full recovery, but in 1919, Paramount executives told director James Cruze to proceed with the filming of scenes they were intending to stage out among the forest. No one was hospitalized. Against the advice of physicians, Wally went back to work the very next day after the accident, his gashed arm hastily patched and dressed with bandages that were hidden by carefully placed costumes, and his head gash was strategically turned away from the camera lens. The picture's scenes were photographed at once, but from that hour on, Wally was never the same.

The accident left him with blinding headaches, and the severe pain threatened to prevent him from finishing the film. Jesse Lasky sent their company doctor to Oregon with a supply of morphine so that Wally could continue working without feeling the full brunt of the pain. It took several weeks for his flesh wounds to heal, and through all that time, Wally continued working on the picture. He never missed a day despite the continual agony from his back injury and from the concussion he suffered on two sides of his head. The morphine helped soften the throbbing aches enough so that he could put in the twelve to fourteen hours needed to shoot each day's scenes. At that time, no one knew the crippling power of morphine or that the drug took only five to seven days to entrench itself. Doctors plied him with the addictive substance several times a day, and by the time the film was finished, Wally was addicted to morphine without even realizing it.

Wally and Grace Darmond in James Cruze's *The Valley of the Giants* (1919). Wally had to finish the film with his head wounds turned away from the camera.

About seven weeks later, he came back to Hollywood, apparently fully recovered. His eyes were bright and his health seemed normal. He had gained weight. Footage taken of him in the aftermath of the train accident was shown on studio projection room screens for inspection: there was the tall, straight form and the frank, boyish, open face audiences had always known and loved. On the surface, nothing had changed, but beneath that facade, Wally's internal injuries were worsening. Most terrible of all, the doctors who plied him with morphine injections did not know about the side effects. In their zeal or ignorance, they were accomplices to the inadvertent physical addiction that had taken an almost irrevocable hold on his nerves. Wally was innocent of any wrongdoing in the matter, and he went on using the pain killer way beyond the brief time that he should have.

After the picture was finished, he took a few weeks off to recover from the injuries, and the studio doctor kept supplying him with morphine for the pain that continued to come at him in unrelenting waves. He should have taken a long rest and had a thorough physical examination to determine the cause of the pounding aches he stoically endured, but there was another picture to make. James Cruze was again to direct him in *The Lottery Man*, and Paramount insisted on proceeding with the picture without any delay to their schedule.

In 1919, Wally visited Miriam Cooper while she was working for her husband, Raoul Walsh, on a Fox film, *Evangeline*. She later recalled in her memoirs that Wally was no longer the happy, smiling young man she had known only five years earlier while they were making *The Birth of a Nation*. He now seemed vague and jittery. While they visited, Miriam drank several cups of coffee from a pot warming over a can of sterno.

"Why do you swill all that coffee?" Wally asked incredulously.

"How else can I stay awake?" Miriam answered. "We've been working since nine this morning and it's nearly midnight now."

"Those slave drivers," he said. "They'll get their money's worth if they have to kill you doing it."

"I don't know about killing me," she told him, "but they are killing this set first thing in the morning and we still have several scenes to do. I've got to keep going."

"Why don't you get my doctor to give you something to keep you going?" Wally suggested. "It'll be better than drinking all that stuff."

At that moment, Miriam was summoned to the set. Wally called back with another friendly offer. "Don't forget to remind me to give you my doctor's phone number."

Wally's interest in the art of pharmaceutical science was a long-standing preoccupation that could be traced to his college studies. At one time, he decided to study chemical engineering. His home laboratory was filled with bottles, test tubes, and beakers cluttering up the place. He spent many hours pouring over compositions and mixing baffling concoctions. He knew the components of morphine, and he thought the small doses he was taking throughout each day were controlled. He believed that he knew exactly how many grams to take, and did so medicinally. What he did not realize was that his body was developing a tolerance to the doses, and gradually, required a little more with each injection to reach the same level of pain reduction.

Dorothy remarked in a 1922 *San Francisco Examiner* story, "It was months before I realized that the change in his disposition dated from that wreck in the lonely mountain wilderness. Now, in the light of later events and developments, I can see, plainly; I can understand how it began, and appreciate how he fell prey to the soothing, deadly sweet promises of drugs."

Nothing changed noticeably on the home front for Wally. He was a good father, and expressed his adoration for his son. "He was very attentive to the education and training of our son," Dorothy later pointed out. "He is very patient and very explicit in answering his childish questions and explaining things to him."

As the passing weeks merged into months, Dorothy was slow to realize the terrible change that had came over him. It was an insidious change, seemingly without any definite beginning. At first, she chalked it up to mere nervousness that seemed to crop up at odd moments. He could not sit still. He fidgeted. He could not read without rocking so violently that she fully expected his chair to tip over. Once, she observed the position of a rocking chair where he sat as he began to read a book. Later, she saw him in the same chair, but his aggressive rocking had gradually shoved him twenty feet away to the other side of the room. He was so absorbed in the book that he did not realize he had inched the chair across the full breadth of the room.

Another manifestation of the drug's effect on him became obvious when he lost his healthy, normal appetite, and the happy ring seemed to go out of his voice, replaced by a pitiful, irritable wail like a spoiled child. He became increasingly touchy, and nothing suited him. His odd, altered disposition baffled Dorothy, yet no one traced his behavioral change to his use of the narcotic.

They continued with their hectic work and social life. On February 12, 1920, The Wallace Reid Ball was held in the Hotel Alexandria on behalf of the Theatrical Charities Fund. Dorothy was one of the hostesses along with Mary Miles Minter. When Dorothy and Wally returned home late that night, he could not sleep. Insomnia became a nightly ordeal. Torturous sleeplessness got to the point that a family doctor had to be called.

"I remember only too clearly the night I watched the doctor give Wally his first shot to quiet his nerves and its astonishing effect,"

Wally and cast in a scene from James Cruze's *Lottery Man* (1919).

she recalled. "The old doctor had been summoned from his bed, and for half an hour, had tried to reason Wally into sleepiness. The argument failed. I lay in bed and watched with a fascinated horror as the doctor opened his little black bag and took out a smaller case. The reading light at the head of Wally's bed glinted from the steel and glass tubes, which lay in the little case in orderly rows. Silently, with a slight frown, the doctor prepared the shot."

Night after night, Wally sat in bed wide-awake after Dorothy had gone to sleep. He tried to pass the hours reading, and he smoked incessantly. On a good night, he dozed in the last few hours before dawn, but by the time the rising sun crept into the bedroom windows, he was again fully awake with the reading lamp still burning at the head of his bed and a book still opened in his nervous hands.

Sleepless nights passed like an eternity. Occasionally, Wally awakened Dorothy in the small hours of the night as he stamped about the room getting into his clothes.

"Where are you going at this time of night?" she asked sleepily.

"Any place; any old place; out to get some air," came his muttered reply.

An advertising billboard going up for one of Wally's popular car racing films.

Minutes later, the lights of his car flashed across the windows, and Dorothy heard the roar of the motor, as he raced down the driveway and disappeared into the night.

On some of those somnambulist-like excursions, he drove furiously for hours. He was unable to understand why he was going through those midnight marathons of inextinguishable alertness. As he drove at high speeds, the scenery flew by in an endless blur that came close to calming him with its hypnotic shadows, but the undeletable awareness hung on.

On another occasion, he put on shooting clothes long before daylight, and then telephoned a friend to get out of bed. Together, they took their guns and drove into the California wilderness to shoot rabbits at dawn. He returned, apparently rested and fresh, just in time to bathe, change clothes, and rush off to the studio for another long day of work. During those months that he was unable to sleep, the stimulant quality of morphine kept him energetic and functioning. He reported for duty at the studio between nine and ten o'clock, and he never missed a single day.

On February 1920, *Double Speed* was released, the first of six 1920 films with Wally in a lead role. Lasky found that Wally struck a continuingly responsive chord with daredevil auto movies. The public could not get enough of them. The films featured flashy cars and dangerous roads, and each one built to a climactic race that held audiences spellbound. The studio reaped a fortune with *The Roaring Road* (1919), *Excuse My Dust* (1920), and *Double Speed* (1920).

"Never, I believe, has an author discovered in the flesh so exactly the hero of his own stories," Byron Morgan, author of those tales, said to writer Kolma Flake in 1940, when he fondly looked back at Wally's work in those racing pictures. "Like the hero of my stories, he was absolutely fearless. Wally was a lover of speed, and did not hesitate to drive the fastest car hub to hub with experienced racing drivers. One day, he was supposed to go into a skid. In the first take he muffed it, so I walked over and said, 'What's the matter, Wally, did you hear the church bells?' He gave me an odd look, then climbed into the car and went into the scene again. He scared us all out of our wits when he skid the car over the curb, sheared off a lamppost, and crashed into the side of a building. With the car practically demolished, he climbed from the wreckage and grinned, 'Well, Byron, does that look like church bells have got me?' But that Wally . . . he'd try anything."

Paramount sent Wally on a publicity tour to Vancouver with Adam Hull Shirk, Director of Publicity. Wally drove, and Adam later remarked ruefully, ". . . he never went less than sixty miles an hour all the way. We were in an open car without a windshield, too. It didn't seem to faze him a bit, but I haven't got my wind back yet. Wally made personal appearances at seventeen theaters, and if I ever doubted his tremendous popularity, never again. It was all I could do to get him away from the mobs, and they almost tore his clothes off for souvenirs."

Paramount kept Wally busily moving from one film to the next, usually with no meaningful break between productions. He appeared in six films in the first year of his Lasky contract, and *the following year he was in ten*. Lasky determined to get the full value of his popular star during the seven-year period of his contract. During those years, Wally continued his secret use of morphine. He felt that he had the drug under control and was just taking it for its pain killing effect and the energy it gave, but he did not realize that it had him hopelessly caught in a powerful grip that was impossible to lose.

"The producers worked their stars until they were ready to drop," Miriam Cooper later stated. She knew first-hand the wrenching schedules to which producers subjected their contract players. "People like Wallace Reid . . . started taking drugs to keep awake to finish a picture. And then there would be another picture, and another pill, until it was too late . . . by then they were hooked on pills."

Miriam Cooper's theory was proving too true in the lives of more than one actor and actress in motion pictures during the 1920s. Like an evil hyena stalking in the shadows of their lives, drugs came in quietly and worked their soothing effect as intended. It was too effective, and doctors at that time knew little about their unstoppable power or the insurmountable, uncontrollable grip they held when once established in a body.

During all that time, his sleepless nights continued unabated. Wally complained of lumps that formed at the base of his skull, on the spot of the wound from the railroad wreck. His right leg also troubled him in the same place where he had been injured way back in 1913 while working on an earlier picture. Sometimes, his leg was numb all night long.

Unpleasant thoughts and fears crowded his mind. He never confided in Dorothy about those agonies, choosing to carry the terrible burdens alone. Sometimes, the lonely hours of the night closed in frighteningly around him. More than once, she opened her eyes to find him sitting on the edge of her bed gently nudging her awake.

"Don't leave me alone, mamma," he whispered, clasping her hand nervously like a child. "I feel so strange. I don't want to be left alone."

On May 22, 1920, Wally lost his father. Hal Reid died, leaving behind four widows, more than a hundred plays, and uncountable movie scenarios on which he had given his talent. Royalties had died off, and what was left of his good-sized fortune had dwindled down to very little to compare to the affluence he once knew. The loss of his father was a terrible blow to Wally, and if he had felt alone before, the sensation of being stranded on an island of hopelessness was never more acute than it was while he was at the height of his fame and popularity. From the outside looking in, people thought Wally had everything. In reality, he lacked the most basic foundation for happiness.

Wally had always experimented with elixirs and compounds in his basement laboratory. Accidentally, he found that mixing alcohol in small quantities tempered the effect of the morphine coursing through his blood. There followed many nights during which Dorothy heard him patter downstairs. After a few minutes, she detected the tinkling sound of a spoon stirring in a tumbler as he mixed a drink. He found that a little whisky taken along with the morphine enabled him to actually catch a few hours of much-needed sleep, and he chose whisky as the lesser of the evils. Wally was not drinking to excess. Prohibition was still new and temperance laws had not been fully embraced by the general population. He routinely had one or two cocktails before dinner, and once in a while, he went to a party at the home of mutual friends, where drinks flowed as part of the entertainment at Thanksgiving, Christmas, and New Year's, just as it was for many other people across the nation. At those parties, he met the Hollywood underworld, people who were living in apartments and hotels and did not maintain homes. There were many of those people, the denizens of Hollywood, who hung onto the fringes of show businesses, hoping for a break. Their company became all too regular. Their habits became expected and accepted.

Late in June 1920, the weather turned very warm, and around the first of July, Dorothy took Billy and went to the mountains for a month, leaving Wally at work. He had renewed his friendship with a San Francisco man he had known since boyhood. The friend dropped whatever work he had been doing and came to Hollywood to be with Wally as his business manager and personal assistant, taking over the reins, paying Wally's bills, and generally attending to his finances. He also served as a much-needed fence to keep unwanted fans from piercing through the thin veil of privacy he had.

After Dorothy went away, Wally finished filming *The Charm School*, and promptly, with the aid of that old friend, decided to stage a wrap party. There were several soirées at their house that week. Dorothy's mother hosted one of them. They were all seemingly harmless affairs, but after Dorothy came home, Wally told her about them in a rather shame-faced way. He was always sorry after he had been drinking too much.

Despite the partying, Wally gave himself equally unashamedly to his tireless efforts to raise funds at various charity drives, such as an American Legion benefit in Los Angeles on Saturday, August 21, 1920. The fundraiser was one of many Wally and his band performed at to elicit contributions for the effort of bond sales.

On September 1, 1920, the night before the premier of D. W. Griffith's *Way Down East*, Griffith and the cast members were in New York. At the hotel, where some of the actors were staying, a light suddenly began to flash on the telephone switchboard from a caller ringing from the room of Robert "Bobby" Harron, one of the stars of *Intolerance* and so many other Griffith pictures, including the many he made with Wally.

"I've shot myself," Bobby gasped. "Send for the doctor."

Bobby was taken by ambulance to Bellevue Hospital while he was in a coma. On his deathbed, he swore to a priest that he had accidentally shot himself with a pistol. Although his death was officially recorded as "accidental," Hollywood gossips wagered that Bobby killed himself in the New York hotel room on the eve of the premiere of Griffith's new film because he was devastated after

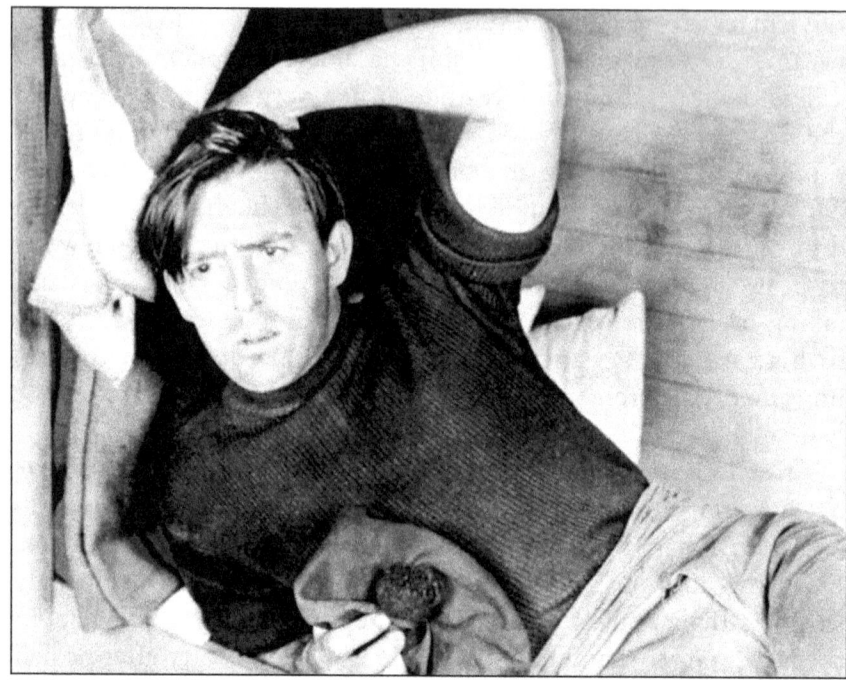

Wally in James Cruze's *Always Audacious* (1920).

being passed over for lead roles in favor of the director's new protégé, Richard Barthelmess. No one ever knew the full truth about the tragedy, but Lillian Gish vigorously denied in her autobiography that there was any possibility of an attempted suicide. Bobby's untimely death remained a heartbreaking mystery, but those who knew him best steadfastly accepted his statement to the priest as truth.

In September 1920, Wally and Dorothy joined many celebrities in a fundraising effort to amass $10,000 for the Disabled Soldiers of the Great War. They went to a ball at the Alexandria in Los Angeles hosted by the Motion Picture Directors Association. The affair was exceedingly gorgeous, and the 700 people who gathered represented the elite of Los Angeles society as well as of the Hollywood film colony.

The *Moving Picture World* reported on November 13, 1920 that a series of conferences among the powerful executives at the studio were quietly held, presided over by their President, Adolph Zukor, developed new policies for the making of Paramount Pictures. The plan called for the elevation of all Paramount stars to the position

Robert "Bobby" Harron, who had appeared with Wally in several D. W. Griffith films.

of "super-stars," the first time the term was coined for film actors.

"I feel that at last my dreams have come true, that now the entire Paramount producing department is in a position to concentrate its efforts upon the making of only the highest type of motion pictures," Lasky proclaimed.

As Wally's career was reaching a creative climax, there were ominous rumblings of wrongdoing erupting in the press. On November 25, 1920, *Variety*, the show business newspaper, reported a mysterious incident concerning the arrest of a strange man:

"HAD DOPE FOR SALE"

"*Los Angeles*: Thomas H. Tyner, alias Claude Walton, alias Bennie Walton, was taken into custody here on a local lot with seven bundles of heroin on his person, according to the arresting officer. He was arraigned before U.S. Commissioner Long and held for $1,000 bail for a preliminary examination. It is said Tyner declared he was delivering the dope to one of the best-known male picture stars on the coast and that it had been the second time he was engaged to deliver to the same star, whose wife, in the hope of having him break the habit, informed the authorities."

That incident sparked a tidal wave of fear among Paramount executives. Jesse Lasky was told that something had to be done about rumors that Wally was taking dope, and that if it was true, the studio was sitting on a powder keg. Lasky was told to do something about it. A few questions brought more information to the Paramount executive about the "best known male picture star," who was unnamed in the article.

Dorothy and Wally continued to live their lives as if there were no undercurrents of misconduct to be concerned about. They celebrated Christmas 1920 in their spectacular new Spanish-style home in West Hollywood. Dorothy was enjoying being a wife and mother, and for a time, virtually retired from pictures. After appearing in *Mothers of Men*, she had made only one brief film appearance in *The Fighting Chance*.

The holidays brought an unprecedented number of visitors to Wally's mansion. One particular night became a watershed because of the quantity and temper of the guests. People were coming into the house already drunk, and some of them became abusive. The situation with those ever-present visitors and their conduct finally reached a crisis point.

"I have never learned whether the chauffeur invited all his

friends, or whether it was the gardener. But they came," Dorothy lamented, looking back. "I have never on any motion picture lot, seen so strange an assembly of humanity as gathered in our drawing room and overflowed into our kitchen that night. It was the most terrible evening in my recollection. I often wondered whether I would live to see another day. Guests began arriving about eight or nine o'clock. They were our friends, the people we knew. Wally's jazz band, in which he alternated with the saxophone and violin, was in full swing. There were three other boys and one girl in the organization. And, of course, there was liquor. What Christmas-time housewarming would be complete without it? Later in the evening, guests began to come from all directions at once—people neither Wally nor I had invited. They had been to other Yuletide affairs, and most of them were already under the influence of liquor. Several young men became hostile, and one or two girls from somewhere or other were ludicrous. One of the strangers barely entered the house when he insulted a young man and the two of them prepared to do mortal combat in our reception hall. I was terribly embarrassed, because the wife of the young man was talking with me at the time. But to save the furniture, I was forced to ask the uninvited guest to leave the house. The young wife, who had not been drinking, was more embarrassed than I, but she whispered to me that she understood."

Wally's jazz band had been tooting away in one corner of the drawing room with him very much in earnest about their music. He busily directed the repertoire while Dorothy had her hands full trying to deal with the drunken guests.

Around two o'clock in the morning, she felt a touch on her arm, and turned around to see Wally, his hair rumpled and his breath coming in pants from his saxophone playing.

"Do you think everybody's having a good time?" he whispered, anxiously questioning the atmosphere. He seemed very much concerned about it.

She assured him the party was a howling success.

"Good," he said mysteriously, and dashed back to his jazz band.

Mercifully, by three o'clock in the morning, most of the guests had gone. An hour later, Dorothy thought she was finally alone with Wally in the kitchen. They were hunting some cold turkey for a quick snack. His arm was around her shoulders, and he had to be repeatedly assured, like a child, that the party had been successful, that everyone had gone away happy. She also learned that he had only taken two drinks over the course of the entire evening. A half hour later, one forgotten young man came wandering into the kitchen to demand a turkey sandwich. He had peevishly refused to come to the table when dinner was served, and he said he was nearly starved.

Hospitality was Wally's watchword, and many of the people he trusted to come into his life and home abused it. From that night on, hospitable evenings at their new home became never-ending. They began with the five or six old friends who were regular guests dropping in during the early evening and then gravitating to the billiard room to play pool until midnight. Occasional drinks were as normal as the jazz music. As the evenings wore on, more and more friends joined the crowd, and many of them were barely acquaintances. They romped into the house on the way to the beach, or on the way home, and proceeded to make themselves very much at home until all hours of the night. Wally's liquor supply diminished very rapidly during their visits. The strangers among their guests often located their stock of supplies, and Dorothy often saw them walking from the house with whole quarts protruding from their pockets. In effect, their home became a roadhouse with no cover charge and everything free.

"Wally would not stop them," Dorothy later pointed out. "He was 'hail fellow, well met' with them all."

On one of those nights at the very coldest part of the year, an unusually boisterous crowd came in late, demanding that Wally go swimming with them, which he did at once. They all found bathing suits and splashed into their ice-cool pool, coming out later blue with cold and strangely sober. That was one of the few nights during all those months that Wally actually slept soundly.

During all that time, he was working, taxing his strength day by day in the studio or on location, and then playing with his guests until all hours of the night. Dorothy observed that his heart was not in any of that. He did not seem to get any kick out of it; he simply had the open, generous heart of a child, and he hated to offend anyone by turning them away.

(TOP) **Wally on the set of Frank Urson's *The Hell Diggers* (1921).**
(BOTTOM) **Wally, Billy, and Dorothy at home and seemingly at peace, but just beneath the idyllic surface lurked the seeds of unspeakable tragedy.**

1921 began with another whirl of Wallace Reid films, one releasing nearly on top of the next. He appeared in six films, one released every few months. In May 1921, Wally and Dorothy were guests of May Allison at The American Society of Cinematographers Ball at the new Ambassador Hotel in Los Angeles. James Kirkwood was the sensation of the evening. There was an audible gasp over the room when he appeared on the floor wearing his long, silky yellow beard, and the grown he wore for his part in *The Money Master*. Alla Nazimova came wearing a yellow satin outfit made exactly like a hula dancer costume. She flitted in with her husband for a few moments, and then gave the spectators a treat by dancing twice, each time giving a very good imitation of a hula. Gloria Swanson arrived wearing fewer clothes than anyone had ever seen in a public place, a shocking outfit made entirely of jet-black beads. The event was one of the outstanding social events of the season.

At home, Wally was like a kid, and he adored all surprises. Every time Dorothy went downtown, she was expected to bring home some kind of surprise for him. The ones he liked best were those that made him laugh, or showed that she had remembered some small wish of his. He loved magic, and she often searched for some new prop or new magic trick that would stimulate his interest in the slight-of-hand art. He loved to read, and she took time to rummage through second-hand bookstores for out-of-print volumes he wanted. Always, Wally was as delighted as any child would be, but lovingly and with appreciation. It seemed like the good times would go on forever.

Then, not long after the heartbreaking death of Bobby Harron, another Hollywood tragedy shocked the nation. On Labor Day in 1921, Roscoe "Fatty" Arbuckle was arrested on manslaughter charges after a party where a disreputable starlet named Virginia Rappe fell seriously ill. She died a few days later. Newspapers, led by the Hearst group, made the incident Hollywood's first truly major scandal. After two sensational trials ended in hung juries, Arbuckle was acquitted.

"But the unfortunate affair occurred at a time when churches, women's clubs, and reformers already had blood in their eyes over Hollywood's alleged sinfulness and the moral laxness depicted in some films," Lasky remembered in his memoirs. "A hundred censorship bills had been introduced in thirty-seven States, and the Arbuckle catastrophe became the flashpoint for the industry. In Massachusetts, one town retaliated by banning all motion pictures. Public scrutiny of actor's lives became intense, and no one escaped the microscopic glare."

To protect their investments, leaders in the film industry chose to head off further calamity. They organized the Motion Picture Producers and Distributors of America with a purpose to formulate a written code of behavior for industry personnel. Will Hays, then Postmaster General under President Harding, was recruited for a position of enforcing ethical and moral responsibility within the industry. Once installed in office, he immediately advised Lasky to shelve the three Arbuckle films that were completed and waiting for release. Lasky argued that his present notoriety might increase profits, but the final decision went to his partner, Adolph Zukor. Reluctantly, Zukor agreed to shelve the films. The Arbuckle films remained unreleased and were written off as a total loss to the studio of over a $1 million.

The worst was yet to come. If anyone had told Lasky that Paramount's greatest individual asset was about to self-destruct, he would have found it hard to believe the charge, but on September 23, 1921, the following cryptic item appeared in *Variety*:

> ". . . It is known the wife of one of the most popular of the younger male stars has time and again had the peddlers of dope supplying her husband arrested, but she has been unable to get her husband to break his habit . . . ."

Prohibition brought a whole set of evils to America, and it touched no place more severely than in Hollywood where a bohemian, gypsy atmosphere prevailed. At home, parties continued into the night at Wally and Dorothy's house. She later blamed the illegal availability of alcohol as one of their miseries. "Before, we had wine in the home, which Wally drank temperately with friends for relaxation after strenuous hours in the studio," she told Herb Howe, "and then, it became a crime, and the bootleggers came with their poisonous Scotch and Bourbon, and their insinuating drugs."

Those hangers-on continued to turn their home into a bar, coming at odd hours and continuing to arrive by scores during the day. They infiltrated the rooms that had once been a place of warm domesticity, and Wally never turned anyone away. There, they lingered, drank, and in the dark shadows of the night, they brought with them other toys for illicit good times.

The parties at the Reid home became commonplace. Because of them, Wally changed, while Dorothy sat grimly silent. She never blamed him for anything he did because she thought he was just trying to be friendly to everyone; his intentions were always right. He wanted to be the perfect host, and he thought it was good to provide an atmosphere for everyone's enjoyment.

Then, there were those oddball hangers-on who did not seem to care much for Dorothy or her stoicism. In some ways, she seemed the opposite of Wally. As his wife, her chief characteristics were clear, common sense, an amazing sense of humor, and a deep, selfless loyalty. Her innate self-control manifested itself in an outer shell that, at times, made people think she was a cold fish, but it was that crust that enabled her to pass unfazed through the confusion at home and Wally's fast-paced professional work. She could not honestly turn it off and pretend to be something other than what she was. Sometimes, when the jazz records were blaring and Wally was caught up in the fun of socializing, she simply left the room. There was always the excuse of checking on their son that gave her an acceptable reason to disappear for long stretches of time. They did not know she was avoiding their company. Sometimes, she left for no other reason than to stay away from witnessing first hand little covert activities that bordered on bawdy or were precariously skirting around the law. It was just that she did not want to be seen obviously frowning at adult behavior that passed for frivolity, but was in reality perilous. She put up with them for the night. There was always tomorrow when they would be gone, the air in the rooms would clear out, and the early morning madness of picture making would again consume their lives to distraction.

In the summer of 1921, director Frank Urson took Wally, cast, and crew to shoot scenes for *The Hell Diggers* in the Sierra Mountain between Yosemite and King's Canyon. Along for the trip was

Charles "Buddy" Post, a genial, roly-poly character actor playing a "Fat Farmer" in the melodrama of mountaineers crossing paths with an inventor of a dredge for re-soiling land that has been stripped by gold mining. They were making the trip on a train with several cars. They had an early morning appointment to begin work while they were able to capture sunrays breaking through tree branches. The trip rolled out of Los Angeles just after nightfall.

Halfway along the route, Wally decided to get away from the crowd and play a little joke on Urson by disappearing. Before long, the director realized that Wally was not in one of the three cars attached to the regular train. A search was launched up and down the aisles of every car, but they could not find Wally. No one thought of looking up on the roof of the rickety, rolling boxcar attached to the coaches.

Above their frantic search, the cool California night air blustered around the heads of the two men roosting quietly on the rooftop of the swaying, lurching boxcar. Buddy Post and Wally took in the lonely, wide-open countryside from their unique vantage point beneath the stars, while below them, panic ensued within the train. The two actors smoked and exchanged confidences. While sailing through the silent night, Wally looked up at the starry sky and marveled at the panorama of nature playing across the landscape. Their talk drifted to philosophy and religion.

"As the conversation progressed, I felt that I had penetrated the happy-go-lucky personality of Wallace Reid," Buddy reminisced. "We talked of every cult from Brahmism to present day 'isms. Epictetus, Epicurus, Plato, Luther, Nietzsche, and Freud figured in his talk. I must admit I am rather ignorant of these writings, and I never in the world suspected Wally of knowing them."

Wally told him of the days when he was a reporter and the pleasure he took out of being broke and on his own for the first time. He spoke of his earlier jobs with much delight, and in those moments on reflection, he commented on the emptiness of his present fame and fortune. Buddy was astonished at his knowledge on nearly every subject they discussed.

"He told me of his troubles—things that I believe he did not tell others. To the outer world, Wally had no troubles. Those things were not of paramount importance, but little annoyances and petty happenings, which in no way would interfere greatly with his course in life. They concerned his ambitions, his next picture, etc. I cannot betray these confidences. He would not have betrayed mine."

While on that location shoot with Buddy Post, Wally came to the rescue of anyone when they were in trouble. There were several times when Buddy witnessed him going to the head office to fight for the needs of some member of their troupe. He helped a prop boy get a well-deserved raise; he kept an errant crewmember from being fired. Buddy suffered a serious burn about the head caused by the misfire of a magnesium flare, and before physicians reached him, Wally administered first aid so proficiently that it saved Buddy's face from ruin. The Paramount production supervisor decided to send him home and replace him with another actor. Nothing could delay the work schedule, they said, and Buddy was expendable. Wally used his clout to force them to take care of him while he was at the location camp and pay him salary for the length of the picture, which they were not going to otherwise do. His generosity, unselfishness, and consideration for everyone were hallmarks of his personality, and those with whom he worked loved him.

Wally still wanted only to direct films, but he was held back by his face and his popularity. He loved motion picture work, but had tired of the kind of parts he was doing. He wanted heavier dramatics, but Paramount kept forcing him into lighthearted stories that were, at best, delightfully bland and devoid of substance. Only a fascinating central figure could carry them to success, and most of them rode to great box office triumph on the sheer force of his personality.

Throughout 1920, other actors were making strides with outstanding work in admirable stories. William Farnum was holding the public fascinated with his wonderful work in *If I Were King*; Richard Barthelmess was earning legions of fans in D. W. Griffith's *Way Down East* and his own *Tol'able David*; John Barrymore won critical and popular acclaim with *Dr. Jekyll and Mr. Hyde*; and Rudolph Valentino stormed the movies in the sensational *The Four Horsemen of the Apocalypse*. By comparison, Wally made *The Dancin' Fool, The Love Special,* and *Don't Tell Everything*, all breezy, light-hearted comedies with trifling stories. He implored those at Paramount to give him meatier roles, but they plunged him into a Cecil B. DeMille trifle, *The Affairs of Anatol*. Wally needed someone to rescue his career from the mush of mediocrity.

Always Audacious, directed by James Cruze, provided Wally with a difficult, dual role as Perry Danton, a millionaire, and Slim Attucks, a crook. Wonderful double-exposure photography that was utilized in the picture won admiration from industry insiders. In one scene, Wally has a tremendous fight with himself, hits himself a terrific blow on the jaw and drops, while at the same time, he stands victorious over his prostrate body. Another very difficult stunt involved opening a door to himself and meeting himself on a landing. Finally, a third, complicated set-up involved the act of throwing a book at himself and catching it. In each camera shot, the book had to be thrown precisely at the same angle and at the same speed, and they accomplished the stunt only after many, repeated attempts.

The flurry of Wallace Reid pictures served to saturate movie theaters with his work. There was still a long slate of upcoming pictures they hoped to grind out with him before his contract ended, and prospects may have begun to look uncertain to Paramount whether he would be able to keep up the pace or not. The rumors of his bad behavior ricocheted like quiet echoes behind closed doors at the studio. They did not want a repeat of the $3,000,000 write-off they had to take after the Arbuckle scandal. They rushed into release as many of the completed Wallace Reid films that were waiting in cans as was possible for them to do. It was as if they had foreknowledge of the horror that was to happen next.

Wally with Cecil B. De Mille during production of *The Affairs of Anatol* (1921).

Chapter 12
A Modern Snare

On May 25, 1921, *The Los Angeles Herald* reported another mysterious, local incident involving a drug sale gone sour:

> Trailing a suspect in a taxicab to the home of a prominent actor in Hollywood, three officers today took into custody a man giving the name of Joe Woods, 34, said by them to be a notorious narcotic distributor, and confiscated $1,000 worth of morphine. Woods was booked at the city jail on a charge of violating the state poison law and was held on default of $500 bail pending arraignment before Police Judge George H. Richardson. Inspectors Fred Borden, and Peoples of the state board of pharmacy, and Detective Sergeants O'Brien, and Yarrow of the police narcotic squad, nabbed Woods, according to records at detective headquarters. Reports received by the state and city officers indicated the suspect was active in the unlawful distribution of narcotics. They followed him in a police automobile to Hollywood, they say, and took him into custody in the pretentious home of the actor while, it is charged, he was attempting to sell his wares. According to the police, Woods, who is well known to them as a narcotic peddler, recently finished serving a term at the county jail after being found guilty of violating a federal law in the unlawful distribution of narcotics. The officers who arrested Woods declined to reveal the name of the actor. It was explained by them that the actor was neither an addict nor a distributor, and played no part in the arrest of the suspect.

The incident was brought to the attention of Jesse Lasky. A little prying on Paramount's part revealed the name and address of the "prominent actor" unnamed in the article. The truth was leaked, and a firestorm of rumors spread quickly. Wally's name was finally mentioned out loud as the one who was buying illegal drugs.

Dorothy tried to fend off the smoldering conflict, and explained the incident her way in a *San Francisco Examiner* letter to Wally's fans:

> ". . . a young man was arrested with narcotics in his possession and explained he was 'going to see Wally Reid.' The explanation was true, but the innuendo was false. Gossips immediately said the young man was taking the drugs to Wally to 'make a delivery,' as the saying goes. That was not true. . . ."

In many later articles and interviews, Dorothy revealed that Wally was using narcotics as far back as the 1919 train wreck, and she pinpointed that incident as the initial reason for his using morphine.

Dorothy tried to hide the real truth, explaining that Wally was fond of "French magazines," and that was the excuse for the meeting. She claimed that their chauffeur knew that young man and brought him to their house to display a large collection of such magazines from which Wally could purchase a selection. Supposedly, Wally bought about $20 worth. He purportedly started to look through the bundle when several little paper-wrapped packages fell out, the kind of pocket-size quantities of narcotics dope peddlers then called "bindles." When Wally was said to have demanded an explanation from the boy, he seemed surprised to see the bindles and professed no knowledge about how they got in with the magazines. Wally called him from the room and they talked privately for quite a while. When he returned, he explained the mysterious appearance of the young man to Dorothy.

According to Dorothy many years later, Wally had his own version of the incident. "He told me a wild story about finding the drugs behind the moldings of the bathroom at his home, and said he brought them here believing that I would buy them. He had heard stories about drug addicts among the picture people. He's coming to the studio tomorrow, and I'm going to try to get him a job." Wally sent the young man away, but arranged to meet him at the studio the next morning, promising him work in the picture business. The next day, the youth was arrested, and gave his statement to the police about "going to see Wallace Reid."

Rumors rebounding from that episode went clear to the top of the Paramount organization, and when the rumors were published, gossiping film fans began to speculate about Wally. In what now sounds like a ruse to divert finger pointing, Dorothy and Wally were said to have investigated the young man, found his wife was expecting a youngster, and offered to help them out of their financial straits as well as assist the wife with taking care of the baby. Wally was reportedly anxious to visit the young man at the jail, but advised by his friends against it. Gossips immediately decided the boy's story was true, and that Wally was afraid to face him, a claim Dorothy persisted in saying was absolutely false.

"I have ceased to play first hypodermic in the narcotic orchestra," the young man wrote in one of the many letters he composed and mailed from prison to Wally. After serving out his term, he continued to write voluminous letters to Wally and delivered them almost every night long after the Reids had gone to bed. The youth stole up to their front door, left a package in the mailbox, and ran madly down the hill. The packages supposedly contained his latest letter. Some people observing those midnight visits jumped to the conclusion the boy was peddling drugs to Wally. The truth has never been revealed about the contents of those frequently delivered packages, but it was believed that they were morphine deliveries.

In 1922, D. W. Griffith's *The Birth of a Nation* was re-released in a special revival eight years after its initial release. It was touted as the "daddy of 'em all," providing a new generation with the same thrills as when it was originally released and causing panic among the censors as it did in 1916. That same year, Dorothy made one film appearance in 1922 in *Every Woman's Problem* as a woman judge battling bootleggers.

Also in 1922, Wally went back on the live theater stage in *The Blue Flame* in Los Angeles. No sooner was the brief vaudeville run on the road than the female actress in the lead part was dismissed. Just before the production went to San Francisco, Dorothy received a call from Wally on a Saturday night urgently asking her to take over the role starting the following Wednesday, and then finish out the tour. Dorothy came to the rescue, ended her sabbatical as a housewife, and returned to the stage to appear with Wally in the play. She was not a member of the original company, and did not start out on tour with them. She agreed to carry out the vaudeville engagement as a last-minute replacement with it understood that she would not permanently be returning to the stage.

A whirlwind of success swept tempestuously throughout every corner of Dorothy and Wally's lives. They were on a treadmill without any end. The responsibilities of raising a child, maintaining a semblance of a home, conducting frequent press interviews, and traveling to locations for picture work mounted. Wally's unrelenting schedule required one picture to be made almost immediately on the heels of each completed picture, and the pace began to take a toll on both of them. Dorothy took time to reflect in October 1922. "So much has been crowded into the short nine years of our married life that it seems that I have been married much longer," she confessed. "We have been through years and years of experiences, it seems. I have been in a position to see the marvelous development, which has taken place in Wally's work from the time when he played that first leading role with me until now. Not only has he shown a remarkable artistic sense and ability in many branches of art, but has also demonstrated a profound interest in things mechanical."

It seemed like their fast track to success was rocket-propelled, and Wally was moving too fast in the sweep of things to spend time reflecting somberly over the direction the course of his life had turned. He also never worried about money. He was earning $3,000 a week in those years when Federal Income Tax was minimal. His contract called for annual increases of $500 per week. At that time, a new model of the latest Jewett-6, Nash, Packard, or Chandler Six cost between $1,065 and $2,390.00. Wally was easily able to afford to buy one every six months and still have plenty of money left over for household expenses in an era when milk was ten cans for $1, bread was 5¢ a loaf, and a prime rib roast only cost 31¢ a pound.

The biggest drain on his income was his habit of loaning money to anyone. He even gave money to people he disliked if they were in need. One was an actor who sporadically worked in comedies.

Broke and unemployed, he came to Wally for support. Wally contributed enough regular money to the man to support him and his family for some time. Wally kept his little black book noted with all the loans he had made to people, someday intending to follow up on collecting repayment. The book was overfilled with the names of many people in the motion picture world who owed money to him, but he never went knocking on their door asking for a return of his generosity.

Secretly, Will Hays went to Jesse Lasky to discuss evidence that Wally was using illegal narcotics. After Hays spilled the definite details he possessed, Lasky wanted to avoid a public relations crisis. He sent for Wally to discuss the looming nightmare. He claimed to be fond of him, and said that he found it very difficult to tell him about the rumors that were swirling into a whirlwind of gossip. As head of production, Lasky reminded Wally that he was responsible for his actions. He claimed that he was on the lookout for anything that might disrupt the non-stop flow of Wallace Reid pictures going out of the Paramount Studios.

According to Lasky, Wally looked him squarely in the eye and said, "It isn't true! And don't you believe it!"

Lasky replied, "I want to believe you, Wally, but the only way the rumors can be stopped is by absolute proof that they're false. Would you mind if I got a doctor to examine you?"

"Why should I? Go as far as you like," the actor challenged.

Lasky gave him the benefit of the doubt, but the actor's loss of weight and unnatural fatigue during the shooting of his current film were symptoms that were known to accompany a narcotic habit. Lasky arranged for the studio's manager, Charles Eyton, to bring a physician from the Southern Pacific railroad in for the examination. Doctor Starr was apprised of the suspicions prompting the examination, and charged with the duty of living with Wally for a time to observe his habits.

Wally's mother recalled in her memoirs, "One day, we were informed that a Dr. Starr was to become a house guest for ten days or two week, sleeping with, and to be every moment with my big, powerful, stalwart boy, with his ruddy out-of-door complexion and his carefree, boyish spirit. It seemed such an unnecessary indignity, to me. There was so much mystery about it all. Wally was advised

Wally, Gloria Swanson, Cecil B. DeMille, and Elliott Dexter discussing *The Affairs of Anatol* (1921).

to be disagreeable to the man. I took the liberty of advising him to treat him as a gentleman, and as a houseguest should be treated so long as he so conducted himself. If not, he should be escorted from the premises."

In her book, *Swanson on Swanson*, Gloria Swanson remembered, "I heard endless rumors that he was an addict, and although I never saw him take drugs, his behavior never seemed quite right during *The Affairs of Anatol*. He was forever offering me rides, and once he sent his valet to my dressing room to ask for a photograph of me. I always found ways to refuse him politely, but he gave me the jitters."

Lasky told Wally of his plan to use the doctor's report to end the rumors that were abounding about his alleged narcotics use, and he informed him that if his behavior led to no further evidence, the studio would have the ammunition needed to squelch the rising whispers of drug addiction. Wally agreed to the constant observation by the doctor. Two weeks passed during which he appeared to be the perfect image of a man with nothing to hide. The doctor was with him constantly, had eaten meals with him, accompanied him to the golf course, and even went to the extreme of searching his belongings while Wally co-operated. At the end of his scrutiny, he reported back to Lasky.

"To the best of my knowledge, Mr. Lasky, Wallace Reid is not using narcotics," he said. "I don't know anyone else I could live with like Siamese twins for two weeks without wanting to murder, but he is unquestionably the nicest chap I've ever known," was the doctor's final conclusion. His final written report said:

> "In accordance with plans made March 16, 1922, I arrived at the home of Mr. Wallace Reid Friday morning, March 17th. From noon of that day until the present time, I have been constantly with him, and can state without reservation that Mr. Reid is not a drug addict. I have slept with him, eaten with him, been with him on the golf course, and everywhere else he has been throughout the twenty-four hours of these days, and at no time has there been any indication of the use or need of any habit-forming drugs. Mr. Reid was examined by myself for morphine, dionin, codeine, heroin and peronin by the Kober test and for morphine by the Huesmann test, and found negative in both cases. Once while Mr. Reid was at his bath, I carefully inspected his entire body, finding only a few puncture marks from injections of vaccine, which had been prescribed by the family physician. From my knowledge and observation of addicts, I can state that Mr. Reid has none of the characteristics of one, and I believe that the reports of certain acts, said to have been committed by him, have been grossly exaggerated."

Wally was given a clean bill of health, which in retrospect did not say much about the doctor's testing capabilities. His report was taken as true, and Lasky, relieved to learn that his profitable star was free from narcotics, notified both Will Hays and Adolph Zukor of the doctor's conclusion. Looking back now, it almost seems as if Zukor and Lasky doubted the report and knew that time was running out for the popularity of Wallace Reid pictures. They

Wally with his son, William "Billy" Reid, at the age of four.

received reports of every rumor and the police arrests of men coming to Wally's home with narcotics, and they were keenly away of the obvious changes in his physical appearance. One touch of scandal and they knew Wallace Reid pictures would have to be blacklisted along with those of "Fatty" Arbuckle. They were still stinging from the money they lost on the unreleased Arbuckle movies, and they may have thought to take steps to insure that the same thing did not happen to the Wallace Reid pictures with which they had tied up millions of dollars. Perhaps it was just greed, but what followed was the usual release of one Reid picture on the heels of another as soon as they were completed.

Unknown to them all, while charming the railroad doctor during the two weeks of close scrutiny, Wally had taken himself to the torturous extreme of attempting to kick his habit by the sheer force of his own will power. Keeping the truth from those who were pouring over his every move, he temporarily stopped using morphine. He was an experienced amateur chemist, and he knew the ruinous havoc the shock of withdrawal would take on his body, yet he tried to make a clean break. He endured the torture for the sake of his reputation and career. As soon as the doctor was out of his life and the close scrutiny subsided, he fell back to his habit.

Paramount gave in and allowed Wally to make a film adaptation of the great novel and play, *Peter Ibbetson*. The film was to be made in New York. As the departure date came near, Billy, his son, had a deep-set attack of whooping cough. At the last moment, Dorothy thought it best not to move him in the summer heat, and so she chose not to go with Wally.

Wally did not want to leave California, his wife, and his son, and go back to New York. After living for years in the easygoing, informal, and relaxed life of the west coast, he was dismayed about returning to the congestion and rush of the big city. He also feared being besieged with people who were thrilled at his sudden appearance in the flesh. He was afraid that they would demand his appearance at various functions when he was supposed to be concentrating on his work, and he knew himself well enough to know that he could not say no. The whole prospect of going to New York filled him with dread.

Billy, Dorothy, and Wally ca. 1921.

"What joy to know that he was to be here several months, and I could see him and he could come down to visit me in his boyhood home," wrote his mother, oblivious to the inner turmoil taking place within her son.

Wally took a furnished apartment near 5th Avenue, a short drive from the Paramount Astoria studio at the eastern end of the 59th Street Bridge.

Billy and Wally alone together, ca. 1921.

At the train station, Adela Rogers St. Johns accompanied Dorothy. "On that day, he looked ill and unhappy. A premonition of danger and disaster hung over him," she later recalled. "'I wish I hadn't agreed to go,'" Wally told them. Adela added, "But, for all that, he was thin and a little drawn, and his eyes were the same steady, clear eyes into which you could look and find the truth about anything." He told them he was going on the wagon for the whole trip.

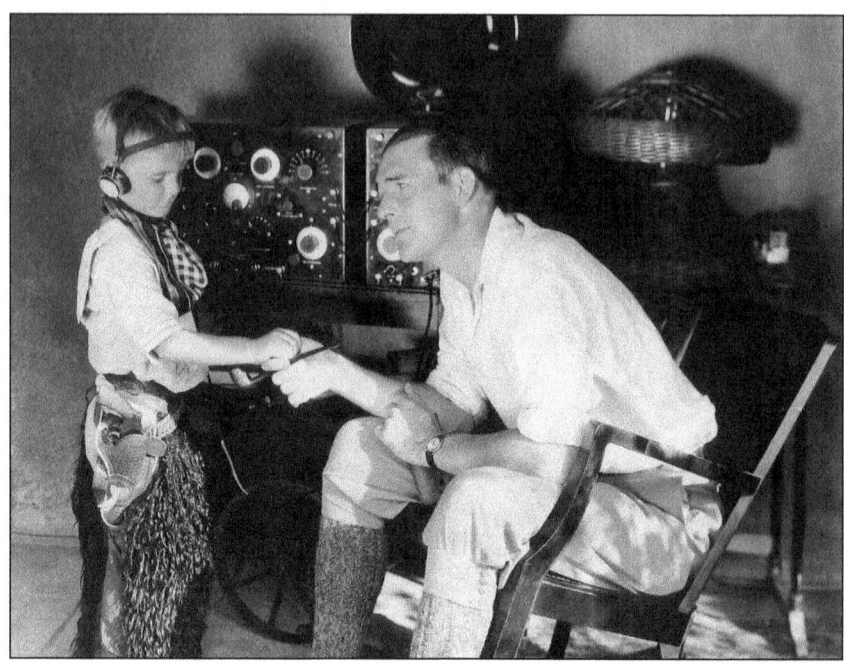
Billy and Wally toying with the latest 1920s electronics.

Wally was not the only film star returning to the East. When he arrived in New York he joined a host of famous actors and writers flocking from the west coast to Lasky's New York studio. Among them were Thomas Meighan, Agnes Ayres, Elliott Dexter, and Elsie Ferguson. Writers, Elinor Glyn, Thompson Buchanan, Rita Welman, and George Pattallo were already there studying film technique and working closely with directors on screen writing.

"The work these authors have done for pictures is only the beginning of a great migration of authors to screen studios," said Jesse Lasky in a 1921 article in the *Mansfield News*. "As a matter of fact, most of the world's best writing brains are now in picture studios, but the example set by these men will influence other writers to give more serious consideration to the immense possibilities which lie in their writing directly for the screen."

On his arrival at the Pennsylvania station, Wally came with his male secretary. The address of the apartment was kept in confidence, but like all juicy tidbits of information, the location soon became one of the best-known secrets in town. Wally's worst fears were realized.

Chapter 13
OVER THE LEDGE

Peter Ibbetson had been performed on Broadway with John Barrymore. The story followed the mutual dream life of two children together in France, who learn a remarkable secret about dreaming true, mutual adventures at the same time. They are later separated for many years, and then a chance encounter reunites them in England. Peter is accused of a murder he has not committed and is condemned to life imprisonment. He and the girl promise to devote their lives together, and a strange but happy existence follows with Peter welcoming hard labor by day so that he can dream nightly along with her in a spiritual love affair that transcends prison bars. In dreams, the two souls, separated by physical and material barriers, journey on and on through the frosts of old age.

Wally liked the change of pace the story afforded. Having made so many lighthearted comedies, the serious role gave him a chance for a dramatically detailed characterization, and along with it, a change of appearance. He had to grow his hair several inches longer than was his personal style, and have it curled in waves.

While he was in New York working on *Peter Ibbetson*, worshipful fans were a constant problem. A certain lady of high social prominence, the wife of a multi-millionaire, called repeatedly on the telephone. His secretary answered all incoming calls to fend off unwanted intrusions and protect Wally. With diplomacy, the woman was told that he could not talk. The determined woman finally came to the apartment in person. There, she found the rooms were filled with other visitors, and she insisted on speaking to him in private. Her excuse for the demand was that her prominence prevented her from being able to discuss her mission in front of others. Under the circumstances, there was nothing Wally could do but see her. His secretary knew that there were rooms adjacent to his apartment and that were vacant at that time. He had the housekeeper open them. The secretary slipped in and hid behind a box against a wall at one end of the room. The danger of blackmailers was ever-present, and the secretary was positioned to witness the discussion from his hiding place.

When Wally came in, the woman poured out the full details of her real mission: she wanted to pay him to escort her to the opera and around town. As a gift for his time, she offered him a Rolls-Royce. The woman wanted nothing more than to be seen by her social constituents with "the great Wallace Reid" in tow. Wally politely declined, and the woman left frustrated and upset.

While his fans went overboard with shows of affection, Jesse Lasky maintained an outward appearance of caring for Wally, but he was not above stooping to disreputable acts once he had made up his mind that Wally was on his way down. While filming progressed at the Astoria studio on *Peter Ibbetson*, the film name was changed to *Forever*. Wally's co-star, Elsie Ferguson, held Lasky to a promise he had hastily made to lure her into making pictures for him. Elsie was famous as a leading actress of the legitimate stage, and she had been in a number of motion pictures. As a concession, Lasky promised and delivered a contract stipulating that she was to have star billing with her name over the title of any picture in which she appeared. Unfortunately for Lasky, Wally also had the same type of top billing guaranteed in his contract, and director George Fitzmaurice also had a clause in his contract calling for his name to appear in larger type than the stars of his films and to be named above the title. The three contracts conflicted, so Lasky had a release form drawn up stating that Wally and Fitzmaurice would waive their rights to top billing. He enlisted the efforts of Lorenzo Del Riccio, an optical and mechanical inventor brought on board his staff, and he conspired to have Del Riccio slip into a projection room where Wally and Fitzmaurice were watching rushes.

"Here George—sign this thing," he told the director.

Annoyed at the interruption, Fitzmaurice signed the waiver without reading it. Then, Del Riccio asked Wally to do the same thing, and the too-trusting star penned his name on another waiver

Elsie Ferguson and Wally in George Fitzmaurice's *Forever* (1922), made in New York under extremely difficult circumstances.

identical to the one snuck under Fitzmaurice's hand. Del Riccio returned to Lasky with the two signed wavers that neither Wally nor Fitzmaurice had bothered to read.

Wally hated above all things to think that his mere physical looks helped him to his success and popularity. He did not like to have pictures of him about the house and never gave photographs of himself to anyone unless they were adamant about possessing one. The only photographs he carried were recent ones from *Forever* in which he was shown in full makeup as a very old man. Those he liked to show off. He carried sets of the prints around and took great delight in showing others how the Paramount makeup artists had transformed his chiseled good looks into the face of a wrinkled old-timer.

Wally plunged into the role despite his dislike of working in New York. The deeply dramatic role demanded the best he had. His in-depth characterization allowed him to age from a splendidly healthy youth to a wrinkled old man warped by madness and living in a musty old prison cell. He made the most of the opportunity and brought to his performance everything he had learned in the eleven years he had been in pictures.

While working on *Forever*, he was feeling the full effects of life in the fast-paced atmosphere that surrounded him. His nerves stretched to the breaking point, and adding to the strain was the loneliness of being away from his wife and son. Making his most valiant effort as an actor and working for the first time for George Fitzmaurice, he felt alone and uncomfortable. He took a fast dislike for Fitzmaurice and his co-star, Elsie Ferguson, and neither of them showed any particular fondness for Wally. Over the previous four years, Elsie had been in twenty pictures, and she was big star who thought the focus of any film in which she worked should be squarely on her.

Wally did not take any time to lavish care on himself. He always pushed to the limit and drove himself harder than necessary. Unfortunately, chronic, long-term use of morphine caused him to suffer a premature loss of tooth enamel, a side effect that was not fully realized at that time, and it resulted in irreversible tooth decay. While he was in New York, a dentist had to pull nine of his teeth in one sitting. The shock to his system and the intense irritation following the extractions only added to his misery.

That summer in New York brought insufferably hot, humid weather. There was no air conditioning in those days, and to one who was used to the cold nights and dry desert heat of California, the weather only added to his depression.

The character he played in the picture had mid-length hair that had to be waved every day. Wally had grown his hair to fit the required length, but the embarrassment and indignity of sitting daily under hair rollers like a woman only added to his despair.

Wally found that coming down from the euphoria of an intense workday was impossible. After nightly socializing and the effects of continued morphine use, he was wracked with unending insomnia, which only added to his woes. A doctor prescribed a sleeping powder for him to help alleviate insomnia when, night after night, he tossed in the clammy, dripping heat without getting any sleep until dawn.

Then, after only a few hours rest, he had to get up and start work by nine o'clock in the morning.

His apartment, as he predicted, was besieged with old acquaintances, new friends, reporters, and the ever-growing parade of fans and idolatrous females. Crowds swarmed the apartment each evening when he was there. Wally entertained, played his saxophone and violin, and basked in the attention, never letting any personal discomfort or vanity inhibit his behavior. His apartment was a perpetual open house. Wally was too thorough a gentleman to show his annoyance with the elaborate parties. How some of those parties could have been given without his consent is hard to comprehend, but Dorothy later said that she heard from friends coming back from New York, who told her that they were there and had seen Wally slip out of the apartment at the height of the festivities and remain away until his guests had gone. The noise and confusion, coupled with his physical agony, was intolerable.

He soon developed a severe cold. For more than a week, his temperature hovered at around 103 degrees. He was very ill, but the studio insisted that he work the entire time. A New York physician kept Wally on his feet by administering small doses of morphine regularly as a painkiller and stimulant. What the doctor did not know was that Wally needed more than was commonplace. Believing his will power was stronger than the insidious ravages of the drug. He resorted to buying morphine from clandestine sellers, and administered it to himself. He was an experimentalist when it came to pharmaceutical compounds. He believed that nothing was going to harm him. He thought of himself as a doctor, and his easy familiarity with medicines gave him a dangerous and overly confident point of view.

In an article by Louella Parsons in the *New York Telegraph*, May 22, 1921, Wally commented about the fact that he had been at Sea Gate with his mother ever since he came to town. "Mother never stopped talking from Sunday night until Tuesday morning," he said with a laugh. "She hadn't seen me in three years and she had so much to say. Last time, Dorothy and the baby came with me, and she directed her attentions to them; but this time she had me alone and she made up for lost time . . . the best time I have had in months. It's great to be with your own people, and, of course, there isn't any one like one's mother." Wally also expressed worry over his role in as Peter Ibbetson in *Forever*. "They have me dissolved in tears most of the time. I shed enough briny drops, according to the script, to fill an ocean. My public expects to see me in comedy, and I wonder how they are going to like this tragedy. I am not very fond of gloom myself and I think I understand how my friends in the small towns feel."

Wally somehow managed to finish making *Peter Ibbetson*, which was definitely set to be released under the title, *Forever*, and then he returned to home in California during the last weeks of July.

Dorothy told *Los Angeles Herald* reporter William Parker, "When Wally returned from the East, he was not the same Wally Reid I had known when he left Hollywood. He seemed to possess a dual nature. To me, he had been always the affectionate suitor. Now there was a change. For no apparently accountable reason he would become irritable, morose, strange. At first I was deeply puzzled."

"I went with Dorothy to meet him at the train," Adela Rogers St. Johns said when looking back years later. "The change in him appalled me. It was like meeting a stranger, or seeing a dear friend through a thick veil. Dorothy had sensed the thing, naturally, much more quickly and deeply than I had. A little white mask seemed to have slipped over her radiant face."

Wally's mother was completely oblivious to the changes taking place in his life, his face, and his demeanor, and she never suspected the truth about what happened to him while he was in New York. "The day came when that same brave figure of my lad went back into that station from whence he had come only yesterday, it seemed," she recalled later. "He vanished into the Pullman—the train receded—growing smaller and smaller, disappearing into the earth—lost to view. His sojourn in New York, in spite of his work, had sent him away in the very 'pink' of condition. I will never believe that Wallace ever left this city with a taint or tarnish of any kind upon him, nor in any way touched with anything abnormal, unless it was a super-abundance of health and joy."

The truth was that he was administering the drugs orally in pills or with hypodermic needles in the soles of his feet, depending on which version of the drug he could obtain.

Dorothy knew the truth about his drug habit, but helped him hide the facts. Stories about him were making the rounds in Hollywood. People asked her about the rumors, but she denied them indignantly. Her brave front fooled no one because the change in Wally was apparent to everyone close to him. He seemed like a distorted image of his old self.

"When Wally returned to Hollywood, I noted a change in his whole manner of life," Dorothy told William Parker. "While previously he had been of a jovial, affectionate nature, now he began to give way to spells of apparent despondency. A sense of irritability developed, a phase of character which was foreign to the real Wally Reid. It must have been that these were the times when he felt the craving for the drug and was trying to ignore its insistent demands."

Dorothy then began to receive a flood of queerly worded telegrams. "Some of them accidentally fell into my hands," she divulged. "They were usually from New York, and were couched in mysterious terms. Most of them contained the word 'shipping'. The senders were always 'shipping' something. One day I realized that the shipments were drugs."

Dorothy's temper exploded. She confronted him over the problem once and for all.

Moviegoers saw this ad for James Cruze's *The Charm School* in the *Wyoming State Tribune,* January 26, 1921.

Dorothy demanded to know the full extent of his drug habit.

Never had she seen emotions flash so swiftly over a man's distorted face as in his reaction to her point-blank question. Written into his expression as he looked back at her were reflections of his sense of having been finally trapped. He was fearful, sorrowful, dumbstruck, and speechless. He flew into a childish tantrum, paced the floor, and denied his addiction. He responded by firing a volley of questions back at Dorothy, and finished by pointing the finger of blame at her.

"You don't love me anymore," he charged.

The long overdue altercation came to a flash point and boiled over into indiscriminant accusations and reproaches, as Wally purged from his system all the pent-up torment he had kept under wraps for so long.

After a while, he quieted down.

Dorothy had seen the guilt written in his eyes. He was not actor enough to fool her anymore.

"I didn't want you to know, mamma," he finally said, revealing everything in a rush of heartfelt words. "I thought I was big enough to fight my own battle and win. I thought I could come back alone, and you would never have to know."

There was another picture to make. Wally braced himself in the seat of the latest racing cars. Along endless stretches of road, he flew at the utmost speed while making scenes with director Philip E. Rosen behind the camera. *Across the Continent*, another Byron Morgan auto story, pictured Wally winning a transcontinental race.

On camera, he was the happy, carefree, boyish Wallace Reid of the old days, but he was quietly caught in the clutches of morphine addiction. He had undergone a complete metamorphosis of his former self. His mental suffering was agony. He grew surly, gritty, despondent, and discontented. His outlook on life became distorted with each new infusion of the narcotic. To Dorothy, he spoke spitefully of his friends and accused them of caring for him "only for what they could get out of him," which, for many of the hangers-on, was true. He doubted Dorothy's love for him despite her dogged support. He was falling victim to delusions, a common side effect of morphine, and he suspected everybody of ulterior motives. He became trapped in a nightmare of distrust, and yet while he was under that torment, he finished *Across the Continent*, and then plunged headlong into making *The Dictator* for director and old friend, James Cruze.

At night, he cautioned his few trustworthy friends on the evil of drugs. More than once, Dorothy overheard him softly sermonizing to his boy, Billy, about the terrible consequences of misusing drugs. Dorothy later said those speeches were "whimsical sermons I am sure the youngster didn't understand. He seemed his old personality only when he was with Bill . . . and I am quite sure the boy didn't have the slightest idea what it was all about."

The routine of work, drugs, and exhaustion continued unabated for the next year and a half. Wally seldom left the house except to work. His friends no longer interested him. He clung to Dorothy and his son like a man losing his grip on reality. One night, after staying up past midnight, she was aroused by the soft touch of his hand on her hair. He was sitting on the edge of the bed. His eyes were red and glassy, and he was beside himself with grief. She rose, and they talked until morning about the future they would have when he was well again. Dorothy felt close to him during those hours, closer than they had been in at least a year. She tried to drive his fears away, to soothe him and fill him with the assurance that they would face together the seemingly insurmountable battle looming on the immediate horizon. They both knew what had to be done.

By dawn, the closeness had become an awakening to the confidence and mutual affection that had originally brought them together back in 1913. Dorothy went forward to face a new day with a renewed assurance, and her spirit soared in a way that was noticed by the house servants. Secretly, she felt certain that his drug habit could be conquered by the sheer power of their combined wills. She knew Wally was mentally strong, and with an infusion of her own strength, the greater bond of love and trust would carry them beyond the evil grip the drug held on his body, mind, and soul. What neither of them realized was that the drug had steel fingers with which to wrench and torture the muscles of the body, preventing any effort to extinguish its fiery hold.

In those post-war years, there was a growing public outrage over the demoralization of society in general, and many were unfairly

Wally in Yosemite Valley in 1922 with cast and crew of Philip E. Rosen's *The World's Champion*.

blaming Hollywood and the influence of motion pictures on young people. Their point was arguable, but there was much evidence to support the belief that morality, as expressed in movie stories, was a far cry from Biblical standards.

As if the industry's outpouring of questionable films had not been enough cause to justify moralists' concerns, one of the worst scandals in Hollywood's history took place on February 1, 1922: Paramount film director, William Desmond Taylor, who had directed Wally in *The World Apart* and *Big Timber*, was shot to death in his bungalow. To add to the mysterious circumstances, his murder remained unsolved despite revelations of his involvement with both Mabel Normand and Mary Miles Minter, two of the screen's most popular young women. All the negative publicity that could be wrung from the tragedy played out in newspapers around the world and reflected terribly on the film industry as a whole.

On March 5, 1922, *Forever* was released to widespread critical acclaim. In the finished film, Elsie Ferguson got her star billing over Wally, the result of the deception Jesse Lasky arranged by obtaining the hastily signed signatures of Wally and George Fitzmaurice while they were too preoccupied with viewing rushes.

In some cities, audiences did not like the change of pace for Wally. Expecting the thrills of his automobile racing pictures, the dreamy-eyed, Peter Ibbetson character with long, wavy hair and stylized period costumes fell flat. In other cities, *Forever* was largely considered charming. Both his wife and mother thought it was the best work he had ever done. "Wally *became* a good actor," Dorothy told Dewitt Bodeen in 1966. "In the beginning, his popularity was based on his good looks and engaging personality, but when he was offered a challenge, as he was with *Forever*, he rose to the occasion."

For his next picture, Paramount had him slip back back to a more action-packed format. On March 12, 1922, *The World's Champion* was released. It reverted to the tried and true formula, but something was missing.

According to Lasky, Wally began to show a change in his appearance that could not be hidden from the camera. He wrote in his autobiography, ". . . he wasn't believable as a heavyweight fighter in *The World's Champion*, taken from a Broadway play. He was rapidly losing weight and couldn't stand on his feet for more than a short time. He made a valiant struggle to get through his scenes, but it was obvious that something was wrong."

In April, all at once, his remaining teeth began to ache excruciatingly. An X-ray was taken, and doctors deemed that an operation on his jaw was necessary. For three days, he lived in a dentist chair while they sliced at his mouth. Eating became an impossible horror, and on the last day, he came back from the dentist so weak that he could hardly walk. Despite his miserable condition, he resumed work the very next day.

The non-stop routine of making one film while several others were released continued unabated. Paramount was determined to squeeze the utmost out of him on the contract he had signed. On June 4, 1922, Wally's picture, *Across the Continent*, a Byron Morgan automobile-racing story, was released while he was in the middle of filming another picture. On July 2, 1922, *Nice People* was released in Los Angeles, and then on August 7, 1922, *The Dictator* was released.

Around that time, Dorothy went back to work in *The Masked Avenger*, directed by Frank Fanning and starring Lester Cuneo. To one reporter she said, "I must have something to do, and the call of the stage is in my blood. I'll have to go back to my makeup box and the Kliegs. It's irresistible . . . the baby doesn't need me anymore, Wally is at work all day, and my house is all furnished and running smoothly—there's not enough to keep a woman occupied now, so I've agreed to go and play a lead for Lester Cuneo in his new production—and what's more, Wally has decided to let me be billed as 'Mrs. Wallace Reid'. . . ."

She was confident in trusting him to his own resources because he had seemingly conquered the drug habit. As far as she knew, he was taking nothing at all, but paying for the abstinence with day and night agony. In her absence, the dental surgery may have pushed him over the edge to reach for morphine in another attempt to drown the insufferable pain. Wally lapsed into the habit again, as usual, figuring it would be temporary, but backsliding broke his heart.

When Dorothy returned in July, he confessed to his fall back. All the brave earnestness of his first victory in defeating the drug's hold on his body had to be done over again. He plunged into a second fight with solemn intensity and fought to clear himself one day at a time. No one but Dorothy knew the depth of the struggle. In spite of his great effort, he still longed to do something creatively striking.

Wally told writer Herb Howe, "They would laugh at you if you told them I ever had a serious thought, but just between you and me, I'd like to do something worthwhile some day—give something to the world besides my face."

One evening, Wally came home with a carload of paintings he had purchased from a local artist "just to keep the poor fellow going," he explained to Dorothy. She often had to look the other way because he was always shouldering someone else's troubles. When difficulties fell their way, Wally was there for them.

Wally's good nature led him into initial contact with people who took advantage of him, but he was not above falling to the temptation to take advantage of them either. On August 26, 1922, the following article appeared in the *New York Times*:

"MR. AND MRS. WALLACE REID TO ADOPT CHILD.

Los Angeles: Mr. and Mrs. Wallace Reid petitioned the Superior Court today for permission to adopt Betty Mummert, 3 years

Betty Ann, shortly after being adopted, with Dorothy, Wally, and Billy.

old, whose parents have consented to the adoption. Mrs. Reid is known to the screen as Dorothy Davenport."

There were rumors in Hollywood at the time that the adopted daughter was in reality Wally's own daughter by an illicit affair, an accident resulting from one of the many out-of-control parties during recent years. Neither he nor Dorothy ever admitted anything to confirm that allegation, but records show that Betty Ann Mummert, age three, came into their lives very suddenly in 1922.

According to Dorothy, Wally always had wanted a baby girl, and while she was playing in vaudeville in Long Beach one night, a tiny curly-haired youngster strayed into her dressing room. Her clothes were dirty, and her hands were black with the grime from the theater alley. Dorothy said she "found the old grandfather who cared for her, and the next night, I took her home—Betty, who is now our own. I wish you could have seen Wally's face that night. I carried Betty, still in her dirty clothes, out of the car and into the house. Some of our friends were there, but Wally forgot them. For an hour he sat on the floor with the youngster, and then, oblivious of his guests, took her upstairs and tucked her into bed. He refused to let the maid touch her. His face was working with emotion when he came back, but he said very little. I think that tiny Betty, with her curly hair and her dimpled cheeks, has played her great big part in Wally's comeback."

A reporter for *Movie Weekly* wrote on August 18, 1923, the following article, which is in sharp contrast to Dorothy's account:

"Real Dramas of Hollywood"

"She heard of her dashing husband's affairs from time to time. She even indulgently answered his 'mash notes' when he was too lazy to write the letters himself, which he frequently was."

"'Here are some more letters from mushy dames!'" he would laugh, and throw the letters into her lap.'"

"But one night came something more serious. The wife was alone in the house, except for the children, who had gone to bed. The servants, Japanese, went home at night. Came a rap on the door—a timid rap—and the wife wondered why the visitor did not ring the bell. But she was no coward, and besides that timid rap did not come from any burly intruder, she was sure of that. She opened the door, and there stood a girl with a baby in her arms. It was so like a melodrama that the wife felt a horribly hysterical desire to laugh when the girl asked for her husband!"

"'So it has come at last!' she said to herself, still with that awful clutching at her throat—the hysterical desire to laugh and weep. She knew now that she had been expecting something of this sort to happen."

"The girl was crying, and looked so helpless—so utterly as a victim of her husband would look, she thought! The wife asked the girl to come in. The girl, young and very pretty and modishly dressed after a cheap fashion, brightened and came in. She felt no pang of jealousy when she looked at the girl, oddly enough, she thought to herself even then—but she felt a terrible, clutching feeling, half anger, half piercing pity, when she looked at the baby! It was all as the wife had expected from the first moment she looked at the girl."

"The baby was her husband's! She never thought to doubt the girl's story. It didn't occur to her until afterward that this was odd. But the girl was so evidently miserable, heart-broken, and her claim was made in such frank, genuine, if heart-broken, fashion, that the wife had to believe her."

"'I'm only an extra girl,'" the girl said hurriedly, after satisfying herself that her seducer was not at home, and that the wife had only pity in her heart for her. 'I do love my baby so, but my mother died last week, and there is no one to care for him! Oh, my darling mamma! She did love my baby so! She was so good to me! Some mothers would have been cross, but she never was. She was just sorry! All the time, she was just sorry. And she loved my baby! Now—I think you just must—you just must adopt my baby and . . . .'"

"The wife started back. She had expected a call for money, but not for this.

'Yes,' the girl said firmly. 'There isn't any other way. I've thought it all out. My baby cannot go to a foundling asylum. I couldn't bear that—nor for anybody but his own father to have him!' The wife was sunk in thought. The baby was a dear baby. 'I'll kill myself if you don't!' the girl threatened desperately."

"'Yes, we'll do it!' the wife suddenly decided."

"What mixed motives there were beneath that decision! It was all generosity on first impulse. Then followed the subtle thought that her husband could never look at the little one without remembering his fault! And he should care for it, and pay its bills. Her husband would not dare refuse, she knew that. For the girl would certainly make a scandal. The girl promised never to see her baby again. As for herself, she had long passed the stage where she could feel any active resentment against the girl. She was only one of many, she thought drearily. And the baby was a dear baby!"

"So the little one found a home. And the child will never know the difference between its own mother and this foster one!"

United Press contacted Dorothy at home to confront her with rumors about a divorce action soon to take place between Wally and her. She wrote out a signed statement, denying the rumor, and it appeared in many newspapers around the country:

"There is absolutely no truth in the stories given prominence in a New York newspaper that a divorce was impending in the Wallace Reid family. Ever since Geraldine Farrar and Lou-Tellegen separated, it seems like every other married couple in the profession is the target for a similar rumor. The fact that I am playing opposite Lester Cuneo means nothing at all. He is Wally's best friend. I needed outdoor exercise and when the opportunity was afforded me to work in Mr. Cuneo's picture I was glad to accept it and have even found a role in it for our little son, William Wallace Reid, Jr. I think these rumors started when Wally went to New York to make a picture and I did not accompany him. Why I did not go was simply because it is too hot in New York.

In 1922, Wally posed for this portrait by renowned photographer, Hartsook.

There is a popular belief that there cannot be two successful people, or, if the seeming flattery be overlooked, two geniuses in one family. Here is one case where happiness rules even though Wally is one of the country's most popular actors and I have returned to the screen."

Ironically, in 1923, the word "scandal" was already creeping into poster art for Wally's films, such as this poster from William C. De Mille's *Nice People* (1923).

Wally's mother came from New York to visit him in California for three months. During her stay, Betty was very much in evidence. The child was brought out to pose for photographs for reporters for the movie magazines in a round of staged poses with the family. The new pictures with Betty were widely circulated.

Wally's consuming interest at that time, aside from non-stop work, was car racing. He struggled earnestly and patiently to earn a genuine racing driver's license. He accomplished the feat, and wore the honor pin proudly. The next step in his pursuit of racing accomplishments was the upcoming Indianapolis event to be held the following summer.

Jesse Lasky's influence over Wally's personal life was unceasing. Wally committed to driving in the 1922 Indianapolis road race, racing his English speed demon, the Sunbeam, in the Decoration Day event. When Lasky heard about it, he blew a fuse. In no uncertain terms, he told Wally that the studio would insist on him remaining on the ground and off the racetrack.

Wally became obsessed with taking part in that race. Company threats failed to move him. Pleas from his family and friends went unrecognized. His decision to go forward with his part in the race was an unprecedented show of stubbornness. He had his mechanics get his car in perfect condition, and planned his departure date for Indianapolis.

Dorothy tried to reason him away from the competition. "You cannot go," she argued. "You would endanger the lives of your friends, Wally. And that I know you would never do!" She did her utmost to dissuade him from driving in a race that could prove to be suicidal in his weakened mental and physical condition. She was the only person who knew of the full size of his drug problem, and she did not hesitate to remind him of the toll it was taking on him. Her appeal stopped him and forced him to face the reality of his situation squarely.

For Wally, it was the last straw. Lasky had telegraphed the racing officials with threats to deploy every resource to have the contest cancelled if they permitted Wally to race. Then, he threatened to sue Wally for breach of contract. With great disappointment, he withdrew from the competition. He issued a long, solemn statement explaining why he had to step down from joining the competitors.

Afterward, he swore that all of his future contracts would have a clause permitting him to race autos and participate in extracurricular activities as he wished.

There was hardly any time for much secondary activity. During his mother's three-month visit, he made three pictures back-to-back. He had just one-half day elapse between the time his work in one picture was finished and work began on the following one.

As the 1922 Holiday's neared, his mother witnessed Wally erecting three Christmas trees in the family home. A bevy of wrapped presents amassed daily beneath the main tree, friends dropped in to chat, sing, and talk moving picture business, which Bertha found exceedingly dull. One night, they ran Mary Pickford's *Little Lord Fauntleroy* on the family projector. The film, in which Mary played both the boy Fauntleroy and his mother, won high praise from everyone, Wally most of all. He raved about the story, her duel-role performance, and the beautiful spirit she displayed.

During his mother's visit, very little alcohol consumption was displayed in front of her in the Reid home. Many of the odd guests who had littered their house during all-night parties were conspicuously absent. He was on his best behavior. After his mother left, his gradual decline over the next few months began. The degeneration of his features that were once so endearing were finally, painfully apparent in his movies. His last four pictures revealed the awful physical crumbling of his once brawny and vigorous physique.

Wally underwent tortures beyond imagination. To his credit, he cut down the use of the morphine drug, and as each day passed, he held himself in check and endured increasing physical agonies. There were times when the wrenching torment caused him to grit his remaining teeth one moment, and then turn to Dorothy in the next moment for encouragement.

"We're going to lick this thing, mamma. We'll win. I'm going to get off liquor and everything."

"It was pitiful and tragic," Dorothy later grieved, "yet, more than that, it was heroic, magnificent. It was the heart-rending effort of a great, fine, brave boy against an intangible horror that clutched him like an octopus, catching its tentacles here, there, everywhere."

His legs ached excruciatingly, and his personal doctor told him it was a certain symptom of withdrawal from drugs. The aches recurred from the accident he suffered back in 1913 when a stunt backfired and a horse fell on his legs, sending him into a hospital. He had never fully recovered from the damage that incident caused, and with the added side effect of degenerative joint and bone misery caused by morphine use, Wally was in unendurable pain.

Incredibly, Wally took to the live theater stage again in a production of *Sick Abed*, which had been the basis of one of his recent films. The farce by Ethel Watts Mumford was staged at the Los Angeles Little Theater Company, and the actors reverted from the film script back to the original stage script. The strain of acting all day long in a film production and then spending the evening performing on stage in the theater version of *Sick Abed* wrung the last ounce of fortitude from Wally. He was bravely carrying on and showed no outward signs of fatigue, but the non-stop running reached an unexpected detour.

One night, Dorothy came home to find the servants fluttering all over the place, and when their Asian houseboy opened the door, she saw that he had turned a ghastly pale white.

"Mistah Reid velly sick man, velly sick," he chattered with fright.

Dorothy ran upstairs, and what she saw caused her jaw to drop and her face to suddenly drain of all color.

Chapter 14
THE WHEEL OF LIFE

Dorothy ran to Wally's bedside as soon as she came into the house and heard the houseboy cry that he had fainted on the drawing room floor. The other servants, fearing he was dead, had laboriously carried him upstairs to the bed. With Dorothy at his side, he recovered, but he had no recollection of the events leading up to his collapse.

As he lay helpless, he grinned gamely, and looked up at her, saying, "We're winning, mamma; we're winning. We'll lick it yet."

No one can fully know what Dorothy bore during the following days. Her first battle was to keep others from knowing the complete extent of his illness. She had to keep him away from work for several days on a leave of absence. Paramount, which owed him so much and had taken so much out of him, put him on half salary for the time he was away.

He was soon back at the studio and working for long hours under the giant Klieg lights erected on an indoor set. Prolonged exposure commonly caused a redness and swelling to the eyes of actors, and although Wally was again abstaining from drugs, the brilliant, dead-white radiance glaring into his eyes for so many extended hours burned his eyes severely. The malady manifested itself fully one morning when Dorothy heard him pattering around the bedroom and into the dressing room.

Suddenly, he gasped, and his voice came with a quick, horrible wail: "Mamma, mamma! Come here. Where's the door?"

The overexposure to the merciless Klieg lights had rendered him blind. Dorothy helped him back into bed that morning, and later he was dressed. He was totally helpless. An eye doctor was summoned, but no fast cure could help bring back his sight. For one week, he was in the dark, seeing nothing, groping his way about the house, his eyes shielded by smoked glasses. Drawn into that terrible blankness, Wally was alone with his thoughts and the agony of his abstinence from drugs. He was like a dependent child, begging Dorothy not to leave him alone in the dark. She stayed with him constantly and led him through those dark days of blindness and withdrawal.

When his vision had barely returned and was still fuzzy, he valiantly went back to work. He could see very little of the things around him. The set was a blur, and he had to be directed at each turn.

"Right, Wally, feel that chair?" or "Left, through that door there!"

Finally, under those desperate conditions, the picture was finished. Incredibly, Wally looked normal in the footage.

They never told Bertha the truth about the calamity, and she only learned of it when she read a news article in one of the papers that told about his blindness from overexposure to the Klieg lights. Her maternal instincts aroused, and she was alarmed and outraged. She determined to intervene and come to his rescue, deciding to close down her country house on the east coast and move to California with his aunt Nell to be at her son's side. Just before they left, she sent a telegram begging for them to have mercy on her and tell her the exact truth about his condition. As usual, they glossed over the truth. Wally and Dorothy wired back this reply:

> "Condition much improved—no cause for worry. Starting today for ten-day motor trip. Ignore all rumors. Love from all . . . ."

Wally insisted on taking a few days off to rest at home, but his condition did not improve. The trip to the mountains for a week to shoot and play tennis brought little change. After eight days, he returned with illness stamped indelibly on his face. Worse, he had contracted dysentery, and his strength was severely undermined by the combination of the ordeals he was going through.

They kept the full truth from Bertha while she was arranging her affairs so that she could move to California and be with Wally by the first of February. Dorothy's mother, Alice, continued to fan the flame of deception, and was the one to write to Bertha this next letter:

> "Wally grows stronger every day and goes back to work in two weeks. The reports were all wrong. We did not realize that you would get them. He will look better than he has in three years. The reports were just killing him—but it's all over, thank God. Now we can rejoice. He will write when he is able. His eyes are not right yet, but they will be in time. They are going out at least twice a week to nice places together. I'm very happy that things look so bright."

The struggle to save Wally was more than Dorothy could face alone. His condition became worse. They tried every known remedy without effect. Publicly, Jesse Lasky, Will Hays, and Adolph Zukor claimed that they were shocked when Wally voluntarily admitted himself to the Banksia Place Sanitarium. He was determined to kick the drug habit he had been carrying in secret. Dorothy made the difficult decision to put him in the sanitarium for two weeks.

"A condition developed which baffled and is still puzzling doctors," Dorothy told Los Angeles Herald writer William Parker. "It first manifested itself as an intestinal disturbance. When this became aggravated, he consulted a physician. He was ordered to a hospital. Other physicians were called in. Every possible test which the doctors knew was given him. Needles half a dozen inches long were driven into his spine. The pain he endured was terrible. The Wasserman test was administered. Not a single test showed a positive result. In the midst of all this, influenza set in. His average weight: 200 pounds, Wally's weight now is about 122 pounds."

On December 10, Alice again wrote to Bertha:

> "Poor Wally had a relapse and he can't go to work for two or three weeks yet, but we hope all will be well in a few days. I'll keep you posted. He is not in danger. He was better today. As soon as the dysentery stops he will begin to gain. His face is like a kid's now. He looks twenty-two. He gains quickly, so don't worry. The worst is past. You will be proud

Three pictures that illustrate Wally's decline: (LEFT) Wally in 1919 before the train wreck that injured him and necessitated the use of morphine as a painkiller; (TOP RIGHT) Wally in early 1922, while making *The Dictator* and showing the effects of three years of debilitation; (BOTTOM RIGHT) Wally in late 1922, while making his second to last film, *Clarence*, only months before his death.

(LEFT TO RIGHT) **Jesse Lasky, Will Hays, and Cecil B. De Mille on the occasion of Hays' 1922 arrival in Hollywood to head the Motion Picture Producers and Distributors of America organization to eliminate objectionable material from films and advise on matters of scandal.**

of your son soon. I shall miss you Xmas, for I learned to love you, you were so just and sweet and wise."

Six days later, the *Los Angeles Times* reported his incarceration in a sanitarium on December 16, 1922:

"Wallace Reid, international screen idol and hero of scores of film plays, has voluntarily given up the use of narcotics and is now playing out the most heroic role of his life in a Hollywood sanitarium where his determined attempt to win out over drugs and whisky have brought him to so low an ebb of physical resistance that his life is in danger. Two months ago Reid determined to break himself of the use of stimulants. Yesterday members of his family talked freely to The *Times* with the purpose of quieting the many false rumors which have grown and spread from coast to coast during the last two years—rumors that have run the gamut of sensationalism from tales of hopeless addiction to morphine and heroin to widely spread and unfounded reports that the Lasky star had reached a stage of partial blindness, and equally untrue tales that his condition had become such that psychopathic treatment had been found necessary. The truth of the situation is that Mr. Reid is perilously weak and suffering from collapse and a high temperature: he is in a sanitarium in Hollywood under the care of two doctors and constantly under the surveillance of two male nurses, but his determination to stage a comeback, both personally and on the screen is unshaken, and his will power and cheerfulness are unimpaired."

A few days later, the *New York Times* quoted Dorothy about how near death Wally really had been:

"He thought he would die the other night," she said. "He was so brave about it, poor boy. For three nights he had expected to die. He isn't afraid to die, but he wants so much to live for Billy and Betty and me," referring to their son and adopted daughter. Mrs. Reid, in describing his condition just before the present breakdown, said that he wept and said: 'How did I happen to let myself go? Why couldn't I have stopped long ago? I thought I was so strong; I thought I knew myself so well; I can't understand it.'"

The same newspaper quoted Wally's doctor, saying:

"Mr. Reid has been near death for the last five or six days. His temperature has repeatedly reached 103 and his pulse 130. His heart action is irregular and weak. He has fainted on an average of three times daily and has lost seventy pounds. Laboratory finds at the present time indicate he is suffering either from a condition of complete exhaustion or from influenza. A re-infection of influenza is possible at any time and could cause his death. This is not anticipated by attending physicians, but must be and is being considered. His present illness has no connection with overindulgences in alcohol or narcotics, although such indulgences have undoubtedly undermined his strength and system in months gone by."

Bertha steeled herself against the onslaught of those reports, and she wrote to Wally before she left the east coast:

". . . the past is gone; let it go, and be not discouraged. Be of good cheer! With that fine brain of yours, which you have kept too long 'marking time' do a little leisurely introspecting, and then begin observing the things that go on immediately about you, and above all, weigh the people who come and go in your home, your social relations, and your business. Weigh clearly, justly, and do not fear to face facts as they are, and not as it is pleasant to imagine they are. Clear out the leeches, for they are many…just because it is nearly New Year when wise people 'take stock' of themselves . . . ."

The paralyzing grip of morphine had taken hold of him. He was no more himself than another person would have been while under ether. If he ever took stock of himself in the cold light of reality, he closed the curtain swiftly, and then sank back into the anesthetizing fog rather than face up to the damage he had caused.

When they returned, Wally decided he wanted get away to the desert. He and Dorothy went to Palm Springs, an oasis away from their whirlwind lives. He seemed to rest there and enjoy himself, but after a week, he became discontented, and talked constantly about home.

"So we came back," Dorothy later recalled, writing in the *San Francisco Examiner*. "In an effort to get him to exercise, I engaged a professional boxer and athletic trainer, who came to the house and lived with Wally. But even that failed. The trainer rigged up a bicycle arrangement and forced Wally to exercise, much against his will. Still the dysentery persisted and Wally grew weaker . . . ."

In 1922, Wally's troubles were complicated by the varying quality in his picture releases. Reviewers finally noticed that there was something wrong with him. They said he seemed to be walking nonchalantly through *The Dictator, Across the Continent, The World's Champion, Rent Free*, and *Don't Tell Everything*. They wrote that he was always competent and professional, but it seemed that he had lost the spark that had once attracted audiences to his pictures. By the time *The Dictator* was released, Paramount was pairing his features with releases of older, dramatic one-reel films that had been turned into travesty comedies with the use of creative comic titles to keep the overall program moving and prop up the feature. More than once, reviewers noted that if this trend toward lackluster, pedestrian posing was to continue, it would spell the end to his career.

Mary Pickford only appeared in one picture in 1922, *Tess of the Storm Country*. Charlie Chaplin only appeared in one picture the same year, *Payday*, a short two-reel comedy. They were the only two performers who topped Wally in overall popularity that year, *yet Wally appeared in nine feature-length films*. He was the ace of the Paramount program. Jesse Lasky exploited Wally as fully as was possible with no concern for the consequences. He had no concern for Wally; his only interest was the tremendous revenue pouring in from Wallace Reid film rentals. In large cities boasting a number of theaters, there were often as many as three or four of his pictures showing at the same time. Exhibitors had to take the rest of the Paramount program in order to get his titles, and his draw at the theaters was so great that they could afford to risk having half-empty theaters for other pictures, knowing that Wally's would bring in the crowds. To satisfy the demand, Paramount released a new picture with Wally about every six weeks. To them, he was a gold mine to be mercilessly excavated for profit. They paid him $3,000 a week, but at the same time, Alla Nazimova, whose box office appeal was weak, got $10,000 a week, and Mary Pickford was annually raking in more than $1 million plus a substantial percent of her films' profits. Wally was not a businessman. He trusted people. Anyone who was pleasant could become his friend, and many of those "friends" continued to take advantage of his naivety. Jesse Lasky and other Paramount executives were the worst offenders.

The last photo Wally sent to his mother, Bertha, before his untimely death. He signed it with his childhood nickname, "Cottontop"

Wallace with his mother, Bertha, a few months prior to his death.

Officially released on October 5, 1922, *The Ghost Breaker* was snuck out to reviewers about a week earlier. An ominous forewarning came from the pen of an anonymous writer for *Variety* reviewing *The Ghost Breaker* in September 1922:

> ". . . the sets are elaborate and the photography good, but it looks as though Reid had made up his mind that he was going to do as little work in this picture as possible, and possibly conspired with the script writer and the director to help him out. Things of this sort are about as sure a road to oblivion, as far as the screen is concerned, as being involved in some unsavory scandal."

On October 21, 1922, despite the fact that some newspaper had already told the truth about Wally's condition, Paramount instructed their press department to deflect any rumors that might still be circulating about the true nature of Wally's illness. They issued to the *Los Angeles Times* this report:

> "Wallace Reid, actor and motion picture star, was stricken with paralysis at his home here shortly after dinner last night, and is at death's door. A consultation of physicians was held, and little hope for his recovery was advanced. Mr. Reid has been at work at the studio all the afternoon and appeared in his usual robust health at dinner and was stricken as he left the table. He is an actor of unusual intelligence and personal charm, and devoted to his wife and son. His popularity both among players and patrons of motion pictures is due not alone to his ability and personality, but to his clean living. His name has never been connected, even remotely, with any of the scandals which infest the picture colony."

The *Los Angeles Examiner* filed this report on the same day:

> **"WALLACE REID SERIOUSLY ILL IN SANITARIUM"**
> "Wallace Reid is seriously ill. Waging a valiant battle against a combination of maladies the debonair, dashing hero of screenland was reported last night as 'doing as well as could

be expected.' From his bedside in a sanitarium Dorothy Davenport, actress, in private life Mrs. Wallace Reid, said in effect: 'Wallace is a very sick man. It is true that his condition is serious but he is not dying, as was the rumor this afternoon.' Attending physicians and Miss Davenport announced that the dangerous illness is a combination of a nervous breakdown and an eye disorder known in cinema circles as 'klieg eye.' 'Klieg eye,' it was explained, is similar to 'snow blindness' and is brought on by long and continued exposure of the eyes to powerful batteries of calcium lights used in moving pictures. The stricken screen star, Miss Davenport said, has been in ill health for several months because of overwork and the eye malady. The combination proved too much for his physique Wednesday and he suffered a 'complete breakdown.' Reid has appeared in more pictures than any male star in the studios here, his friends assert, and his eyes, never strong, failed completely about two weeks ago. For several days he was blind, they say, but during the last week his eyes grew stronger, but his nervousness was accentuated. The climax came when he started to work on the Lasky lot a week ago on a picture known as *Nobody's Money*. He was cast for the lead, but was unable to continue after the first day or so. Scenes in which he was not scheduled to appear were shot while the supporting company waited for his recovery. But yesterday it was announced that Jack Holt had been signed to play the lead in *Nobody's Money*. Reid requested and obtained a four weeks' vacation from the Lasky Corporation, which ended Wednesday. During that period he camped and hunted in the mountains in an attempt to stem the onrushing nervous breakdown."

On November 19, 1922, Paramount released *Clarence*. Still photographs taken during production can be scrutinized more closely than watching fleeting shots that have been carefully edited into the finished motion picture film. Those stills show the face of a man wasting away, especially when the Wally of 1922 are compared to the Wally of 1918 before his ordeals began.

The usually astute reviewers for the *New York Times* found nothing unsettling about Wally or his appearance, which is a tribute to William de Mille's skillful direction of the picture. The newspaper reviewer wrote,

> "In the role of Clarence . . . Wallace Reid qualifies beyond expectations. He fits into the part of the meek, yet exceedingly competent, Clarence with apparent ease and is able in several places to indulge in the light comedy pantomime at which he is adept . . . ."

In December 1922, United States Congressmen were incensed over the revelations about Wally and drug abuse. The *Indiana Evening Gazette* reprinted an article by William K. Hutchinson, "Wallace Reid Case Stirs Up Congressmen." The report ran up a red flag about drug use in Hollywood, and called for the enactment of more stringent anti-narcotic laws in the wake of Wally's illness. Congressional circles, led by California Republican, Senator Shortridge, recommended harsher enforcement of existing laws and new Federal restrictions to wipe out the drug trade throughout the nation. The same action was also suggested by Idaho Republican, Senator Borah, of the Senate Committee on Education and Labor. Borah frowned on Federal censorship of the movies as a means of eradicating the evils of Hollywood. He considered "American motherhood fully capable of protecting children from undesirable films. Senator Myers of Montana, after attacking the Hollywood film colony from the floor of the Senate, declared the Reid case indicated the need of a major clean up of "undesirable characters in the movies."

A bill by Senator Myers to provide Federal censorship of films in the District of Columbia was then pending before Borah's committee. He said, "The Reid case will focus the attention of Congress on the need of more drastic anti-drug laws. There should also be stricter enforcement of existing laws. Reid's sudden collapse is a danger signal to the rest of the movie colony and the whole nation of the frightful punishment inflicted by these deadly drugs. The moral to be learned from his case should not be an attack on the movies but a warning to those who traffic and use deadly drugs." Senator Borah

Wally in his final film, James Cruze's *30 Days* (1922).

stopped short of calling for the outright ban or censoring of films in which Wally appeared. "I am not censoring the movies," Senator Borah declared. "I don't know of any better censor than the motherhood of America. I doubt whether any Government contrivance could be compared to the heart and mind of a mother. If she doesn't want her child to see a certain class of movies, the child won't. The remedy probably lies in stricter anti-drug laws and better enforcement of present laws. "I think the charges that Wallace Reid is a drug addict justify the claims that there should be a clean-up in the character of men and women who furnish attractions for the motion picture business." Senator Borah concluded by pointing the finger of responsibility for this clean-up squarely at Will Hays.

The public furor took its toll on Wally. While making *30 Days* (1922), he was hardly able to stand, let alone act. The strain is all too obvious on his face even in the still photographs taken of him during those hours while making that picture. Those working with him winced visibly when they witnessed the gallant and losing struggle he waged throughout the making of the picture. He suffered so constantly that a physician was on the set each day to attend to him as soon as the camera stopped grinding. When asked, Wally insisted that nothing serious was wrong, and assured friends that he would soon be well. They tried to persuade him to give it up and seek rest, but he refused to listen to them. He told them he needed the money, and explained the troubling situation away by stating that "his teeth were hurting, and that was all." He would be all right as soon as they were fixed, he assured them. Perhaps he believed that explanation himself. To those around him, he was falling apart.

Rather than halt production and see that he got medical attention, they literally propped him up in front of the camera to perform the last bits needed to complete the picture. His health was taking such a turn for the worse that they had to change the action of the script to fit his condition. In the last scene of the comedy, the story was changed to show him carried comically from a room, but the truth was that he was unable to stand, so the rewritten script had him carried off the set in what was supposed to be an amusing bit of action. To those who watched with tear-dimmed eyes, the rewriting was a tragic necessity. Director James Cruze barely managed to get the required footage "in the can" before Wally suffered a complete breakdown.

Despite his obvious inability to work, Paramount plunged him headlong into the next picture. *Nobody's Money*, a comedy about a young man who has a nervous breakdown, was to go into production right on the heels of Wally's completion of *30 Days*. One of the first scenes to be filmed involved a scene called for him to cross a drawing room. The cameraman began to crank, and with an attempt at his old jauntiness, Wally took a few steps. Then, to the horror of those watching, his knees buckled, and then he sank to the floor. He could not get up. Alone on the stage with the klieg lights mercilessly glaring down on him, Wally looked up into the blinding rays and openly wept. He could not stand. On that third day of heart-breaking effort, he took off his makeup for the last time.

Dorothy took control, and went into action to save Wally from completely slipping away. She obtained another leave of absence from the studio for him.

". . . the trainer carried him in his arms up and down the steps and through the gardens at the house," Dorothy revealed in her *San Francisco Examiner* article. "I suppose I grew panicky. At any rate, I took him to a hospital, and the best specialists obtainable poked him and probed him and pierced him with needles in an effort to diagnose his illness. They failed. The nerve-racking days in the hospital sapped what little strength he had left . . . ."

Then in early December, she took him back to rest at the Banksia Place Sanitarium in the mountains where he began his final, magnificent fight with death.

Cecil B. DeMille remembered many years later the brave determination that he heard in Wally's voice just before he entered the sanitarium. "I'll either come out cured," the heroic man said, "or I won't come out."

Chapter 15
THE HOUSE OF SILENCE

Wally was confined to a dark room for about a week, while Dorothy sat at his bedside in a day and night vigil. He had never experienced the full agony of total withdrawal from morphine, and she had never witnessed it, but the sanitarium doctors had seen it first-hand—many times. They admitted that there was little that could be done then to ease Wally's withdrawal, and complete cessation was the only known cure. Unfortunately, the result often was death. Both his mother and the public were kept from knowing the full, horrible truth of the terrible ordeal he was going through while he was in confinement.

He was under treatment for more than a month, attended by Dr. G. S. Herbert. As the weeks passed, his normal weight of nearly 200 pounds had reduced to 135 pounds. Dorothy came and went, maintained the household, and took care of the children, but she spent as much time with him during that hellish nightmare as possible.

"I'm winning the fight, Mama," was his invariable, optimistic greeting when Dorothy visited him, but day by day, she could see that he was actually losing the battle.

". . . but his condition is much improved," stated Paramount in a press release, "and the specialists attending him declare that he will return to work in better condition than he has been for a long time."

In reality, he was dying. Teddy Hayes, former trainer for Jack Dempsey, was chief aid to Dorothy in helping Wally with a desperate attempt to rebuild his body with a careful physical culture routine, an almost hopeless effort to keep him from succumbing to the ravages of withdrawal. He was subjected to regular hours and absolute quiet. He saw no one other than Dorothy, the doctor, Buddy Post, and his trainer.

In public, Dorothy put up a brave front. The mask required all the actress skills she could muster. She flatly lied to reporters, who dutifully published her every word as if they were fact.

"It's been a rest cure," told a smiling Dorothy, when facing inquisitive reporters, "and Wally's improvement is remarkable. He had us pretty well worried when we took him there—he will never take care of himself until it's just forced on him—but I am so pleased and happy over the way he is getting along. He is putting on weight, climbing mountains, sleeping twelve hours a night, and beginning to look like himself again."

Her overly optimistic report was a valiant front, but in other interviews, she spoke the truth in veiled terms, such as this excerpt from an article by William Parker that appeared in the *Los Angeles Herald*, December 18-21, 1922:

> "I am opening the book of Wallace Reid's life so that the public will read and know the truth," Dorothy said. "My husband is battling as a man has never battled before. He has traversed the 'land of darkness and the shadow of death.' The horrors of the hell he has gone through would long ago have broken the heart of an ordinary man. But I know as surely as I know there is a God he will win out . . . He fully realized, poignantly, desperately that he had come to the turn in the road in his life. He reiterated his determination in the sanitarium where he now lies critically ill . . . Some whisky was given him in medicine. Wan, weary, and so weak he would faint from exertion when his pillow was turned under his head, he roused himself to protest. In almost a passion of rage, he demanded to know what was in the medicine. Someone replied, 'Scotch whisky.' 'What are you trying to do?' he exclaimed. 'Do you want me to get started again?' Then, nerving himself for a final effort, he clenched his teeth and said grimly, 'I'll beat it. I've never been licked yet—and I'm not licked now.'"

> "No matter what the public hears, no matter what it reads,"

Dorothy went on to say, "I want it to keep before it the Wally Reid I know, a man of heroic determination, a man who one day suddenly recognized his foe, met it face to face, clenched his teeth, and declared, 'We will fight it out now—till one of us is dead.'"

Dorothy further explained, "In telling you the story I am relating what he had hoped to do. He knew of the rumors which had spread like wildfire to all parts of the country. It was his plan, as soon as he gained strength, to invite a representative of every Los Angeles newspaper to come to him and hear the true story, the truth of his slavery. He recognized impersonally—as I do—that by reason of his prominence, such a story from him would serve to bring forcibly before the people the dangers of the drug evil. He felt that through such a story he would be able to prompt his thousands of screen 'fans' to use their vote and moral and financial influence in behalf of any campaign being waged against the traffic in drugs and liquor. The premature publication of his condition forestalled his plan. Now, it has fallen to me to tell the truth. And I want to tell it. I want to tell it more as a mother than as a wife. I want to tell it with all the compassion and tender affection for the one who has always been in my heart and thoughts, 'My boy.'"

According to an article that appeared in the *Oakland Tribune*, Gloria Swanson got into the Christmas spirit to cheer Wally and others. She went through the property room at Paramount to retrieve assorted model homes, buildings, and miniature cities used in various films, and had them sent to youngsters at the Lark Ellen Home. Then, she sent a small Christmas tree to Wally at the sanitarium where he languished. It was placed on a white enameled table in his sickroom, arriving on the morning that his son, Billy, and daughter, Betty, arrived to visit him. His room had been inundated with flowers from associates and fans, and Dorothy cleared out the foliage by donating all the flowers to the local Children's hospital. Wally seemed able to rally for the Holidays, and together, they took him home.

During Christmas 1922, Wally knew it might be his last Holiday season. Looking back, Dorothy said, "The generous, sensitive nature that gave friendship for the asking was often disillusioned because his humility and sweetness never allowed him to judge others, to question worth; the idealism that never allowed him to become embittered or discouraged into not giving friendship again and again. On the last Christmas he was with us, ill as he was, knowing as he did that it might be his last Christmas, he thought of those whom he feared might be lonely or might miss his gift or word of love. The gaiety that was of the heart, that sweet and simple gaiety that fell upon everyone around him like sunshine, that shone in his eyes and in his smile, a real cheerfulness of the heart."

Christmas was always a great time for him, and on that one, he spent hours trimming the tree elaborately to surprise Billy and Betty.

"Dorothy, can't you just see their faces when they come in that door?"

He had tremendous pride in Billy, and regarded him as more of a pal than a son. He wanted above all things to make a man of him, to instill manliness into him from his first months. He had taught Billy to shoot a .22 rifle, to swim and dive, and had instructed him in mechanics and mathematics. He had soothed Billy's fears of the dark by explaining how God watched over him.

"Billy, it's just like a mother hen covering her chickens, the way God's wings are over us at night. I suppose it's dark under the mother hen's soft protecting feathers, too, but the baby chicks are safe and happy there. And so, though it's dark at night, we can always know that we are safe and happy because we are in the shadow of God's wings."

Betty was another source of great pride. His eyes flashed angrily the few times she was crassly referred to as an "adopted child." Betty worshiped her daddy with all her heart, and never forgot to speak of him in her nightly prayers.

There was in Wally a highly developed spiritual side, half hidden, and half understood only by himself. He had no fear of death. God, to him, was a great, understanding heart of love, who would help, understand, forgive, and teach His children.

About that time, he wrote to his friend, Adela Rogers St. Johns, "I don't know why I have failed like this. Sometimes I think you do. Pray for me that, somewhere in the strange land into which I am going alone, I may become at last the man I have always wanted to be."

Dorothy continued to be open about the nightmare when talking with the press, especially William Parker from the *Los Angeles Herald*. "I am being criticized severely by some of our acquaintances for having talked so much, but I feel that if the public knows the truth it will not condemn Wally any more than I have condemned him. His is not an individual case symptomatic of a community. The battle Wally is making is the battle that thousands—I might say a million—of men and women are making. My heart goes out to them in sympathy. I know the horrors of the hell they must be suffering because I saw this dread enemy attack my husband. If then through telling the truth I can do my part to arouse public sentiment against this nefarious traffic I am willing to suffer criticism."

The *Los Angeles Times* reported on December 24, 1922, in an article by Harry Carr:

". . . Some months ago, there was formed an organization called the "Federated Arts," which was made up of directors, camera men, scenario writers, electricians, etc. The stated purpose was to boycott any picture stars who were not conducting themselves in a manner to bring credit to the industry. Everybody understood that it was directed at Wally Reid and two or three other stars. A delegation went to Lasky and asked him to remove Wally Reid from the films—at least, until he cured himself of the dope habit. According to the story told by the survivors, Mr. Lasky promised to investigate, but did nothing. The truth is that Reid presented himself at "the front office" with heated denials, threats, and demands for an investigation. He offered to allow physicians to examine him, etc. So the affair came to nothing. After that, an informal scheme was proposed by some of Wally's friends to forcibly kidnap him and take him to some hospital for treatment. This also fell through. The remnants of the Federated Arts have burned with the rebuff ever since . . . ."

On January 8, 1923, Paramount released the James Cruze comedy, *30 Days*. It was not realized by anyone at the time that, other than two previously filmed, brief cameo appearances in other pictures, *30 Days* would be the last time audiences would see Wally in a new movie. The studio still tried to cover up the truth of his troubles. Paramount, which had millions of dollars invested in Wally's schedule of pictures, issued more euphemisms about his rest from "overwork."

"Wallace Reid is in a foothill sanitarium near Los Angeles," reported one movie magazine in January 1923, adding, "suffering from a combination of severe Klieg eyes and a serious nervous breakdown."

Barely over thirty years old, the young man with the magnetic personality that charmed the whole country had tried to salvage his reputation on his own. He was too late.

Then suddenly, the graphic truth of his hospitalization exploded in front page headlines in nationally published reports in nearly every city around the country. At first, the Reid family wanted to spare the public the full details of his ordeal, but finally, they had to reveal the truth in a tidal wave. The news broke in a peculiar manner to newspapers, beginning with a wild rumor that Wally had broken away from his nurses and gone into Los Angeles to buy an ounce of morphine for $300. He was said to have gone crazy.

Reporters for the *Chicago Tribune*, the *New York News*, and associated newspapers descended on the Reid home and met Alice at the door. She denied the story, and claimed that Wally was too weak to get off his bed. She declared with much weeping that she would never allow another bottle of whisky to come into the house, and that she would try to keep Wally from his friends.

"It was his friends that ruined him," she told reporters for the nation's leading newspapers. "When we sell this house, I'll see we get one with a high iron fence around it, a fence his friends cannot penetrate. This wasn't a home, it was a roadhouse. Wally's friends would troop in here by the scores at any old hour of the day or night or the early hours of the morning. They would come whether they were invited or not. . . ."

After the reporters had left, Dorothy communicated with Alice and learned of the interview. She flew into action, went down to the offices of the *Los Angeles Times*, and begged to have the story suppressed. They refused to cooperate with her plea, so she decided to go to the public with the full truth and reveal the facts as she knew them. She insisted on making an official announcement about Wally's battle to conquer the dope habit.

The sensational news stunned the nation because he was not just a movie star; he was the living model of Young American Manhood. To the pleased surprise of the Reid family, the news brought him sympathy and help from all over the country.

In Danville, Virginia, the local newspaper, The *Bee*, wrote:

> "Wallace Reid near death in struggle against morphine. Screen idol in sanitarium at Los Angeles facing his greatest battle, a victim of his friends. Wallace Reid, one of the brightest of film stars, the idol of millions of movie fans, for years, the slave of whisky and morphine, lies near to death tonight in an obscure little sanitarium, fighting to come back."

Similar accounts carried by wire reports ran in every newspaper around the country. Thousands of letters and telegrams poured in when he reached the point where he was bedridden. They expressed love and sympathy, and offered heartfelt prayers for his recovery. He gently touched the letters, and told Dorothy in utter amazement, "I didn't know so many felt like that about me. How kind of them, dear; how kind they all are to me."

Wally underwent the final agonies of drug withdrawal, but the torture left him physically debilitated. He also caught influenza, and after a high fever set in for several days, he lapsed into a coma. His pal, Buddy Post, came forward to offer his blood in a last-ditch endeavor to save Wally's life. When he came back to consciousness, he first saw Dorothy, who had kept a bedside vigil during his delirium. Doctors told them the only way he was going to survive was to go back on morphine in small, controlled doses. They frankly told him he was ruined, and only a return to the drug habit he was fighting could save him. He refused. He chose to let go of life, if all he could look forward to was a killer monkey of a habit and no freedom from the curse of it. As he had done so many times, he looked to Dorothy for a decision, but this time she shook her head. The burden was too much for her to assume. For once, he had to make the choice on his own.

Wally chose a clean death rather than a return to morphine slavery.

"I'll go out clean," he told her. "I'd rather my body died than to go back to the thing that almost killed me. At least, I'm myself now. I'll—go out clean. I believe in God now. No one but God could have made the love you've given me. I'm not afraid."

His weight sank to 120 pounds, and in deliriums, his failing brain recalled the music he loved most. He longed for music, and he lay for hours listening to great masterpieces on phonograph records played on a gramophone that was moved into his room. In-between concertos and saxophone records played on the gramophone, his lips murmured along with the sounds as if he were playing one of his beloved instruments again. For weeks, his iron will and determination to live were all that kept him from dying.

In a 2010 interview with Terry Kottler, whose mother was Dorothy and Wally's daughter, Betty, an interesting fact came to light about Wally's death. Terry recalled Dorothy telling her that she and Wally had retreated to a cabin in the mountains that they both loved. They thought the hideaway would be an ideal place for him to rest undisturbed, but they were visited by a woman who brought narcotics to Wally. Dorothy remembered that Wally took more of the drug than he should have, and that act probably sped his untimely death.

When it became clear that the end was in sight, Wally asked if he might have a Christian Scientist practitioner come to him in his final hours. Dorothy and her mother, Alice, both of whom were Christian Scientists, assured him that he could, but then he changed his mind. He asked Dorothy to read poetry by Keats and Mrs. Browning. Dorothy's voice softly resounded off the deadened walls, and her audience of one listened quietly, as the life flow slowly ebbed out of him and the clock ticked away his final hours.

On Thursday, January 18, 1923, shortly after one o'clock in the afternoon, not yet thirty-one year old Wally died in Dorothy's arms. His best friend, Charles "Buddy" Post, was also at his side. The official cause was listed as "hypostatic congestion of the lungs and renal suppression."

". . . he stood by his colors and gave his life rather than retreat," his mother said afterward.

"He faced the end, when he knew it must come, with a blessed spiritual courage which was beautiful to see," wrote Dorothy in 1923.

"Prohibition, hypocrisy, Hollywood?" recounted Herb Howe, as he thought back. "There is something wrong with a scheme that can destroy such charming, great-hearted children. Perhaps that is why the loving God took them out of the mess."

"One could not help but sympathize with Wallace," recalled Adolph Zukor later, "a big, likable fellow who photographed much slimmer than his 180 pounds. Wally may have had too much money for his own good, for he was a thrill seeker—though not in conquest of women, fascinated as they were with him . . . Wally was a great lover of the outdoors. He liked to hunt and fish, and above all, to race automobiles. He lived his life to the hilt. Perhaps excitement overtaxed his nerves, or, as was widely reported, he may have had too many thrills."

Cecil B. DeMille recalled the mood of the times when he looked back on Wally's death from the distance of 1959: "There was a sickness in Hollywood, but it was a sickness that infected the whole postwar world. I am neither excusing nor accusing. There was throughout the world a crumbling of standards, aggravated in America, I have always believed, by the Eighteenth Amendment and the Volstead Act, by which government attempted to regulate the personal habits of individuals, and succeeded only in teaching many of them disrespect for all law. But the germ of that sickness was older than Prohibition, older than World War One. Theologians call it original sin. If someone in Hartford became addicted to narcotics, it was a grievous trial to his family and friends . . . but anything that happened in Hollywood was magnified far beyond the family concerned. . . ."

"This is one of the saddest things I have ever known," said Theodore Roberts in an interview with the *Lincoln Star*. Theodore appeared with Wally in a dozen pictures, and between them was affection almost like father and son. "I have known Wally since he was two years old, then a little blonde-haired baby just learning to prattle and walk. Among the host of friends I have on the other side, Wally is one of the closest and best thought of."

"My heart goes out in sympathy to the widow and mother of Wallace Reid," said Mary Pickford. "His death is a great tragedy

The urn holding Wally's cremated ashes was designed by him before his untimely death.

because I know he would have lived down every mistake he made. He was a charming boy with great genius."

At first, little Billy and Betty, Wally's two children, were not told of their father's death. Dorothy led them to believe that he had gone "on location," and that it would be a long trip. The legacy he left his son and daughter was perhaps the greatest bequest of all: a model of genuine courage. In time, Betty and Billy came to know the bravery with which their father died, and they understood that he would not be coming back.

Funeral services were in charge of the Elks Lodge No. 99, of which Wally was a member. While the services were in progress, every motion picture studio in the country closed as a show of respect to his memory. When the studios shuttered temporarily, his funeral became fodder for cynics.

Wally's body lay in state from ten o'clock in the morning to after two o'clock in the afternoon in the First Congregational Church. Pallbearers were announced from the ranks of Wally's fellow workers: active Pallbearers were William Desmond, William S. Hart, Edward Brady, Noah Beery, Eugene Pallette, and Benjamin Frazee. Honorary Pallbearers were Jack Holt, Sam Wood, Theodore Roberts, Conrad Nagel, Antonio Moreno, and Victor Clarke.

An article in the *Indianapolis Star* stated, "His body lay in a casket of deep purple whose fittings were of plated gold, while around the casket were placed more flowers than have ever been in a church in Los Angeles."

As he lay in state, wearing one of the tweed sport suits he loved so well, traffic stopped for blocks in Los Angeles because of the many thousands of people trying to get a last look at what remained of the handsome, boyish face that had brought so many happy hours to them in the movie theaters. Men, women, and children gathered for miles in all directions just to stand uncovered as the car drove through the streets bearing their idol to his final resting place. Traffic policemen were nearly torn to shreds by the ferocity of women trying to push their way through the crowd. At one point, a band of shop girls got together behind the line and formed a flying wedge in football fashion, charging headlong into the police and knocking them out of their way in order to catch a glimpse of the casket as it was being taken to the rear of the hearse. Dorothy and her mother were marooned in a corner of a side street, and nothing less than the heroic efforts of the police enabled them to succeed in getting into the church at all.

The First Congregational Church was filled with flowers, and great stars knelt beside millionaire producers, grips, and electricians, who had worked with Wally and loved him dearly. At the foot of the casket sat Wally's faithful friend, his hunting dog, Spike. The pews were packed to the doors, while out in the streets, crowds pushed and shoved to get past the police barriers.

Rev. Neal Dodd, a scholarly pastor of Hollywood's Little Church Around the Corner, read the funeral service of the Episcopal church.

In the church during the service were seen "Fatty" Arbuckle, Pola Negri, Charlie Chaplin, Harold Lloyd, Bebe Daniels, Mary Pickford, Douglas Fairbanks, and Sid Grauman, to name just a few of the stars who came to pay their last respects. Drawn and haggard, Dorothy sat with her mother, Alice. Wally's mother, Bertha, could not cross the continent in time to be present at the funeral, and neither could the Reids' closest friend, Adela Rogers St. Johns, who was in British Columbia and could not get there in time.

In one heartbreaking moment, a pitiful scene played out in front of the open casket. All eyes riveted on Dorothy, worn and tired from the ordeal, as she looked down one last time at the wasted form of the beautiful man she had loved more than anyone on Earth, and whispered, "Goodbye, Wally . . . dear. . . ."

Following the funeral service, Wally's body was cremated late in the evening on January 21 in accordance with his last wish, and the ashes were kept in a bronze urn, which he had designed. On the Forest Lawn memorial grounds was the Church of the Flowers, a small, quaint structure in which a marriage or funeral could take place. The church was an exact replica of the little church that Henry W. Longfellow told about in *Evangeline*. A winding road led to the top of a hill on which the unusually beautiful, Greek mausoleum stood. At the entrance of the north door, the memorial and urn holding Wally's ashes were interred. There were many other persons buried in the mausoleum, but Wally's was built on a more elaborate scale and of more expensive and beautiful marble.

Dorothy managed to express her grief in a written letter to fans that was published in *Photoplay* in 1923. "Losing him, the real Wally, the world lost a bright and brilliant spirit, a gentle and loving soul, a rare and gifted nature, which might have given to the world something immeasurably great, but which at least did give much of happiness, joy, beauty to many who loved him and whom he loved."

Wally left no will. Of all the sums that he must have made over the years for himself and for the various picture companies for which he worked, nothing was left for Dorothy and the two children except an estate of $58,500, the bulk of which was a home valued at $40,000 and attached to two mortgages, and his furniture and automobiles valued at $18,599. He also left a life insurance policy of about $70,000.

After the excitement of his funeral settled down, some friends found that Dorothy seemed unusually bitter, and they were not

A grieving Dorothy walked a lonely road after Wally's untimely death.

mistaken. She was not concerned about money because there was plenty to sustain her and the two children for a while. Her focus landed squarely on a group of hangers-on, who she was certain were responsible for his downfall. Wally's best friend, Buddy Post, agreed.

Buddy said, "A certain class, who liked Wally, enjoyed the hospitality of his home, borrowed everything he owned, and basked in the reflected glory of his association, were the first to leave him when he started his death struggle . . . only a few staunch friends remained with him throughout."

Dorothy directed her harshness at those who hastened his entrapment by narcotics. At a press conference, she announced her intent to avenge Wally's death. She turned over to the police a scathing list of names of Wally's "friends," who she claimed drew him into debauchery and destruction. Dorothy was out for blood, and those denizens on the infamous list became known as the "Hollywood Hell-Raisers." At her urging, the witch-hunt began.

"What happened to Wally had happened to many a soldier released from hospitals after World War One, and had happened to patients—both men and women—released from hospitalization, cured perhaps of their ailments and injuries, but made into hopeless addicts through the then abysmal ignorance of the medical profession. I don't mean to minimize a terribly tragic situation, but I want to get one thing straight: my husband did not get morphine through any underworld connection. His source was neither illicit nor illegal—it didn't have to be. Wally could charm any doctor into giving him the tablets he wanted. He knew just enough about medicine to convince doctors that he knew exactly how many grams he could safely take every day. Nor were there any great financial outputs for the narcotic. That I know, for I kept the family books, and would have been the first to know had there been any large payments to any peddler, some of whom may have tried to ensnare Wally in the hope of blackmailing him. But they never succeeded. He got what he wanted—and on his own. He took the morphine orally. It was worse, in a way, with Wally, because he had always been the picture of health, and he was confident that he knew enough about medicine to believe that addiction wouldn't happen to him. But it did. And when he found he couldn't put a stop or even a check to the morphine, he began to use liquor as a cover-up for what he was really doing. Before that, he had only drunk for relaxation and fun. Drinking now made things even tougher for him. Today, most people recognize morphine and alcohol as two forces that work dangerously and destructively against one another."

According Richard Koszarski in his book, *An Evening's Entertainment*, Film Daily Yearbook of Motion Pictures, in 1923, shortly after Reid's death, the Russell Sage Foundation, the National Board of Review of Motion Pictures, and Associated First National Exhibitors surveyed 37,000 high-school students in seventy-six cities across the country. When asked whom they considered their favorite actors, Wally came in second on both lists compiled by boys and girls, unique in his ability to appeal strongly to both sexes.

Herbert Howe wrote a tribute to Wally in 1923:

"He was the exemplar of American youth: reckless, genial, carefree, democratic, with an unfailing sense of humor, and a spirit that never said die. In appearance, he was a young god with all the gifts that the gods could bestow, and yet with the great lovable good nature that made him—just Wally. He didn't take himself seriously. He didn't take life seriously. He lavished his gifts freely and offered his hand to all. An athlete, a musician, an artist, an actor—and yet he would laugh at his own accomplishments. There was no ego in Wally Reid. He accepted everyone as a friend and his door was open to all. Who you are or where you came from never mattered to Wally. He was not only a hero to the millions who saw him in films; he was a hero to his own valet and to every extra around the studio. Whenever charity called Wally Reid came. He never spared himself; he never considered his prestige; he was the friend of every man. Yet few people knew the real Wally Reid, who once said to me, 'They would laugh at you if you told them I ever had a serious thought, but just between you and me I'd like to do something worthwhile some day—give something to the world beside my face and figure.' And now he has. He lived to delight millions. He died with the whispered hope that he might save at least a few from the agony that was his. His last role was the greatest he ever played. Never on the screen did he wage such a brave and splendid fight. The loyal love of millions will follow the star that is forever—just Wally."

Paramount promised to mollify his large fan following by announcing it would erect a memorial to his memory. Three years later, nothing had been done, and no memorial ever came into being. Many of his pictures were reportedly destroyed, although prints of a few have survived despite the deliberate destruction and negligence by the studio that made them. When requested, some of his old films were resurrected at a few retrospective showings, but Paramount took no special effort in promoting the few battered prints remaining in their vaults.

Quietly, Dorothy slipped into the Hospital for Wounded Veterans and the convalescent homes of the American Legion, and she distributed Wally's enormous wardrobe to the boys who wanted to have something of his by which to remember him.

She set at once to mounting an anti-dope propaganda picture, and she rallied to campaign around the country aiding social reform groups to fight the growing problem of drug use in America. She produced the film, *Human Wreckage*, starring Bessie Love, and it was released in 1923 to great critical acclaim.

"It is not my own wish to make an anti-dope picture," Dorothy told reporters. "I am very, very tired, and I should like to retire from the field for a little while. But during these days since my husband's going, my home has been flooded with appeals to me to do something. Everyone has been so kind to me. They have commended my struggle, sympathized with me in my grief. But from every class—from legislators, from statesmen, from men and women who for years have been fighting this evil—comes the cry, 'Do something. They will listen to you. They loved Wally, and they admired his brave fight and they hate the thing that killed him. Tell what you know for the good of humanity.' So, I am going to make this production. I have asked Thomas H. Ince to aid me in making this picture, and I can only pray it will stand as a real message from me and a memorial to my Wally's great fight."

The *Human Wreckage* story attempted to pull the veil of silence from the problem of drug addition. The film revealed in graphic

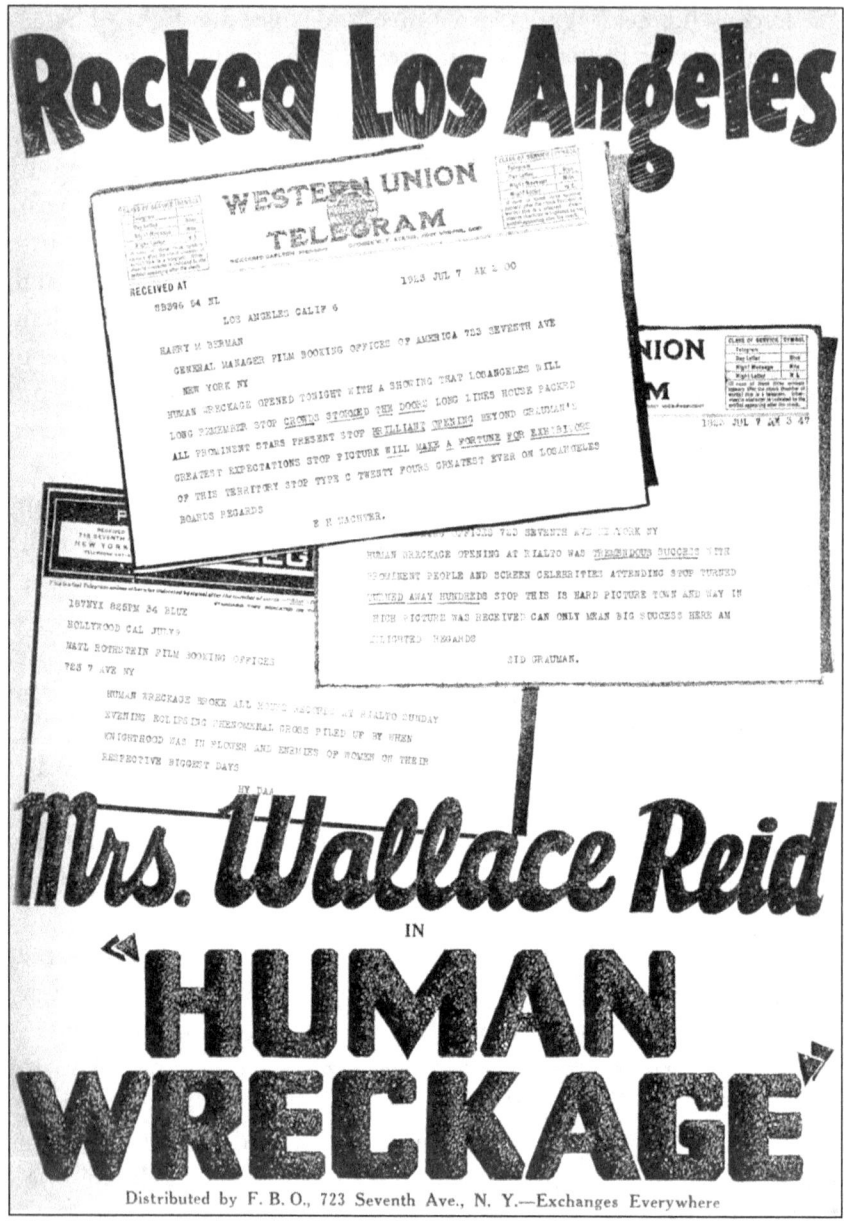

A motion picture trade magazine advertisement for John Griffith Wray's *Human Wreckage* (1923).

detail the horrors of drug addiction, and ultimately served to stimulate public reforms. She often accompanied the film to deliver lectures to the film audience.

Bessie Love in John Griffith Wray's *Human Wreckage* (1923).

The cast of *Human Wreckage* read like a Who's Who of Hollywood. Aside from Dorothy, it boasted James Kirkwood, Bessie Love, George Hackathorne, Claire McDowell, Robert McKim, Victor Bateman, Harry Northrup, Eric Mayne, and others. Not content with a list of stars, the story also brought into play notables, George

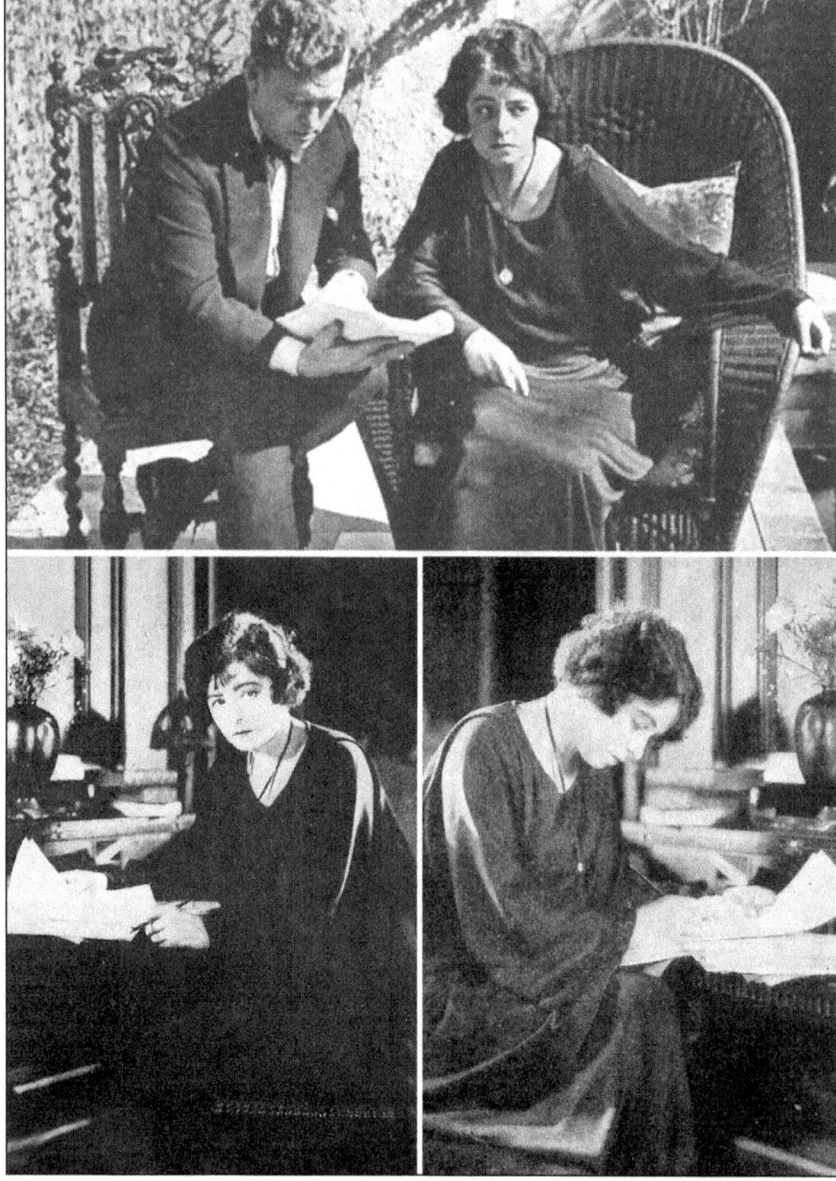

Three photographs of Dorothy while she was making *Human Wreckage*, (TOP) **with director Thomas Ince.**

E. Cryer, Mayor of the City of Los Angeles, Dr. R. B. Von Kleinsmid, President of the University of Southern California, Benjamin Bledsoe, United States Judge, Louis D. Oaks, Chief of Police, and Martha Nelson McCan, Los Angeles Park Commissioner.

Dorothy went on tour after Wally's death to promote her anti-drug film, *Human Wreckage*.

"Treat narcotic addicts as sick people," she told reporters. "Remove their fear of having the world know of their addiction; encourage them to freely seek medical help. Then, throw the limelight of publicity mercilessly upon this menace, and much of the charm that it has for young people, who think they merely are getting a kick out of life, will be banished." Dorothy took her message to City Halls, club women, town mayors, and civic groups in a determined effort to strip away the mystery surrounding the evil and lead the nation's first crusade against the narcotic menace.

Human Wreckage was criticized by the *New York Times* in a 1923 review: "To deliver a lecture through a motion picture against the traffic in drugs, Mrs. Wallace Reid appears in this film that might appeal to an audience of those who need narcotics, but to the average person who has a night off and goes to the theater for entertainment, it is not pleasing. A valiant attempt has been made to render this production effective, and James Kirkwood's performance in certain sequences is unusually good. The story, however, wanders along until it becomes tiresome, and the dramatic climax is spoiled."

Variety noted in its review: "The best impression left by the film is that of a ghost-like hyena stalking through every scene where drugs come in to wreak their worst. This was frequent. A title said the hyena is the ugliest of animals, inferring the drug habit is the ugliest of the diseases."

Moving Picture World, August 11, 1923, said, "Crowds that flocked to the theater on the opening date were so large that it was necessary to build an extra box office on the sidewalk, for which a special permit had been granted by city authorities."

Dorothy was a reasonably astute businesswoman and a great artist. She made the family money fare as well as possible and added to their available income money that she made producing several independent pictures. The two children were raised well. They understood that their father left them a legacy of honor and courage, if not great material wealth.

Dorothy carried out his wishes in devoting as much money earned from *Human Wreckage* as she could to helping the cause of saving other addicts from the snares that killed Wally. She went to tireless lengths to educate the public on the pitfalls that lay waiting for unsuspecting victims. Billy, Dorothy's mother, and Bertha went on many of those trips to principal cities in the northwest and Canada in support of her film. The call for her services in connection with the picture were so strong that she felt obligated to take up the cause and champion the effort to bring the drug plague out into the open. Almost everyone knew someone who had been touched by the scourge. So many men had emerged from past wars with dependencies on morphine that use of the drug had become a silent, nationwide curse, one which was routinely swept under the carpet. It was considered a shameful condition, and aided by filthy street merchants, who trafficked illegally in the drug, it had earned a reputation as one of the great evils infecting society. Until Dorothy began her crusade, most people spoke of the blight in veiled tones.

Human Wreckage made enough money for Dorothy to support her children, finance her own production company, and support the Wallace Reid Foundation Sanatorium. A remarkable monument to Wally's memory, the sanatorium was in planning stages soon after he died. A permanent institution was realized on a beautiful knoll in the heart of the Santa Monica Mountains in a big, rambling cottage covered with vines and surrounded with flowers. Up to sixteen patients were cared for at a time, and experimental cures for drug addiction were tested and perfected on penniless patients suffering as Wally had. It was her hope that the institution would grow into a lasting home of salvation and hope to all unfortunate sufferers who were in need of a saving cure.

Unrecognized and festering, the drug problem in America was already at a boiling point when Wally died from the affliction, but it was kept under cover so well that few realized the full extent of the plague. The attention his battle with drugs brought to the subject drew back the curtain of secrecy and shame and made the curse a topic to be openly discussed. It was suddenly no longer an issue to be cloaked in secrecy. The revelation of his struggle unmasked similar efforts undertaken in private silence by thousands of people. With her respectful and admirable focus on the subject came awareness, and with the newfound consciousness came a hoped-for cure.

Life went on in the sunny California gardens of the home Wally and Dorothy shared. The children were told of their loss when they were old enough to understand the courage Wally rallied to fight

Billy Reid at age fifteen, after his father's death.

the narcotic that had taken him from them. As head of the household in the lonely absence of their husband and father, Dorothy carried on bravely.

"There has been no consolation for me in the months since Wally left me more helpful or more beautiful than the loyal affection and steadfast devotion of those who knew him only on the screen," she told readers of *Photoplay* in 1923. "This love, enduring through the years, they still extend to me daily. . . ."

For several years, Dorothy refused to change anything in their home. Every article remained exactly as Wally had left it. She wrote

After Wally's death, Dorothy bravely went on with her life.

with his fountain pen, and his musical instruments were carefully maintained as testaments to his greatest loves. Little reminders nestled about the house: the blue vase he gave her on their second anniversary; the big chair on which he used to sprawl with his legs and arms spilling over it; the funny rag doll he brought to her one day when she was feeling ill; his basement laboratory where he used to experiment with test tubes and strange concoctions. Everything rested exactly where it was placed the last moment when his hands touched it.

Broken Laws (1924), directed by Roy William Neill, and produced by the Thomas H. Ince Corporation, brought Dorothy back onto movie screens as Joan Allen, the mother of an eight-year-old spoiled and willful son. At age sixteen, he becomes arrogant and lawless. With a Stutz Bearcat given to him by his mother, he takes to the road with an extravagant flapper to party at a roadhouse. On the way, he runs into a wagon and kills an old woman. Brought up on manslaughter charges, he is convicted. "Spare the rod and spoil the child" is her motto until fate takes a toll on his weakness, and brings her to the realization of the havoc that her lenience has brought. Only her pleading convinces the judge to reverse the charges and apply them to her for her willful overindulgence on the boy, which she vows is the reason for his misconduct. Suddenly, she awakens from a dream and realizes that her nightmare was only an illusion.

"There have been so many blurbs printed in the past about the screen stars' ideals that it sounds bromidic," she confessed in a 1925 *Picture-Play* article, "but really, work is a salvation. That, and having children dependent upon you not only for the necessities of life, but in the greater personal sense."

Dorothy carried on, standing with a sort of rock-like stability and dependability in the middle of the ever-changing, artificial, high-keyed movie world. "I am still a young woman, and I have spent years very close to this profession, acting before my marriage, and afterwards, preserving that contact through Wally's interests. I have had dark hours this past year when it did not seem to me that anything was worthwhile. But life and health assert themselves, the virile strain of one who has been accustomed to activity and keeping busy, and the call to get back into the studios was too strong to

Dorothy having her palms read by "Sandra," famous psychic to the stars, in 1928.

resist, aside from our material needs. Besides, I feel that, though the primary mission of the screen is to entertain, my pictures are going to do a little good. *Human Wreckage* has made money, which has enabled me to further my work for the Wallace Reid Foundation sanitarium for the saving and restoration to health of drug victims. And, perhaps, it taught a lesson to a few wayward boys."

Broken Laws, a film Dorothy made to awaken laggard interests in combating the drug evil, was not a propaganda film, but the story was tenderly written with much attention to little details that lent reality to the story.

In 1930, the depression fell hard on everyone. Dorothy was forced to file a petition for bankruptcy. The stock market crash had wiped out what little savings Wally had left her. In a lawsuit over the character depicted in one of her films, *The Red Kimono*, Dorothy lost more tens of thousands of dollars. She ultimately had to sell the family home to Clive Brook and his family in order to pay the lawsuit damages. Nearly broke, she went on with what life she had.

Dorothy and Billy in 1928, five years after Wally's death.

Years passed, and on the occasion of their twelfth wedding anniversary, Dorothy celebrated alone. Tenderly and with consideration, she sent her two youngsters to the beach with their grandmother so that she could be alone with her memories of him. Dorothy still clung to him in her heart. Taken so abruptly and so needlessly, he remained cherished in her spirit as he was, unchanged, and forever at his best.

CHAPTER FIFTEEN: THE HOUSE OF SILENCE | 269

Dorothy established a remarkable monument to Wally's memory: the
Wallace Reid Foundation Sanitarium in the heart of the Santa Monica
Mountains. The facility provided much-needed housing and money for
rescuing drug victims and aiding their families.

Friends were conscious of the pervasive feeling of his vibrant and vital personality the minute they entered the door to their home, and most of them admitted that they would not prefer it any other way. "Wally, fleeting of mood, changeable of impulse, chameleon of talent, one minute touched very deeply, the next a spirit of fun—cuddling his head in my arms and begging to be petted when he was hurt or tired like a small boy—bursting from this to that, in constant activity like a dynamo," Dorothy reminisced. "One of his main charms was this flashing type of interest, but it kept him going. Few people know that he was within a few months of receiving a doctor's degree, with a professional opportunity promised him in the office of a famous medical man of New York City, when he suddenly tired of it. No other business but pictures could have held him. It was the varied panorama that entranced him, something new every day."

Dorothy was deeply impressed by the strong hold that his memory exerted over the great public heart, which she encountered daily while on a personal appearance tour promoting *Human Wreckage*. "Most particularly," she recalled, "by the deference of the young boys to whom he is still an idol."

Wally earned the affection of the millions of people who adored watching him in the movies. He gave them his best, even though he did not want to be an actor. His personal descent into the secret agony of morphine addiction was accidental and born at the insistence of Paramount film producers, who initially plied him with the drugs to keep film production moving at the breakneck pace they required. The public understood the tragedy of his decline and wept all the more because of the unfortunate circumstances. There has never been anyone to replace him because the place he held is also gone.

Today, it is difficult to imagine what it was first like nearly a hundred years ago to see thoughts expressed in terms of youth and on faces enlarged on a motion picture screen. Since the days when Adam and Eve perhaps made shadow puppets on cave walls by the light of a flickering fire and the idea of projecting images was born, nothing like movies had ever been witnessed by mankind. Wally was one of the first-born of that fascinating new art, and after his death, people still thought that he was the most magnetic, charming, personable, and handsome young man in the movies.

Epilogue

JACK HOLT stepped in at the last moment to finish the picture Wally was making at the time of his final collapse. All stills photos and motion picture film taken of Wally during the three days of shooting were destroyed by Paramount.

ANTONIO MORENO, one of Wally's friends, who served as an Honorary Pallbearer at the funeral service, was given his dressing room at Paramount.

JOE WOODS, the dope peddler, who was hustled off to jail in 1921 after being arrested for attempting to sell Wally drugs, served six months in a local jail instead of a lengthy sentence that would have been given by a Federal judge had Wally not intervened. Deeply grateful for all that had been done for him, he protected Wally's name until the day of his death. Then, twenty-four hours after Wally passed away, he committed suicide.

ROBERTO FIRPO, a musician and artist in Buenos Aires, wrote in Wally's honor an excellent waltz called *Eternamente (Eternally)*. The original music sheet was published in 1923 and featured a still photograph of Wally over two Paramount Pictures logos. The waltz became extremely popular, and Firpo recorded it several times, last in 1950. EMI reprinted it in 1974 as an LP, and recently, it was reprinted in a CD.

DOROTHY DAVENPORT REID appeared as an actress in at least 123 motion pictures, beginning with *A Mohawks Way* (1910). After Wally's

Dorothy posed for this glamour portrait in the early 1930s, and signed it as "Mrs. Wallace Reid."

death, she appeared in two silent pictures and three sound pictures, ending with *The Road to Ruin* (1934). An expensive lawsuit cost her most of her life savings, and she was forced to sell the mansion she and Wally built. Living more modestly, she contributed as a writer to at least seventeen known films, produced two others, and directed *Linda* (1929), *Sucker Money* (1933), *Woman Condemned* (1934), and *The Road to Ruin* (1934). She worked as a producer and writer throughout the 1930s, notably as a story editor for Monogram, and she continued to contribute to a number of films as a writer and

Cecil B. DeMille and Billy Reid in the late 1920s, as they looked over photographs of Wally that were taken during their years together.

dialogue coach in the 1940s and 1950s. She lived in a pleasant cottage only two blocks from the lot in North Hollywood where she and Wally helped Carl Laemmle turn the first spade of earth for Universal's new studio. Dorothy died on October 12, 1977 at Woodland Hills, California at the Motion Picture & Television Country House and Hospital. She is interred with her husband in the Forest Lawn Memorial Park, Glendale.

WILLIAM WALLACE REID, JR., Wally's son, married, had a son, Brian, and a daughter, Kathe, and had an odd career of sorts in motion pictures. Having made his film debut in *Excuse My Dust* in the youthful incarnation of the same character his father played in the film, he was closely observed by industry insiders in the years after

(LEFT TO RIGHT) **sons of famous stars: Erich Von Stroheim, Jr., Billy Reid, Carlyle Blackwell, Jr., and Bryant Washburn, Jr., appeared in Joseph Santley's *We Went to College* (1936).**

Wally's death. They wondered if he would grow up to succeed his father in popularity. In 1932, he took a role in *The Racing Strain*, a youth-oriented, auto-racing film written by Dorothy Davenport and directed by Jerome Stern. His full list of credits include:

His Extra Bit (1918) as himself
Young Hollywood (1927) as himself
Excuse My Dust (1920) as "Toodles Jr."
The Masked Avenger (1922) as the School Boy

Billy became "Bill" Reid as an adult. Here he is shown finishing construction of a bridge that led to the home of friends, Alice and Peter Gowland.
PHOTO COURTESY OF ALICE AND PETER GOWLAND.

The Racing Strain (1932) as The Big Shot
This Day and Age (1933) in an unaccredited role as a student
The Hoosier Schoolmaster (1935) as Hank
The Adventures of Frank Merriwell (1936)
Black Friday (1940) in an unaccredited role as a student
Gold Rush Maisie (1940) as Matt Sullivan
King of the Royal Mounted (1940) in an unaccredited role as Constable Doyle
North West Mounted Police (1940) as Constable Rankin
The Yukon Patrol (1942)
The Outlaw (1943) in an unaccredited role as a bystander
Bomber's Moon (1943) in an unaccredited role as a pilot

(LEFT) **Dorothy Davenport next to Betty** (CENTER) **holding Terry, her three-week-old baby, when they were surrounded by other family members at the wedding of Wallace Reid, Jr.**

Later, he was an architect, remodeling and building many canyon homes in the Hollywood Hills, and he helped build air bases in South Vietnam in the 1960s. On February 26, 1990, at the age of seventy-two, he was flying in a home-built single-engine experimental airplane in heavy fog over the ocean near the Santa Monica coast. After about half an hour, at about 11:30 a.m., he lost contact with Jeff Mathieu, Director of the Santa Monica Airport control tower. His airplane encountered deep fog and crashed into the ocean, where he died. Ironically, family members later retold that he had always said "that was the way he would prefer to go when his time was up."

BETTY REID, Wally and Dorothy's daughter, was remembered by her family as "petite and shy." She attended a British school, and later, graduated from Hollywood High School. At age twenty-two,

The short book Wally's mother published after his death was a warm and loving tribute to him, as only a mother could write about her beloved son.
PHOTO COURTESY OF CHRISTOPHER J. DAVIS.

she married Bob MacDonald, and they had one child, Terry. Betty worked as a bank teller, and later as an escrow officer before going into the real estate business. She supported Dorothy with her meager salary after Dorothy suffered many financial setbacks, and she instilled good values in her small daughter, who she raised alone after she and Bob divorced. At age thirty-six, Betty was diagnosed with breast cancer. According to her daughter, she never suffered from depression or mental illness, as has been reported erroneously by others. She took part in brain mapping, and was an early recipient of chemotherapy, which gave her an extra five years to live. She was known for her generosity, supported a Korean orphan, and loved her two small grandsons. At age forty-eight, she lost her fight with brain cancer.

BERTHA WESTBROOK REID, Wally's mother, who was kept from knowing much of what transpired during his final months, successfully published a memoir shortly after his death, explaining, in her own way, his youth and rise to fame.

CHARLES "BUDDY" POST, Wally's intimate friend, after working on *The Hell Diggers* in 1921, appeared in many other silent pictures until the end of the era. After a five-year hiatus, during which he continued to work in motion pictures as an editor, writer, and production manager, he returned for two appearances in talking pictures, and then was not heard from again for many years. In 1940, he suddenly reappeared as Earthquake McGoon in *Li'l Abner*. Buddy passed away on December 20, 1952, in Los Angeles, California.

ADOLPH ZUKOR went on to serve as executive producer on nearly 500 known films. He continued to serve on the Paramount Pictures executive staff, and died on June 10, 1976 in Los Angeles.

JAMES CRUZE, who's real name was James Bosen, directed Wally in fourteen pictures, and he also acted in at least ninety-four known films. He directed seventy-four films, working steadily from 1914 to 1938. Many of the films Cruze directed in the 1920s and 1930s have been lost. He died August 3, 1942.

LILLIAN GISH held a stellar position in silent pictures until talking pictures. She made *One Romantic Night* (1930), and then *His Double Life* (1933). For ten years, she went back to the stage where her peculiar beauty was cherished for decades. When she did return to films in 1943, she played in two big screen films, *Commandos Strike at Dawn* (1942) and *Top Man* (1943). In 1946, she won an Oscar nomination as Best Supporting Actress for her role of Laura Belle McCanles in *Duel in the Sun* (1946). One of her best later roles was in *The Night of the Hunter* (1955). In 1969, Lillian published her autobiography, *The Movies, Mr. Griffith, and Me*. In live television in the 1950s, she appeared in many roles, and returned to motion pictures in a number of films in the 1960s and 1970s. Her last, *The Whales of August* (1987), surprised many by its quality and poignancy. She died on February 27, 1993, in New York.

DOROTHY GISH remained a top star in silent pictures until the end of the era. She appeared in a few talking pictures in the 1930s, but returned to the stage for a long and stellar career that lasted for decades. She returned to films with director Otto Preminger in his 1946 film, *Centennial Summer*. 1950s television brought her to a new audience with a number of roles, and she continued in many stage roles until she was in a successful summer tour with her sister in *The Chalk Garden*. One night, shortly after Lillian was closing in a Broadway play called *I Never Sang for My Father*, a summons from overseas alerted her to a collapse Dorothy suffered. A few days after Lillian reached her on June 4, 1968 in Rapallo, Italy, Dorothy died of bronchial pneumonia.

D. W. GRIFFITH, after directing *The Struggle* (1931) found no further work in the art he helped create. The industry he helped establish bestowed accolades at him, including a 1936 Special Academy Award, and an Honorary Life Member of the Directors Guild of America honor in 1938. In his later years, Griffith lived off income from an annuity he had wisely established when he was earning top money in Hollywood. He died in Los Angeles on July 21, 1948 of a cerebral hemorrhage, virtually forgotten by the world. Mary Pickford, Richard Barthelmess, Lillian Gish, Mae Marsh, and a few other admirers flew to his burial in his hometown in Kentucky.

MAE MURRAY, who began in films with a starring role in *To Have and to Hold* (1916) with Wally, continued as a top silent film star until the end of the 1920s. She starred in a few early talkie films, *Peacock Alley* (1930), *Bachelor Apartment* (1931), and *High Stakes* (1931), but after the crash of the stock market and the horrors of the depression in the early 1930s, her film career as an exotic, fantasy creature had passed its vogue. In her later years, a sort of dementia seemed to overcome her. She co-wrote her autobiography in 1959, and spent her last days in the Motion Picture Country Home, in Woodland Hills, California. Frances Marion observed her slow demise wistfully in her autobiography: "Mae Murray never knew that she had found her way home; her disturbed mind was aware of nothing beyond her pitiful vanity. 'Step aside, peasants! Let the Princess Mdivani pass!' she demanded imperiously of the nurses who came forward to help her into the hospital. 'Where are the cameras? Where are my flowers? I must be photographed with flowers! Get them before I'm surrounded by cameramen!' A doctor came forward. 'If you're a Hearst reporter, be sure to mention that I've just finished my memoirs.' She wheeled on the nurses. 'Music! I always make my entrance with music! Have your orchestra play *The Merry Widow Waltz*. That's the number I made famous.' She held out her hand to the doctor. 'May I introduce myself? I'm Mae Murray, the young Ziegfeld beauty with the bee-stung lips—and Hollywood is calling me.' He caught her in his arms as she slumped forward. 'Poor old thing,' said one of the nurses. . . ." She died in 1965.

CECIL B. DEMILLE had one of Hollywood's longest careers as a producer, director, editor, writer, and actor. He appeared as himself most notably in *Sunset Boulevard* (1950), and loved performing the voice-over narrations for many of his talking pictures. Best known for the Biblical epics, *The King of Kings* (1927), and *The Ten Commandments* (1923) and (1956), he was also an institution in American homes on radio from 1936 to 1945 as the host and director the hour-long *Lux Radio Theatre*, which brought audio dramatizations of popular movies to the airwaves. He died on January 21, 1959 from a heart ailment.

JESSE LASKY was executive producer on at least 441 movies, and official producer on 129, including all of Wally's Paramount films. He died on January 13, 1958.

LOU-TELLEGEN appeared in a number of Fox films throughout the remainder of the silent era. Then, after a return to the stage, he came down with cancer and endured three operations. After token appearances in a couple of talking pictures, the depression took its toll on his career. By May 1934, his funds were nearly depleted. He found a free room within the home of an old friend of fifteen years, Floria Cudahy, the widow of John P. Cudahy, the Chicago meet packer's son. There, on one dismal morning on November 2, 1934, a butler found Lou lying on the floor of the bathroom clad in his silk bathrobe. In the sink below the mirror laid the bloody pair of golden scissors with which he had stabbed himself seven times until dying.

GERALDINE FARRAR retired from the screen after only a few years. Her film career was entirely in fifteen silent pictures, and she never made a talking picture that captured her singing voice. Her marriage to Lou-Tellegen ended in a drawn-out, bitter divorce that played across front-page headlines for many months. She never remarried. Although she abhorred microphones and records, there are many recordings of her voice in its splendidly youthful tones. She retired from performing, and devoted her life to working for the Red Cross, hosting radio broadcasts of famous operas, delivering lectures, and writing two autobiographies. She died on March 11, 1967.

GLORIA SWANSON remained a top star to the end of the silent era. She was nominated for an Academy Award for *The Trespasser* (1929), made five pictures during the 1930s, one in 1941, and then experienced a major comeback in *Sunset Boulevard* in 1950. Over the next three decades, she successfully recast her public image as businesswoman, artist, and food faddist with three occasional film appearances. Gloria died April 4, 1983.

PORTRAIT GALLERY

FILMOGRAPHY

FILMOGRAPHY

Most of Wally's films are no longer in existence, or they are held in archives and are not available for viewing. Still photographs and film reviews from issues of *Moving Picture World*, *Motion Picture News*, *Variety*, the *New York Times*, and other newspapers and magazines from 1910-1923 have been the only means for analysis for many of those lost films. This Filmography details reviews from most of Wally's feature films from 1915 to 1923. The reviews contain valuable and fascinating information about the producers, cast, and story content. To show how he and his work were received in their time, comparisons are made between the industry publications, major city newspapers, and small town newspapers.

THE PHOENIX (1910)
SELIG POLYSCOPE
DIRECTOR: Milton Nobles
CAST: Milton Nobles, Dollie Nobles, Wallace Reid, Sam Pickens, Fred Walton, Karl King, Barbara Swager.
SYNOPSIS: Reid portrays a youthful reporter for a major newspaper. While working on a story, he saves a girl from drowning and from being burned to death.

THE COURTING OF THE MERRY WIDOW (1910)
VITAGRAPH
DIRECTOR: Unknown
CAST: Wallace Reid and unknown players
SYNOPSIS: A brief fight follows for two men after their attentions for the affection of a rich widow conflict with each other.

This advertisement for the Alvin Japanese Theater appeared in the *Mansfield News*, July 22, 1910, and it heralded *The Phoenix*, Wally's first appearance in a motion picture, as "a drama of unusual merit."

THE LEADING LADY (1911)
VITAGRAPH
DIRECTOR: Ned Finley
CAST: John Bunny, Van Dyke Brooke, Wallace Reid, Robert Gaillard.
SYNOPSIS: Bunny convinces an Irish cook to take a major role in a stage play. Her display of temperament proves that women of her type are more volatile than professional actresses.

THE REPORTER (1911)
SELIG POLYSCOPE
DIRECTOR: Unknown
CAST: Fred Waltan, Sam Pickens, Karl King, Barbara Swager, Wallace Reid.
SYNOPSIS: As an assistant to a newspaper reporter, Reid appears along side the journalist as he essays a story, "How It Feels to Be a Burglar."

WAR (1911)
SELIG POLYSCOPE
DIRECTOR: Unknown
CAST: Wallace Reid, Edward Brady, Mary Maurice, Rose Tapley, Charles Kent

THE PATHFINDER (1911)
VITAGRAPH
DIRECTOR: Laurence Trimbler
CAST: Wallace Reid, Hal Reid

LEATHER STOCKING TALES (1911)
VITAGRAPH
DIRECTOR: Laurence Trimble
CAST: Wallace Reid and unknown cast

A RED CROSS MARTYR; OR ON THE FIRING LINES OF TRIPOLI (1911)
VITAGRAPH
DIRECTOR: Laurence Trimble
CAST: Wallace Reid, Rosemary Theby, Anita Stewart, Florence Turner, Robert Gaillard

HIS SON (1912)
RELIANCE
DIRECTOR: Milton J. Fahrney
CAST: Henry B. Walthall, Wallace Reid, Dorothy Davenport

(TOP) **William Shea, John Bunny, Wallace Reid, Marshall P. Wilder, and Leah Baird in *Chumps* (1912).** (BOTTOM) **John Bunny, Wallace Reid, Van Dyke Brooke, and unknown actor in *The Leading Lady* (1911).**

CHUMPS (1912)
VITAGRAPH
DIRECTOR: George D. Baker; Written by Wallace Reid
CAST: Wallace Reid, Leah Baird, William Shea, John Bunny, Marshall P. Wilder.
SYNOPSIS: Appearing as George The Denouement, Reid portrays a flying trapeze artist.

> **NEW PHOTOPLAY**
>
> Vitagraph   Gaumont   Pathe
>
> Chumps - - - - Vitagraph Comedy
> Marshall P. Wilder and John Bunny. A ripping good laugh.
> Uncle Ned's Diplomacy - - Gaumont Comedy
> A pleasant comedy, pretty well acted and interesting.
> Bonoparte and Pichegru - - - - Pathe
> An unusually good historical drama.
> Here and there in China - - - Travelog.
>
> *Three Splendid Reels*

"*Chumps*, one of Wallace Reid's first pictures at Vitagraph, starred rotund comic, John Bunny, and it was advertised in *The Gettysburg Times*, April 15, 1912, on page 1. "A pleasant comedy, pretty well acted and interesting," the advertisement claimed.

JEAN INTERVENES (1912)
VITAGRAPH
DIRECTOR: Unknown
CAST: Hal Reid, Florence Turner, Edith Halleran, Jean the Vitagraph Dog, Wallace Reid.
SYNOPSIS: Jean plays cupid, bringing about reconciliation for a couple who quarrel when the man becomes jealous over the Collie's bond with the woman.

INDIAN ROMEO AND JULIET (1912)
VITAGRAPH
DIRECTOR: Laurence Trimble
CAST: Florence Turner, Wallace Reid, Harry T. Morey, Hal Reid, Mrs. Adelaide Ober, Harold Wilson.
SYNOPSIS: William Shakespeare's *Romeo and Juliet* is transposed by scenarist, Hal Reid, into a tale of American Indians with Wally appearing as a Huron Indian in love with a girl from the Mohawk tribe.

A scene from the Vitagraph drama, *The Seventh Son* (1912), with Earle Williams, William R. Dunn, Mary Maurice, Wallace Reid, James Morrison, and Robert Gaillard.

THE TELEPHONE GIRL (1912)
VITAGRAPH
DIRECTOR: Unknown
CAST: Edith Storey, Wallace Reid
SYNOPSIS: After bravely warning all tenants of a burning building to escape to safety, a telephone operator becomes trapped. Reid appears as her boyfriend, a fireman who rescues her.

THE SEVENTH SON (1912)
VITAGRAPH
DIRECTOR: Hal Reid
CAST: Wallace Reid, Mary Maurice, Earle Williams, James Morrison, William R. Dunn, Robert Gaillard, Tefft Johnson, Ralph Ince.
SYNOPSIS: In a story by Hal Reid, Mary Maurice plays a widow who sacrifices six of her seven sons to the Union Army in the Civil War. Her seventh son enlists, proves to be a coward while under fire, and

is condemned to die. The widow pleads with Abraham Lincoln to spare her sons life.

THE ILLUMINATION (1912)
VITAGRAPH
DIRECTOR: Charles L. Gaskill
CAST: Wallace Reid, Tom Powers, Helen Gardner, Rosemary Theby, Harry Northrup, Rose Tapley.
SYNOPSIS: A drama about a Heavenly light emanating from a Christ figure and touching the lives of all who cast their gaze on It.

AT SCROGGINS CORNER (1912)
VITAGRAPH
DIRECTOR: Unknown
CAST: Wallace Reid and unknown cast

THE BROTHERS (1912)
CHAMPION
DIRECTOR: George Field
CAST: Wallace Reid, Frank B. Coigne, Miss Orlamond, Charles Hoskins, Evelyn Francis.
SYNOPSIS: Two brothers are separated in their youth. As adults, one becomes a soldier while the other joins the priesthood. Later, they reunite when the wounded turncoat of a soldier finds refuge in his brother's church.

THE VICTORIA CROSS (1912)
VITAGRAPH
DIRECTOR: Hal Reid
CAST: Wallace Reid, Edith Storey, Tefft Johnson, Julia Swayne Gordon, Rose Tapley.
SYNOPSIS: In a story by Hal Reid, a Lieutenant crosses paths with Queen Victoria and Florence Nightingale before saving the life of a Colonel and wining both the Victoria Cross and the hand of the colonel's daughter.

THE HIEROGLYPHIC (1912)
VITAGRAPH
DIRECTOR: Charles L. Gaskill
CAST: Wallace Reid, Zena Keefe, Tom Powers, Harry Northrup, Edwin R. Phillips.
SYNOPSIS: A young man overcomes the temptation to wrangle the heroine out of her inheritance.

DIAMOND CUT DIAMOND (1912)
VITAGRAPH
DIRECTOR: Unknown
CAST: John Bunny, Flora Finch, Wallace Reid, Richard Rosson, Ray Ford, Jack Standing, Mae Costello, Kate Price.
SYNOPSIS: Bunny's wife masquerades as a man to win a bet.

CURFEW SHALL NOT RING TONIGHT (1912)
RELIANCE
DIRECTOR: Hal Reid
CAST: Wallace Reid and unknown cast
SYNOPSIS: A dramatic film written by Hal Reid and based on the famous poem by Rose Hartwick Thorpe in which the heroine prevents the execution of her lover by swinging on the clapper of a bell to silence its chime at dawn.

KAINTUCK (1912)
RELIANCE
DIRECTOR: Hal Reid
CAST: Wallace Reid, Gertrude Robinson, Robert Tabor, Virginia Westbrooke.
SYNOPSIS: In a story by Reid, Wally plays a mountaineer who is resentful of a city artist painting his girlfriend until he learns the artist is actually in love with the girl's younger sister.

BEFORE THE WHITE MAN CAME (1912)
RELIANCE
DIRECTOR: Otis Turner
CAST: Wallace Reid, Gertrude Robinson.
SYNOPSIS: In a story by Reid, Wally portrays an Indian who kills

himself after his sweetheart dies rescuing him from harm.

A MAN'S DUTY (1912)
RELIANCE
DIRECTOR: Hal Reid
CAST: Wallace Reid, Hector Dion, Charles Herman, George Siegmann, Sue Balfour, Edward P. Sullivan.
SYNOPSIS: In the Civil War, a Union officer disguised as a Confederate officer is captured and sentenced to death by his Confederate father but saved from execution by a last-minute pardon.

AT CRIPPLE CREEK (1912)
RELIANCE
DIRECTOR: Hal Reid
CAST: Wallace Reid, Sue Balfour, Gertrude Robinson.
SYNOPSIS: A Western melodrama scenario by Reid based on a Hal Reid play.

HIS ONLY SON (1912)
NESTOR-UNIVERSAL
DIRECTOR: Milton H. Farhney
CAST: Wallace Reid, Dorothy Davenport, Jack Conway, Victoria Forde, Hoot Gibson.
   Noteworthy as the first film Wally made in Hollywood, and the first film pairing him with Dorothy Davenport.
SYNOPSIS: An Easterner comes out West, and is mistaken for an outlaw. His arrest spurs a rancher's daughter to prove his innocence and win his love.

MAKING GOOD (1912)
IMP-UNIVERSAL
CAST: Wallace Reid, Jane Fernley, William R. Dunn, Joseph S. Chailee.
SYNOPSIS: The hero romances a girl and faces objections by her father. After he rescues her at Brighton Beach, her father relents and consents to their love.

THE SECRET SERVICE MAN (1912)
RELIANCE
DIRECTOR: Unknown
CAST: Wallace Reid, Rodman Law.
SYNOPSIS: An enemy undercover agent steals top-secret plans, and is pursued and captured in a thrilling chase on automobile, motorcycle, horse, plane, and train.

INDIAN RAIDERS (1912)
BISON / UNIVERSAL
DIRECTOR: Tom Ricketts
CAST: Wallace Reid and unknown cast
SYNOPSIS: Two cowboys in love with the same girl fight for her affection.

EVERY INCH A MAN (1912)
VITAGRAPH
DIRECTOR: William Humphrey
CAST: Hal Reid, Wallace Reid, Rose Tapley, Robert Gaillard, Morris McGee, Frank Mason.
SYNOPSIS: In a story by Hal Reid, two detectives go on the hunt for a criminal, and a country boy helps bring the culprit to justice.

THE TRIBAL LAW (1912)
BISON / UNIVERSAL
DIRECTOR: Otis Turner (some sources claim Wallace Reid)
CAST: Wallace Reid, Margarita Fischer, Charles Inslee.
SYNOPSIS: In this story of an Indian romance, an Apache brave and a Hopi squaw suffer a death penalty exacted by their tribes when they marry. They escape to Mexico and freedom.

LOVE AND THE LAW (1912)
AMERICAN
DIRECTOR: Wallace Reid
CAST: Wallace Reid, Lillian Christy, Edward Coxen.
SYNOPSIS: Reid appears as a sheriff who must decide between love and justice when his girlfriend's brother is captured for committing a theft.

THE COWBOY GUARDIANS (1912)
BISON /UNIVERSAL
DIRECTOR: Unknown
CAST: Wallace Reid, Charles Inslee, Sylvia Ashton.

HIS MOTHER'S SON (1912)
RELIANCE
DIRECTOR: William Christy Cabanne
CAST: Wallace Reid and unknown cast
SYNOPSIS: A family's security is threatened by the wanton ways of their degenerate son. He reforms, and raises their status to a respectable one.

THE GAMBLERS (1912)
VITAGRAPH
DIRECTOR: Unknown
CAST: Wallace Reid, Zena Keefe, Earle Williams, Julia Swayne Gordon, Leah Baird.
SYNOPSIS: A Western based on a play by Charles Klein.

AN UNSEEN ENEMY (1912)
BIOGRAPH
DIRECTOR: D. W. Griffith
CAST: Lillian Gish, Dorothy Gish, Robert Harron, Elmer Booth, Harry Carey, Grace Henderson, Adolph Lestina, Walter Miller. Appearing as unaccredited extras are Antonio Moreno, Charles Hill Mailes, Mary Gish, and some sources claim Wallace Reid as a man on the bridge.
SYNOPSIS: A physician dies and leaves his two adolescent daughters orphaned. Money from the estate is stored in a safe, which is burglarized by a drunken, slattern maid and her accomplices. The two orphans are terrorized before help arrives in a last minute rescue.

The film is noteworthy as the first starring motion picture of both Lillian and Dorothy Gish.

EARLY DAYS IN THE WEST (1912)
BISON / UNIVERSAL
DIRECTOR: Unknown

CAST: Wallace Reid, Dolly Larkin, George Field, Ray Francis, W. G. Rice, Paul Machette.
SYNOPSIS: A Western about a girl, a young pioneer, and an Indian scout.

HUNTED DOWN (1912)
BISON / UNIVERSAL
DIRECTOR: Unknown
CAST: Wallace Reid, Charles Inslee, William Clifford, Margaret Manners, Lizette Thorn.

AN INDIAN OUTCAST (1912)
BISON / UNIVERSAL
DIRECTOR: Unknown
CAST: Wallace Reid, Charles Inslee, William Steel, Chief Harvey, Ravena, Margarita Fischer, Edward H. Philbrook, Harry Tenbrook.

ALL FOR A GIRL (1912)
VITAGRAPH
DIRECTOR: Frederick A. Tomson; Written by Wallace Reid
CAST: Wallace Reid, Dorothy Kelly, Leah Baird, Harry T. Morey, Kate Price, Earle Foxe, Darwin Karr.

THE SEEPORE REBELLION (1912)
VITAGRAPH
DIRECTOR: unknown
CAST: James Morrison. Wallace Reid appears as an unaccredited extra.

THE COURSE OF TRUE LOVE (1912)
VITAGRAPH
DIRECTOR: Unknown
CAST: Wallace Reid, Edith Halleran, Hal Reid, Laurence Trimble, Florence Turner.

VIRGINIUS (1912)
VITAGRAPH
DIRECTOR: Hal Reid
CAST: Wallace Reid, Hal Reid

SYNOPSIS: In a story by Hal Reid from a play by James Sheridan Knowles.

THE DEERSLAYER (1912)
VITAGRAPH
DIRECTOR: Hal Reid
CAST: Florence Turner, Hal Reid, Wallace Reid, Harry T. Morey, Ethel Dunn, Edward Thomas, Evelyn Dominicus, William F. Cooper.
SYNOPSIS: Eugene Mullin fashioned this adaptation of the famous James Fennimore Cooper tale of frontiersmen in the 1740's. Reid appears as Chingachgook, the Delaware Indian chief.

A DAUGHTER OF THE REDSKINS (1912)
BISON / UNIVERSAL
DIRECTOR: Frank Montgomery
CAST: Wallace Reid, Charles Inslee, Harry Tenbrook, William Messick, Lizette Thorn, Dolly Larkin.
SYNOPSIS: A Western about a conflict between the U.S. Army and Sioux Indians.

THE HIDDEN TREASURE (1912)
AKA THE PHILANDERINGS OF PUDDENFOOT PETE
FLYING A / FILM SUPPLY COMPANY OF AMERICA
DIRECTOR: Wallace Reid and Allan Dwan
CAST: Lillian Christy, Edward Coxen, Wallace Reid
SYNOPSIS: After selling his ranch, Bill Binks runs into trouble with his cash, but ends up giving what remains of the money to an injured man and his wife, and then falls to sleep on his lumber pile.

THE PATH OF TRUE LOVE (1912)
UNIVERSAL
CAST: Wallace Reid, Florence Turner, Laurence Trimble, Edith Halleran, Hal Reid.

LOVE AND THE LAW (1913)
AMERICAN
DIRECTOR: Wallace Reid
CAST: Wallace Reid, Lillian Christy, Edward Coxen.

Wallace Reid in a loincloth in Vitagraph's *The Deerslayer* (1912), in one of the many Indian roles he played for that studio.

HIS MOTHER'S SON (1913)
BIOGRAPH
DIRECTOR: D. W. Griffith
CAST: Wallace Reid, Gertrude Robinson.

THE WAYS OF FATE (1913)
AMERICAN
DIRECTOR: Wallace Reid
CAST: Wallace Reid, Vivian Rich, Pauline Bush, Lon Chaney, Murdock McQuarrie.
SYNOPSIS: When his father is killed, a young man hunts down his murderer. His pursuit leads into the mountains where he falls in love with a girl whose father is the killer.

THE WALL OF MONEY (1913)
REX-UNIVERSAL
DIRECTOR: Allan Dwan
CAST: Wallace Reid, Pauline Bush, Marshall Neilan, Jessalyn Van Trump, James McQuarrie.
SYNOPSIS: In a story by Marshall Neilan, a young man returns from college to visit his father's factory. The penny-pinching conditions cause workers to resort to a violent strike, prompting the young man to influence his father to upgrade to more modern methods.

THE MYSTERY OF THE YELLOW ASTER MINE (1913)
BISON / UNIVERSAL
DIRECTOR: Frank Borzage
CAST: Wallace Reid, Pauline Bush, Arthur Rosson, Frank Borzage.
SYNOPSIS: In a story by Bess Meredyth, an innocent Indian is executed, and white settlers face an epic battle with his tribe.

THE GUERILLA MENACE (1913)
BISON / UNIVERSAL
DIRECTOR: Allan Dwan
CAST: Marshall Neilan, Wallace Reid

THE ANIMAL (1913)
REX-UNIVERSAL

Pauline Bush and Wallace Reid in Allan Dwan's *The Wall of Money* (1913).

DIRECTOR: Allan Dwan
CAST: Wallace Reid, Pauline Bush, Marshall Neilan, Jessalyn Van Trump.
SYNOPSIS: In a story by Allan Dwan, a brawny but uncomplicated brute becomes resentful of his wife's affection for their newborn son.

MAN'S DUTY (1913)
REX-UNIVERSAL
DIRECTOR: Allan Dwan
CAST: Wallace Reid, Marshall Neilan, Jessalyn Van Trump, Pauline Bush.
SYNOPSIS: When a self-centered man in the old West ignores his responsibility to a woman, his point of view is changed by the intervention of a blind girl.

Marshall Neilan and Wallace Reid in Allan Dwan's two-reel Bison film, *The Guerilla Menace* (1913).

THE PICKET GUARD (1913)
BISON / UNIVERSAL
DIRECTOR: Allan Dwan
CAST: Wallace Reid, Pauline Bush, Marshall Neilan, Jesselyn Van Trump, David Kirkland.

SYNOPSIS: In a story by Arthur Rosson, based on a poem by Ethel Lynn Beers, the life story of a Civil War soldier is told in flashbacks before he is killed while on sentry duty at the Potomac.

IN LOVE AND WAR (1913)
AKA THE CALL TO ARMS
BISON / UNIVERSAL
DIRECTOR: Allan Dwan
CAST: Wallace Reid, Pauline Bush, Marshall Neilan
SYNOPSIS: In a story by Allan Dwan, a one-armed journalist in the Civil War overcomes his handicap to perform a heroic deed that surprises his comrades and his sweetheart.

THEIR MASTERPIECE (1913)
AMERICAN
DIRECTOR: Allan Dwan
CAST: J. Warren Kerrigan, Wallace Reid, Pauline Bush.

PIRATE GOLD (1913)
BIOGRAPH
DIRECTOR: Wilfred Lucas
CAST: Blanche Sweet, Charles Hill Mailes, J. Jiquel Lanoe, Hector Sarno, W. Chrystie Miller, Harry Carey, Donald Crisp, Joseph MacDermott, Wallace Reid.

WHEN THE LIGHT FADES (1913)
AMERICAN
DIRECTOR: Allan Dwan
CAST: Wallace Reid, Lillian Christy, Eugene Pallette, Edward Coxen.

NEAR TO EARTH (1913)
BIOGRAPH
DIRECTOR: D. W. Griffith
CAST: Lionel Barrymore, Robert Harron, Gertrude Bambrick, Mae Marsh, Kathleen Butler, Walter Miller, Dorothy Bernard, Christy Cabanne, Harry Carey, Donald Crisp, Charles Hill Mailes, Joseph McDermott, Frank Opperman, Mabel Normand, Wallace Reid, Blanch Sweet.

WHEN JIM RETURNED (1913)
AMERICAN
DIRECTOR: Wallace Reid
CAST: Wallace Reid, Vivian Rich, Eugene Palette.
SYNOPSIS: In a story by Reid, the title character returns from college to face a coming-home party at his family ranch. Comic mix-ups follow.

THE KISS (1913)
AMERICAN
DIRECTOR: Wallace Reid
CAST: Wallace Reid
SYNOPSIS: Ralph Walters, an artist from the big city, falls in love with the daughter of a country trapper.

THE SPIRIT OF THE FLAG (1913)
BISON / UNIVERSAL
DIRECTOR: Allan Dwan
CAST: Wallace Reid, Pauline Bush, Jessalyn Van Trump, Arthur Rosson, David Kirkland, Marshall Neilan.
SYNOPSIS: In a story by Reid, a teacher and a doctor working with islanders in the Philippines fall in love and share the meaning of freedom with the natives.

WOMEN AND WAR (1913)
BISON / UNIVERSAL
DIRECTOR: Allan Dwan
CAST: Wallace Reid, Pauline Bush, Jessalyn Van Trump, Marshall Neilan.
SYNOPSIS: A story by Reid of love, heartache, and intrigue surround a Virginia soldier during the Civil War.

MENTAL SUICIDE (1913)
POWERS-UNIVERSAL
DIRECTOR: Allan Dwan
CAST: Wallace Reid, Pauline Bush, Jessalyn Van Trump, Marshall Neilan, David Kirkland.
SYNOPSIS: In a story by Reid, a young contractor accepts a corrupt

Pauline Bush and Wallace Reid in Allan Dwan's *Women and War* (1913).

kickback, which accidentally causes the death of his sweetheart.

THE HARVEST OF FLAME (1913)
REX-UNIVERSAL
DIRECTOR: Wallace Reid
CAST: Wallace Reid, Pauline Bush, Marshall Neilan, William Walters.

SYNOPSIS: In a story by Reid, a cigarette smoker causes a disastrous fire in an overall factory, prompting a safety inspector to save a girl in a last-minute rescue.

THE CRACKSMAN'S REFORMATION (1913)
POWERS-UNIVERSAL
DIRECTOR: Willis Robards
CAST: Wallace Reid, Dorothy Davenport, Edward Brady, James Neill.
SYNOPSIS: In a story by Reid, a suave cracksman uses a gun to force a wealthy man to help a needy person.

A CRACKSMAN SANTA CLAUSE (1913)
POWERS-UNIVERSAL
DIRECTOR: Willis Robards
CAST: Wallace Reid, Dorothy Davenport, Gertrude Short, Frank Borzage, Edward Brady.
SYNOPSIS: In a story by Reid, a suave cracksman saves a poor girl from a life of crime.

DEAD MAN'S SHOES (1913)
AMERICAN
DIRECTOR: Wallace Reid
CAST: Wallace Reid, Vivian Rich, George Field.
SYNOPSIS: In a story by Wallace Reid, a hobo finds a place in the world and the love of a woman when he switches identity with a dead man.

A ROSE OF OLD MEXICO (1913)
AMERICAN
DIRECTOR: Wallace Reid and Allan Dwan
CAST: Wallace Reid, Lillian Christy, Edward Coxen, Chet Withey.
SYNOPSIS: A father disapproves of the marriage plans of Paquita, his daughter, and disowns the girl. The daughter and her fiancé are accused of his death after he accidentally kills himself.

THE GRATITUDE OF WANDA (1913)
BISON / UNIVERSAL
CAST: Wallace Reid, Arthur Rosson, Pauline Bush, Jessalyn Van

Dorothy Davenport and Wallace Reid in *A Cracksman Santa Claus* (1913).

Trump, Frank Borzage.
SYNOPSIS: In a story by Bess Meredyth, a cowboy befriends an Indian maiden who comes to his rescue when his cabin is attacked in a hostile raid.

THE HEART OF A CRACKSMAN (1913)
POWERS-UNIVERSAL
DIRECTOR: Wallace Reid
CAST: Wallace Reid, Cleo Madison, James Neill, Edward Brady, Marcia Moore.
SYNOPSIS: In a story by Reid, a suave crook visits the home of a decadently extravagant heiress and foils the efforts of other thieves to rob her.

CROSS PURPOSES (1913)
POWERS-UNIVERSAL
DIRECTOR: Wallace Reid
CAST: Wallace Reid, Cleo Madison, James Neill.
SYNOPSIS: In a story by Bess Meredyth, a man and woman are brought together for an arranged marriage but find love erupts despite their initial reluctance.

RETRIBUTION (1913)
NESTOR-UNIVERSAL
DIRECTOR: Wallace Reid
CAST: Wallace Reid, Dorothy Davenport, Edward Brady, Phil Dunham.
SYNOPSIS: When a jealous landowner dynamites a Mexico mine owned by a man and his daughter, a young man comes to their rescue.

THE LIGHTNING BOLT (1913)
NESTOR-UNIVERSAL
DIRECTOR: Wallace Reid
CAST: Wallace Reid, Dorothy Davenport, Edward Brady, Phil Dunham, Frank Borzage.
SYNOPSIS: A love triangle is broken when a lightning bolt kills a mounted policeman who attempted murder on another Mountie.

YOUTH AND JEALOUSY (1913)
AMERICAN
DIRECTOR: Wallace Reid
CAST: Wallace Reid and Vivian Rich, Frank Borzage.
SYNOPSIS: In a story by Theodosia Harris, Bill Higgins, a jealous

Wallace Reid and Cleo Madison in *The Heart of a Cracksman* (1913).

rival thwarts romance between a pretty girl and another cowboy.

WHEN LUCK CHANGES (1913)
AMERICAN
DIRECTOR: Allan Dwan, Wallace Reid
CAST: Wallace Reid, Vivian Rich, George Field.
SYNOPSIS: In a story by Hal Reid, Wally appears as a young prospector who marries the wife of a deceased gambler after he finds fortune with his mining expedition.

VIA CABARET (1913)
AMERICAN
DIRECTOR: Wallace Reid
CAST: Wallace Reid, George Field.
SYNOPSIS: In a story by Hal Reid, Wally plays Harry Reeder, a cabaret performer who clashes with another performer for the affections of a female entertainer.

THE TATTOOED ARM (1913)
AMERICAN
DIRECTOR: Wallace Reid
CAST: Wallace Reid, Vivian Rich, Eugene Pallette, George Field.
SYNOPSIS: In a story by Reid, a tattoo on the arm of a thief is the tell-tale clue that enables Ben Hart, a mining expert, to catch the crook and save the mine for a girl.

PRIDE OF LONESOME (1913)
AMERICAN
DIRECTOR: Wallace Reid
CAST: Wallace Reid, Vivian Rich, Frank Borzage.
SYNOPSIS: In a story by Hal Reid, an orphan girl befriends Ed Daton, a cowboy, and later, when she has matured into womanhood, she again turns to him for protection against an unwanted suitor.

A MODERN SNARE (1913)
AMERICAN
DIRECTOR: Wallace Reid
CAST: Wallace Reid, Vivian Rich, George Field.
SYNOPSIS: When new sheriff of a town finds his reputation harmed by the old sheriff, his wife gets involved in the conflict and helps bring about a happy conclusion.

THE POWDER FLASH OF DEATH (1913)
AKA THE MENACE
BISON / UNIVERSAL
DIRECTOR: Allan Dwan
CAST: Wallace Reid, Pauline Bush, Marshall Neilan, David Kirkland, Jessalyn Van Trump.

SYNOPSIS: In a story of the Civil War by Allan Dwan, soldiers on opposing sides die together on the same battlefield and share their love of a Dixie girl.

A HOPI LEGEND (1913)
NESTOR-UNIVERSAL
DIRECTOR: Wallace Reid
CAST: Wallace Reid, Dorothy Davenport, Edward Brady, Phil Dunham, Frank Borzage
SYNOPSIS: In a story by Reid, an Indian maiden dies after saving her sweetheart from harm.

HER INNOCENT MARRIAGE (1913)
AMERICAN
DIRECTOR: Wallace Reid and Allan Dwan
CAST: Wallace Reid, Vivian Rich, George Field.
SYNOPSIS: In a story by Theodosia Harris, a girl's life is nearly ruined when she passes the chance to marry the best man for her and takes up with a drunkard.

HEARTS AND HORSES (1913)
AMERICAN
DIRECTOR: Allan Dwan and Wallace Reid
CAST: Wallace Reid, Vivian Rich, George Field.
SYNOPSIS: Thieves steal the horse belonging to Wally's sweetheart, and although he is jealous of her attentions to the horse, he pursues the culprits and returns the steed to the girl.

A FOREIGN SPY (1913)
AMERICAN
DIRECTOR: Wallace Reid
CAST: Wallace Reid, Vivian Rich, Frank Borzage.
SYNOPSIS: In a story by Hal Reid, intrigue and espionage come between the daughter of an army man and her sweetheart.

THE PICTURE OF DORIAN GRAY (1913)
NEW YORK MOTION PICTURE COMPANY
DIRECTOR: Phillips Smalley

CAST: Wallace Reid, Lois Weber, Phillips Smalley.
SYNOPSIS: Based on the famous novel by Oscar Wilde, Wally plays the man who sees his disintegrating face in a portrait.

THE EYE OF A GOD (1913)
PYRAMID-WARNERS
DIRECTOR: Joseph A. Golden
CAST: Chester Barnett, Octavia Handworth, Earl Metcalfe, Wallace Reid.

THE FIRES OF FATE (1913)
REX-UNIVERSAL
DIRECTOR: Wallace Reid
CAST: Wallace Reid, Dorothy Davenport, Edward Brady.
SYNOPSIS: In a story by Reid, Wally rescues a pretty girl from a fire in one of her father's dilapidated tenement buildings.

JUDITH OF BETHULIA (1913)
BIOGRAPH
DIRECTOR: D. W. Griffith
CAST: Blanche Sweet, Henry B. Walthall, Mae Marsh, Robert Harron, J. Jiquel Lanoe, Harry Carey, Lillian Gish, Dorothy Gish, Kate Bruce, Elmo Lincoln, Wallace Reid.
SYNOPSIS: Judith, Queen of the Judean fortress of Bethulia, becomes the savior of the city when she seduces and beheads Assyrian king, Holofernes.

SONG BIRD OF THE NORTH (1913)
NESTOR-UNIVERSAL
DIRECTOR: Ralph Ince
CAST: Anita Stewart, Ralph Ince, Wallace Reid, E. K. Lincoln, Harry T. Morey, Gladden James, Rose Tapley, Ned Finley, Josie Sadler, Mary Maurice.

THE GREATER LOVE (1913)
DIRECTOR: Allan Dwan
CAST: Mabel Brown, Charlotte Burton, Edward Coxen, George Field, Wallace Reid.

Wallace Reid and Dorothy Davenport in the Wallace Reid-directed *The Countess Betty's Mine* (1914).

THE INTRUDER (1914)
Nestor-Universal
Director: Wallace Reid
Cast: Wallace Reid, Dorothy Davenport, Edward Brady, Phil Dunham.
Synopsis: A woodsman nearly loses his sweetheart to a man from the city when he leaves town to build a home in the country.

THE COUNTESS BETTY'S MINE (1914)
Nestor-Universal
Director: Wallace Reid

CAST: Wallace Reid, Dorothy Davenport, Edward Brady, Phil Dunham.
SYNOPSIS: In a story by Bess Meredyth, an English girl inherits a mine out West and goes to the claim with her brother. The brother clashes with a mining superintendent and attempts to blow up the mine, dying in the explosion.

THE WHEEL OF LIFE (1914)
NESTOR-UNIVERSAL
DIRECTOR: Wallace Reid
CAST: Wallace Reid, Dorothy Davenport, Edward Brady, Frank Borzage, Lucile Wilson, John G. Blystone.
SYNOPSIS: In a story based on a play by James B. Fagan, an intruder on a mining territory kidnaps a prospector's wife and child. When they die, the prospector avenges the crime and brings the man to justice.

FIRES OF CONSCIENCE (1914)
NESTOR-UNIVERSAL
DIRECTOR: Wallace Reid
CAST: Wallace Reid, Dorothy Davenport, Gertrude Robinson, Edward Brady.
SYNOPSIS: In a story by Henry Warnack, love and the lust for gold erupt in the desert as two prospectors vie for the attentions of a pretty girl.

THE GREATER DEVOTION (1914)
NESTOR-UNIVERSAL
DIRECTOR: Wallace Reid
CAST: Wallace Reid, Dorothy Davenport, Fred Gamble, Edward Brady, Phil Dunham.
SYNOPSIS: Love, Wealth, and Devotion are put to the test in an allegorical drama of life in old California.

A FLASH IN THE DARK (1914)
NESTOR-UNIVERSAL
DIRECTOR: Wallace Reid
CAST: Wallace Reid, Dorothy Davenport, Edward Brady, Frank Borzage.

SYNOPSIS: In a story based on a play by James Dayton, a mine explosion leaves a newly married prospector blind, but he uses his wits and senses to protect his bride. A gunfight in the dark puts him on equal ground with another man challenging his rights.

BREED O' THE MOUNTAINS (1914)
NESTOR-UNIVERSAL
DIRECTOR: Wallace Reid
CAST: Wallace Reid, Dorothy Davenport, Edward Brady, Lucile Wilson.
SYNOPSIS: In a story by Harry G. Stafford, a woodsman finds an abandoned baby and searches for a bride to give the child a proper home.

THE MOUNTAINEER (1914)
NESTOR-UNIVERSAL
DIRECTOR: Wallace Reid
CAST: Wallace Reid, Dorothy Davenport, Phil Dunham, Lucile Wilson, Edward Brady.
SYNOPSIS: In a story by Reid, a remake of *Kaintuck*, Wally plays a mountaineer who is resentful of a city artist painting his girlfriend until he learns the artist is actually in love with the girl's younger sister.

REGENERATION (1914)
POWERS-UNIVERSAL
DIRECTOR: Wallace Reid
CAST: Wallace Reid, Helen Taft, Edward Brady, Phil Dunham.
SYNOPSIS: A fallen woman's regeneration results when she models for a painter and his portrait of the Madonna.

THE VOICE OF THE VIOLA (1914)
NESTOR-UNIVERSAL
DIRECTOR: Wallace Reid
CAST: Wallace Reid, Dorothy Davenport, William Gettinger, Edward Brady, Phil Dunham, William Steele.
SYNOPSIS: In a story by Bess Meredyth, three woodsmen fall in love with a blind girl but she returns the affection of only one when her sight returns.

THE HEART OF THE HILLS (1914)
REX-UNIVERSAL
DIRECTOR: Wallace Reid
CAST: Wallace Reid, Dorothy Davenport, Phil Dunham, Edward Brady, Lucile Wilson.
SYNOPSIS: In a story by Reid, a female revenuer comes between a woodsman-turned-moon shiner and the law as he to raises money for his crippled brother.

THE WAY OF A WOMAN (1914)
NESTOR-UNIVERSAL
DIRECTOR: Wallace Reid
CAST: Wallace Reid, Dorothy Davenport, Edna Maison, Antrim Short.
SYNOPSIS: In a story by Bess Meredyth, love grows between an injured woodsman and the girl he loves after he kidnaps her and she nurses him through recovery from an injury.

WHO SO DIGGETH A PIT (1914)
POWERS-UNIVERSAL
CAST: Wallace Reid, Lurline Lyons, James Neill, Edward Brady.
SYNOPSIS: Wally comes to the rescue of a girl who is falsely charged with the murder of her father.

THE SPIDER AND HER WEB (1914)
REX-UNIVERSAL
DIRECTOR: Phillips Smalley
CAST: Wallace Reid, Lois Weber, Dorothy Davenport, Phillips Smalley, William Wolbert, Rupert Julian.
SYNOPSIS: In a story by Lois Weber, a gambling queen snares men into her web of romance and intrigue.

WOMEN AND ROSES (1914)
NESTOR-UNIVERSAL
DIRECTOR: Wallace Reid
CAST: Wallace Reid, Dorothy Davenport, Lillian Brockwell, Vera Sisson, Phil Dunham.
SYNOPSIS: In a story by Bess Meredyth, based on a poem by Robert

Browning, a philandering husband returns to his wife when his mistress proves unfaithful.

CUPID INCOGNITO (1914)
NESTOR-UNIVERSAL
DIRECTOR: Wallace Reid
CAST: Wallace Reid, Dorothy Davenport, Phil Dunham, John G. Blystone, William Wolbert, Edna Maison, Lucile Wilson.
SYNOPSIS: In a story by Bess Meredyth, a young heiress to a mine is saved from ruin when a young man intervenes.

A GYPSY ROMANCE (1914)
NESTOR-UNIVERSAL
DIRECTOR: Wallace Reid
CAST: Wallace Reid, Dorothy Davenport, Edward Brady, William Gettinger, Phil Dunham.
SYNOPSIS: A jealous gypsy attempts to lure the bride from a king of the gypsies.

THE TEST (1914)
NESTOR-UNIVERSAL
DIRECTOR: Wallace Reid
CAST: Wallace Reid, Dorothy Davenport, Frank Lloyd, Tom Santschi, Edward Brady, Antrim Short, Gertrude Short, Gladys Montague.
SYNOPSIS: Two errant husbands face a bizarre test of faith when one robs the other and their families fall apart.

THE SKELETON (1914)
NESTOR-UNIVERSAL
DIRECTOR: Wallace Reid
CAST: Wallace Reid, Dorothy Davenport, Phil Dunham, William Wolbert.
SYNOPSIS: A newborn baby brings a surprising turn of events for a young couple.

THE FRUIT OF EVIL (1914)
NESTOR-UNIVERSAL
DIRECTOR: Wallace Reid

Wallace Reid and Frank Lloyd in the Wallace Reid-directed *The Test* (1914).

CAST: Wallace Reid, Dorothy Davenport, Edward Brady, Gladys Montague, Antrim Short, Gertrude Short.
SYNOPSIS: In a story by Reid, based on a fiction work by Elaine Sterne, a licentiousness husband causes a marriage to end in separation, and a daughter and son are raised with opposite parents. The children grow up, fall in love, and when they learn they are siblings, they commit suicide.

THE DAUGHTER OF A CROOK (1914)
NESTOR-UNIVERSAL
DIRECTOR: Wallace Reid
CAST: Wallace Reid, Phyllis Gordon

THE QUACK (1914)
NESTOR-UNIVERSAL
DIRECTOR: Wallace Reid
CAST: Wallace Reid, Dorothy Davenport, William Wolbert, Phil Dunham, Robert Chandler, Lucille Bolton

SYNOPSIS: An attorney and his father, a quack doctor, go to court over an argument. The attorney's fiancé testifies in his behalf, the father comes clean about his guilt, and reconciliation is won.

THE SIREN (1914)
NESTOR-UNIVERSAL
DIRECTOR: Wallace Reid
CAST: Wallace Reid, Dorothy Davenport, Lillian Brockwell, David Kirkland, Lucille Bolton, William Wolbert, Page Peters.
SYNOPSIS: A young woman causes the suicide of her mother's fiancé, and in a turn-about, the man's older brother woos then jilts her, leaving her alone with her transgressions.

THE MAN WITHIN (1914)
NESTOR-UNIVERSAL
DIRECTOR: Wallace Reid
CAST: Wallace Reid, Dorothy Davenport, Phil Dunham, William Gettinger, Clarence Burton.
SYNOPSIS: An outlaw sacrifices his freedom so the girl he loves and her father can earn the prize for his capture.

THE SPARK OF MANHOOD (1914)
POWERS-UNIVERSAL
DIRECTOR: Wallace Reid
CAST: Wallace Reid, Dorothy Davenport.
SYNOPSIS: A misfortune turns a good-for-nothing into a hero and earns him newfound love with a beautiful girl.

PASSING OF THE BEAST (1914)
NESTOR-UNIVERSAL
DIRECTOR: Wallace Reid
CAST: Wallace Reid, Dorothy Davenport, Joe King, John G. Blystone, William Gettinger, Phil Dunham, Edgar Keller, William Wolbert.
SYNOPSIS: A woodsman and a Canadian Mountie are at odds with each other over a woman until the woodsman saves the Mountie's life, and a reconciliation soothes their conflict.

LOVE'S WESTERN FLIGHT (1914)
NESTOR-UNIVERSAL
DIRECTOR: Wallace Reid
CAST: Wallace Reid, Dorothy Davenport, Joe King, Phil Dunham, William Wolbert, Frank Borzage.
SYNOPSIS: In a story by Harry G. Stafford, based on a previous work by James Oliver Curwood, a woman's drunkard husband, long presumed dead, turns up after she has fallen in love and married another man. His accidental death follows, resolving the catastrophe.

A WIFE ON A WAGER (1914)
NESTOR-UNIVERSAL
DIRECTOR: Wallace Reid
CAST: Wallace Reid, Dorothy Davenport, Joe King, John G. Blystone.
SYNOPSIS: In a story by Calder Johnstone, a man from the East travels to the West where good fortune and success earn him the love of a beautiful girl.

'CROSS THE MEXICAN LINE (1914)
NESTOR-UNIVERSAL
DIRECTOR: Wallace Reid
CAST: Wallace Reid, Dorothy Davenport, William Gettinger, Phil Dunham, Edgar Keller.
SYNOPSIS: In a story by Harry G. Stafford, a Mexican woman nurses a U. S. soldier after he suffers wounds in battle. Her jealous love erupts to sabotage his relationship with another woman but she ultimately resigns her affections to foster their reconciliation and ultimate happiness.

THE DEN OF THIEVES (1914)
NESTOR-UNIVERSAL
DIRECTOR: Wallace Reid
CAST: Wallace Reid, Dorothy Davenport, Lillian Brockwell, David Kirkland, William Wolbert, Phil Dunham.
SYNOPSIS: In a story by F. McGrew Willis, a woman of low morals schemes to undermine the disgrace and defeat of a younger woman until she learns the object of her plot is her own daughter and rescues her from a certain downfall.

THE AVENGING CONSCIENCE (1914)
Mutual-Majestic
Director: D. W. Griffith
Cast: Henry B. Walthall, Spottiswoode Aitken, Blanche Sweet, George Siegmann, Ralph Lewis, Mae Marsh, Robert Harron, George Beranger, Josephine Crowell, Wallace Reid, Donald Crisp, Walter Long.
Synopsis: Based on Edgar Allen Poe's *The Tell-Tale Heart*, the story of a man nearly driven mad by the sound of a buried, beating heart.

FOR HER FATHER'S SINS (1914)
Mutual-Majestic
Director: John B. "Jack" O'Brien
Cast: Wallace Reid, Blanche Sweet, Billie West, Al Fillson.
Synopsis: In a story by Anita Loos, a romantic entanglement is played against an expose of labor practices in American sweatshops.

THE ODALISQUE (1914)
Mutual-Majestic
Director: William Christy Cabanne
Cast: Wallace Reid, Blanche Sweet, Henry B. Walthall, Miriam Cooper, Robert Harron.
Synopsis: In a story by Leroy Scott, a stock girl is lured into the lifestyle of a kept woman when a scoundrel entices her with misleading temptations.

OVER THE LEDGE (1914)
Mutual-Majestic
Director: Fred A. Kelsey
Cast: Wallace Reid, Irene Hunt, Ralph Lewis, Donald Crisp.
Synopsis: Bob and Mabel catch a kite snagged on a lofty ledge, and then discover they are a brother and sister who have been separated since their childhood.

AT DAWN (1914)
Mutual-Majestic
Director: Donald Crisp

CAST: Wallace Reid, George Seigmann, Billie West, William Lowery, Claire Anderson, Eagle Eye, Fred Burns.
SYNOPSIS: In a story by Hal Reid, a sympathetic Marine on duty in the Philippines shields a young woman from the truth about the degradation and death of her fiancé.

THE EXPOSURE (1914)
MUTUAL-MAJESTIC
DIRECTOR: Fred A. Kelsey
CAST: Wallace Reid, Irene Hunt, Howard Gage, Ralph Lewis, William Lowery, Raoul Walsh.

SIERRA JIM'S REFORMATION (1914)
MUTUAL-RELIANCE
DIRECTOR: John B. "Jack" O'Brien
CAST: Wallace Reid, Gertrude McLynn, Raoul Walsh, Eagle Eye, Dark Cloud, Fred Burns.
SYNOPSIS: In a story of the old West, the sister of a pony-express rider reforms an outlaw.

THE SECOND MRS. ROEBUCK (1914)
MUTUAL-MAJESTIC
DIRECTOR: William Christy Cabanne
CAST: Wallace Reid, Blanche Sweet, Mary Alden, Raoul Walsh.
SYNOPSIS: In a story by W. Carey Wonderly, two women haggle for control of a household when a well-heeled widower takes a second wife and brings her into a home with his older sister.

THE NIGGARD (1914)
MUTUAL-MAJESTIC
DIRECTOR: Donald Crisp
CAST: Wallace Reed, Cora Drew, Billie West, William Lowry, Donald Crisp.
SYNOPSIS: A young man overcomes his stigma as a spendthrift by overspending at a vacation resort and regrets his irresponsibility.

A MOTHER'S INFLUENCE (1914)
MUTUAL-MAJESTIC

Wallace Reid and Mae Marsh in William Christy Cabanne's *Moonshine Molly* **(1914).**

DIRECTOR: John "Jack" O'Brien
CAST: Wallace Reid, Billy West.
SYNOPSIS: A man's disinherited son burglarizes his home, is apprehended, and finds ultimate forgiveness.

MOONSHINE MOLLY (1914)
MUTUAL-MAJESTIC
DIRECTOR: William Christy Cabanne
CAST: Wallace Reid, Mae Marsh, Robert Harron, Fred Burns, Eagle Eye.
SYNOPSIS: Romance blossoms in the Kentucky hills among moon shiners, revenue hunters, and murder.

HOME, SWEET HOME (1914)
RELIANCE-MAJESTIC
DIRECTOR: D. W. Griffith
CAST: Lillian Gish, Dorothy Gish, Robert Harron, Mae Marsh, Henry B. Walthall, Spottiswoode Aitken, Josephine Crowell, Fay Tincher, Miriam Cooper, Mary Alden, Donald Crisp, James Kirkwood, Jack Pickford, Fred Burns, Courtenay Foote, Blanche Sweet, Owen Moore, Edward Dillon, Wallace Reid.
SYNOPSIS: Three stories based on the life of composer, John Howard Payne, are told in separate episodes that reflect a common theme. Wally Reid appears in an unaccredited role.

THE LITTLE COUNTRY MOUSE (1914)
MUTUAL-MAJESTIC
DIRECTOR: Donald Crisp
CAST: Blanch Sweet, Wallace Reid, Mary Alden, Raoul Walsh.
SYNOPSIS: High society gamblers threaten an innocent girl who is quickly saved from ruin by a handsome military man.

HER AWAKENING (1914)
MUTUAL-MAJESTIC
DIRECTOR: William Christy Cabanne
CAST: Wallace Reid, Blanche Sweet, Ralph Lewis.
SYNOPSIS: A beautiful girl nearly loses her life and her inheritance.

DOWN THE ROAD TO CREDITVILLE (1914)
MUTUAL-MAJESTIC
DIRECTOR: Donald Crisp
CAST: Wallace Reid, Dorothy Gish, Donald Crisp, Kate Price
SYNOPSIS: In a story by George Terwilliger, a perky and materialistic bride-to-be spends excessively on credit until her fiancé owes everyone, including a clergyman, who repossesses the girl as his payment.

DOWN BY THE SOUNDING SEA (1914)
MUTUAL-MAJESTIC
DIRECTOR: William Christy Cabanne
CAST: Wallace Reid, Robert Harron, Mae Gaston.

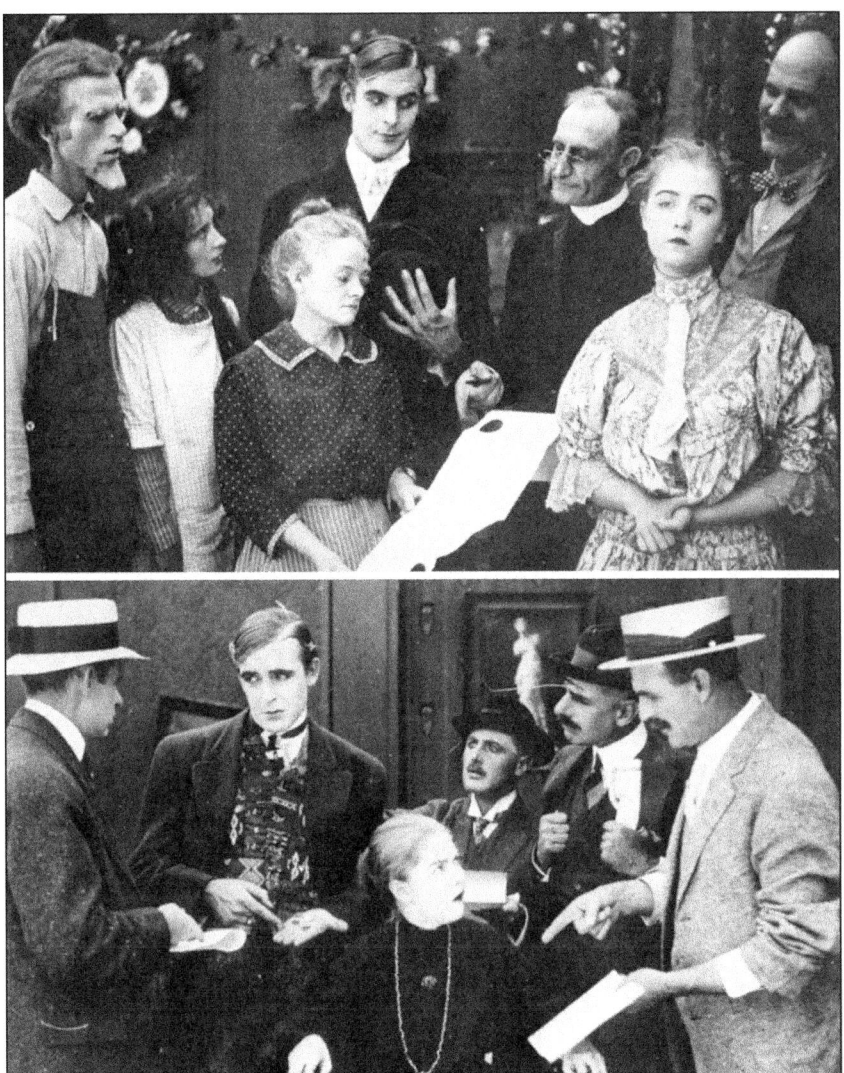

Wallace Reid with Dorothy Gish in two scenes from *Down the Road to Creditville* (1914).

SYNOPSIS: A shipwreck maroons a man on a distant island where natives lead him to rescue and romance.

THE CITY BEAUTIFUL (1914)
MUTUAL-MAJESTIC
DIRECTOR: William Christy Cabanne
CAST: Wallace Reid, Dorothy Gish

SYNOPSIS: In a closely autobiographical story, a young man finds romance and success in Los Angeles when he finds work in the motion picture business.

BABY'S RIDE (1914)
MUTUAL-MAJESTIC
DIRECTOR: George Beranger
CAST: Wallace Reid, Loretta Blake.
SYNOPSIS: A child runaway surprises her family when a rug is unfurled and she rolls out safely returned home.

THE JOKE ON YELLENTOWN (1914)
RELIANCE
DIRECTOR: Arthur Mackley
CAST: Vester Pegg, Joseph Belmont, Richard Cummings, Howard Gage, Joseph Henabery, Wallace Reid

THE HIGH GRADER (1914)
RELIANCE
DIRECTOR: Unknown
CAST: Charles Courtwright, Florence Crawford, Wallace Reid

ARMS AND THE GRINGO (1914)
MUTUAL-MAJESTIC
DIRECTOR: William Christy Cabanne
CAST: Wallace Reid, Dorothy Gish, F. A. Lowery, Fred A. Kelsey, Howard Gaye.
SYNOPSIS: In a story by Anna Tupper Wilkes, a Mexican lovers tangle romance and intrigue along the border territory.

ANOTHER CHANCE (1914)
MUTUAL-MAJESTIC
DIRECTOR: Donald Crisp
CAST: Donald Crisp, Wallace Reid, William Lowery, Mary Alden, Jane E. Wilson, Maxfield Stanley.
SYNOPSIS: In a story by Hal Reid, a jobless man and a hobo rescue a newsboy, and then the newsboy and the vagrant save the unemployed man from a false counterfeiting charge.

FOR THOSE UNBORN (1914)
MUTUAL-MAJESTIC
DIRECTOR: William Christy Cabanne
CAST: Blanche Sweet, Wallace Reid, Robert Harron, Irene Hunt.

THE BIRTH OF A NATION (1915)
EPOCH FILM CORPORATION
DIRECTOR: D. W. Griffith
CAST: Henry B. Walthall, Lillian Gish, Miriam Cooper, Mae Marsh, Mary Alden, Ralph Lewis, George Siegmann, Walter Long, Robert Harron, Wallace Reid, Joseph Henabery, Elmer Clifton, Josephine Crowell, Spottiswoode Aitken, George Beranger, Maxfield Stanley, Jennie Lee, Donald Crisp, Howard Gaye, Sam de Grasse, Raoul Walsh, Elmo Lincoln, Olga Grey, Eugene Pallette, Bessie Love, William de Vaull, Tom Wilson.
SYNOPSIS: Based on a story and play by Rev. Thomas F. Dixon, Jr., the fictional story of the Cameron and Stoneman families are depicted against a panorama of the Civil War, the reconstruction period, the assassination of Abraham Lincoln, and the rise of the Ku Klux Klan. Wallace Reid plays Jeff, the blacksmith, in a rousing fight scene, and is said to be the unaccredited actor appearing as Christ in an allegorical finale.

A reviewer for the *Atlanta Constitution* wrote, "The genius behind this great undertaking is David W. Griffith, son of Colonel Jacob Griffith . . . to what degree Griffith injected his inbred patriotism into his work is shown by the phenomenal success *The Birth of a Nation* has enjoyed, not alone in the South, but in the leading cities of the north as well. The Northerner enjoys the spectacle for its massiveness, its strong human appeal, and its splendid superiority over anything of the kind that has ever been unfolded to the public; but there is another and a far stronger reason why the Southerner praises it and warns his neighbor not to miss it. In swift panorama, the Southerner sees grievous wrongs of history righted and historical events enacted that have lived heretofore only in tradition. With the theatric and photographic arts combined, Griffith has breathed into phantoms of the past, and seated comfortably in his orchestra chair, the spectator sees General US Grant saunter across the room to shake hands with General Robert E. Lee at Appomattox; and he

Poster art from D. W. Griffith's *The Birth of a Nation* (1915).

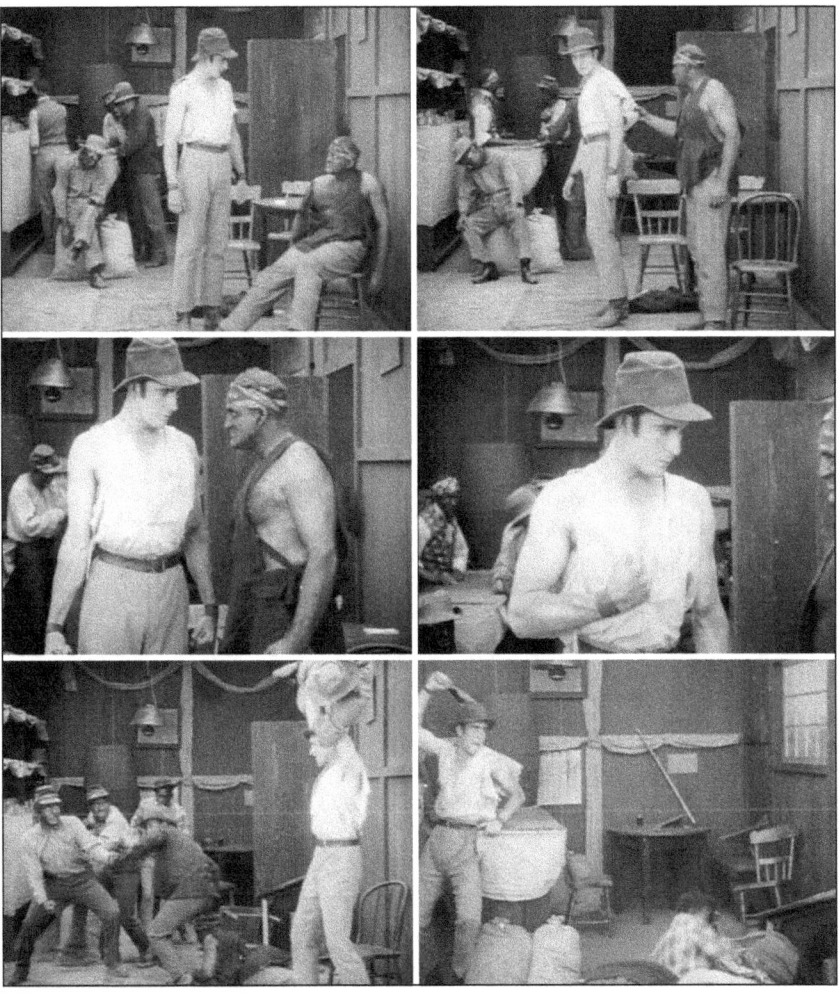

Frame enlargements from D. W. Griffith's *The Birth of a Nation* (1915) show Wallace Reid as Jeff, the blacksmith, approaching Gus in One-Arm Joe's gin mill after he has caused the death of a white girl. Gus grabs Jeff, which causes him to turn and look at him menacingly. In seconds, the tension erupts into an epic brawl with Jeff single-handedly taking on an entire roomful of renegades.

The gin mill brawl ends tragically as Jeff wins the fight and leaves victorious, only to be viciously gunned down by two shots, one fired in his back as he exits the mill, and a second time as Gus shoots him point blank in the chest.

Dorothy Davenport claimed in 1966 that the Christ figure appearing in the allegorical epilogue of *The Birth of a Nation* was impersonated by Wallace Reid in heavy beard, long hair, and robe.

sees the great hosts of the North and South meet in deadly conflict at Petersburg; and he hears the roar of the cannon and the rattle of musketry because stage effects of the most realistic sort are employed by Griffith throughout the two hours and forty minutes that the spectacle runs."

THE LOST HOUSE (1915)
MUTUAL-MAJESTIC
DIRECTOR: William Christy Cabanne
CAST: Lillian Gish, Wallace Reid, O. O. Sears, Fred Turner, Elmer Clifton.
SYNOPSIS: In a story by Richard Harding Davis, a girl held prisoner in a burning house in Kentucky is saved from certain death.

A reviewer writing in the *Indianapolis Star* said, "Richard Harding Davis' pet story, *The Lost House*, has been placed upon the screen . . . none of this distinguished author's ability to build up a cumulative, interest-compelling narrative is lost sight of in handling this drama . . . in a wonderful scene, Ford and Dosia leap from the fourth story through the flames and are caught in the fire net while doctor and uncle perish. To bring this thrilling narrative to an attractive conclusion, Mr. Davis leaves the two young people, not unnaturally, clasped in lovers' embrace."

ENOCH ARDEN (1915)
MUTUAL-MAJESTIC
DIRECTOR: William Christy Cabanne
CAST: Wallace Reid, Lillian Gish, Alfred Paget, Mildred Harris, Betty Marsh, D. W. Griffith.
SYNOPSIS: After many years, a man presumed to be lost at sea returns to find his wife married to another man.

A reviewer for *Moving Picture World* wrote, "As visualized by Cabanne, it is a splendid composite of imagery and illustrations, just what the distinguished poet intended it should be. The very simplicity of the story is artfully preserved. The simplicity, however, is not in atmosphere, feeling, and humanity. In its avoidance of sensation and false sentiment, it is all the more impressive and more in accord with the author's own mood when he wrote it. The pictured version, in fact, becomes a formidable rival to the poem, instead of a poor and inadequate reflection, as are most transformations from literature to the screen. Because of its background, it is manifestly impossible to present this story of other days without resorting to studio costumes and settings, but these do not jar by their artificiality. They are overlooked because of the evident sincerity of the producer. He has taken infinite pains in the small details of household equipment, and has even attempted, though less successfully, to 'plant' a tropical island. Mr. Cabanne has made an effort that deserves high praise because he has absorbed his subject and given to it the soul and feeling of a genuine artist. A strong factor in the success is Lillian Gish as Annie Lee. I feared at the outset that she could not respond to the exactions of the role, but she gathers strength as the story goes on, and her slight figure gradually becomes the center of sympathetic attention. She has caught the idea of mental revelation without effort—her face is very

Wallace Reid in William Christy Cabanne's *Enoch Arden* (1915).

expressive—but she still adheres to a painful eccentricity of Griffith's pupils: that of bent elbows and clutching hands. What is done with hands and arms depends entirely upon the character to be depicted, and to repeat a peculiarity under all circumstances, gives a sameness to characterizations. Miss Lillian is admirably supported by Alfred Paget and Wallace Reid. Both men act with convincing sincerity and dignity."

A review for the *Mansfield News* wrote, "Lillian Gish, whose golden beauty has added distinction and charm to many a society drama, graces a part decidedly in contrast to those she has recently been so much associated with when she appears as Annie Lee, the heroine of *Enoch Arden*, the four-reel Mutual master picture based on Lord Tennyson's famous poem. Histrionically, her performance measures up to the high standard established by D. W. Griffith."

A YANKEE FROM THE WEST (1915)
MUTUAL-MAJESTIC
DIRECTOR: George Siegmann
CAST: Wallace Reid, Seena Owen, Tom Wilson, Josephine Crowell, Christopher Lynton, William Brown, George Seigmann, Al Fillson.
SYNOPSIS: In a story by Mary O'Connor based on a novel by Opie Reed, Wallace appears as "Hell-in-the-Mud" Billy Milford, a prize-fighter falsely accused of a hold-up and. Billy Milford robs money from a railroad, goes to prison, and then escapes. He meets a pretty Norwegian refugee who inspires him to confess his crime and make restitution.

THE CHORUS LADY (1915)
FAMOUS PLAYERS-LASKY-PARAMOUNT
DIRECTOR: Frank Reicher
CAST: Wallace Reid, Cleo Ridgely, Marjorie Daw, Richard Grey, Mrs. Lewis McCord.
SYNOPSIS: In a story by Marion Fairfax based on a play by James Forbes, an striving chorus girl struggles to keep her younger sister from stage-door-Johnnies, and nearly loses her detective boyfriend when circumstances compromise her position.

"Cleo Ridgely is a likeable and level headed 'Pat' in the picture," wrote a reviewer in *Variety*. "She looks well, and it is easily believable she could accomplish the discomfiture of the 'John' as she did, over the immature looking Nora. Miss Daw's chorus girl type is perfect of its class, the younger chorus girl with a baby face and not a brain in her head. Miss Daw's face is a study . . . Messrs. Wallace Reid and Mr. Grey perform to the full requirements of their role . . . considerable comedy during the running has been lost through improper or careless attention to captions.

Wallace Reid and Cleo Ridgely in Frank Reicher's *The Chorus Lady* (1915).

Pat is ultra-slangy. This should have been reduced to laughs in captions."

OLD HEIDELBERG (1915)
TRIANGLE
DIRECTOR: John Emerson
CAST: Wallace Reid, Dorothy Gish, Erich von Stroheim, Karl Forman, Raymond Wells, Madge Hunt, Erik von Ritzau, Kate Toncray, Harold Goodwin, Francis Carpenter, Joseph McDermott, James Gibson, Franklin Arbuckle, Harold Goodwin.
SYNOPSIS: In a story by John Emerson, based on a novel by W. Meyer-Forster and a play by Richard Mansfield, a student prince falls in love with a tavern waitress. When he becomes king he is forced to conduct his life along prescribed patterns befitting a monarch and must reluctantly forsake her.

"With the hand of Griffith at the helm, it makes for premiere excellence," wrote a reviewer for *Variety*. "Whoever is directly responsible for the casting of the other male members of the organization is a positive genius for selecting types. The majority of them are unmistakably Teutonic, and the visualization of college life at Heidelberg is admirably depicted. No Griffith feature would be complete without a battle scene. *Old Heidelberg* is no exception, and as before stated, this feature is a complete one. The weakest spot of the entire production is the casting of Dorothy Gish for Kathie. She doesn't suggest anything Teutonic, thereby failing to preserve the otherwise strongly created atmosphere of German student life."

CARMEN (1915)
FAMOUS PLAYERS-LASKY-PARAMOUNT
DIRECTOR: Cecil B. DeMille
CAST: Geraldine Farrar, Wallace Reid, Pedro de Cordoba, William Elmer, Horace B. Carpenter, Jeanie Macpherson, Anita King, Milton A. Brown.
SYNOPSIS: In a story by William C. de Mille, based on the play by Prosper Mérimée, the story closely follows the love affair of Carmen, a gypsy girl, and Don Jose, a Spanish soldier. When Carmen becomes smitten with Escamillo, a bullfighter, Don Jose stabs her in a fit of jealousy.

Variety's review raved about the production. "Geraldine Farrar's picture, *Carmen*, hasn't a single redeeming trait of character. It isn't

Four scenes from John Emerson's *Old Heidelberg* (1915) with Dorothy Gish and Wally.

Dorothy Gish and Wallace Reid in John Emerson's *Old Heidelberg* (1915).

that of a woman with an overpowering sexual desire, but an unmoral female who gives herself to the highest bidder. She consorts with Jose to help the smugglers, and for that reason alone, and quarrels with them over the cash payment they offer her for the job. She goes to Seville with Escamillo, the toreador, only because he is able and willing to shower wealth and luxury upon her. She boasts that she is free and belongs to no man. And it is all magnificently enacted by the three central actors, and ably supported by a host of minor artists. The magnificence of the scenic investiture as a whole reflects much credit upon the producers and praise is due the director."

A reviewer writing in the *Fort Wayne News* said, *Carmen* ". . . contains two fights as vehement and sterling as the reel has ever unrolled, and adds inspiration to the story. The first is between Carmen and a taunting cigarette girl. Never in the history of pictures has such a realistic encounter been enacted by two women. It fairly makes one grip his seat in intense interest. The second between Don Jose and a brother officer who quarrel over the affections of Carmen is just as exciting, but it is all done so cleverly, so artistically, that criticism cannot be made. These scenes positively electrify with their ferociousness."

THE GOLDEN CHANCE (1915)
FAMOUS PLAYERS-LASKY-PARAMOUNT
DIRECTOR: Cecil B. DeMille
CAST: Wallace Reid, Cleo Ridgely, Edythe Chapman, Horace B. Carpenter, Raymond Hatton, Ernest Joy.
SYNOPSIS: In a story by Jeanie Macpherson, a judge's daughter marries a good-for-nothing who turns out to be a thief. When poverty overtakes her, she becomes a seamstress, masquerades as a well-dressed lady, and falls in love with Roger Manning, a millionaire.

"Two more capable leading players could not be secured than Cleo Ridgely and Wallace Reid," wrote a reviewer in *Variety*. "This production is said to be their first as co-stars. Their work in this would warrant many more. The production stands out nicely with the picture on a whole giving satisfaction. Some well-done silhouette close-ups add materially to the picture."

Four scenes from Cecil B. DeMille's *Carmen* (1915) with Geraldine Farrar and Wallace Reid.

Geraldine Farrar's famous song and dance in Cecil B. DeMille's *Carmen* (1915). Wallace Reid as Don Jose is to her right.

LEFT:
Cleo Ridgely, early silent film star.

BELOW
Wallace Reid in a scene from Cecil B. DeMille's *The Golden Chance* (1915).

Two scenes from Cecil B. DeMille's *The Golden Chance* (1915): (TOP) **Cleo Ridgely, Edythe Chapman, Wallace Reid, Ernest Joy, and Horace B. Carpenter, and** (BOTTOM) **Cleo Ridgely, Raymond Hatton, Horace B. Carpenter, and Wallace Reid.**

According to a reviewer in the *Lima Times Democrat*, ". . . it is one of the best pictures that has ever been shown upon a screen . . . it is a picture among a thousand. Its dramatic story is so absorbing, the acting of Miss Ridgeley, Mr. Reid, and the other members of the all-star cast, which was provided for the play, is so convincing, and the production and photography is of such exquisite character that it will be many moons before a picture will be found that contains so many elements of success."

THE THREE BROTHERS (1915)
MUTUAL-RELIANCE
DIRECTOR: William Christy Cabanne
CAST: Wallace Reid, Claire Anderson, Josephine Crowell, Allan Sears, William Hinckley.
SYNOPSIS: One girl entangles three brothers in a quarrel over her affections.

STATION CONTENT (1915)
MUTUAL-RELIANCE
DIRECTOR: Fred A. Kelsey
CAST: Wallace Reid, Catherine Henry, Ben Lewis.
SYNOPSIS: The frustrated and unhappy wife of a railroad man plans to end their marriage, but in a turn of events, saves his life by preventing a train wreck from destroying him.

SHERIFF FOR AN HOUR (1915)
DIRECTOR: Wallace Reid
CAST: Wallace Reid, Arthur Mackley

THE CRAVEN (1915)
MUTUAL-RELIANCE
DIRECTOR: William Christy Cabanne
CAST: Wallace Reid, Seena Owen, William Hinckley, Allan Sears, Claire Anderson, Josephine Crowell.
SYNOPSIS: A shy but brawny blacksmith avenges his sister and is killed in rousing fight.

MARIA ROSA (1915)
FAMOUS PLAYERS-LASKY-PARAMOUNT
DIRECTOR: Cecil B. DeMille
CAST: Geraldine Farrar, Wallace Reid, Pedro de Cordoba, Ernest Joy, Anita King, Horace B. Carpenter.
SYNOPSIS: In the title role, Farrar falls in love with a man condemned to die for a murder he did not commit. Then, she accepts a marriage proposal from the real killer, and when she learns of his deception, she stabs him to death. William de Mille crafted the scenario from material gleaned from individual plays by Wallace Gilpatrick, Angel

Two scenes from Cecil B. De Mille's *Maria Rosa* **(1915):** (TOP) **Wallace Reid, Pedro de Cordoba, and Geraldine Farrar, and** (BOTTOM) **Geraldine Farrar and Wallace Reid.**

Guimerá, and Guido Marburg.

According to a review in the *Lima Times Democrat*, "The big outstanding impression created by this picture is the consummate finish of Geraldine Farrar's acting, and this is all the more remarkable when it is taken into consideration that although this is the third picture shown starring this operatic songbird it was the first one in which she acted before the camera...there can be only one explanation: she is a born actress, and has the adaptability of one so gifted by nature... Wallace Reid handled the leading male role of Andres most effectively, although at times he was a little too cold for a naturally hot-blooded Spaniard... the photography and lighting were well up to the usual standard of excellence so prevalent in Lasky features."

"The producer, Cecil B. DeMille, has altered the story in deference to popular screen demand for a happy ending, and in so doing, has taken considerable strength out of the play," reported a *Variety* reviewer. "Nevertheless, with Miss Farrar in the name part, it ranks with the best of the Lasky releases, and far above their recent output. Miss Farrar has what few of our American screen stars possess—temperament, augmented by a genius for projecting it upon the film ... the best of the Lasky photography and atmospheric detail is employed, as well as the selection of an excellent supporting company."

TO HAVE AND TO HOLD (1916)
FAMOUS PLAYERS-LASKY-PARAMOUNT
DIRECTOR: George Melford
CAST: Wallace Reid, Mae Murray, Tom Forman, William Bradbury, Raymond Hatton, James Neill, Lucien Littlefield, Robert Fleming, Camille Astor, Robert Gray.
SYNOPSIS: In a story by Margaret Turnbull, based on a novel by Mary Johnson, Lady Jocelyn, a favorite in the court of England's King James, escapes a forced marriage to the hated Lord Carnal by fleeing to American colonies on a ship with other young women destined for marriage to American frontiersmen. Once arrived, she becomes involved with a dashing landowner who becomes a pirate.

According to a review in the *Middletown Daily Times*, "... it is an elaborate picturing of the famous novel by that name, but the book never could compare to the picture. Like all Lasky productions, it is accurate and complete in every detail. Mae Murray was very

Mae Murray and Wallace Reid in George Melford's *To Have and to Hold* (1916).

petite and graceful . . . her gowns were very pretty but the one worn at the court of St. James in the sixteenth century surely was a picture or perhaps an encumbrance. However, it was an exact reproduction. We liked her best in the simple Quaker frock. Wallace Reid as Captain Ralph Percy was splendid. Everybody likes Wallace Reid. We cannot help doing so. The boat used was an exact replica of the old time Galleon which once sailed the Atlantic to discover America. The scenes of the boat at sea were jus like famous paintings and the scenes on board were very picturesque. The costuming of the vast mob was wonderful, and the brilliant uniforms of the Lords of the early seventeenth century were perfect even to the stiff neck stuff . . . a big and flawless production."

A reviewer in *Variety* thought highly of the picture. "The fight with the pirate crew who have come ashore to bury their dead leader, the final victory and the taking command of the pirate ship, the wreck of the latter, and the rescue by the English vessel bearing the new Governor of Virginia, are all faithfully depicted in the picture, which is a rattling swashbuckling yarn that is sure to thrill and interest the country over . . . Miss Murray screens very well indeed, and after another picture or two, she will develop into a motion picture actress of no uncertain caliber, for she is possessed of a certain wistfulness that is sure to appeal."

"The erstwhile dancer did not betray the confidence her managers put in her," wrote a reviewer for the *New York Times*. "Her natural grace is an asset in an art where movement means so much, and she possesses a certain girlish and piquant beauty, in itself appealing but especially so through a suggestion of pathos she is able to put into her facial expression . . . Wallace Reid fought almost as many duels during the photographing of the picture as a German soldier . . . there are some fine pictures of the four-mast schooner riding at anchor and of the wicked band with their long mustachios and knives who roam her decks."

STARLIGHT'S MESSAGE (1916)
UNIVERSAL
DIRECTOR: Frank Montgomery
CAST: Wallace Reid, Mona Darkfeather

Wallace Reid and Cleo Ridgely in Frank Reicher's *The Love Mask* (1916).

THE LOVE MASK (1916)
FAMOUS PLAYERS-LASKY-PARAMOUNT
DIRECTOR: Frank Reicher
CAST: Wallace Reid, Cleo Ridgely, Earle Foxe, Robert Fleming, Dorothea Abril, Lucien Littlefield.
SYNOPSIS: In a story by Jeanie Macpherson, a sheriff who earns a living as a blacksmith helps a young girl protect her virgin gold mine from claim jumpers.

"Are we going back to first principles in motion picture drama?" asked a reviewer in *Variety*. "The latest Lasky release tends toward that. It is the old, old story of the romantic road agent who robs stage coaches, clad in a comic opera cloak, a girl whose mining claim has been jumped by unscrupulous miners, the girl beloved by the sheriff, the blood of the bandit being traced to the girl's hut, and so on. The Lasky company must have invested fully two dollars and forty cents' worth of atmosphere in the making of that

Canton flannel opera cloak worn by the bandit and possibly another fifty cents for the rental of a pair of spurs. The girl rides a white horse while disguised as the bandit and so does the bandit himself. It was evidently deemed cheaper to have them both use the same equine, or else but one white mount was available. One of the inconsistent things in the scenario was the allegation that the road agent had held up a saloon single-handed and stolen twenty kegs of whiskey. How he managed to tote them off on that single white charger without the aid of a brewery wagon should make an interesting problem. What is the matter? Isn't the Lasky outfit trying to keep up to the Paramount standard any longer? This one is way off."

A reviewer writing for the *Fitchburg Daily Sentinel* said, "some of the scenes that stand out are the Western saloon holdup, the trial incident, and the attack on the cabin. Wallace Reid is growing bigger and handsomer every day while Miss Ridgely has made rapid advancement in her work . . . *The Love Mask* is a pretty story, nicely pictured, and full of realism and atmosphere. The cast is one of Lasky's best. . . ."

THE SELFISH WOMAN (1916)
FAMOUS PLAYERS-LASKY-PARAMOUNT
DIRECTOR: E. Mason Hopper
CAST: Wallace Reid, Cleo Ridgely, Edythe Chapman, Charles Arling, Joe King, Jane Wolff, William Elmer, Horace B. Carpenter, Robert Fleming, Milton A. Brown.
SYNOPSIS: In a story by Hector Turnbull, the career of a civil engineer is nearly destroyed by his wife's extravagances.

"The story is not as good as most Lasky scenarios, but it is so capably handled that this is not altogether apparent," wrote a *Variety* reviewer. "The visualization is much more effective than the telling in cold type."

A review in the *Decatur Daily Review* said, "Wallace Reid, well known to photoplay audiences, provides some interesting scenes in this photoplay . . . the Lasky directors are among the first to hazard the making of motion pictures at night but it is said that the burning of the railroad camp is the most spectacular thing of its kind every made."

A theater poster for E. Mason Hopper's *The Selfish Woman* (1916).

THE HOUSE WITH GOLDEN WINDOWS (1916)
FAMOUS PLAYERS-LASKY-PARAMOUNT
DIRECTOR: George Melford
CAST: Wallace Reid, Cleo Ridgely, James Neill, William Jacobs, Mabel Van Buren, Robert Fleming, Marjorie Daw.
SYNOPSIS: In a story by Charles Sarver, based on an old fairy tale, a couple struggled to climb a hill to a house with golden windows, only to discover its disappointments.

"This is a peculiar sort of picture," wrote a reviewer in *Variety*, "in that it is difficult to determine the status of the production. It starts off with a prologue fairy tale theme, switches to conventional melodrama, and winds up as a dream. Much of its demerits are redeemed by the excellent handling in the manner of acting, photography, and direction. It preaches the doctrine of dissatisfaction with one's condition in life—showing that love in a cottage enjoys about the same degree of happiness as discontent in a mansion, no more, no less."

INTOLERANCE: LOVE'S STRUGGLE THROUGH THE AGES (1916)
WARK PRODUCING CORPORATION
DIRECTOR: D. W. Griffith
CAST OF THE MODERN STORY: Mae Marsh, Fred Turner, Robert Harron, Sam de Grasse, Vera Lewis, Mary Alden, Pearl Elmore, Lucille Brown, Luray Huntley, Mrs. Arthur Mackley, Miriam Cooper, Walter Long, Tom Wilson, Ralph Lewis, Lloyd Ingraham, Rev. A. W. McClure, Max Davidson, Monte Blue, Marguerite Marsh, Tod Browning, Edward Dillon, Clyde Hopkins, William Brown, Alberta Lee.
THE WOMAN ROCKING THE CRADLE: Lillian Gish;
CAST OF THE JUDEAN STORY: Howard Gaye, Lillian Langdon, Olga Grey, Gunther von Ritzau, Erich Von Stroheim, Bessie Love, George Walsh.
CAST OF THE MEDIEVAL FRENCH STORY: Margery Wilson, Eugene Pallette, Spottiswoode Aitken, Ruth Handforth, A. D. Sears, Frank Bennett, Maxfield Stanley, Josephine Crowell, Constance Talmadge, W. E. Lawrence, Joseph Henabery.
CAST OF THE BABYLONIAN STORY: Constance Talmadge, Elmer

Wallace Reid and Cleo Ridgely in George Melford's *The House with the Golden Windows* (1916).

Clifton, Alfred Paget, Seena Owen, Carl Stockdale, Tully Marshall, George Siegmann, Elmo Lincoln, George Fawcett, Kate Bruce, Ruth St. Denis, Loyola O'Connor, James Curley, Howard Scott, Alma Rubens, Ruth Darling, Margaret Mooney, Mildred Harris, Pauline Starke, Winifred Westover, Wallace Reid.

SYNOPSIS: In a story by Griffith with titles by Anita Loos, four stories illustrating bigotry, prejudice, and narrow-mindedness are woven together with parallel action accelerating to breathtaking, simultaneous climaxes and an allegorical ending. Unaccredited in the film, Wallace Reid was later credited in programs as a Boy Killed in the Fighting.

"Stupendous, tremendous, revolutionary, intense, thrilling, and you can throw away the old typewriter and give up with the dictionary because you can't find adjectives enough," wrote a reviewer in *Film Daily*. "Mr. Griffith has put on the screen what is, without question, the most stirring human experience that has ever been presented in the world."

"For in spite of its utter incoherence, the questionable taste of some of its scenes, and the cheap banalities into which it sometimes lapses, *Intolerance* is an interesting and unusual picture. Its stupendous panoramas, the grouping and handling of its great masses of players, make it an impressive spectacle," wrote one reviewer in the *New York Times*.

"This new work is a departure from all previous forms of legitimate or film construction," wrote *Variety*'s reviewer, "in that it attempts to tell four distinct stories at the same time—more or less successfully—accomplished by the aid of flashbacks, fade-outs, and fade-ins . . . a detailed analysis would occupy pages and then fall short. Mr. Griffith has a film spectacle that goes a step beyond his contemporaries."

THE YELLOW PAWN (1916)
FAMOUS PLAYERS-LASKY-PARAMOUNT
DIRECTOR: George Melford
CAST: Wallace Reid, Cleo Ridgely, William Conklin, Tom Forman, Irene Aldwyn, Clarence Geldart, George Webb, George Kuwa, Olive Carey.
SYNOPSIS: In a story by Margaret Turnbull, based on a novel by Frederic Arnold Kummer, a renowned artist is chosen to paint the portrait of a woman with whom he had a romance in his youth.

A review in the *Fitchburg Daily Sentinel* said, "*The Yellow Pawn* follows the usual action of eternal triangle plots until the climax where a genuine surprise is sprung in a scene which recalls the judgment

Cleo Ridgley and Wallace Reid in George Melford's *The Yellow Pawn* (1916).

of Solomon. This scene, combined with the introduction of sinister Chinese figures, adds a touch of the unusual to the production . . . in *The Yellow Pawn*, life is represented as played on a gigantic chessboard with the characters as pawns, and the final checkmate coming through the yellow pawn. Cleo Ridgley is half roguish and half seductive in the leading role while Mr. Reid is as handsome as ever. Mr. Kuwa plays the part of Sen Yat with Asiatic cunning and stoicism, and adds a touch of real pathos in the Celestial's devotion to his master. *The Yellow Pawn* is a drama of intrigue and jealousy. It is presented with all the Lasky skill . . . ."

THE WRONG HEART (1916)
FAMOUS PLAYERS-LASKY-PARAMOUNT
DIRECTOR: Wallace Reid
CAST: Wallace Reid, Dorothy Davenport.

THE WALL OF FLAME (1916)
FAMOUS PLAYERS-LASKY-PARAMOUNT
DIRECTOR: Wallace Reid
CAST: Wallace Reid, Pauline Bush

A WARRIOR'S BRIDE (1917)
FAMOUS PLAYERS-LASKY-PARAMOUNT
DIRECTOR: Wallace Reid
CAST: Wallace Reid and unknown cast

JOAN THE WOMAN (1917)
FAMOUS PLAYERS-LASKY-PARAMOUNT-ARTCRAFT/CARDINAL FILM CORP.
DIRECTOR: Cecil B. DeMille
CAST: Geraldine Farrar, Wallace Reid, Raymond Hatton, Hobart Bosworth, Theodore Roberts, Charles Clary, James Neill, Tully Marshall, Lawrence Peyton, Horace B. Carpenter, Lillian Leighton, Marjorie Daw, Stephen Gray, Ernest Joy, John Oaker, William Conklin, Walter Long, William Elmer, Jane Wolff, Cleo Ridgely, Hugh B. Koch, Emilius Jorgensen, Clarence Geldart, Fred Wilson, Ernest Butterworth.
SYNOPSIS: Jeanie Macpherson and William de Mille crafted the Joan of Arc story so it can be told in flashback from the point of view of a Eric Trent, a French soldier.

The usually eloquent *Variety* reviewer could barely compose a fitting monument in print to *Joan the Woman* after seeing a preview performance. "Hardened motion picture and dramatic critics, who imagined they were proof against any possible surprise from the other side of the footlights, came out of the 44th Street Theater last Saturday afternoon in a state of bewilderment . . . the surprise was pleasurable . . . it is impossible to describe in detail what producer DeMille accomplished with such a wealth of material. Suffice it to say that no one else could have done more and few, if any, could have done as much."

Geraldine Farrar as Joan of Ark in Cecil B. DeMille's *Joan the Woman* (1917).

A review in the *Decatur Daily Review* said, "*Joan the Woman* is by far the greatest super-picture ever attempted at any time. The coloring and scenic splendor are beyond comprehension, especially where Joan is burned at the stake the coloring is so natural that one

Wallace Reid as an English soldier in love with his sworn enemy, Joan of Arc, in Cecil B. DeMille's *Joan the Woman* (1917).

Poster art from Cecil B. DeMille's Joan the Woman (1917).

imagines the fire a reality. Joan of Arc stands supreme as the greatest woman who ever lived since history began. Today, it is told beautifully, wonderfully, by the marvelous acting of Miss Farrar in the most massive production ever shown on the screen."

THE MAN WHO SAVED THE DAY (1917)
UNIVERSAL (BIG U)
DIRECTOR: Wallace Reid
CAST: Wallace Reid, Pauline Bush, and John Burns.

THE GOLDEN FETTER (1917)
FAMOUS PLAYERS-LASKY-PARAMOUNT
DIRECTOR: Edward J. LeSaint
CAST: Wallace Reid, Anita King, Tully Marshall, Guy Oliver, Walter Long, Mrs. Lewis McCord, Clarence Geldart, Lawrence Payton, Lucien Littlefield.
SYNOPSIS: In a story by Charles Maigne and Charles Tenney Jackson, a Western mining engineer helps a New England schoolteacher overcome the men who have robbed her mine.

A reviewer for *Variety* panned the picture. "Wallace Reid's smile and Lucien Littlefield's artistic work in what was intended to be only a 'bit' are the only things which lift this feature out of the pit of banality. They bring it into the 'fair' class. E. J. Le Saint's direction is perhaps all that could be expected with the material at his disposal, for the story is the old combination of a fake western mine, unscrupulous exploiters, a confiding Easterner, and a Yankee schoolmarm."

A review in the *Middletown Times Press* said, "A sensational western story . . . Mr. Reid is seen as a young mining engineer who has come west to seek his fortune . . . an unusual incident in this feature is when the two are handcuffed together and Mr. Reid severs the chain by a shot from his revolver. An excellent cast support the stars."

BURIED ALIVE (1917)
FAMOUS PLAYERS-LASKY-PARAMOUNT
DIRECTOR: Wallace Reid
CAST: Wallace Reid, Dorothy Davenport

THE PRISON WITHOUT WALLS (1917)
MOROSCO-PARAMOUNT
DIRECTOR: E. Mason Hopper
CAST: Wallace Reid, Myrtle Stedman, William Conklin, Marcia

Manon, William Elmer, James Neill, Clarence Geldart, Camille Ankewich, Lillian Leighton.
SYNOPSIS: In a scenario by Beulah Marie Dix, based on a story by Robert E. MacAlarney, a prison reform expert voluntarily submits to incarceration to investigate rumors of payoffs, vice, and other misdeeds behind bars.

"There is nothing remarkable about it from any point of view, and it is simply fair program material," wrote a reviewer for *Variety*.

A review in the *Lima Daily News* said, ". . . how the grafter, jealous, tries to have him done away with, and how the guilty are finally brought to justice, and the true conditions divulged is brought about in a gripping and unusual manner . . . it is felt that this stellar duo of Wallace Reid and Myrtle Stedman will be popular with the amusement public."

THE PENALTY OF SILENCE (1917)
FAMOUS PLAYERS-LASKY-PARAMOUNT
DIRECTOR: Wallace Reid
CAST: Wallace Reid, Dorothy Davenport, Edward Brady.

THE WORLD APART (1917)
MOROSCO-PARAMOUNT
DIRECTOR: William Desmond Taylor.
CAST: Wallace Reid, Myrtle Stedman, John Burton, Eugene Pallette, Florence Carpenter, Henry A. Barrows, Phyllis Daniels.
SYNOPSIS: In a story by Julia Crawford Ivers, based on a novel by George Middleton, a mine superintendent saves a mine from being robbed by a woman's despicable husband. He is killed, she nurses him back to health, and they discover newfound love and romance.

A review in the *Oakland Tribune* said, "When George Middleton sat down to write *The World Apart* he had a story to tell that was worth telling. Life in a Western mining camp is contrasted with existence in a New England village. Wallace Reid is attractive and entertaining, and with Myrtle Stedman following his lead and the rest of the cast trailing along for all they are worth, results in acting of a very superior sort."

(TOP LEFT) **A movie poster from William Desmond Taylor's *Big Timber* (1917),** (TOP RIGHT) **Kathlyn Williams with Wally, and** (BOTTOM) **Joe King with Wally in the same film.**

THE BRAND OF DEATH (1917)
FAMOUS PLAYERS-LASKY-PARAMOUNT
DIRECTOR: Wallace Reid
CAST: Wallace Reid, Dorothy Davenport

THE BIG TIMBER (1917)
Morosco-Paramount
Director: William Desmond Taylor
Cast: Wallace Reid, Kathlyn Williams, Joe King, Alfred Paget, Helen Bray, John Burton.
Synopsis: In a story by Gardner Hunting, based on a novel by Bertrand W. Sinclair, a marriage of convenience between a logger and a young society girl takes on a new dimension when their soured relationship pushes her to the arms of another man. When her husband's land is nearly destroyed by a fire, rain comes, saves the day, and reveals the true depth of their feelings for one another.

"From a pictorial standpoint, *Big Timber* is a corker," wrote a *Variety* reviewer. "The same can be said for the greater part of the production, with the exception of one final touch, the rainstorm. This is the one flaw, but in view of what has preceded it, one is quite ready to forgive this slip. Wallace Reid and Kathlyn Williams play the principal roles in the piece, which is just what the title implies, a story of the big timber country. . . ."

THE SQUAW MAN'S SON (1917)
Famous Players-Lasky-Paramount
Director: Edward J. LeSaint
Cast: Wallace Reid, Anita King, Dorothy Davenport, Lucien Littlefield, Clarence Geldart, Donald Bowles, Frank Lanning, Ernest Joy, Mabel Van Buren, Raymond Hatton.
Synopsis: In a scenario by Charles Maigne, based on a novel by Edwin Milton Royal, a half-breed Indian reared in England returns to the tribal roots of his mother and falls in love with an Indian girl.

"The name of the picture, the Lasky trademark, the careful production and direction, should all contribute to make it a very successful feature. Produced by another concern and without the *Squaw Man* name it wouldn't attract any unusual attention," wrote a reviewer in *Variety*.

A review in the *Iowa City Citizen* said, "Wallace Reid is the most popular of the younger masculine screen stars . . . he has a part exactly suited to his personality and ability . . . by a strange coincidence, *The Squaw Man*, Edwin Milton Royle's famous drama, was the first story every picturized by the Lasky Company. So great was its

Anita King and Wallace Reid in Edward J. LeSaint's *The Squaw Man's Son* (1917).

success and so great was the demand of the amusement-seeking public to know what became of little Hal, son of the Squaw Man, that Edwin Milton Royle was easily induced to continue the story . . .how Hal returns to England only to be called back again to protect his people and how he is finally free to Marry Wah-na-gi and save her from death on the grave of his mother, is brought about in a most exciting and gripping manner."

THE TELL-TALE ARM (1917)
FAMOUS PLAYERS-LASKY-PARAMOUNT
DIRECTOR:
CAST: Wallace Reid, Vivian Rich

THE HOSTAGE (1917)
FAMOUS PLAYERS-LASKY-PARAMOUNT
DIRECTOR: Robert Thornby
CAST: Wallace Reid, Dorothea Abril, Gertrude Short, Clarence Geldart, Guy Oliver, Marcia Manon, Noah Beery, George Spaulding, Lillian Leighton, Lucien Littlefield, Camille Ankewich.
SYNOPSIS: In a story by Beulah Marie Dix, mountaineers hold a lieutenant from the lowlands hostage in a dispute between two family tribes.

"Wallace Reid, this time, proves himself a real screen star," wrote a reviewer in *Variety*. "The man who can play a hero who is called upon to violate a trust and who can still retain the sympathy of his audience as Reid does is something besides a good-looking figurehead. Reid does some acting in this picture that will boost him still further along in the hearts of his admirers . . . actors, star, director, author, and cameraman have contrived to make an absorbing story of *The Hostage* with a proper mixture of thrills and heart interest. It has the right amount of martial spirit to make it popular in these times."

"More action than has even been injected into five reels," wrote a reviewer for the *Fort Wayne News*. "Action, Love, and Suspense, the three greatest requisites for a great picture. Mr. Reid attains heights he has never reached. His best production to date. . . ."

According to a review in the *Lima Daily News*, "*The Hostage* is a cleverly devised and handsomely produced drama of wartime conditions of in the mountains of a European principality. Mr. Reid appears to great advantage and Mr. Lasky has surrounded him with one of his justly famous casts."

THE WOMAN GOD FORGOT (1917)
PARAMOUNT-ARTCRAFT
DIRECTOR: Cecil B. DeMille
CAST: Geraldine Farrar, Wallace Reid, Hobart Bosworth, Raymond

Three scenes from Robert Thornby's *The Hostage* (1917) with Dorothea Abril and Wallace Reid.

Hatton, Theodore Kosloff, Walter Long, Charles B. Rogers, Olga Grey, Julia Faye, James Neill.

SYNOPSIS: In a story by Jeanie Macpherson and William C. de Mille, explorer Cortez invades Mexico, Montezuma, and the Aztecs. Montezuma's daughter sacrifices her responsibility to her people for the love of one of Cortez' soldiers, and struggles to chose between him an Aztec prince who is betrothed to her.

"A truly magnificent production," wrote a reviewer in *Variety*. "In the matter of direction, Mr. DeMille has left much to be desired, and his battle scene is very much lacking in action. One thing about the picture that will take some explanation is the reason for Miss Farrar appearing in white skin, while all the others of her tribe are bronze in hue. There are details in the picture overlooked in the making. Otherwise, the story is one of those fanciful thrillers that one might imagine from the pen of H. Rider Hagard . . . the one big scene is a long staircase (evidently build on the side of a hill) on which the battle takes place. That alone is worth the price of admission. The supporting cast, outside of Kosloff, was about on a par with the star as far as acting went."

According to a reviewer writing in the *Lima Daily News*, "Farrar, De Mille, and Macpherson have combined their super talents in behalf of a giant cinema spectacle based on a page of the history of America when Montezuma and his Aztecs were conquered by the Spaniards, headed by Cortez. The first use of gunpowder in America is shown, and greater battle scenes than have ever been disclosed are shown. Although the production presents immense spectacular displays, including the highest set ever built for a motion picture, its interest is not confined to this feature alone. A stirring romance between the Aztec princess and the Spanish captain brings in many dramatic situations and fastens the spectator's interest upon the leading characters in the play. Never in her career has Geraldine Farrar been afforded a vehicle that carries to better advantage her wonderful histrionic talents . . . Wallace Reid heads the fine cast assembled for the play . . ."

The *New York Times*, said in their review, ". . . Miss Farrar, although a trifle light-skinned to be a daughter of Montezuma, meets all of the other requirements of the role, and Theodor Kisloff, the dancer, makes his first screen appearance and proves himself a

(TOP) **Wallace Reid in Cecil B. DeMille's *The Woman God Forgot* (1917), and** (BOTTOM) **Ramond Hatton, Theodore Kosloff, Geraldine Farrar, and Wallace Reid in the same film.**

surprisingly good film actor. Miss Farrar's leading man is again Wallace Reid, who makes a handsome but quite unconvincing Spaniard."

(TOP) **A movie slide for George Melford's** *Nan of Music Mountain* **(1917), and** (BOTTOM) **Theodore Roberts, Ann Little, and Wallace Reid in a scene from the same film.**

NAN OF MUSIC MOUNTAIN (1917)
FAMOUS PLAYERS-LASKY-PARAMOUNT
DIRECTOR: George Melford
CAST: Wallace Reid, Ann Little, Theodore Roberts, James Cruze, Charles Ogle, Raymond Hatton, Jack Hoxie, Ernest Joy, Guy Oliver, James P. Mason, Henry Woodward, Horace B. Carpenter, Alice Mark, Charles McHugh.

SYNOPSIS: In a scenario by Beulah Marie Dix, based on *Whispering Smith* by Frank H. Spearman, a railroad deputy and hired gunman takes on a mountaineer clan and terrorizing outlaws before falling in love with the clan leader's daughter.

"There is a very fascinating love story with the daughter of the worst thief in the gang as the hero's fiancé," wrote a reviewer in the *Sheboygan Press*. "The way these two alone, after de Spain has at last won the girl's love, make the gang reform and find a way to commence their lives together without any of the ever-present feuds or robberies, makes a vivid and unusual photoplay."

"The last reel is enough to make the whole picture a drawing card, even if the rest were lacking—which it isn't," claimed one reviewer in *Variety*. "The last reel is taken up almost entirely with the scenes of a blizzard working in with the action of the story, and is done in a manner probably never before seen on the screen. Inside gossip has it that Cecil DeMille had a hand in the staging of these blizzard scenes, and he has certainly put a punch that is new in the picture . . . Wallace Reid, in the character of Henry deSpain, has a chance to show at his best, a quiet, forceful, heroic representation . . . pictorially, it is a splendid picture done by artists from Wallace Reid, Theodore Roberts, and Ann Little, down to the camera man who braved the storm to get a real blizzard on the screen."

THE DEVIL-STONE (1917)
PARAMOUNT-ARTCRAFT
DIRECTOR: Cecil B. DeMille
CAST: Geraldine Farrar, Wallace Reid, Hobart Bosworth, Tully Marshall, James Neill, Raymond Hatton, Gustav von Seyffertitz, Ernest Joy, Mabel Van Buren, Lillian Leighton, Burwell Hamrick, Horace B. Carpenter, Ernest Joy, Burwell Hamrick, Theodore Roberts.
SYNOPSIS: In a story by Jeanie Macpherson, based on another story by Beatrice DeMille, a woman and her lover find romance and intrigue follow the theft of an emerald gem that carries a satanic curse.

In the *Oakland Tribune*, a review wrote, ". . . a detective story of weird fascination . . . based on superstition brought down from ancient folklore and made to influence the events in the life of a

Wallace Reid and Geraldine Farrar in Cecil B. DeMille's *The Devil Stone* (1917).

modern woman. The underlying motif of the narrative, the effect of the world-old stumbling block of man, superstition, furnishes the basis for a story of interesting study since it links with the ancient tale of a modern development of the curse placed upon the possessor of the Devil stone and handed down to the Breton fisher girl, as portrayed by the star . . . the plot is thrilling . . ."

Variety's reviewer wrote, "It serves Miss Farrar well and gives Tully Marshall an opportunity for some bully good work, but the proverbial busy-bee, Wallace Reid, who generally has the work of several men to do in picture acting, seems to be on a vacation. Not his fault. The scenario wasn't framed that way. But what Reid did was done with good grace and he made a handsome figure opposite Miss Farrar . . . Miss Farrar handles her emotional and suppressed scenes effectively. She wears some becoming wardrobe. Some of the scenes are splendidly staged, the atmosphere being for the most part complete and satisfactory. Some of the connections between the visionary and traditional and the present date reality were vague but conveyed graphically enough for the audience to keep the story well in mind."

RIMROCK JONES (1917)
FAMOUS PLAYERS-LASKY-PARAMOUNT
DIRECTOR: Donald Crisp
CAST: Wallace Reid, Ann Little, Charles Ogle, Paul Hurst, Guy Oliver, Fred Huntley, Edna Mae Cooper, Tote Du Crow, Gustav von Seyffertitz, Ernest Joy, George Kuwa, Mary Mersch.
SYNOPSIS: In a story by Frank X. Finnigan, based on a novel by Dane Coolidge, a young miner is tricked into losing his copper mine in the town of Gunsight. With the help of a caring secretary, he finds a second copper mine and restores his fortunes.

"While utterly different from anything Reid has ever done, *Rimrock Jones* reflects the vital life and characteristics of a certain section of the great West," wrote one reviewer in the *Newark Advocate*. "It's author, Dane Coolidge, is quite at home in this environment, as he has traveled through it many times not only as a writer in search of material but also as a naturalist and photographer working for the Smithsonian Institute and other scientific organizations . . . Miss Little particularly has added more than a little to the success of the production as Mary Fortune, the girl stenographer, who saves Rimrock's mine and stands valiantly by when all comes dark and hopeless. Needless to say, a happy ending has been supplied and the photoplay winds up most satisfactorily."

Variety's reviewer wrote, "This picture marks the advent of the latest Paramount star, Wallace Reid, a dashingly handsome leading man with much personality, long leading man with some of the best of the Paramount women stars . . . the direction was in the hands of Donald Crisp, who turned out a fast moving picturization that abounds in action . . . *Rimrock Jones* is a good feature for the Paramount program, and Reid will win many friends in the title role . . . it is his first bid on Broadway as a star, and he more than made good . . . Rimrock will be especially strong with the women folk."

THE THING WE LOVE (1918)
FAMOUS PLAYERS-LASKY-PARAMOUNT
DIRECTOR: Lou-Tellegen
CAST: Wallace Reid, Kathlyn Williams, Tully Marshall, Mayme Kelso, Charles Ogle, William Elmer.

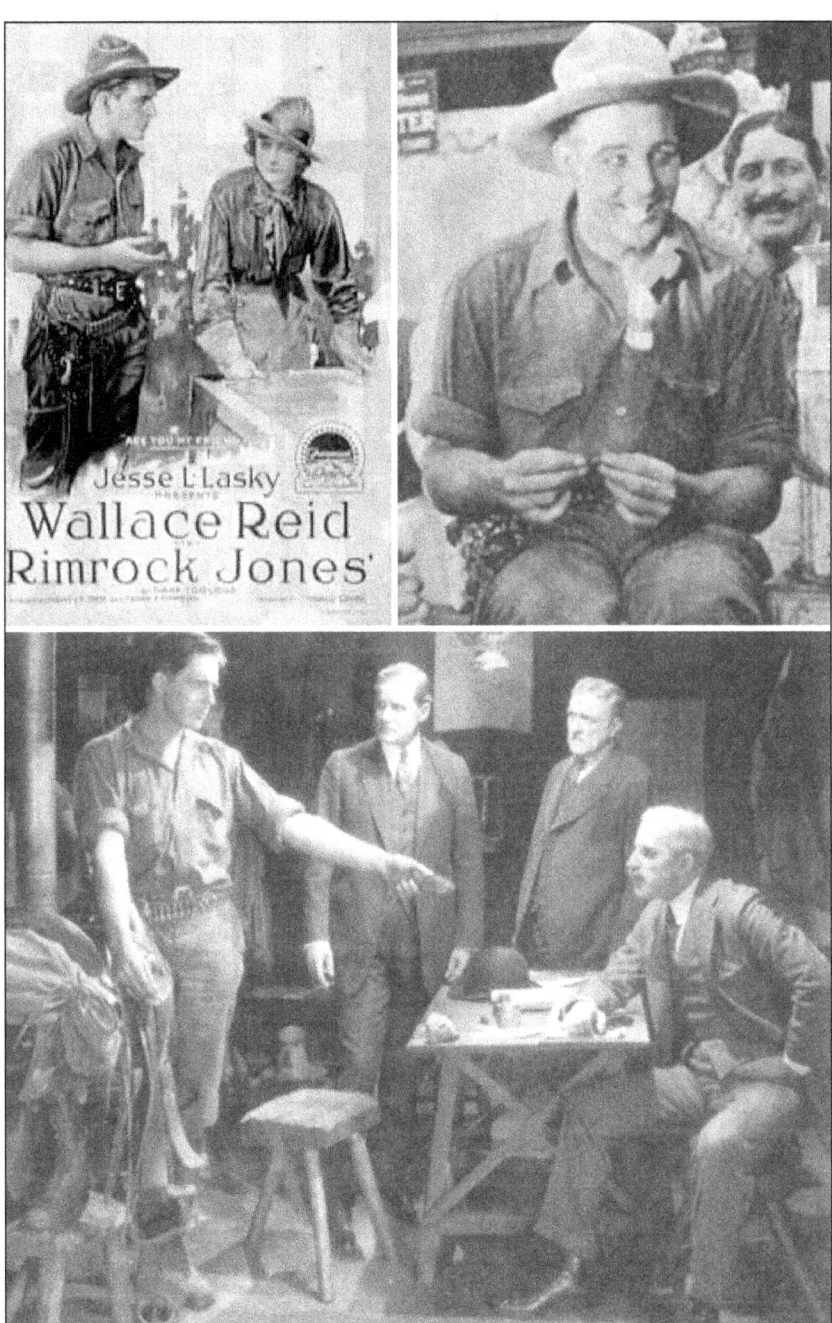

(TOP LEFT) **A studio poster from Donald Crisp's *Rimrock Jones* (1918), and** (TOP RIGHT) **Wallace Reid, and** (BOTTOM) **Wallace Reid with Charles Ogle in the same film.**

A vintage glass slide with Wally and Kathlyn Williams in Lou-Tellegen's *The Thing We Love* (1918).

SYNOPSIS: In a story by H. B. Daniel, an ex-con embittered against the Federal government has a change of heart at the outbreak of war and proves his worth with newfound patriotism.

A reviewer for *Variety* wrote, "Lou-Tellegen makes his debut as a director with this feature, which has Wallace Reid and Kathlyn Williams as the stars. The production is a Lasky-Paramount release, and about as botched up an affair as has been placed on the market in a long, long time. There is an effort to put the picture over through the medium of an allegorical, patriotic touch at the beginning and finish. But it is hardly probable this will have the desired effect . . . it is hardly probable Lou-Tellegen will direct any further features for the Lasky firm unless he develops a greater insight in the art of staging a film production than the knowledge that he exposes in the feature . . . it is a very ordinary feature, and it is rather surprising the Paramount didn't shelve the production rather than let it go on the market in the shape that it is in."

THE HOUSE OF SILENCE (1918)
FAMOUS PLAYERS-LASKY-PARAMOUNT
DIRECTOR: Donald Crisp
CAST: Wallace Reid, Ann Little, Adele Farrington, Winter Hall, Ernest Joy, Henry A. Barrows.
SYNOPSIS: In a story by Margaret Turnbull, based on a novel by Elwyn Alfred Barron, a detective investigating a stabbing in a house where masked men and women rendezvous falls in love with a girl prisoner.

"Those who like mystery will find plenty of it and its attendant fascination," wrote a reviewer for the *Oakland Tribune.*

According to a reviewer in the *Indianapolis Star*, "It is said the history of detective fiction made famous by Gabortau, Poe, and Sir Conan Doyle contains few more thrilling incidents than those which are disclosed in Wallace Reid's picture . . . in this photoplay, Reid portrays the role of a wealthy clubman whose hobby is the investigation of crime. He learns of a supposed murder in a mysterious house and with a hatpin and nurse as the sole clews to the perpetrator of the crime, begins his inquiry. Numerous complicating, thrilling incidents are then unraveled."

"It starts out with the strongest piece of absorbing mystery that Paramount has offered in a feature in many a day," proclaimed a reviewer in *Variety*. "It is exceedingly interesting and full of suspense. Well acted, directed and photographed, but it is questionable if the detailed scenes in the house of ill fame are at all necessary or won't be seriously objected to in some quarters."

BELIEVE ME, XANTIPPE (1918)
FAMOUS PLAYERS-LASKY-PARAMOUNT
DIRECTOR: Donald Crisp
CAST: Wallace Reid, Ann Little, Ernest Joy, Winter Hall, Henry Woodward, Henry Barrows, James Farley, Noah Beery, Charles Ogle, James Cruze, Winifred Greenwood, Clarence Geldart.
SYNOPSIS: In a story by Olga Printzlau, based on a play by John Frederick Ballard, a wealthy young man wagering $20,000 that he can execute a crime and escape discovery for one year succeeds with his boast and falls in love with a sheriff's daughter.

In a smaller town, the *Warren Evening Times* reviewer called it

Wallace Reid in Donald Crisp's *Believe Me, Xantippe* (1918).

"an enthralling screen romance," and added, "Wallace Reid and Ann Little do some excellent acting in the principal roles. They have been provided with excellent support, and the splendid direction the picture received at the efficient hands of Donald Crisp adds a great deal to its attractiveness."

"The action is brisk throughout and there is not a dull moment from start to finish. The photography is fine, and should make a good program feature," wrote a reviewer for *Variety*.

"The merriest farce in the city . . . it came out of Harvard, but there is nothing of the academic about it. Breezy as the prairies, it swept everything before it, and woke the audience to gales of laughter," wrote a reviewer in the *Lincoln Daily Star*.

By comparison, the *New York Times* reviewer wrote that the film had too many subtitles, saying it, ". . . has elements of amusement, but falls far short of the play as presented on the stage some seasons ago. It depends too much upon its conversation, and sentences flashed on the screen are not as effective as words spoken by good actors."

THE FIREFLY OF FRANCE (1918)
FAMOUS PLAYERS-LASKY-PARAMOUNT
DIRECTOR: Donald Crisp
CAST: Wallace Reid, Ann Little, Charles Ogle, Raymond Hatton, Winter Hall, Ernest Joy, William Elmer, Clarence Geldart, Henry Woodward, Jane Wolff.
SYNOPSIS: In a story by Margaret Turnbull, based on a work by Marion Polk Angelotti, murder, espionage, and love surround an American aviator when he joins the allies in the war effort and searches for The Firefly, a missing aviator.

"*The Firefly of France*, produced serially in the *Saturday Evening Post*, is a story of American pluck, perseverance, and Yankee ingenuity, an unbeatable combination. The photoplay will raise you right off your seat. It is a special in every instance . . . five million have read the story, a hundred million want to see Wallace Reid in the play.

A reviewer writing in the *New York Times* found the film flawed. "Donald Crisp, or some other director could have made a very good melodrama . . . but as produced the play is marred by a number of rough spots, which, it seems, were avoidable . . . a newspaper story announcing the disappearance of the Firefly offers the conjecture that he has either been killed or has turned traitor, and of course, no newspaper would have printed the latter suggestion about a man concerning whom there was no ground for suspicion and every

Three scenes from Donald Crisp's *The Firefly of France* (1918) with Wallace Reid, Ann Little, and Charles Ogle.

evidence of loyalty. Notwithstanding this and other weaknesses, it is still a good melodrama, and it would be better if Wallace Reid could succeed in not looking so much like a matinee idol all of the time."

"There is a far-fetched aspect from time to time, but it all runs for the good of the feature, and as expected, the real love is reciprocated in the finale," wrote a reviewer in *Variety*. "Photography at times splendid, with some sections off color. But the story is abreast of the times, and with Reid and Miss Little making a nice pair of sweethearts, the feature will be acceptable in all American neighborhoods."

LESS THAN KIN (1918)
FAMOUS PLAYERS-LASKY-PARAMOUNT
DIRECTOR: Donald Crisp
CAST: Wallace Reid, Ann Little, Raymond Hatton, Gustav von Seyffertitz, Noah Beery, James Neill, Charles Ogle, Jane Wolff, James Cruze, Guy Oliver, Jack Herbert, Calvert Carter.
SYNOPSIS: In a story by Marion Fairfax, a fugitive from justice assumes the name of his identical look-alike until he encounters romance and must reveal his turn true identity.

A reviewer for the *Daily Kennebec* wrote that the picture was an ". . . absorbing photodrama of romance, love, thrill, and laughter. 'If I take a dead man's name, I'll escape', figured Robert Lee when he got into trouble. It was a great idea—until the window appeared! Then he knew what real trouble was! Romance, fun, mystery, and the lure of a Central American Revolution are happily mingled . . . the ever-popular Wallace Reid is starred, with dainty Ann Little as his leading woman, both of whom will be enthusiastically received by Augusta admirers . . . all of you who love fascinating stories of soldiers of fortune—and that includes everybody—will like this colorful new picture, for it certainly gives Wallace Reid one of the best acting parts of his career in the role of the buoyant daredevil, Lewis Vickers, who gets into bunches of trouble in both the United States and Central America, and then gets out of it through his own nerve and resources. The difficulties of getting this 'sweat army in the world', as Mr. Reid calls them during rehearsal, in shape, provides some screamingly funny situations, which will be heartily appreciated by all who see the picture . . . a strong supporting cast and excellent photography by the clever little Japanese cameraman, Kotani, showing Central America, makes this play an instantaneous hit."

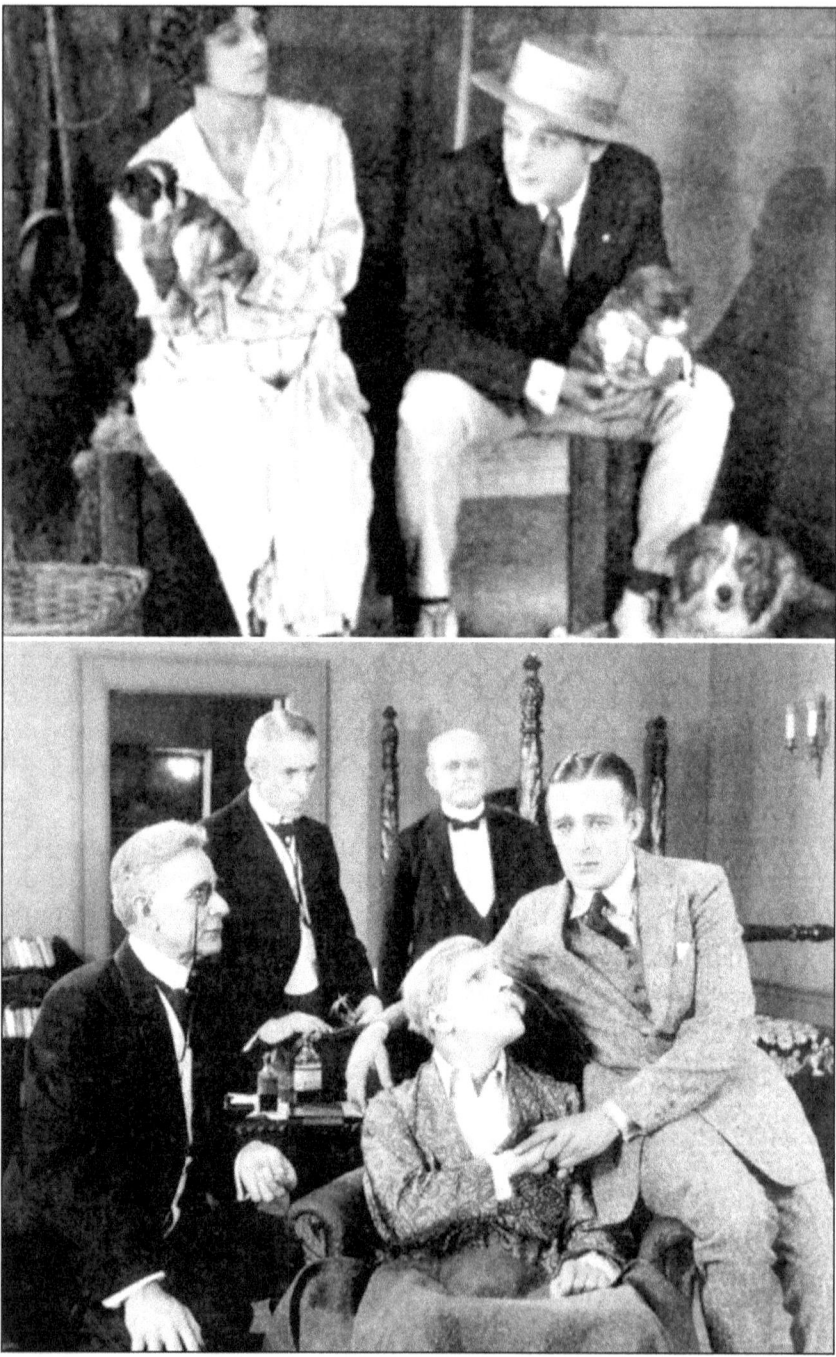

Two scenes with Ann Little and Wallace Reid in Donald Crisp's *Less Than Kin* (1918).

"Wallace Reid has a capital vehicle for the exploitation of his positive and distinctive talents," wrote a reviewer in *Variety*. "It is a dual role, in this case evolved and played with great plausibility and with a grip on the interest that does not lag for an instant. The direction is worthy of comment, while the photography is way above average. The scenic effects are often very striking . . . the acting of an excellent company gives a semblance of reality to a manifestly improbable plot. As Nellie, Ann Little is both pretty and clever. A number of funny types are excellently portrayed and the picture abounds in really good comedy scenes."

The *New York Times* reviewer wrote, "Less Than Kin is a photoplay with a rather good but not unusual story, in which Wallace Reid gives a poor imitation of John Barrymore's light-comedy manner."

THE SOURCE (1918)

FAMOUS PLAYERS-LASKY-PARAMOUNT
DIRECTOR: George Melford
CAST: Wallace Reid, Ann Little, Theodore Roberts, James Cruze, Noah Beery, Raymond Hatton, Charles West, Charles Ogle, Nina Byron, G. Butler Clonblough (Gustav Von Seyffertitz).
SYNOPSIS: In a story by Monte M. Katterjohn, based on a novel by Clarence Kelland, an alcoholic finds love, and his newfound sobriety inspires him to interfere with German wartime sabotage of U.S. property.

In the *Lima Daily News*, a reviewer wrote, ". . . Wallace Reid shows that he has lost none of his ability to visualize the hero of an engrossing and virile tale . . . a fine supporting cast."

The *New York Times*' reviewer wrote, ". . . Reid appears as a tramp, although, like the hero of *He Comes Up Smiling*, he could boast a higher social position if he wished . . . Reid is a bit too anxious to be elegant to appear convincing as a tramp, but as soon as he is permitted to remove his beard his work picks up noticeably. Then, getting down to work in the good old movie manner, he saves the spruce forests for Uncle Sam. The picture enlists the services of several good actors in the star's support. . . ."

"Virility, strong action, and fascinating romance are three of the characteristics which stand out in this comedy-drama," wrote a

Two scenes with Wallace Reid, Ann Little, and Noah Beery in George Melford's *The Source* (1918).

Wallace Reid and Ann Little in Walter Edwards' *The Man from Funeral Range* **(1918).**

reviewer in *Variety*, "splendidly handled, in fact, the whole production is unusually well done. Wallace Reid's leading role allows him to do some real acting. As Van Twiller Yard, a logger, he is a manly hero without any heroics. Ann Little and Nina Byron show talent, and their work is highly creditable . . . the locations secured have the proper atmosphere for the story, where all the scenes are laid in a western lumber camp and the photography is pleasing . . . the story is absorbing."

THE MAN FROM FUNERAL RANGE (1918)
FAMOUS PLAYERS-LASKY-PARAMOUNT
DIRECTOR: Walter Edwards
CAST: Wallace Reid, Ann Little, Willis Marks, George McDaniel, Tully Marshall, Lottie Pickford, Phil Ainsworth, Tom Guise.
SYNOPSIS: In a story by Monte M. Katterjohn, based on a play by W. E. Wilkes, a man takes the rap for a murder he wrongly believes his girlfriend committed, and after his conviction, he escapes prison and brings the true killer to justice.

Lottie Pickford, who was Mary Pickford's sister, appeared with Wally in Walter Edward's *The Man from Funeral Range* (1918).

In the *Indianapolis Star*, a reviewer said the film ". . . is a drama dealing with circumstantial evidence as it relates to miscarriage of justice. In this instance, such evidence is skillfully employed by a lawyer to send an innocent man to the chair. The victim escapes his prison guards, and in a series of interesting scenes, succeeds in establishing his claim of innocence and brings about restitution."

A reviewer in *Variety* wrote, "Mr. Reid is seen to fine advantage in a part which suits him admirably . . . the picture, while glaringly improbable, should prove a winner. As a production, it is of high merit . . . has scenes partly in the West and in the city. The picture is thus saved from monotony, at any rate."

TOO MANY MILLIONS (1918)
FAMOUS PLAYERS-LASKY-PARAMOUNT
DIRECTOR: James Cruze
CAST: Wallace Reid, Ora Carewe, Tully Marshall, Charles Ogle, James Neill, Winifred Greenwood, Noah Beery, Percy Williams, Richard Wayne, Ernest Pasque.
SYNOPSIS: In a story by Gardner Hunting, based on Porter Emerson Browne's *Someone and Somebody*, a struggling book salesman inherits $40,000,000 and is besieged with troubles, which he avoids by disassociating from the legacy, escaping with his sweetheart, and finding work as an automobile mechanic.

". . . a dandy picturization of Porter Emerson Browne's widely read novel," wrote a reviewer for the *Capital*. "It isn't at all possible that there is such a thing as having too many millions, and yet that is just the way Walsingham Van Dorn felt when the sudden death of his two wealthy uncles left him a fortune of forty millions, large, round, fat shining samoleons. You will enjoy greatly watching Wallace Reid spend that fortune quite as much as Wally enjoys spending it. Ora Carewe is the girl in the case, and Tully Marshall is the absconding cashier. *Too Many Millions* is an extremely interesting and fascinating story, with Wallace Reid in a role that fits him admirably."

"Mr. Reid is fitted to his every requirement with this part, as is Ora Carewe, who plays opposite him. All the quaint types are shown with the naturalness of life. With fine photography and direction, the picture is sure of being a winner as a feature anywhere," wrote a reviewer in *Variety*.

The *New York Times* reviewer wrote that the film, ". . . is a pleasantly impossible farce in which Reid actually wraps himself in a blanket in one scene and gets into overalls in another and does not seem always to be concerned about his reputation as a matinee idol."

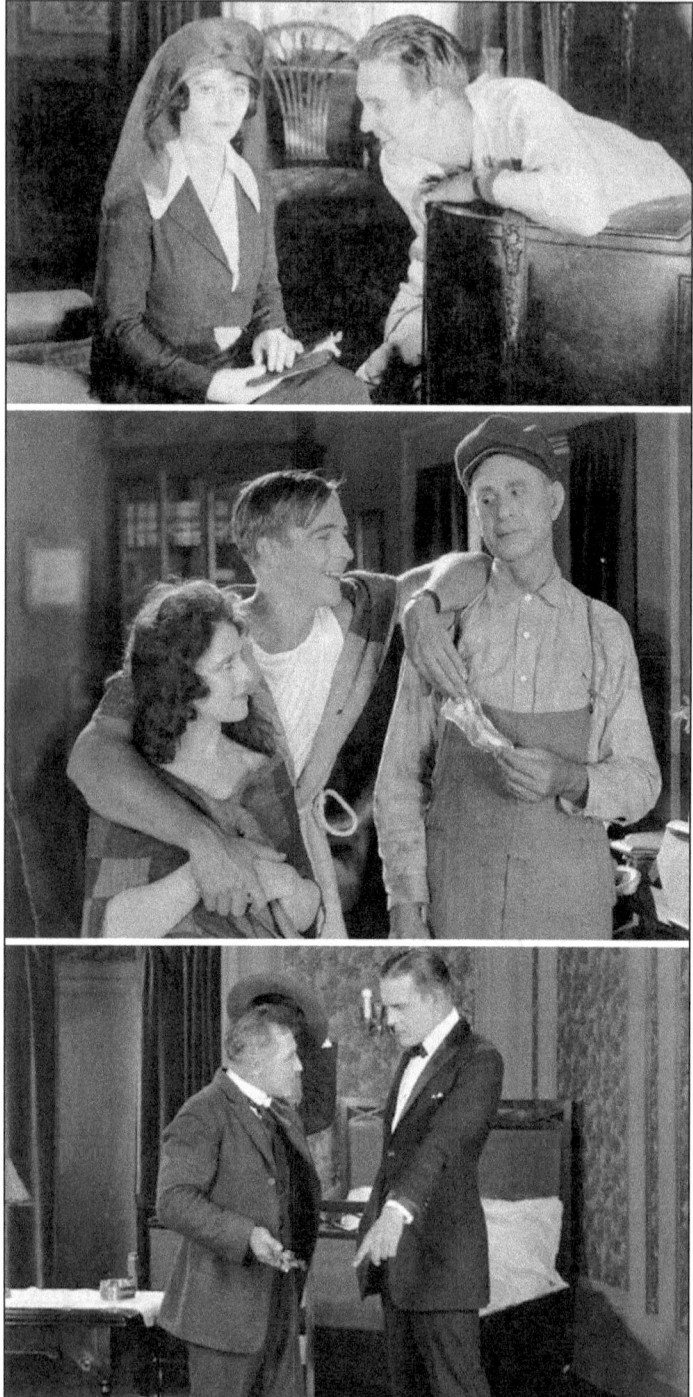

Three scenes with Wallace Reid in James Cruze's *Too Many Millions* (1918).

UNITED STATES FOURTH LIBERTY LOAN DRIVE (1918)
DIRECTED BY FRANK LLOYD
CAST: Roscoe Arbuckle, Alice Brady, George M. Cohan, Dorothy Dalton, Douglas Fairbanks, William Farnum, Geraldine Farrar, William Faversham, Elsie Ferguson, Pauline Frederick, Lillian Gish, William S. Hart, Sessue Hayakawa, Madge Kennedy, Harold Lockwood, Mae Marsh, Tom Moore, Mae Murray, Mabel Normand, Mary Pickford, Wallace Reid, Emily Stevens, Edith Storey, Norma Talmadge.
SYNOPSIS: a United States Government production supervised by E.L. Hyman, Director of Pictures Division of the Commission on Training Camp Activities, featured stars showing support for war-time bond sales.

HIS EXTRA BIT (1918)
LASKY-PARAMOUNT
DIRECTOR: Frank Lloyd
CAST: Wallace Reid, Dorothy Davenport, Wallace Reid, Jr.
SYNOPSIS: The entire Wallace Reid family appears in this patriotic, war-time short, showing them quarrelling over buying bonds until a family cook tells them that even servants buy bonds.

THE DUB (1919)
FAMOUS PLAYERS-LASKY-PARAMOUNT
DIRECTOR: James Cruze
CAST: Wallace Reid, Nina Byron, Charles Ogle, Ralph Lewis, Raymond Hatton, Winter Hall, Guy Oliver, William Elmer, Harry O'Connor, Clarence Geldart.
SYNOPSIS: In a scenario by Will M. Richey, based on a story by Edgar Franklin (aka Edgar Franklin Stearns), a girl is held prisoner by mine thieves and rescued by her sweetheart, John "The Dub" Craig.

"He's got more fight in him than a young white hope," wrote a reviewer in the *Oakland Tribune*, "in fact, they call him a fightin' fool, but he's still 'the Dub.' It's a fast-moving story full of pep and energetic action. The 'Dub' is no side-stepper, he goes after what he wants, whether its love or money."

In the *Trenton Evening Times,* a reviewer wrote, "A chance

Wallace Reid and Nina Byron in James Cruze's *The Dub* (1919).

happening sometimes results in the directing of a man's entire life. This truth is well illustrated in *The Dub*, Wallace Reid's new Paramount Picture. A strong quartet of acting talent is represented ... all of them are well known to admirers of the best in screen acting and teamwork they do in the picture is worthy of praise."

"This Wally Reid starring feature is a pippin of a comedy drama that could have been made a whale of a picture had it had comedy titling," summed up a reviewer in *Variety*. "Here was a chance for the title writer to have spread himself and turned out a picture that would have been a scream for laughs from start to finish. Then, it would have been a comedy of real value, but now it is just a corking good comedy drama ... James Cruze was the director, and he certainly turned out a mightily cleverly constructed production. It would have been easy to overplay this one with too much melodrama, but Cruze handled it with just sufficient humor here and there to put it over in great shape . . . one unusual thing about the picture is that there is but one woman in it and all the other characters men. The picture runs along with men, men, and nothing but men for so long that one wonders whether or not it is to be a stag affair. But when the girl does arrive she steps into a situation that is rather interesting, and, of course, at the finish, she falls for handsome Wally . . . there is a lot of rough-and-tumble fight stuff, but it was surrounded with sufficient humor to take away any grim touch, and when all is said and done, it must be admitted that, as a comedy drama, it is 'there.'"

ALIAS MIKE MORAN (1919)
FAMOUS PLAYERS-LASKY-PARAMOUNT
DIRECTOR: James Cruze
CAST: Wallace Reid, Ann Little, Emory Johnson, Charles Ogle, Edythe Chapman, William Elmer, Winter Hall, Jean Calhoun, Guy Oliver.
SYNOPSIS: In a scenario by Will M. Ritchey, based on a story by Frederick Orin Bartlett, an ex-convict and a draft dodger switch places; both achieve acclaim and polish the reputation of the other.

"No matter how weak a man's character or how mean he is, one can be reasonably assured that some day, sooner or later, the strong and good traits within him are going to overwhelm the evil," wrote a reviewer in the *Warren Evening Mirror*. "This is a strong point clearly conveyed by Wallace Reid in his portrayal of Larry Young . . . a man who turns yellow when he is drafted and bribes another man to take his place."

"One must admire the nerve that Wallace Reid displays in accepting a role that makes him appear as an absolute weakling for the greater part of this five-reel Paramount production," wrote *Variety*'s reviewer. "For the bigger part of three reels all the heroics go to an ex-convict who steps into the gap that Mr. Reid was to have filled in the draft army. Reid, in the meantime, displays nothing except the face that he is a self-centered coward and fortune hunter, a role that absolutely alienates the sympathy of the audience. Before

Wallace Reid as a draft-dodger in James Cruze's *Alias Mike Moran* (1919).

the finish, he manages to come back with a wallop and lands with the audience . . . James Cruze handled the direction most capably. Both the director and the scriptwriter are to be congratulated on the fact that they did not insist on trying to make the roles of Mike Moran and Larry Young a dual one for the star. This would have been one of the easiest errors to fall into, for in the original the two men are described as bearing a marked resemblance to each other . . . Reid gives a very clever characterization of the role . . . right now, with the troops returning to their homes all over the country, the picture is timely. The big punch is the fact that here is a boy given up for dead who returns to his sweetheart and parents. There are hundreds of those all over the country that haven't given up hope yet as to their boys, no matter what the official reports have said, and they are living in hope. The picture is well worthwhile playing."

THE ROARING ROAD (1919)
FAMOUS PLAYERS-LASKY-PARAMOUNT
DIRECTOR: James Cruze
CAST: Wallace Reid, Ann Little, Theodore Roberts, Guy Oliver, Clarence Geldart.
SYNOPSIS: In a scenario by Marion Fairfax, based on a story by Byron Morgan, the 400-mile Santa Monica Road Race is the setting for thrills and romance for racecar driver, "Toodles" Walden.

"It is exciting . . . the spectators seemed to feel themselves on the train when the passengers were seen scampering from one side of the car to the other or crowding eagerly at windows to watch the tearing automobile," wrote a reviewer in the *New York Times*. The big race was especially praised, with credit going to Frank Urson. "He knew just when and where and how to use the camera, when to show a flash of the car, when to cut in with the train, when to give a glimpse of the excited passengers, where to throw highlights, and how to use darkness to intensify the suspense . . . the race is one of the distinct triumphs of the moving pictures . . . Wallace Reid has the featured role, and is satisfactory, but the major acting is done by Theodore Roberts and notably well done."

"The picture is supposed to star Wallace Reid, but according to the number of close-ups of Theodore Roberts smoking a cigar, I should say it was starring a new brand of tobacco," wrote a reviewer for *Motion Picture Magazine*. "I quarrel with the infrequency with which the handsome Wally is allowed to come within camera range, I cannot but admit that the production as a whole is a mighty interesting piece of work . . . some of the photography is unnecessarily harsh on Ann Little, and Wally Reid is conspicuous because of the distance they keep him from the camera, otherwise *The Roaring Road* is satisfactory . . . ."

Two scenes from James Cruze's *The Roaring Road* (1919): (LEFT) **Clarence Geldart and Wallace Reid, and** (RIGHT) **Ann Little, Theodore Roberts, and Wallace Reid.**

A reviewer in *Variety* pointed out, "Several of the Byron Morgan stories, appearing recently in the *Saturday Evening Post*, have been incorporated into one and furnished the basis for a Wallace Reid—Paramount screen vehicle . . . the combination makes an interesting, clean, wholesome, suspense-interest picture story, but it is not a stellar vehicle for Wallace Reid, who is utterly eclipsed by Theodore Roberts in the role of 'The Bear', the character around which the Morgan stories were written. This is no reflection upon Reid's talents, which he utilizes neatly and acceptably, but 'The Bear' is a character role, and when handled by one of the greatest living character actors, if not the greatest, the result was inevitable he would walk away with the show . . . the finish is a race between an auto and a train from Los Angeles to 'Frisco, in which are shown some remarkable bits of photography. The picture is first-rate comedy with a lot of corking thrills. It will please any picture audience."

YOU'RE FIRED (1919)
FAMOUS PLAYERS-LASKY-PARAMOUNT
DIRECTOR: James Cruze
CAST: Wallace Reid, Wanda Hawley, Henry Woodward, Theodore

Three scenes with Wallace Reid as a happy-go-lucky, rich idle forced to hold a job in James Cruze's *You're Fired* (1919).

Roberts, Lillian Mason, Herbert Pryor, Raymond Hatton, William Lesta.

SYNOPSIS: In a story by Clara Kennedy, based on a story by O. Henry, comedy complications follow a wealthy playboy, when he is compelled by his fiancé's father to hold a job for one month or loose the girl's hand in marriage.

"*You're Fired* provoked long applause . . . and revealed Wallace Reid as one of the few men stars in motion pictures who knows how to dress like a man accustomed to smart society," conceded a reviewer in *Variety*. "Other actors in pictures would do well to study Reid's wardrobe . . . he was well supported by Wanda Hawley, who is getting roly-poly, but somehow conceals the fact on the screen, and by the one and only, inimitable Theodore Roberts. The photography was of that rare, clear, richness that makes pictures restful, not tiring. Wilfred Buckland contributed some remarkable effects in the backgrounds for the titling and inserts which were written with a charming an delightful humor . . . this picture has another virtue in that it gets started right at the beginning and without delay."

The *Washington Post* reviewer wrote about the adaptation of the O. Henry plot: "*You're Fired* is the screen title of *The Halbardier of the Little Rheinschloss*, and in order to add tension and drama to the story, it being photographically impossible to duplicate the writer's quaint style, a bit of a crime touch is added to the picture, which vastly increases its suspense and does not detract fro the theme selected by the master writer."

"Reid used to do more posing that acting," wrote a reviewer for the *New York Times*, "but recently he has been showing that he can act in comedy, and *You're Fired* is about his best demonstration of talent."

THE LOVE BURGLAR (1919)
FAMOUS PLAYERS-LASKY-PARAMOUNT
DIRECTOR: James Cruze
CAST: Wallace Reid, Anna Q. Nilsson, Raymond Hatton, Wallace Beery, Wilton Taylor, Edmund Burns, Alice Taaffe, Richard Wayne, Henry Woodward, Loyola O'Connor.
SYNOPSIS: In a story by Walter Woods, based on a play by Jack Lait, a writer in disguise as a gun moll investigates the criminal underworld soaking up their local color when a man pretending to be a convict arrives to rescue his wandering brother from a life against the law.

According to a reviewer in *Variety*, "It makes a very pleasing and highly entertaining screen entertainment, and Mr. Reid scores effectively in the heroic role of the production . . . Anna Q. Nilsson is also delightful . . . James Cruze has handled the story in great shape, getting over his dive and crook atmosphere with a wallop. His types are perfection, and the fight stuff that he staged is so realistic it reminds one of the old days at Sweeney's . . . the development of the love story from this point on is filled with suspense and capably handled by the director. The society features are full of color, and there are occasional comedy touches that fit the picture perfectly."

"The story is too long drawn out," wrote a reviewer in the *New York Times*, "but gets such a good running start that it is able to reach its end before it becomes tiresome."

THE VALLEY OF THE GIANTS (1919)
PARAMOUNT-ARTCRAFT
DIRECTOR: James Cruze
CAST: Wallace Reid, Grace Darmond, William Brunton, Charles Ogle, Ralph Lewis, Alice Taaffe, Kay Laurel, Jack Hoxie, Noah Beery, Guy Oliver, William Brown, Richard Cummings, Virginia Foltz, Ogden Crane, Lillian Mason.
SYNOPSIS: In a story by Marion Fairfax, based on a novel by Peter B. Kyne, a lumberman's son builds a railroad, fights a number of fights, gets into dirty politics, rescues his girl, loses her regard, and wins her back again, all to save from destruction his mother's grave in a valley of the California redwoods.

A reviewer writing for the *Bridgeport Standard Telegram* said, "Wallace Reid ascended to new heights of popularity in his latest picture, which has been filmed from Captain Peter B. Kyne's best-seller of the same name. The play is even better than the book because it is photographed in the Californian outdoors. The story is a succession of dramatic incidents—the red-blooded stuff that the fans adore—and the audience went wild over it."

". . . a peach of a story," wrote one reviewer in *Variety*. "Score that point to begin with. In addition, it has been adequately turned into a screenplay by Marion Fairfax, skillfully directed by James Cruze, and admirably photographed by Frank Urson who has made

(TOP LEFT) **A studio poster for James Cruze's *The Valley of the Giants* (1919).** (TOP RIGHT) **Grace Darmond, and** (BOTTOM) **Wally in a scene from the same film.**

the best of the California scenery, of the night scenes, and the thrilling adventures that fill this romance to the full with excitement. In the acting line, Reid's own pleasant personality is charmingly supplemented by the blonde Grace Darmond . . . in brief, this feature is far above the average."

Two scenes from James Cruze's *The Valley of the Giants* (1919), (BOTTOM) a fight scene with Noah Beery in the same film.

Two scenes from James Cruze's *The Lottery Man* (1919) with Wanda Hawley and Wallace Reid.

THE LOTTERY MAN (1919)
PARAMOUNT-ARTCRAFT
DIRECTOR: James Cruze
CAST: Wallace Reid, Wanda Hawley, Harrison Ford, Wilton Taylor, Clarence Geldart, Fanny Midgely, Sylvia Ashton, Carolyn Rankin, Virginia Flotz, Winifred Greenwood, Marcia Manon, Fred Huntley, Tully Marshall, Lila Lee, Charles Ogle, Guy Oliver.
SYNOPSIS: In a story by Elmer Harris, based on a play by Rida Johnson Young, love wins against all odds when a handsome bachelor auctions himself to an old maid for $50,000, and then learns she stole her lottery ticket from the cookie jar of his sweetheart.

". . . the action is fast from beginning to end, with the laughs coming readily," wrote one reviewer in *Variety*. "Wallace Reid plays the young hero to perfection, and Wanda Hawley as his leading woman gives a very clever performance . . . James Cruze has directed the picture in such a manner as to keep the action going along at top speed at all times."

The *New York Times* reviewer wrote, "Ever since Wallace Reid discovered his comedy genius he has been unfailingly entertaining, and the record is not broken by his performance in *The Lottery Man* . . . in this production, in fact, he abandons himself to farce more completely even than in other recent photoplays and the result is thoroughly agreeable . . . all of this may give the impression that The Lottery Man is a classic of wit, originality, and skill, but that is not quite the truth. It is good fun, however, most of the time, and keeps up its spirit better than most so-called screen comedies. It does not take itself seriously, it is seldom heavy, and there are a number of really noteworthy scenes in it . . . it must be confessed, before passing on, that the production is not all that it might be. It needlessly descends to crudeness, if not coarseness, in places, and it would move at a faster clip with fewer and better subtitles."

HAWTHORNE OF THE U.S.A. (1919)
PARAMOUNT-ARTCRAFT
DIRECTOR: James Cruze
CAST: Wallace Reid, Lila Lee, Harrison Ford, Tully Marshall, Charles Ogle, Guy Oliver, Edwin Stevens, Clarence Burton, Theodore Roberts, Ruth Rennick, Robert Brower.

Wallace Reid in James Cruze's *Hawthorne of the U. S. A.* (1919).

SYNOPSIS: in a story by Walter Woods, based on a play by James B. Fagan, a gambler breaks the bank at Monte Carlo; a small kingdom is saved from revolution; and a king declares democracy, all of which paves the way for the hero to marry a princess.

". . . it has the virtue of laugh producing qualities, though the picture slides from a genuine comedy vein to farce," explained a *Variety* reviewer. "The feature has much pointed humor, with situations that are improbably enough, but sufficient to pass too sedulous criticism in its smooth and rapid denouement. The star's work is satisfying, but furnishes him a role less genuine than *The Lottery Man*. The rest of the players are of the usual efficient stock . . . ."

THE CRUCIFIX OF DESTINY (1920)
PARAMOUNT-ARTCRAFT
DIRECTOR: R. Dale Armstrong
CAST: Antonio Corsi, Wallace Reid

DOUBLE SPEED (1920)
PARAMOUNT-ARTCRAFT
DIRECTOR: Sam Wood
CAST: Wallace Reid, Wanda Hawley, Theodore Roberts, Tully Marshall, Lucien Littlefield, Guy Oliver, Maxine Elliott Hicks.
SYNOPSIS: In a scenario by Clara Kennedy, based on a novel by Byron Morgan, "Speed" Carr, a racing car driver, loses his car on the brink of a cross-country drive only to win it back when his sweetheart buys the stolen automobile.

"This is my idea of a truly original, peppy, entertaining, and wholesome movie," wrote Hazel Naylor in *Motion Picture Magazine*. "Wallace Reid is in great danger of becoming more popular than ever if he continues to decorate such comedies as these, and little Wanda Hawley is intensely likable."

Variety wrote a positive profile of the story with their reviewer commenting, "The story breezes along at a refreshing rate, and laughs follow each other . . . the plot is full of novel twists, the action doesn't lag, and there is a pretty little love story with humor aplenty . . . Wanda Hawley is extremely easy to look upon. Miss Hawley shares the honors with Reid, and the latter does not seem in the least reluctant to go 50-50 with his good-looking leading woman. It is a picture that has taxed the ability of the photographer, as it involves shots of racing automobiles, a crash in which a summer house is demolished by a speeding car, and some colorful

(TOP) **An advertising slide for Sam Wood's *Double Speed* (1920), and** (BOTTOM) **Wallace Reid with Wanda Hawley in the same film.**

scenes on the Western desert. Then, there are neat, long shots with rich interiors and timely close-ups. Elaborate sets and good lighting distinguishes the production throughout."

"Its title is misleading to those who have Reid's *The Roaring Road* and *The Lottery Man* in mind," wrote a *New York Times* reviewer. "Its speed is generally about half that of those productions, and sometimes much less. The story does become merry in places, though, and the general opinion will probably be that if one has to wait for the laughs, they prove worth waiting for. This is principally because of Reid, but it is also due to clever complications of the story.'

EXCUSE MY DUST (1920)
PARAMOUNT-ARTCRAFT
DIRECTOR: Sam Wood
CAST: Wallace Reid, Ann Little, Tully Marshall, Theodore Roberts, Walter Long, Byron Morgan, William Ritchey, Wallace Reid, Jr., Guy Oliver, Otto Brower.
SYNOPSIS: In a scenario by Will M. Ritchey, based on a story by Byron Morgan, a racecar driver lets his father-in-law win an important race.

"*Excuse My Dust* relates a plausible and interesting incident . . . no sex stuff here, and no suave young villain. Just a good, interesting, at times exciting, and always well-told short story, wrote Burns Mantle in *Photoplay*. "The ingratiating Reid is as cheering a screen hero as usual . . . ."

As reviewed in *Variety*, some of the comments were, ". . . the direction was handled by Sam Wood. He has carried the action along in a logical manner and achieved several comedy touches here and there that stand out . . . Reid handles the role of the light hearted 'Toodles' delightfully but the support given him by Theodore Roberts, Tully Marshall, and Ann Little aids materially in putting over the picture. Roberts is especially good . . . the picture from a production standpoint is a real thriller, the auto race scene being responsible for this. The race was particularly well handled by the director and the suspense is maintained throughout it."

(TOP LEFT) **A Swedish advertising poster for Sam Wood's *Excuse My Dust* (1920), and the three stars in the film, Wallace Reid, Ann Little, and Theodore Roberts.**

THE DANCIN' FOOL (1920)
PARAMOUNT-ARTCRAFT
DIRECTOR: Sam Wood
CAST: Wallace Reid, Bebe Daniels, Raymond Hatton, Lillian Leighton, Tully Marshall, Ernest Joy.

(LEFT) **A newspaper advertisement for Sam Wood's *The Dancin' Fool* (1920), as seen in the *Wyoming State Tribune* on January 18, 1921.** (RIGHT) **Wallace Reid in two scenes from the same film.**

SYNOPSIS: In a scenario by Clara Kennedy, based on a story by Henry Payson Dowst, fame and fortune follow a clerk with a passion for ballroom dancing when a dancer arrives at his uncle's old-fashioned restaurant and jazz music takes to the air.

A reviewer in the *Daily Kennebec* wrote, "Really, it is almost hopeless to attempt to describe *The Dancin' Fool* . . . Augusta people who have been charmed by the handsome features of this most likeable young chap will find him more pleasing than ever as Sylvester Tibble. All those who have read Henry Payson Dowst's famous story will recall the real fascination of the tale, jugs, jazz, and joy—that's what it's about, and there is a whole lot of each. There is also plenty of action, too, for Wally no sooner enters a New York cabaret than he gets into a fight. But then, he lands a girl, and what follows about everyone knows who has read the story. The screen version is far more fascinating than was the original romance."

"The Lasky studio might have done better than cast Wallace Reid for the lead . . . he isn't the hick rube type; doesn't look the part; acts it but passably, and the majority of Reid admirers won't care particularly for it," summarized a reviewer writing in *Variety*. "The comedy possibilities are overlooked through Reid being starred, In the original story there were any number of laughs that do not show on the screen . . . Wood did the best he could with the picture but Reid isn't a dancer of the type that was required to fill the titular role properly . . . from a production standpoint, the picture shows nothing remarkable and it could not have cost a lot to place on the screen."

"Director Wood had material here suited to Reid's aptitude for foolishness, but he let the story take itself seriously in places and drag along under the impression that it was becoming a romance or something related to life," wrote a reviewer in the *New York Times*. "The result is that *The Dancin' Fool* is interesting only in spots."

SICK ABED (1920)

PARAMOUNT-ARTCRAFT
DIRECTOR: Sam Wood
CAST: Wallace Reid, Bebe Daniels, John Steppling, Winifred Greenwood, Tully Marshall, Clarence Geldart, Lucien Littlefield, Robert Bolder, Lorenza Lazzarini, George Kuwa.
SYNOPSIS: In a story by Clara Kennedy, based on a play by Ethel Mumford, a rich hypochondriac is cured of his imaginary ailments when he finds romance with his pretty nurse.

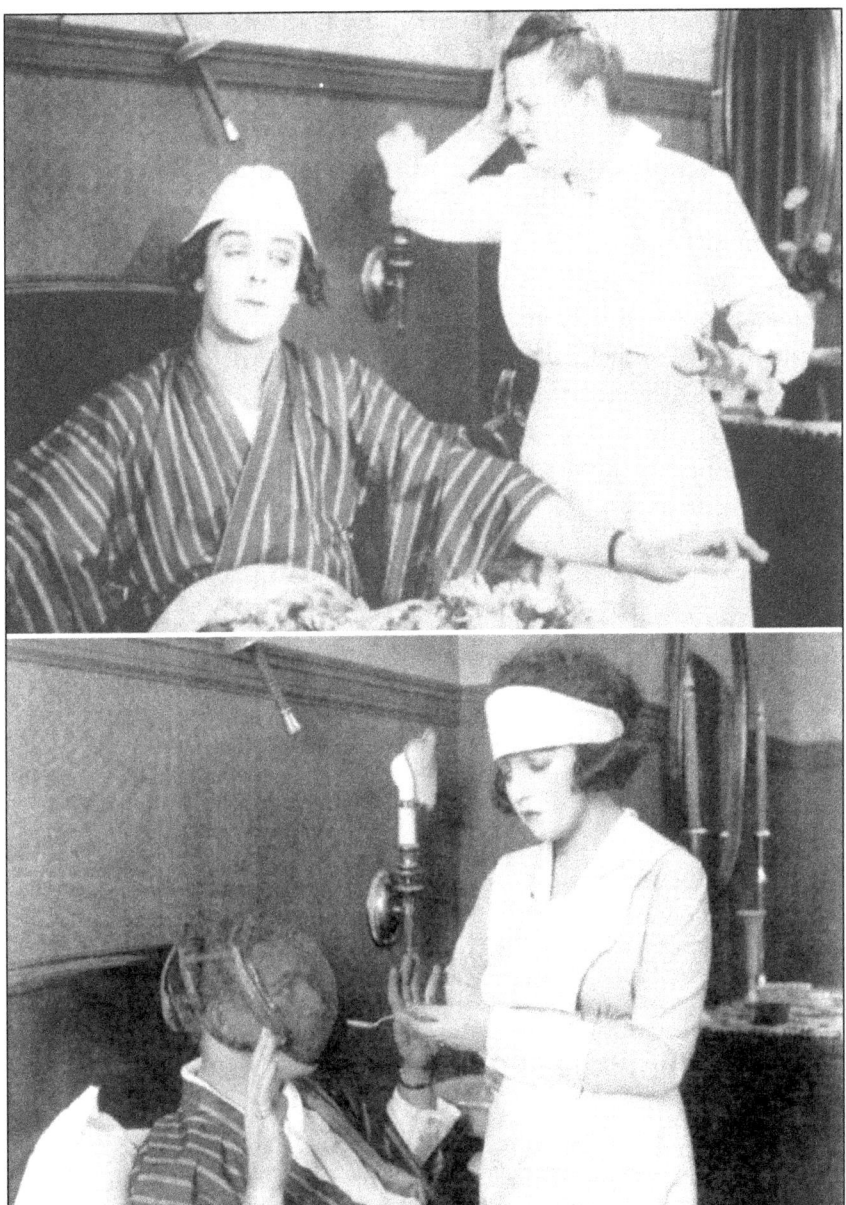

Two scenes from Sam Wood's *Sick Abed* (1920) with Wallace Reid and Winifred Greenwood.

A review in the *Trenton Evening Times* said, "There is never an idle or sad moment in Wallace Reid's new screen farce . . . the story is frankly for entertainment purposes only. That it succeeded in its efforts to amuse was attested by the gales of laughter with which it was greeted by last night's audience. Wallace Reid has the role of Reginald Jay, the young friend of John Weems, a businessman. The latter gets into difficulties through being caught out in a rainstorm with a pretty lady customer and seeking shelter in a notorious roadhouse."

"Handsome Wallace Reid lying in bed, a towel around his head and a pretty nurse and two doctors in attendance," wrote a reviewer in the *Elyria Chronicle Telegram*. "This is the sight that would have met your eye had you visited the Lasky studios recently. And you might have wondered if Wallace had paid the price at last for the reckless daring that he displays in those automobile racing pictures of his. But you would quickly have learned a different story. Mr. Reid was just making scenes for his new picture . . . not that the picture's one of those depressing dramas with half the cast dying off before the third reel. On the contrary, *Sick Abed* is one of the liveliest Reid pictures ever screened. Wally isn't ill a moment, not even for film purposes. He's just shamming, according to the story, in order not to incriminate a friend of his in a divorce suit, and the pretty nurse by his bedside is none other than Bebe Daniels . . . *Sick Abed* will make real invalids forget their pains and cause well folks to roar with mirth."

WHAT'S YOUR HURRY? (1920)
PARAMOUNT-ARTCRAFT
DIRECTOR: Sam Wood
CAST: Wallace Reid, Lois Wilson, Charles Ogle, Clarence Burton, Ernest Butterworth, Jack Young, Ernest Joy.
SYNOPSIS: In a story by Byron Morgan, a racing hero saves a dam from bursting with the aid of a caravan of motor trucks and their last-minute delivery of emergency supplies.

"Another breezy automobile romance," began a review in the *Trenton Evening Times*, "which thrilled the capacity audience at the Trent Theater yesterday afternoon and evening. Further automobile atmosphere is provided by showing of the Trenton Fair Motor Races in motion pictures. Wallace Reid appears at his best in this picture. Lois Wilson makes a charming heroine."

A reviewer in *Variety* praised the scenario by Byron Morgan who also wrote the original story that appeared in the *Saturday Evening*

(TOP LEFT) **Wallace Reid in Sam Wood's *What's Your Hurry?* (1920), and** (TOP RIGHT) **Lois Wilson, and** (BOTTOM) **Lois Wilson and Wallace Reid in the same film.**

Post. "This tale of the auto business is a splendid melodrama with plenty of action in its final reel, and an interesting love story with genuine comedy values in the earlier passages . . . the scenes at the new Los Angeles Speedway are thrilling. The progress of the five motor trucks through a raging storm forms a striking series of views, and the performance of the hero in driving one of the trucks into a breach in the dam gives just the right dramatic punch at the right moment. Tension is skillfully worked up."

"Another automobile story on a dead level with many that have gone before it, so far as its plot and people are concerned," wrote a reviewer for the *New York Times*, "but raised above them by a succession of exceptionally well-made scenes . . . in picturing the progress of the trucks, the struggle at the dam, and the contrasting festivity in the endangered houses and in assembling his scenes, Mr. Wood has displayed noteworthy cinematographic skill. *What's Your Hurry?* winds up with a genuine thrill."

MOTHERS OF MEN (1920)
ROBARDS-REID PICTURES
DIRECTOR: Willis Robards; Written by James Halleck Reid
CAST: Willis Robards, Dorothy Davenport, Hal Reid, Marcella Russell (as Mrs. Hal Reid), Katherine Griffith, Grace Blake, George Utel.

ALWAYS AUDACIOUS (1920)
PARAMOUNT ARTCRAFT
DIRECTOR: James Cruze
CAST: Wallace Reid, Margaret Loomis, Clarence Geldart, J. M. Dumont, Rhea Haines, Carmen Phillips, Guy Oliver, Fanny Midgely, Charles Bennett.
SYNOPSIS: In a story by Thomas J. Geraghty, based on a work by Ben Ames Williams, a look-alike switches place with a clubman in South America. The identical face of the imposter fools everyone until the clubman's dog identifies friend from the fraud.

"San Francisco has been a frequent locale in Paramount pictures starring the popular Wallace Reid," began a review in the *Trenton Evening Times*. "All of the action was supposedly transferred to the Bay City and the company photographed many scenes in the

(TOP) **Wallace Reid in a fight scene from James Cruze's *Always Audacious* (1920), and** (BOTTOM) **Wallace Reid and Margaret Loomis in the same film.**

beautiful St. Francis Hotel . . . Mr. Reid plays a duel role and portrays with characteristic energy both the millionaire and a crook. Many complications develop when the latter shanghais the former and seeks to gain possession of his immense fortune."

". . . the picture seems patchy," complained one reviewer writing in *Variety*. "No moving main purpose seems to actuate all of it, and hold it together. Possibly this is due to the immediate introduction of the two chief characters. On the whole, a better result might have been obtained if one of them had been firmly established and then the other brought to bear on his life . . . Mr. Reid himself played both parts straight and had a difficult task in keeping them distinct. He used fairly obvious methods to accomplish his purpose, but accomplish it he did. Margaret Loomis has real screen charm and looks like a gentlewoman. The photography, as usual, touched the high Paramount standard."

THE CHARM SCHOOL (1921)
PARAMOUNT-ARTCRAFT
DIRECTOR: James Cruze
CAST: Wallace Reid, Lila Lee, Adele Farrington, Beulah Bains, Edwin Stevens, Grace Edwards, Tina Marshall, Patricia Magee, Lincoln Stedman, Kate Toncray, Minna Redman, Snitz Edwards, Helen Pillsbury, Tina Marshall.
SYNOPSIS: In a story by Thomas J. Geraghty, based on a play by Alice Duer Miller, a young man becomes heir to a school for girls and replaces traditional courses with a curriculum of charm.

"Wallace Reid, as an automobile salesman, shoes her into 'high' and lets the 'gas' escape undismayed and unabashed in *The Charm School*," began a review in the *Bridgeport Telegram*, "a versatile, handsome auto salesman does not seem to jibe at first glance but by adjusting one's rimmed spectacles, one discovers that the adjustment takes place with fine precision when Wally's aunt wills him a female seminary filled with fair seminarians. It may be imagined how many feet of frivolous film and corking entertainment can be gotten out of a situation like this with Wally as the headmaster of such a chicken coop. One must see Wally in harness to know how proficient he is as a schoolmaster."

According to *Variety*, "If this is the Lila Lee of the Lasky end,

A studio poster for James Cruze's *The Charm School* (1921).

who was aimed for stardom, it looks somewhat peculiar to see her in support and not mentioned in the billing. Nothing about her performance to call for anything extra. In fact, there is nothing to anyone's performance as a whole, excepting Reid's. He has it all. Edwin Stevens is the banker, looking and playing the role but it's just incidental, as are all of the others. It's strictly a Wally Reid picture and a good one as a program release."

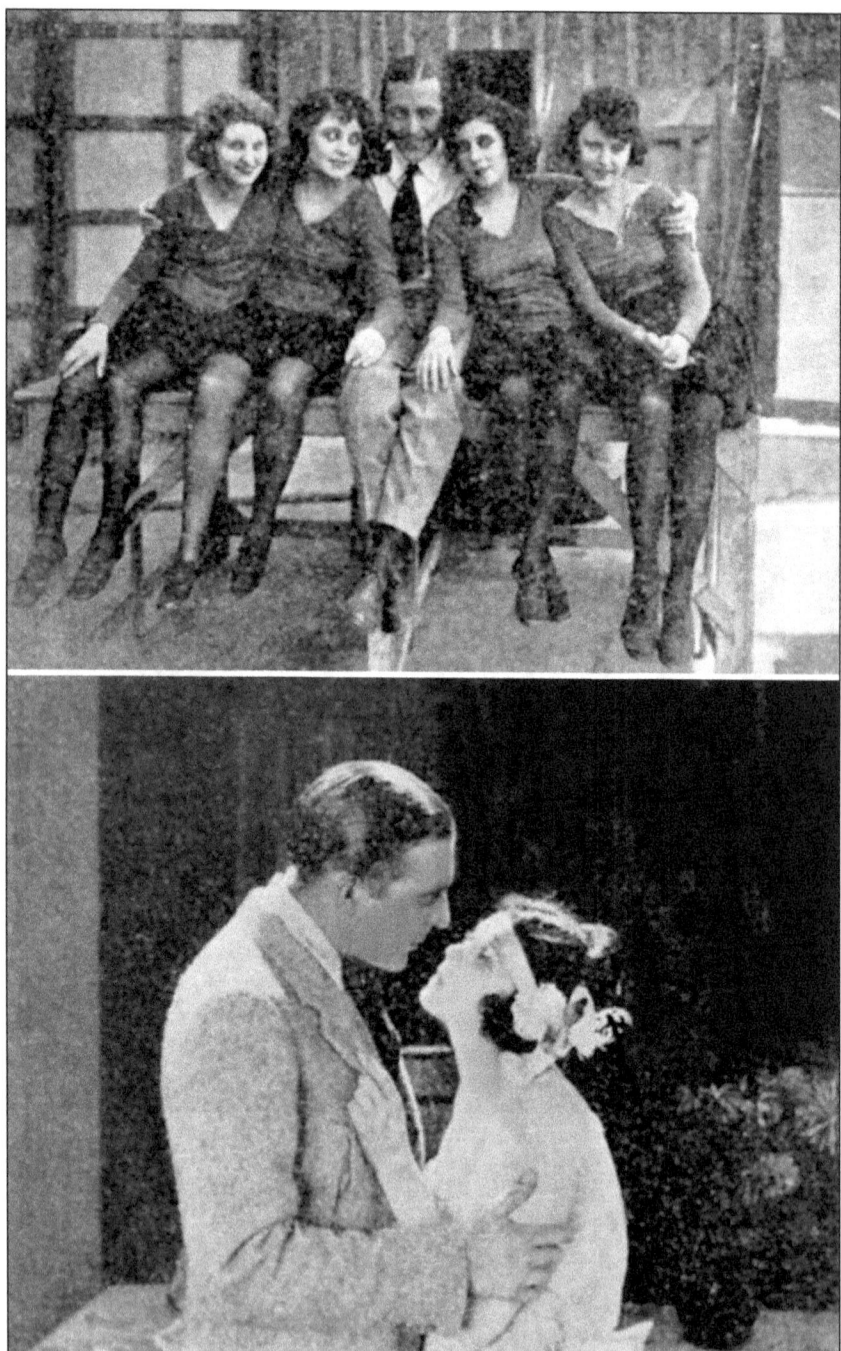

Two scenes with Wallace Reed and Lila Lee in James Cruze's *The Charm School* (1921).

Wallace Reid and Agnes Ayres in Frank Urson's *The Love Special* (1921).

THE LOVE SPECIAL (1921)
PARAMOUNT
DIRECTOR: Frank Urson
CAST: Wallace Reid, Agnes Ayres, Theodore Roberts, Lloyd Whitlock, Sylvia Ashton, William Gaden, Clarence Burton, Snitz Edwards, Ernest Butterworth, Zelma Maja.
SYNOPSIS: Based on a story by Frank H. Spearman, a civil engineer finds romance on the rails when he mistakes the pretty daughter of the president of the rail line for his stenographer.

In *Progress*, a reviewer wrote, "One is mightily puzzled before a Wallace Reid picture these days, puzzled, that is, in distributing credit for the acting. Steam engines and racing cars, bursting dams, and snowstorms are, to be sure, the chief actors, but Mr. Reid smilingly takes what bows there are. Whether he is bowing for himself or for the steam engines—well, anyhow, *The Love Special* is another unblushing hero picture with something of our own Rocky Mountains and railroads in it, something of recklessness with Mr. Reid at the throttle, and something of suspense, but not enough to deceive. Agnes Ayres is the heroine, one so lovely and capable of creatures deserves better than so safe and sane a trip through so uninspired a story."

"Jesse Lasky has provided the male star with a picture that may pass as an average program feature and be acceptable to the Reid fans," wrote a reviewer in *Variety*, "It will never cause comment to arise concerning the merit it contains, either as to direction, action, interest or photography . . . the cast, which comprises enough known ability, must have found it easy going in the making, as they have all gone through the identical action time and again, and it is in that respect, the repetition of many films that have gone before, where most of the fault will be found . . . Mr. Roberts, as usual, gave a sterling performance and runs Reid an even race for honors. Miss Ayres impresses with her photographing value, though not to the extent she did in Forbidden Fruit, and played easily here in a part not calling for any special effort."

"Wallace Reid often gives one the impression that he is an aimless, cheerful fellow who doesn't seem to care very much, or know, whether he is doing finished farcing or simply living up to his reputation as a matinee idol," wrote one reviewer in the *New York Times*. "And in its careless good cheer and general aimlessness, his latest picture has some bright comedy touches and a strikingly well-made scene of a locomotive driving through a blizzard; there are also a number of other effective scenes and a quantity of adroit acting by Theodore Roberts, Agnes Ayres, and others in the cast but the photoplay as a whole does not proceed smoothly and never reaches any climax."

(TOP) **Agnes Ayres and Wallace Reid in Frank Urson's** *Too Much Speed* **(1921), and** (BOTTOM) **Theodore Roberts and Wallace Reid in the same film.**

TOO MUCH SPEED (1921)
PARAMOUNT
DIRECTOR: Frank Urson
CAST: Wallace Reid, Agnes Ayres, Theodore Roberts, Jack Richardson, Lucien Littlefield, Guy Oliver, Henry Johnson, Jack Herbert.

SYNOPSIS: In a story by Byron Morgan, a racing enthusiast, "Dusty" Rhodes, wins a contract in South America for his father-in-law's automobile manufacturing plant.

"A pippin of a feature," wrote a reviewer in *Variety*. "A1 summer entertainment . . . it affected the imagination the way candy does a child . . . the racing scenes are immense. So is the handling of the continuity, which keeps things alive every foot. The net result is a feature so full of movement it is good for any type of audience or house, yet undeniably first class."

"The Adonis of the screen in a cyclonic yarn of the auto race track," wrote a reviewer in the *Bridgeport Telegram*. "*Too Much Speed* but not too much action, nor too much romance, nor too much love, nor too many thrills—just enough of everything good to make this a whirlwind piece of jolly entertainment."

The *New York Times* reviewer thought the film lacked human element but said the cast gave ". . . the old story new life by treating it lightly. It has lost its power to thrill, except intermittently, but there's still fresh comedy in it and it has been allowed to bubble up brightly . . . the scene of the wreck of the limousine is alone worth the price of admission."

THE HELL DIGGERS (1921)
PARAMOUNT
DIRECTOR: Frank Urson
CAST: Wallace Reid, Lois Wilson, Alexander Broun, Frank Leigh, Lucien Littlefield, Clarence Geldart, Charles Post, Frank Geldart.
SYNOPSIS: In a story by Byron Morgan, a construction superintendent inventor creates a machine that will re-soil land that has been stripped from gold mining ventures, and battles efforts to sabotage his invention and farmers who support his fight to oppose the destruction of their land.

A *Variety* reviewer wrote, "The story in screen form is told in a direct manner but the author in adaptation has failed to retail the suspense quality which Frank Urson's written effort contained. The result is that the production is a program picture and that is all. It is hardly worthy of a full week's run. Wallace Reid plays the heroic role in a very matter-of-fact fashion, denoting that he is so sure of himself that it matters not what sort of a screen performance he

(TOP) **Wallace Reid and Lois Wilson in Frank Urson's *The Hell Diggers* (1921), and** (BOTTOM) **Alexander Broun and Wallace Reid in the same film.**

delivers. A continuance of this attitude at this particular time and he will discover the vogue he has enjoyed in the last few years has slipped away from him. He'll be high and dry on the lot. Lois Wilson, who plays opposite him, manages to present a rather pleasing performance in a role that requires little. Frank Leigh as the heavy delivers with a wallop and a character role played by Alexander Broun is a real delight."

"Wallace Reid motored almost the entire length of California to make the exterior scenes," began a reviewer writing in the *Oakland Tribune*. "This is one of those red-blooded roles . . . a fine opportunity for the display of those typical characteristics in setting which have made him so popular. There is plenty of excitement in the story, and the author has made a careful study of the first hand of the local conditions and the work of the dredging companies."

THE AFFAIRS OF ANATOL (1921)
AKA THE PRODIGAL NIGHT (UNITED KINGDOM)
PARAMOUNT
DIRECTOR: Cecil B. DeMille
CAST: Wallace Reid, Gloria Swanson, Elliott Dexter, Bebe Daniels, Monte Blue, Wanda Hawley, Theodore Roberts, Agnes Ayres, Theodore Kosloff, Polly Moran, Raymond Hatton, Julia Faye, Charles Ogle, Winter Hall, Guy Oliver, Patsy Ruth Miller, Lucien Littlefield, Zelma Maja, Shannon Day, Elinor Glyn, William Boyd, Maude Wayne, Fred Huntley.
SYNOPSIS: In a story by Jeanie Macpherson, based on a play by Arthur Schnitzler, a man dallies with different young women before returning to his wife.

"It was no easy task for the photographers, Alvin Wycoff and Karl Struss, to get the best effects from their cameras," said Jesse Lasky in an interview with the *Atlanta Constitution*. "From the standpoint of the cameraman, every one of these luminaries offered an individual problem. The case can best be explained by stating that Wallace Reid has certain lighting arrangements under which he appears to best advantage. Gloria Swanson requires an entirely different gradation of lights. Wanda Hawley, a blond of the most pronounced type, requires still another arrangement, and Bebe Daniels who is as markedly a brunette as Wanda Hawley is a blond,

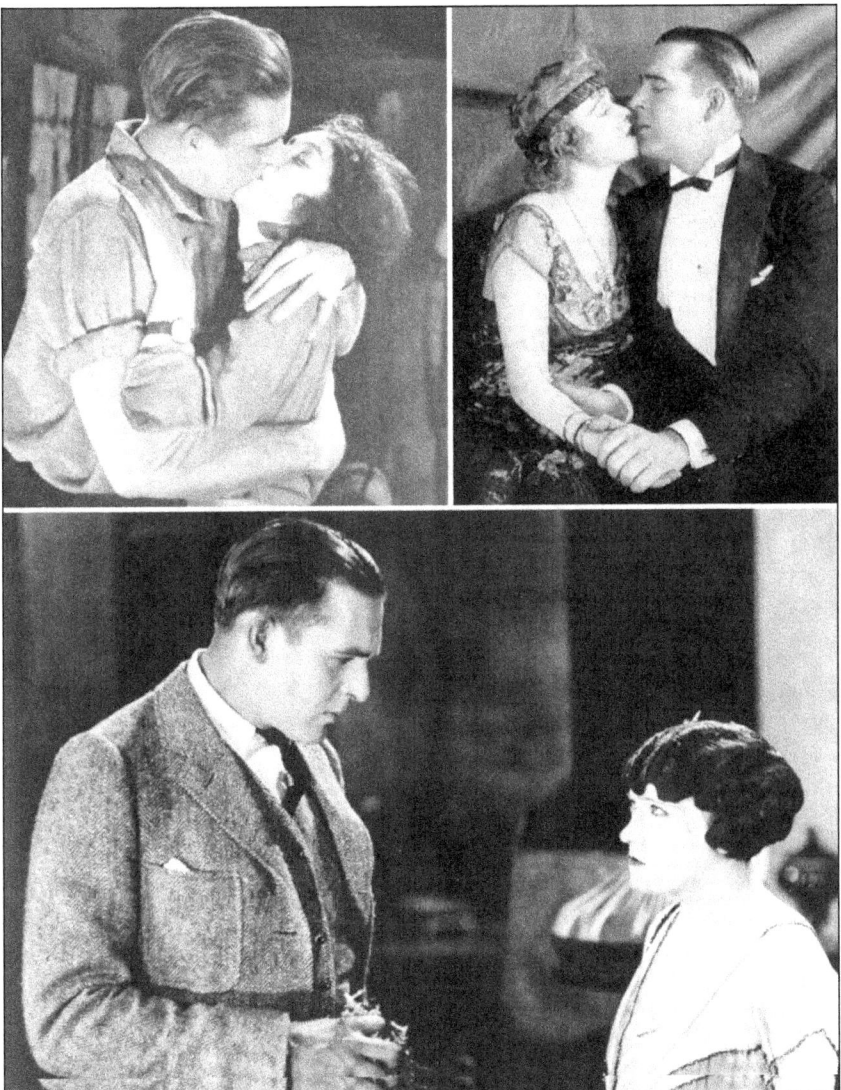

Three scenes with Wallace Reid in Cecil B. De Mille's *The Affairs of Anatol* (1921): (TOP LEFT) **with Bebe Daniels,** (TOP RIGHT) **with Wanda Hawley, and** (BOTTOM) **with Gloria Swanson.**

again takes best under different conditions. To the photographers was given the seemingly impossible task of synchronizing the lighting effects so that all appeared on an equal photographic footing that would still show up each individual to the greatest advantage. The difficulty was increased by the fact that each important character had his or her favorite style of makeup. One of the leading characters

Wallace Reid and Bebe Daniels in Cecil B. De Mille's *The Affairs of Anatol* (1921).

has a decided preference for yellow grease paint. Another favors pink. The resulting complexity of having several characters appear in different shades of makeup practically multiplies the cameraman's difficulties. The work was, in large measure, facilitated by the spirit of cooperation that permeated the cast. Every member was an experienced screen actor or actress and had learned the value of sacrifice. The result was that, in some cases, where it was necessary to alter the makeup from the individual's favorite style in order to ensure the success of the photography, the changes were made willingly for the success of the production."

The *New York Times* heralded the film when it premiered in New York at two theaters simultaneously, an unusual marketing ploy for the time. "Here is Mr. DeMille at his best," the newspaper review said. "Whether you will like it is another matter. If you like a glorified movie that you can take as a movie and are not asked to take as a genuinely human photoplay, you will probably be among the large number who will find enjoyment in Anatol and his innocent escapades. Mr. DeMille, it appears, must be ornate and artificial, theatrical at all times, and his style is not suited, therefore, to stories of real people and serious import . . . but the case of the present offering is different. Here is an extravagant story that never by any chance could be taken seriously, ornamented by elaborate and expensive sets, and such an assemblage of screen favorites as has never before been brought together in one picture for the worship of idolatrous fans. And, incidentally, a number of the screen's best pantomimes are among them. So it's a magnificent puppet show, legitimately and logically excessive in every way. For once Mr. DeMille's theatricalities are in harmony with his subject. He is free, for example, to indulge his love of trick furniture and bizarre costumes to his heart's content without giving offense. They're all part of the show." The review went on to point out, "Wallace Reid, as Anatol, farces some of his scenes delightfully."

FOREVER (1921)
PARAMOUNT
DIRECTOR: George Fitzmaurice
CAST: Wallace Reid, Elsie Ferguson, Montagu Love, George Fawcett, Dolores Cassinelli, Paul McAllister, Elliott Dexter, Barbara Dean, Charles Eaton, Jerome Patrick, Nell Roy Buck.
SYNOPSIS: In a scenario by Ouida Bergère, based on Daphne Du Maurier's *Peter Ibbetson*, an architect rediscovers his childhood sweetheart only to be separated from her when he is imprisoned for a murder he did not commit. His love visits him in dreams while he languishes in prison.

A lobby card and three scenes from George Fitzmaurice's *Forever* (1922) with Elsie Ferguson, George Fawcett, and Wallace Reid.

The *New York Times*, seeing the film in advance while it was still titled *Peter Ibbetson*, wrote in its review, "How persuasive the story on the screen is will depend for each individual upon how much his or her loyalty to the book or the play is . . . for one thing, the photography is beautiful. George Fitzmaurice, who directed the production, is a director of pure pictures. His scenes are gracefully composed, effectively lighted, and softly toned without sacrifice of clearness. Many of the sets of *Peter Ibbetson* are a treat to the eye, and some of them are dramatically expressive, too. The story is largely verbal, but whenever it does get into moving pictures it is alluring. The effect is strengthened by the players. Though only a few of them do any noteworthy acting, George Fawcett, as old Major Duquesnois, being among those emphatically worthy of note, they all look their parts . . . Wallace Reid, as Peter, is esthetic enough, almost, to banish rude memories of his irresistibly visible farcing in other pictures."

A review in the *Wellsboro Gazette* said, "A delicate touch of symbolism appears in the picture, *Forever* . . . the symbolism enters the picture in a manner frequently seen in literature but seldom in a motion picture production. The scenic atmosphere of the picture was made to correspond with the lives of the characters and their moods. It is a story of all you've ever dreamed a great love could be. Told in enthralling action and scenes of exquisite beauty."

Forever is considered forever "lost." A 35mm print of *Forever* was given by Wally's widow to a proposed museum in Hollywood, but when the museum collection was dispersed, the film had mysteriously disappeared. Fans of the film's stars hope that one day the print will show up.

DON'T TELL EVERYTHING (1921)
PARAMOUNT
DIRECTOR: Sam Wood
CAST: Wallace Reid, Gloria Swanson, Elliott Dexter, Dorothy Cumming, Genevieve Blinn, K. T. Stevens, Charles De Briac, Raymond De Briac.
SYNOPSIS: In a story by Albert LeVino based on a work by Lorna Moon, a wandering husband momentarily leaves his wife to explore a fascinating, athletic-minded girl.

The *Washington Post* reviewer wrote, "The author, Lorna Moon, has satirized in brilliant and appealing fashion the engagement period in the career of a young, when the question of telling each other all they know is a moot one, and when the idea that 'what you don't know will never hurt you is frequently relied on to gloss over the confessional shortcomings of one or the other members of the informal matrimonial understanding . . . The satirical nature of Miss Moon's theme has been carried through with conviction and force, though it is never permitted to eclipse for a moment the brilliantly romantic and splendid scenic elements of a gorgeously executed photoplay production."

A reviewer in *Variety* wrote, ". . . this is a first-class offering for all houses. It is clean, wholesome, well-conceived character comedy with a society touch. It is knit together with every incident related to the central idea. This is the result, probably, of Mr. Buchannan's ability to boss the works. Sam Wood directed, handling the actors

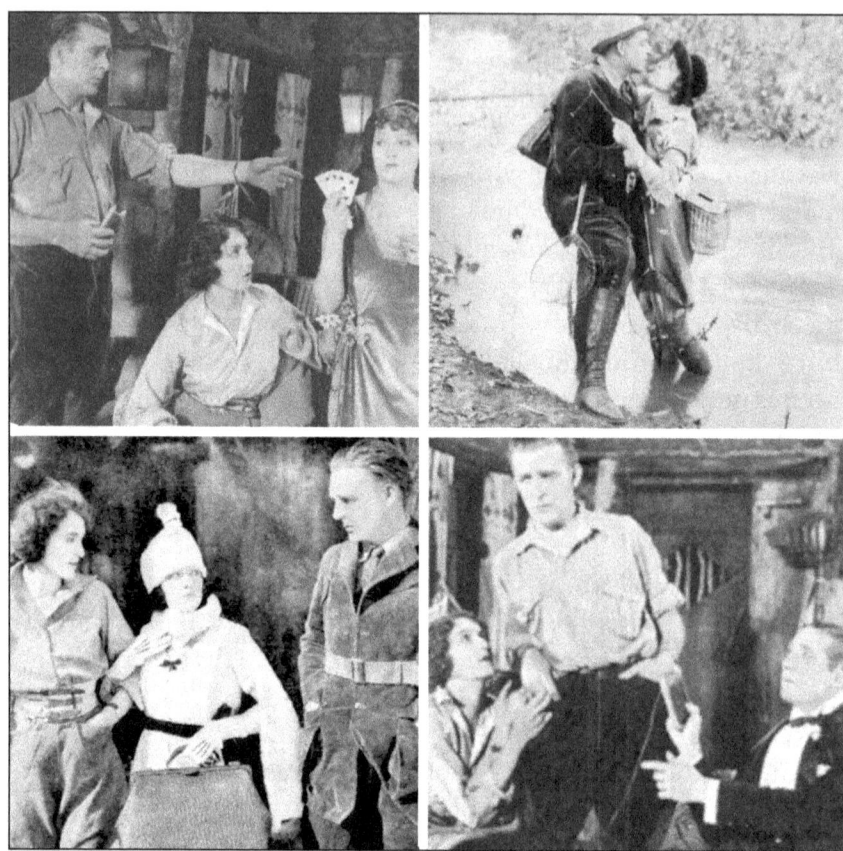

Four scenes from Sam Wood's *Don't Tell Everything* (1921): (TOP LEFT) **Wallace Reid, Dorothy Cumming, Gloria Swanson,** (TOP RIGHT) **Wallace Reid and Dorothy Cumming,** (BOTTOM LEFT) **Dorothy Cumming, Gloria Swanson, Wallace Reid, and** (BOTTOM RIGHT) **Dorothy Cumming, Wallace Reid, and Elliott Dexter.**

competently." The review also took special note of the clothing worn by Gloria Swanson. ". . . they are reconciled up at the hunting lodge of the vamp in the mountains to which Miss Swanson proceeded in the most extraordinary ermine wrap. This was the flashlight of costuming, the sort of thing no one in their senses would wear anywhere save at a masquerade—certainly never to go motoring in. Evidently this is one of the things Mr. Buchannan didn't supervise. Outside of that, what Miss Swanson contributed was very much to the point. This comedy is mostly by-play, comedy touches. Miss Swanson managed them very well. So did Mr. Reid. Mr. Dexter had little to do, but did it acceptably enough."

"It is especially good to see Wallace Reid get back to farcing," wrote a reviewer for The *New York Times*. "He always seems self-conscious and soon grows monotonous as a romantic or melodramatic hero, but as a farceur he is delightful. And he is agreeably aided and abetted by Gloria Swanson and Elliott Dexter."

RENT FREE (1922)
PARAMOUNT
DIRECTOR: James Cruze
CAST: Wallace Reid, Lila Lee, Henry Barrows, Gertrude Short, Lillian Leighton, Clarence Geldart, Claire McDowell, Lucien Littlefield.
SYNOPSIS: In a scenario by Mann Page, based on a story by Elmer Rice, a successful lawyer changes careers in mid-life and becomes a struggling artist living in a mansion with two women.

A review in the *Lima New* said, "There can be no question but that Wallace Reid makes the very most of his role in *Rent Free*, his new picture . . . true, the story is along Cinderella lines, and not the kind of story one would naturally associate with the popular Mr. Reid, but its entertaining, at least, and that's what you're looking for."

"The long arm of coincidence is pretty thoroughly stretched in unfolding the plot," wrote a reviewer in *Variety*. "Running but 50 minutes, it peters out as it approaches the clinch, and were it not for the uniformly high grade acting and painstaking direction would fail to hold interest half way through. As it is, you laugh heartily several times at the ludicrous situations, which would be well nigh impossible in actual life but the moment your thoughts resume their functioning you realize how far-fetched it all is, and it becomes necessary to win you back all over again. Wallace Reid is one of our most popular male picture stars, but he won't continue so unless he is given more consistent stories to appear in . . . ."

THE WORLD'S CHAMPION (1922)
PARAMOUNT
DIRECTOR: Philip E. Rosen
CAST: Wallace Reid, Lois Wilson, Lionel Belmore, Henry Miller, Jr., Helen Dunbar, Leslie Casey, William J. Ferguson, Guy Oliver, Stanley Sandford.

(TOP LEFT) **A studio poster for James Cruze's *Rent Free* (1922, and** (TOP RIGHT AND BOTTOM) **Wallace Reid in the same film.**

SYNOPSIS: In a story by Albert LeVino, based on a play by A. E. Thomas and Thomas Louden, a young Englishman rises to the top of his game in America, and then returns to England to succeed in winning the love of a noblewoman.

Variety's reviewer wrote, "The film has not realized on the comedy value instances the show held, but on the other hand, has come through for laughs where the stage presentation was unable to connect. The story is fitting for Reid, who ambles through without being called upon for any exceptional effort, though lending a deft touch to the character, possibly due to direction, that keeps the theme continuously amusing, backed of course, by his appearance. Well dressed, having most of the action take place within interior sets, and nicely cast, the picture has the punch laughs placed down near the finish previous to a non-clinch ending which leaves a satisfactory and wholesome impression . . . it is a program feature that doesn't infringe on the double-feature racket. It'll get over by itself and register for a society comedy the censors won't have to annoy anyone about."

The *New York Times* said the picture was an ". . . often tedious photoplay in five or six reels of film. In its bright spots—and they are bright—Wallace Reid is seen in a quietly humorous role, such as he is easily capable of, and such as is keenly missed whenever he essays a seriously romantic part. There are also a number of amusing incidents in the story that derive their vitality from the way in which they are presented. For example, there is a bloody battle of fists between the hero and the villain, not one blow of which is pictured on the screen. Yet the spectator does not miss a moment of the fight, and he enjoys it a great deal more than if it had been literally detailed."

ACROSS THE CONTINENT (1922)
PARAMOUNT
DIRECTOR: Philip E. Rosen
CAST: Wallace Reid, Mary MacLaren, Theodore Roberts, Betty Francisco, Walter Long, Lucien Littlefield, Jack Herbert, Guy Oliver, Sidney D'Albrook.
SYNOPSIS: In a story by Byron Morgan, a car-racing enthusiast drives his father's speedy machine in a transcontinental race.

(TOP LEFT) **A foreign language movie poster from Philip E. Rosen's *The World's Champion* (1922).** (TOP RIGHT) **Wallace Reid, and** (BOTTOM) **Lois Wilson and Wallace Reid in the same film.**

A review in the *Davenport Democrat* said, "If a transcontinental race were staged between entries by all the leading makes of automobiles, what type of a car would win? This question is pictorially answered in *Across the Continent* by Wallace Reid, Paramount star,

Two scenes from Philip E. Rosen's *Across the Continent* (1922): (TOP) Theodore Roberts, Mary MacLaren, and Wallace Reid, and (BOTTOM) Wallace Reid.

who thunders over the roads in a small flivver and drives it to victory. Wallace Reid has proven popular in all of the preceding automobile race stories in which he has appeared, but his latest is the most unique of them all. The action doesn't take place on a circular race track, but involves all kinds of roads in the United States, all kinds of weather, and a good many thrilling stunts and incidents. Action, fast and spicy, is its principal ingredient."

"Wallace Reid in mad dash risks his life . . . races his flivver through great fire curtain in race," blared headlines in the *Mexia Evening News* review. "One of the most thrilling scenes ever in pictures is shown when Mr. Reid, who is driving a flivver in a transcontinental race, dashes through a blazing roadway at more than eighty miles an hour . . . *Across the Continent* marks the return of Mr. Reid to his now famous automobile speed driving pictures."

"A coast-to-coast auto race for the family honor and the love of a girl is deftly framed to provide one of the best moments of suspense the screen has ever designed," praised a reviewer in *Variety*. "There was an audible stir of excitement during the big passage, eloquent tribute to the skill of the people concerned in the presentation from author to actor. It is worth nothing that the author also made the scenario and a few other names are disclosed as having had a part in the production."

THE DICTATOR (1922)
PARAMOUNT
DIRECTOR: James Cruze
CAST: Wallace Reid, Lila Lee, Theodore Kosloff, Kalla Pasha, Sidney Bracey, Fred Butler, Walter Long, Alan Hale.
SYNOPSIS: In a story by Walter Woods, based on a play by Richard Harding Davis, a young American millionaire follows his sweetheart to South America and becomes involved in their revolution.

A review in the *Woodland Daily Democrat* said, "When Richard Harding Davis wrote *The Dictator* he couldn't have written a better character to fit Wallace Reid than that of Brooke Travers, the son of the Banana King who fixes the price of the fruit according to the cost of tropical precedents. The scenes are laid in California and in South America. Mr. Reid, as the hero, a carefree adventurer chap, becomes embroiled in a South American revolution and has many exciting adventures, eventually falling in love with and winning the beautiful of a self-styled liberator. The action is rapid and many of the situations are thrilling to a degree. It's just the sort of story old and young alike enjoy."

The *New York Times* wrote in its review, "Wallace Reid, as the hero, is back at his farcing and this means that he is altogether enjoyable.

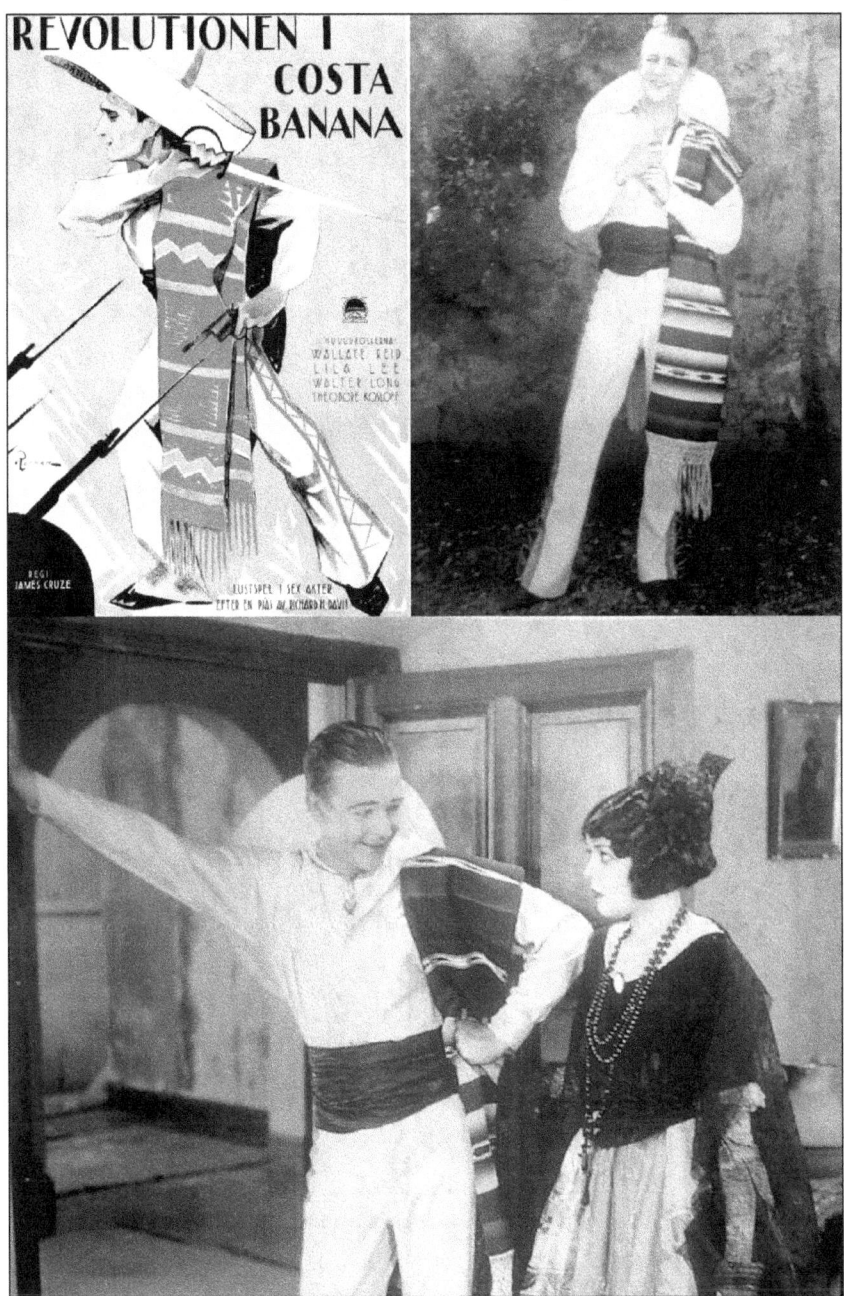

(TOP LEFT) **A foreign language movie poster from James Cruze's *The Dictator* (1922),** (TOP RIGHT) **Wallace Reid, and (bottom) Wallace Reid and Lila Lee in the same film. Wally looked visibly weak in this film made when his health was failing.**

Two scenes from James Cruze's *The Dictator* (1922) with Wallace Reid and Lila Lee.

Reid, the gay comedian, is worth a dozen of Reid, the romantic lover, and in *The Dictator*, he is as gay as he has ever been."

"The revolution itself is a riot of absurd spectacle," summed up a reviewer in *Variety*, "and the whole thing is surrounded by magnificent palaces and beautiful tropical scenery which give an added touch to a situation already comic. Reid plays the blundering young American with just the right touch of casual nonchalance to give point to its broad absurdity. Lila Lee makes a charming dark-eyed heroine, and the picture is rich in pictorial surprises. The whole bill was framed to keep comedy to the fore . . . the title writing also contributed greatly to the comedy."

NICE PEOPLE (1922)
PARAMOUNT
DIRECTOR: William C. de Mille
CAST: Wallace Reid, Bebe Daniels, Conrad Nagel, Julia Faye, Claire McDowell, Edward Martindel, Eve Southern, Bertram Johns, William Boyd, Ethel Wales.
SYNOPSIS: In a story by Clara Beranger, based on a play by Rachel Crothers, the petting parties and free drinking of Easterners shocks a shy Westerner when he is caught with them in a farmhouse during a thunderstorm.

Variety's reviewer thought the picture plot "rather thin," and thought the performers tried valiantly to rise above the material, praising Bebe Daniels, Julia Faye, and Conrad Nagel. Special kudos were given to old Griffith actress, Claire McDowell, for her conception of the aunt role. "Nice People compared to some of the stuff Paramount has been pre-releasing this summer at its Broadway twin weekly change houses, suffices as a one-week feature, although compared to regular fall and winter stuff, it is just a good society program release."

THE GHOST BREAKER (1922)
PARAMOUNT
DIRECTOR: Alfred Green
CAST: Wallace Reid, Lila Lee, Walter Hiers, Arthur Carewe, J. Farrell MacDonald, Frances Raymond, Snitz Edwards.
SYNOPSIS: In a story by Walter DeLeon, based on a play by Paul Dickey and Charles Goddard, a freewheeling young man and his manservant help a pretty Spanish girl dispose of ghosts haunting her castle. When he exposes the spirits as robbers in disguise, he wins the girl's love.

(LEFT) **A studio advertising poster from William C. de Mille's *Nice People* (1922).** (TOP RIGHT) **William Boyd, Conrad Nagel, Julia Faye, Bebe Daniels, and Wallace Reid, and** (BOTTOM RIGHT) **Wallace Reid with Bebe Daniels in the same film.**

"You can hear them laugh a block away at the Rialto," began a review in the *Lincoln Evening State Journal* and *Lincoln Daily News*. "The feature which is attracting capacity houses and causing explosions

Three scenes from Alfred Green's *The Ghost Breaker* (1922) with Wallace Reid and Lila Lee.

of laughter is *The Ghost Breaker,* a gay tale of adventure and love, with Wallace Reid supported by Lila Lee and Walter Hiers."

"This is one of those usual Wallace Reid starring pictures, fairly well done, with considerable comedy element that prevents the picture from falling into the classification of ordinary," considered a reviewer in *Variety*. "To the Reid fans the feature will prove pleasing; to others it will be but mildly entertaining. As a box office attraction, the draw depends whether or not the exhibitor's average audience is strong for the star. There is noting in the production that will pull additional business . . . if it wasn't for the world of Walter Hiers, who does a blackface valet to the star, there wouldn't be anything to the story . . . his work in this picture pulls all the laughs there are . . . the sets are elaborate and the photography good but it looks as though Reid had made up his mind that he was going to do as little work in this picture as possible, and possibly conspired with the script writer and the director to help him out. Things of this sort are about as sure a road to oblivion as far as the screen is concerned, as being involved in some unsavory scandal."

"You will probably be bothered by the intrusive and persistent reflection that it could have been a great deal better than it is," wrote a *New York Times* reviewer. "And this is disturbing to anyone's enjoyment of a comedy. But you can't get away from it. The reflection sticks. For the fact is that the Dickey-Goddard play offered almost boundless opportunities for fun and thrills on the screen, and they have been taken advantage of only half-way and half-heartedly. Whereas the comedy ought to move rapidly with mystery and humor merrily mixed and spinning always, it proceeds deliberately and dwells upon each detail of its strung-out story until the impatient spectator wants to stick spurs in it to make it go . . . Wallace Reid, Walter Hiers, and Snitz Edwards have all been much gayer, much more pointedly meaningful as pantomimes than they are in *The Ghost Breaker*."

CLARENCE (1922)
PARAMOUNT
DIRECTOR: William C. de Mille
CAST: Wallace Reid, Agnes Ayres, May McAvoy, Kathlyn Williams, Edward Martindel, Robert Agnew, Adolphe Menjou, Bertram Johns, Dorothy Gordon, Mayme Kelso.
SYNOPSIS: In a story by Clara Beranger based on a play by Booth Tarkington, a returning war veteran becomes comically employed with a wealthy family. In a mix-up of identities, Clarence is believed to be a deserter and then revealed to be a university professor.

(TOP LEFT) **An advertisement for William C. de Mille's *Clarence* (1922), as it appeared in the *Lima News*.** (TOP RIGHT) **Wally with Agnes Ayres,** (BOTTOM LEFT) **Agnes Ayres, and (bottom right) Wally with May McAvoy in the same film.**

". . . Wallace Reid, Agnes Ayres, and May McAvoy form a triumvirate of stars that cannot fail to dazzle and attract the most seasoned picturegoer," wrote a reviewer in the *Lima News*. "These three popular players not only appear together in *Clarence* but they are credited with scoring a success even more pronounced than they have ever achieved in individual appearances . . . Mr. de Mille has preserved all of the Tarkington flavor in his screen adaptation . . . he has made it a thoroughly enjoyable comedy that should find a welcome from all classes of picturegoers."

A reviewer in *Variety* thought the picture version of the play was remarkably amusing. "The picture is a demonstration of the fact that the screen can be the medium of fine character delineation and gentle humor and is not by any means restricted to horseplay and crude melodrama . . . the character of Clarence is rather a departure for Reid. He does get into the spirit of the part, which calls for quiet effectiveness and absence of emphasis, no easy role for a pantomimist trained to flamboyant technique of the studio. The same comment applies to the others of a singularly excellent cast rich in film notables. All the care that went to the casting shows for full value. The company is an eminent example of what can be done in high comedy in the pictures there was not a false note in the five reels . . . the sparing use of titles is notable throughout the picture."

"They've made a pleasant screen comedy out of material taken from Booth Tarkington's play," wrote a reviewer for the *New York Times*. "As might be expected, the picture is not as good as the original play was, and, be it hoped, still is, which is due in large part, to the fact that the play needs the speaking stage. Inevitably, much of it is lost in the process of adapting it to the silent, pictorial screen . . . but it's a good substitute . . . in the role of Clarence, the returned soldier who innocently looks for a job and finds himself on the domestic battleground of the perpetually agitated Wheeler family, Wallace Reid qualifies beyond expectations. He fits into the part of the meek, yet exceedingly competent, Clarence with apparent ease and is able in several places to indulge in the light comedy pantomime at which he is adept."

30 DAYS (1922)
PARAMOUNT
DIRECTOR: James Cruze
CAST: Wallace Reid, Wanda Hawley, Charles Ogle, Cyril Chadwick, Herschel Mayall, Helen Dunbar, Carmen Phillips, Kalla Pasha, Robert Brower.
SYNOPSIS: Based on a play by A. E. Thomas and Clayton Hamilton, a young man tries to avoid a jealous boyfriend and gets his friend, a judge, to put him in jail. There, he discovers the jealous boyfriend is also incarcerated for the same length of his term.

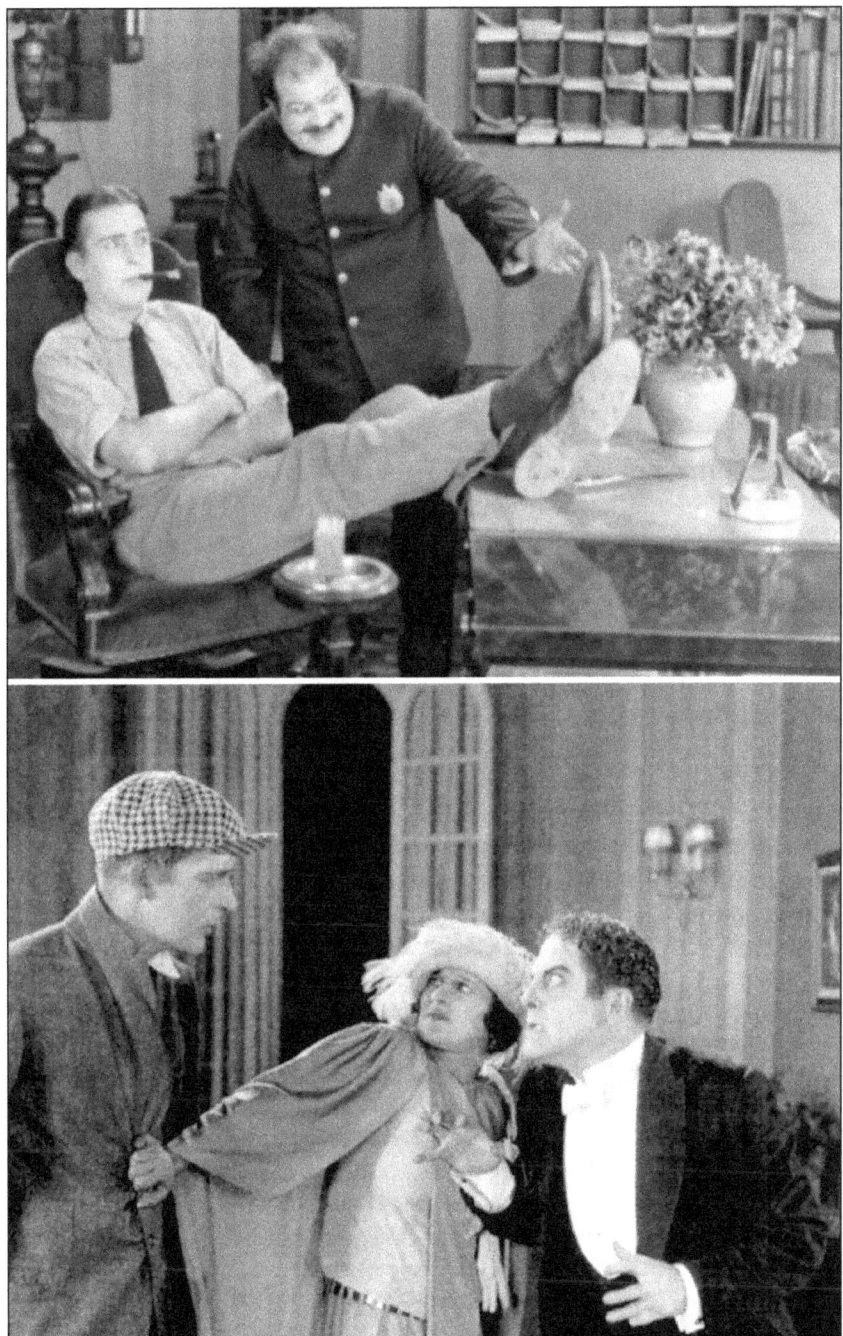

Two scenes from James Cruze's *30 Days* (1922) with Wallace Reid, Wanda Hawley, and Charles Ogle.

The picture landed with a thud in the mind of the reviewer for *Variety*. "It is merely a program picture of average merit," he wrote. "If Wallace Reid is satisfied to continue in pictures of this type he will soon join the stars of yesteryear. Not that his acting is bad, but he seems to think it sufficient in some scenes to merely make a personal appearance. Despite a few typical Reid touches most of his work is commonplace, and mediocrity neither makes nor maintains a star. Furthermore, he seems at times to think he is Harold Lloyd. The story itself is an amusing conception, but utterly misses fire in the telling . . . the titles are mediocre . . . the direction is uneven . . . several gags, quite extraneous to the real plot, are introduced to little point."

According to a reviewer from the *Syracuse Herald*, "It's a fast-moving comedy that deals with the operations of a villainous Italian knife man . . . Herschel Mayall of *Kismet, Queen of Sheba*, and *Civilization* fame, has a part of fights, knives, and laughs as the pursuing Polenta...as the warden who persecutes John Floyd, then presents him with a gramophone; who breakfasts in bed, and has a valet, easy chair, and all the luxuries and comforts of home, Mr. Cruze has cast Kalla Pasha, the veteran of many Mack Sennett slapstick comedies."

The *New York Times* film critic wrote that the picture ". . . doesn't get anywhere in particular nor go very fast as a story, but it is a gay piece of foolishness and keeps the spectator in pretty continuous good humor. You don't often laugh out loud at its aimless nonsense, but you are likely to find yourself chuckling most of the time. Wallace Reid is at his farcing again, which means that he is doing the thing he seems cut out for, and James Cruze, one of the most spirited directors in the business, has made some more of his sharp-edged pictures . . . there really isn't any coherent story to the piece. There isn't any plot that matters. However, it may be reported that Wallace Reid is a young man in love, who has a sympathetic nature which makes him do things that his sweetheart and others call flirting."

An advertisement for Fred Caldwell's *Night Life in Hollywood* (1922).

NIGHT LIFE IN HOLLYWOOD (1922)
PARAMOUNT
DIRECTOR: Fred Caldwell
CAST: J. Frank Glendon, Josephine Hill, Gale Henry, J. L. McComas, Elizabeth Rhodes, Jack Connolly, Delores Hall.
SYNOPSIS: A star-struck family meanders through Hollywood and encounters dozens of stars. Wallace Reid appears in a cameo role.

A TRIP TO PARAMOUNTOWN (1922)
PARAMOUNT
DIRECTOR: Jack Cunningham
CAST: T. Roy Barnes, Alice Brady, Betty Compson, Dorothy Dalton, Bebe Daniels, Marion Davies, Cecil B. DeMille, William C. de Mille, George Fawcett, Julia Faye, Elsie Ferguson, Wanda Hawley, Jack Holt, Leatrice Joy, Lila Lee, Walter Long, Bert Lytell, May McAvoy, Thomas Meighan, George Melford, Mary Miles Minter, Tom Moore, Conrad Nagel, Nita Naldi, Anna Q. Nilsson, Wallace Reid, Theodore Roberts, Milton Sills, Gloria Swanson, Rudolph Valentino.
SYNOPSIS: Paramount stars appear in humorous scenes as part of a behind-the-scenes newsreel.

An advertising poster for James Cruze's *Hollywood* (1923).

HOLLYWOOD (1923)
PARAMOUNT
DIRECTOR: James Cruze
CAST: Hope Brown, Luke Cosgrave, George K. Arthur, Ruby Lafayette, Harris Gordon, Bess Flowers, Eleanor Lawson, King Zany.
SYNOPSIS: Thomas J. Geraghty wrote a scenario, based on a story by Frank Condon in which an aspiring movie actress and her family come to Hollywood. The girl fails to find work, but her entire family finds success in films. Along the way, they have brief encounters with more than fifty stars. Wallace Reid appears in a cameo role.

BIBLIOGRAPHY

"$12,500,000 Merger of Film companies." The *New York Times*, June 29, 1916.

"30 Days." The *Syracuse Herald*, December 31, 1922, page 50.

"Across the Continent." The *Davenport Democrat and Leader*, June 6, 1922, page 3.

"Across the Continent." The *Mexia Evening News*, July 19, 1922, page 3.

"Across the Continent." *Variety*, April 28, 1922.

"Affairs of Anatol, The." The *Atlanta Constitution*, August 21, 1921, page 36.

"Affairs of Anatol, The." The *New York Times*, September 12, 1921.

Agnew, Frances. *Motion Picture Acting*. New York: Reliance Newspaper Syndicate, 1913.

Aitken, Roy E. *The Birth of a Nation*. Virginia: William W. Denlinger, 1965.

"Alias Mike Moran." The *Warren Evening Mirror*, April 9, 1919, page 3.

"Alias Mike Moran." *Variety*, March 28, 1919.

"Always Audacious." The *Trenton Evening Times*, November 8, 1920, page 2.

"Always Audacious." *Variety*, November 12, 1920.

Arvidson, Linda. *When the Movies Were Young*. New York: Dover Publications, Inc., 1969.

"Ambassador Theater Opening." The *Los Angeles Examiner*, March 16, 1921, page 1.

"American Cinematographers Ball." *Photoplay*, May 1921, page 11.

American Film Institute Catalog of Feature Films. Berkley: University of California Press, January, 1997.

Ardmore, Jane Kesner Morris. *The Self-Enchanted: Mae Murray, Image of an Era*. New York: McGraw-Hill, 1959.

"A Veteran's View." By Ray C. King in *Reclamation Era*, July 1948, page 137.

"Bandits Kidnap, Rob, Then Free Lottie Pickford." The *Lima Ohio News*, November 10, 1928, page 1.

Bangley, Jimmy. "The Rise to Stardom of Mae Murray." *Classic Images*, August, 1996.

Barry, Iris. *D. W. Griffith American Film Master*. New York: Doubleday, 1965.

"Believe Me, Xantippe." The *Lima Daily News*, November 15, 1918, page 16.

"Believe Me, Xantippe." The *Lincoln Daily Star*, December 29, 1915, page 6.

"Believe Me. Xantippe." The *Warren Evening Times*, June 17, 1918, page 6.

"Believe Me, Xantippe." *Variety*, June 7, 1918.

"Big Reception for Human Wreckage." *Moving Picture World*, July 1923, page 321.

"Big Timber." *Variety*, June 29, 1917.

"Birth of a Nation, The." The *Atlanta Constitution*, December 5, 1915, page 20.

"Birth of a Nation, The." *Variety*, March 12, 1915.

Blaisdell, George. "At the Sign of the Flaming Arcs." *Moving Picture World*, January 3, 1914.

"Blue Flame, The" The *Nebraska State Journal*, July 23, 1922, page 19.

Blum, Daniel. *A Pictorial History of the Silent Screen*. New York: Alfred A. Knopf, 1989.

Bogdanovich, Peter. *Allan Dwan the Last Pioneer*. New York: Praeger Publishers, Inc., 1971.

"Boston Welcomes Mrs. Reid Warmly." *Moving Picture World*, August 18, 1923, page 583.

"Brentwood Country Club." By Marguaret Ettinger in the *New York Telegraph*, July 13, 1919, page 1.

Brown, Karl. *Adventures with D. W. Griffith*. New York: Farrar, Straus and Giroux, 1973.

"Browning Now Given in Moving Pictures." The *New York Times*, October 10, 1909. page 11.

Brownlow, Kevin and John Kobal. *Hollywood: The Pioneers*. New York: Alfred A. Knoph, 1980.

Brownlow, Kevin. *The Parade's Gone By*. New York: Ballentine Books, Inc., 1968.

"Buffalo Bill Returns as Shoshone Dam is Renamed." *Reclamation Era*, June 1946, page 136.

"Bureau Reclaims Its Own, The." By Carl J. Thye in *Reclamation Era*, April 1947, pages 90-92, 94.

"Carmen." The *Fort Wayne News*, November 3, 1915, page 4.

"Carmen." The *Lima Daily News*, October 17, 1915, page 14.

"Carmen." The *Lincoln Daily Star*, July 16, 1916, page 27.

"Carmen." *Variety*, November 5, 1915.

Carr, Harry. "Griffith: Maker of Pictures." *Motion Picture Magazine*, August, 1922, page 11.

Carroll, David. *The Matinee Idols*. New York : Arbor House, 1972.

Casanova, Eve. "I Married the World's Greatest Lover." *True Story*. New York: True Story Publishing Company, February, 1935, page 22-25, 73-75.

Casselton, Harold. *Remembering Dorothy Gish*. Minneapolis, MN: The Society for Cinephiles, 1986.

"Charm School, The." The *Bridgeport Telegram*, May 19, 1921, page 9.

"Charm School, The." The *Wyoming State Tribune*, January 26, 1921, page 5.

"Chumps." The *Gettysburg Times*, April 15, 1912, page 1.

"Church of Flowers." The *Circleville Herald*, August 16, 1932, page 12.

Churchill, Beryl Gail. *The Dam Book: The Construction History of Corbett, Buffalo Bill, and Willwood Dams*. Cody WY: Rustler, 1986.

"Clarence." The *Lima News*, November 19, 1922, page 16.

"Clarence. The *New York Times*, October 16, 1922, page 20.

"Clarence." *Variety*, October 20, 1922.

"Col. Selig's Stories of Movie Life—Wallace Reid." *Screenland*. Chicago: Screenland Publishing Company, April 1923.

"Confession, The." The *Fitchburg Daily Sentinel*, September 20, 1911, page 6.

Cooper, Miriam with Bonnie Herndon. *Dark Lady of the Silents*. New York: The Bobbs-Merrill Company, Inc., 1973.

"Cracksman Santa Claus." The *Elyria Evening Telegram*, December 29, 1913, page 1.

"Craven, The." The *Wichita Daily Times*, March 21, 1915, page 18.

Croy, Homer. *Star Maker: The Story of D. W. Griffith*. New York: Duell, Sloan and Pearce, 1959.

Cugat, F. "Mae Murray's Victory. *Movie Weekly*, 19 August 1922.

Cuniberti, John Michael. *The Birth of a Nation Shot-By-Shot Analysis*. Woodbridge, Connecticut: Research Publications, 1979.

Curzon, Julian. *The Great Cyclone at St. Louis.* Carbondale: Southern Illinois University, 1997.

"Dancin' Fool, The." The *Daily Kennebec Journal,* May 19, 1920, page 12.

"Dancin' Fool, The." The *New York Times,* May 3, 1920, page 18.

"Dancin' Fool, The." *Variety,* May 7, 1920.

"Dancin' Fool, The." The *Wyoming State Tribune,* January 18, 1921, page 5.

DeMille, Cecil B. *The Autobiography of Cecil B. DeMille.* New Jersey: Prentice-Hall, Inc., 1959.

"Devil Stone, The." The *Oakland Tribune,* January 9, 1918, page 9.

"Devil Stone, The." *Variety,* December 21, 1917.

"Dictator, The." The *New York Times,* July 3, 1922, page 8.

"Dictator, The." The *Woodland Daily Democrat,* October 24, 1922, page 6.

"Disabled Soldiers of the Great War Ball." *Photoplay,* December 1920, page 11.

"Don't Tell Everything." The *New York Times,* December 12, 1921, page 20.

"Don't Tell Everything." The *Washington Post,* December 12, 1921, page 10.

"Double Speed." By Hazel Simpson Naylor in *Motion Picture Magazine,* June 1920, page 110.

"Double Speed." The *New York Times,* February 2, 1920, page 10.

"Double Speed." *Variety*, February 6, 1920.

"Dub, The." The *Oakland Tribune*, March 24, 1919, page 5.

"Dub, The." The *Trenton Evening Times*, January 25, 1919, page 7.

"Dub, The." *Variety*, January 17, 1919.

Easton, Carol. *The Search for Sam Goldwyn*. New York: William Morrow and Co., Inc., 1976.

"Editorial in Praise of Human Wreckage." *Moving Picture World*, July 21, 1923, page 241.

"End of the Film, The." The *Mexia Evening News*, January 24, 1923, page 4.

"Enoch Arden." By Louise Reeves in *Moving Picture World*, April 24, 1915, page 568.

"Enoch Arden." The *Mansfield News*, July 31, 1915, page 9.

"Excuse My Dust." By Burns Mantle in *Photoplay*, June 1920, page 68.

"Excuse My Dust." *Variety*, March 26, 1920.

"Famous Players Revolutionizes Policy of Production." *Moving Picture World*, November 13, 1920, page 173.

"Famous Players Output Unaffected by Studio Fire." *Motion Picture News*, September 25, 1915, page 51-52.

Farrar, Geraldine. *Such Sweet Compulsion*. New York: The Greystone Press, 1938.

"Federated Arts Boycott." By Harry Carr in the *Los Angeles Times*, December 24, 1922, page 11.

"Film Stars Appear to be Deserting the West." The *Mansfield News*, May 22, 1921, page 28.

"Firefly of France, The." The *Indiana Evening Gazette*, December 24, 1918, page 1.

"Firefly of France, The." *Variety*, June 21, 1918.

"Fires of Fate, The." The *Perry Daily Chief*, December 17, 1913.

"Forever." The *New York Times*, October 17, 1921, page 18.

"Forever." The *Wellsboro Gazette*, May 4, 1922, page 5.

Franklin, Joe and William K. Everson. *Classics of the Silent Screen*. New York: Citadel Press, 1971.

"Frightful Calamity — St. Louis Struck by Cyclone." The *Reno Weekly Gazette* Stockman, June 4, 1896, page 8.

Frohman, Daniel. *Daniel Frohman Presents*. New York: Claude Kendall and Willoughby Sharp, Inc., 1935.

Geduld, Harry M. *Focus on D.W. Griffith*. New York: Prentice-Hall, 1971.

"Ghost Breaker, The." The *Lincoln Evening State Journal and Lincoln Daily News*, December 14, 1922, page 3.

"Ghost Breaker, The." The *New York Times*, September 11, 1922, page 20.

"Ghost Breaker, The." *Variety*, September 1922.

Gish, Lillian. *Dorothy and Lillian Gish*. New York: Charles Scribner's Sons, 1973.

Gish, Lillian with Ann Pinchot. *The Movies Mr. Griffith and Me.* New Jersey: Prentice-Hall, 1969.

"Gloria Swanson Christmas Tree at Sanitarium." The *Oakland Tribune*, December 25, 1922, page 1.

"Golden Chance, The." The *Fort Wayne News*, January 19, 1916, page 4.

"Golden Chance, The." The *Lima Times Democrat*, June 17, 1916, page 3.

"Golden Chance, The." *Variety*, December 31, 1915.

"Golden Fetter, The." The *Fort Wayne News*, January 30, 1917, page 6.

"Golden Fetter, The." The *Middletown Times Press*, July 13, 1917, page 9.

"Golden Fetter, The." *Variety*, March 9, 1917.

Goldwyn, Samuel. *Behind the Screen.* New York: George H. Doran Company, 1923.

"Greater Devotion, The." The *Frederick Post*, March 25, 1914, page 2.

"Griffith, David Wark." In *Theater Arts*, April 1945, pages 242-249.

Griffith, Richard. *The Film Til Now.* Great Britain: Fletcher & Sons, Ltd., 1967.

"Had Dope for Sale." *Variety*, November 25, 1920.

"Hal Reid—Father of the Sport Shirt." By Arabella Boone in *Photoplay*, January 1919, page 11.

"Hawthorn of the U.S.A." *Variety*, November 21, 1919.

Hays, Will H. *The Memoirs of Will H. Hays*. New York: Doubleday and Company, Inc., 1955.

"Hearts of the World Premier." By Antony Anderson in the *Los Angeles Times*, March 13, 1918, page 1.

"Hell Diggers, The." The *Oakland Tribune*, November 27, 1921, page 48.

Henderson, Robert M. *D. W. Griffith His Life and Work*. New York: Oxford University Press, 1972.

"Heroes Don't Die." By Kolma Flake in *Hollywood*, June 1940, pages 32, 48.

Hayes, Helen. *On Reflection*. New York: M. Evans and Company, Inc., 1968.

"Hidden Treasure, The." *Moving Picture World*, November 23, 1912.

"Hostage, The." The *Fort Wayne News*, September 20, 1917, page 6.

"Hostage, The." The *Lima Daily News*, May 22, 1918, page 9.

"Hostage, The." The *Warren Evening Mirror*, November 23, 1917, page 2.

"Hostage, The." *Variety*, September 14, 1917.

"House with Golden Windows, The." *Variety*, August 11, 1916.

"House of Silence." The *Evening State Journal*. June 10, 1920, page 4.

"House of Silence, The." The *Indianapolis Star*, May 29, 1918, page 11.

"House of Silence, The." The *Oakland Tribune*, June 1918, page 19.

"House of Silence, The." *Variety*, April 26, 1918.

"Human Wreckage Has Notable Opening." *Moving Picture World*, July 21, 1923. Page 242.

"Human Wreckage." *Moving Picture World*, August 11, 1923.

"Human Wreckage." The *New York Times*, August 10, 1923.

"Human Wreckage." *Variety*, August 9, 1923.

"How I Got In." By Wallace Reid in *Motion Picture Magazine*, 1917.

"Intolerance." *Variety*, September 8, 1916.

"Intolerance." The *New York Times*, September 6, 1916, page 6.

"Intolerance." *Film Daily*, September 7, 1916, page 7.

"Jack and Lottie Pickford to be Called Before Grand Jury in Rum Investigation." The *Bridgeport Telegram*, March 17, 1923, page 1.

"Jerry on the Job." By Kenneth McGaffey in *Photoplay*, January 1917, pages 33-42.

"Joan the Woman." The *Decatur Daily Review*, June 28, 1917, page 17.

"Joan, the Woman." The *Mansfield News*, May 23, 1917, page 6.

"Joan the Woman." *Variety*, December 29, 1916.

"Kisses According to Cecil B. DeMille." By Hazel Simpson Naylor in *Motion Picture Magazine*. New York: Brewster Publications, Inc., June 1921.

Knight, Arthur. *The New York Times Directory of the Film.* New York: Arno Press, Inc., 1971.

Koszarski, Richard. *An Evening's Entertainment: The Age of the Silent Feature Picture 1915-1928.* Berkeley: University of California Press, 1990.

"La Belle Marie." The *Newark Daily Advocate*, February 20, 1895, page 8.

"La Belle Marie." The *Oakland Tribune*, June 5, 1896, page 4.

"Lasky Home Guard Company." The *California Home Guard News*, December 22, 1917.

Lasky, Jesse L. *I Blow My Own Horn.* New York: Doubleday & Company, Inc., 1957.

"Less Than Kin." The *Daily Kennebec Journal*, August 9, 1918, page 9.

"Less Than Kin." *Variety*, July 26, 1918.

"Life Story of Wallace Reid, The." By Adela Rogers St. Johns in *Liberty*, June 30, 1928, pages 36-42.

"Life Story of Wallace Reid, The." By Adela Rogers St. Johns in *Liberty*, July 7, 1928, pages 60-66.

"Life Story of Wallace Reid, The." By Adela Rogers St. Johns in *Liberty*, July 14, 1928, pages 50-54.

"Little Colonel Marches Back, The." By Ruth Rankin in *Photoplay*, June 1934, pages 70, 95-97.

"Love Mask, The." The *Fitchburg Daily Sentinel*, May 10, 1916, page 11.

"Lost House, The." The *Indianapolis Star*, July 11, 1915.

"Lottery Man, The." The *New York Times*, October 6, 1919, page 15.

"Lottery Man, The." *Variety*, October 10, 1919.

"Lottie Pickford, Former Star of the Movies, Dies." The *Nevada State Journal*, December 11, 1936, page 10.

"Lottie Pickford Kidnap Plot Is Disclosed." The *Reno Evening Gazette*, November 17, 1930, page 1.

"Lou Tellegen Stabs Self to Death With Shears; Feared Insanity." The *New York Tribune*, October 30, 1934, page 1.

"Love Burglar, The." The *New York Times*, July 28, 1919, page 8.

"Love Burglar, The." *Variety*, August 1, 1919.

"Love Special, The." *Progress*, April 1, 1921, page 7.

"Love Special, The." The *New York Times*, March 21, 1921, page 11.

Magill, Frank N. "The Affairs of Anatol." *Magill's Survey of Cinema Volume 1*. New Jersey: Salem Press, 1982.

"Man From Funeral Range, The." The *Indianapolis Star*, November 17, 1918, page 50.

"Man From Funeral Range, The." The *Oxnard Courier*, February 24, 1919, page 4.

"Man From Funeral Range, The." *Variety*, October 11, 1918.

"Many Stars Attend Human Wreckage." *Moving Picture World*, July 1923, page 324.

"Maria Rosa." The *Lima Times Democrat*, June 5, 1916, page 7.

"Maria Rosa." *Variety*, April 28, 1916.

Marion, Frances. *Off with Their Heads!* New York: The Macmillan Company, 1972.

Marsh, Mae. *Screen Acting.* New York: Frederick A. Stokes Company, 1921.

McGowan, Kenneth. *Behind the Screen.* New York: Delacourte Press, 1965.

"Memories of Wallace Reid." By Bertha Westbrook Reid in *Pictures and Picturegoer*, March 1924, pages 20, 21.

"Memories of Wallace Reid." By Dorothy Davenport Reid in *Picture-Play*, January 1926, pages 66- 67, 109, 110.

Miles, John P. "D. W. Griffith's Twenty-Year Record." In *D. W. Griffith Papers, 1897-1954.* Frederick, Md.: University Publications of America, 1982.

"Mr. and Mrs. Wallace Reid to Adopt Child." The *New York Times*, August 26, 1922, page 1.

"Mrs. Wally Reid Denies Rumor of Divorce Action." The *Oakland Tribune*, August 29, 1921, page 1.

"Nan of Music Mountain." The *Sheboygan Press*, January 15, 1918, page 7.

"Nan of Music Mountain." *Variety,* December 21, 1917.

"Nice People." *Variety,* August 16, 1922.

"Nice People." The *Wisconsin Rapids Daily Tribune*, January 13, 1923, page 3.

"Nothing to Say for Publication." By Wallace Reid in *Pantomime*, April 15, 1921, pages 9, 30.

"Of a Different Color." The *Daily Northwestern*, August 21, 1920, page 6.

"Old Heidelberg." *Variety,* October 8, 1915.

O'Leary, Liam. *The Silent Cinema*. New York: E.P. Dutton and Co., 1965.

"Pair of Scissors Used By Tellegen to End His Life." The *Dallas Morning News*, October 30, 1934, page 1.

"Peddlers of Dope." *Variety*, September 23, 1921.

"Phoenix, The." The *Mansfield News,* July 22, 1910, page 12.

"Phoenix, The." The *Middletown Daily Argus*, December 23, 1898, page 3.

"Pilot Dies in Crash of His Home-Built Plane at Sea." By Julio Moran in the *Los Angeles Times*, February 27, 1990.

Pratt, George C. *Spellbound in Darkness*. New York: New York Graphic Society, 1966.

"Prince of the World, The." The *New York Times*, June 4, 1901, page 5.

"Prison Without Walls, The." The *Lima Daily News*, June 17, 1917, page 12.

"Prison Without Walls, The." *Variety*, May 4, 1917.

"Queen Elizabeth." By W. Stephen Bush in *Moving Picture World*, August 3, 1912, pages 428-429.

"Queen Elizabeth." *Moving Picture News*. New York: Moving Picture News Publishing, March, 1912.

Ramsay, Terry. *A Million and One Nights*. New York: Simon and Schuster, 1926.

"Real Dramas of Hollywood." *Movie Weekly*, August 18, 1923, page 11.

"Real Wally, The." By Dorothy Davenport Reid in *Photoplay*, 1923, pages 58, 100.

Reid, Bertha Westbrook. *Wallace Reid His Life Story*. New York; Sorg Publishing Company, 1926.

"Reiding Between the Lines." By H. C. Witwer in *Picture-Play*, August 1921, pages 11-12.

"Rent Free." The *Lima News*, April 10, 1922, page 9.

"Rent Free." The *Lincoln Star*, March 26, 1922, page 31.

"Rent Free." *Variety*, January 6, 1922.

"Retribution." The *Perry Daily Chief*, January 2, 1914, page 4.

"Rimrock Jones." The *Elyria Evening Telegram*, February 18, 1918, page 6.

"Rimrock Jones." The *Newark Advocate*, March 6, 1918, page 8.

"Rimrock Jones." *Variety*, January 25, 1918.

"Roaring Road, The." By Hazel Simpson in *Motion Picture Magazine*, July 1919, page 62.

"Roaring Road, The." The *New York Times*, April 14, 1919, page 11.

"Roaring Road, The." *Variety*, April 18, 1919.

"Romances of Famous Film Folk The Story of the Courtship and Marriage of Wally Reid and Dorothy Davenport." By Grace Kingsley in *Picture-Play*, July 1921, pages 51-53.

Scott, Evelyn F. *Hollywood When Silents Were Golden*. New York: McGraw-Hill, 1972.

"Selfish Woman, The." The *Decatur Daily Review*, July 16, 1916, page 22.

"Selfish Woman, The." *Variety*, July 7, 1916.

Sell, Henry Blackman with Victor Weybright. *Buffalo Bill and the Wild West*. New York: Oxford University Press, 1955.

"Shoshone Project." The *Nebraska Sate Journal*, May 8, 1909, page 4.

"Shoshone Dam Logical Survey." The *Oakland Tribune*, August 13, 1906, page 12.

"Shoshone Dam on Irrigation Projects." The *Reno Evening Gazette*, August 13, 1906, page 2.

"Shoshone Dam." The *Syracuse Herald*, June 21, 1908, page 25.

"Sick Abed." *Elyria Chronicle Telegram*, November 12, 1920, page 8.

"Sick Abed." The *Syracuse Herald*, December 31, 1922, page 50.

"Sick Abed." The *Trenton Evening Times*, July 9, 1920, page 15.

"Sick Abed Stage Play." The *Washington Post*, August 1, 1920, page 54.

Slide, Anthony. "Mae Marsh in an Interview with Robert B. Cushman." *The Silent Picture*. New York: Arno Press, 1977.

Slide, Anthony. *The Griffith Actresses*. New York: A.S. Barnes and Company, 1973.

Smith, Albert E. *Two Reels and a Crank*. New York: Doubleday & Company, Inc., 1952.

Smith, Frederick James. "Intolerance In Review." The *New York Dramatic Mirror*, 16 September, 1916.

"Son of Silent Film Star Dies in Pacific Crash." The *Associated Press*, February 26, 1990.

"Source, The." The *Lake Shore News*, September 19, 1918, page 6.

"Source, The." The *Lima Daily News*, January 29, 1919, page 7.

"Source, The." *Variety*, August 16, 1918.

"Spider and Her Web, The." The *Indianapolis Star*, April 1, 1914, page 5.

"Special Studios Built for Geraldine Farrar—Filmdom's Latest Captive." In *Photoplay*, August 19115, page 42.

Spehr, Paul C. *The Movies Begin*. Newark, NJ.: The Newark Museum, 1977.

"Squaw Man's Son, The." The *Coshocton Morning Tribune*, October 18, 1917, page 5.

"Squaw Man's Son, The." The *Iowa City Citizen*, September 15, 1917, page 5.

"Squaw Man's Son, The." *Variety*, August 3, 1917.

"Station Content." The *Atlanta Constitution*, May 9, 1915, page 30.

"Station Content." The *Lancaster Daily Eagle*, May 13, 1915, page 7.

Stern, Seymour. *Griffith: The Birth of a Nation Part 1*. New York: Film Culture, 1965.

St. Johns, Adela Rogers. "Mae Murray-A Study in Contradictions." *Photoplay*, July 1924, 43.

"St. Louis in Ruins." The *Daily Review*, May 26, 1896, page 1.

Swanson, Gloria. *Swanson on Swanson*. New York: Random House, 1980.

Talmadge, Margaret L. *The Talmadge Sisters*. New York: J. B. Lippincott Company, 1924.

"Tellegen Dead Alone With Faded Glory." The *Evening Herald and Express*, October 30, 1934, page 1.

"Tellegen, Former Stage Idol, Stabs Himself to Death." The *Los Angeles Examiner*, October 30, 1934, page 1.

Tellegen, Lou. *Women Have Been Kind*. New York: The Vanguard Press, 1931.

"The Man Who Has Everything." The *Picturegoer*, June 1922, pages 43-46.

"The Shoshone Dam, U.S. Reclamation Service, Near Cody, Wyoming." By H. N. Savage in *Engineer News*, December 9, 1909, pages 627-32.

"Thing We Love, The." The *Bridgeport Telegram*, November 30, 1918, page 6.

"Thing We Love, The." *Variety*, March 15, 1918.

"Thirty Days." The *New York Times*, December 11, 1922, page 22.

"Thousands Attend Funeral Services for Wallace Reid." The *Indianapolis Star*, January 21, 1923, page 1-2.

"To Have and to Hold." The *Middletown Daily Times*, April 28, 1916, page 4.

"To Have and To Hold." *Variety*, March 3, 1916.

"Too Many Millions." The *Capital*, January 10, 1919, page 4.

"Too Many Millions." The *Sheboygan Press*, February 3, 1919, page 7.

"Too Many Millions." *Variety*, December 13, 1918.

"Too Much Speed." The *Bridgeport Telegram*, September 27, 1921, page 11.

"Too Much Speed." The *New York Times*, June 6, 1921, page 16.

"Tragedy of Wallace Reid, The." *Picture Show*, March 30, 1929, page 9.

"Tragic Mansions." By Cal York in *Photoplay*, September 1929. Pages 33-34, 128.

"Trailing a Suspect in a Taxicab." The *Los Angeles Herald*, May 25, 1921, page 11.

"Train Accident." The *New York Telegraph*, March 11, 1919, page 11.

"Opera Singers on the Screen-Geraldine Farrar. By Roi A. Uselton in *Films in Review*. New York: April 1967, pages 196-197.

"Valley of the Giants, The." The *Bridgeport Standard Telegram*, November 1, 1919, page 34.

"Valley of the Giants, The." The *Oakland Tribune*, September 25, 1919, page 2.

"Valley of the Giants, The." *Variety*, September 5, 1919.

Wagenknecht, Edward. *The Movies in the Age of Innocence*. Oklahoma City: The University of Oklahoma Press, 1962.

"Wallace Reid." By Louella Parsons in the *New York Telegraph*, May 22, 1921.

"Wallace Reid Ball." The *New York Telegraph*, February 22, 1920, page 1.

"Wallace Reid." By Dewitt Bodeen in *Films in Review*, April 1966, pages 205-230.

"Wallace Reid." By Tom Scalzo in *Hollywood Studio Magazine*, January 1988, page 7.

"Wallace Reid Case Stirs Up Congressmen." The *Indiana Evening Gazette*, December 19, 1922, page 1, 5.

"Wallace Reid Collapses at home." The *Oakland Tribune*, October 20, 1922, page 1.

"Wallace Reid Dies in Fight on Drugs." The *New York Times*, January 19, 1923.

"Wallace Reid Horseback Injury." *Motography*, January 18, 1913.

'Wallace Reid In Sanitarium." The *Los Angeles Times*, December 16, 1922, page 1.

"Wallace Reid." *Motion Picture*, December 4, 1920, page 608.

"Wallace Reid Near Death." The *Bee*, December 18, 1922, page 12.

"Wallace Reid Near Death." The *New York Times*, December 19, 1922, page 1.

"Wallace Reid Seriously Ill in Sanitarium." The *Los Angeles Examiner*, October 21, 1922, page 1.

"Wallace Reid's Funeral." By Louis Weadock in the *Los Angeles Examiner*, January 21, 1923, page 1.

"Wallace Reid's Struggle Against Drug Addiction." By William Parker in the *Los Angeles Herald*, December 18-21, 1922.

"Wallace Reid's Widow to Carry On." The *Chronicle Telegram*, February 14, 1923, page 6.

"Wallace Reid." *The Blue Book of the Screen*, page 224.

"Wally." By Mrs. Wallace Reid in *Pictures and Picturegoer*, October 1922, pages 20-21.

"Wally Reid, My Friend." By Charles "Buddy" Post in *Motion Picture Magazine*, December 1923, page 20-22, 84.

"Wally Reid Near Death at His Home." The *Los Angeles Times*, October 21, 1922, page 2.

"Wally Reid, Star of Silver Screen, Dead in Hospital. The *Lincoln Star*, January 19, 1923, page 16.

"Wally's Widow Is Carrying On." *Picture-Play*, January 1925, pages 31, 105.

"Wally, the Genial." By Maude S. Cheatham in *Motion Picture Magazine*. New York: Brewster Publications, Inc., October 1920.

Weitzel, Edward. "Elinor Glyn Throned on Her Tiger Skin Sets a New Pace for Speedy Interviews." *Moving Picture World*, December 11, 1920, page 13.

Welsh, Robert E. "David W. Griffith Speaks." The *New York Dramatic Mirror*, 14 January 1914.

"What Price Film Fame?" *Picture Show*, June 11, 1927, pages 14-15.

"What's Your Hurry?" The *New York Times*, August 16, 1920, page 8.

"What's Your Hurry?" The *Trenton Evening Times*, October 12, 1920, page 6.

"What's Your Hurry?" *Variety*, August 20, 1920.

"Wife Pens Dramatic Story of Wallace Reid's Drug Ruin." By Dorothy Davenport Reid in the *San Francisco Examiner*, December 31, 1922.

"Winning Farrar." By Morris Guest in *Photoplay*, July 1915, pages 115-117.

"Woman God Forgot, The." The *Lima Daily News*, December 23, 1917, page 16.

"Woman God Forgot, The." *Variety*, November 2, 1917.

"World, Apart, The." The *Fort Wayne News*, June 9, 1917, page 3.

"World, Apart, The." The *Mansfield News*, July 21, 1917, page 7.

"World Apart, The." The *Oakland Tribune*, June 25, 1917, page 7.

"World Apart, The." The *Washington Post*, June 6, 1917, page 14.

"World Champion, The." The *New York Times*, February 27, 1922, page 13.

"World War Two Internees to Return to Wyoming Camp." By John C. Ensslin in the *Rocky Mountain News*, June 21, 1986, page 48.

"Yankee from the West, A." The *Elyria Chronicle*, September 16, 1915.

"Yankee from the West, A." The *Sandusky Register*, December 3, 1915, page 4.

"Yankee from the West, A." The *Warren Evening Times*, January 13, 1916, page 6.

"Yellow Pawn, The." The *Fitchburg Daily Sentinel*, December 20, 1916, page 9.

"You're Fired." The *New York Times*, June 16, 1919, page 11.

"You're Fired." The *Washington Post*, June 8, 1919, page 51.

"You're Fired." *Variety*, July 20, 1919.

Zukor, Adolph. *The Public Is Never Wrong*. New York: G. P. Putnam's Sons, 1953.

INDEX

'Cross the Mexican Line 352
"Come on Papa" 143
"Comin' Through the Rye" 137
"Eternamente" (Eternally) 272
"It's a Long Way to Tipperary" 143
"Lullaby" poem 147
"Merry Widow Waltz, The"
"Over There" 143
"Star Spangled Banner, The" 125
"St. Louis Cyclone Blues" 24
"Three Wonderful Letters from Home" 143
"Uncle Sam's Ships" 143
"You'll Find Old Dixieland in France" 143
30 Days 239, 240, 246, 247, 470-472, photos 239, 471
About Town 137
Abril, Dorothea 379, 395, 396, photo 396
Across the Continent 7, 212, 213, 215, 233, 459, 460-462, photos 461
Adamas, Stella photo 76
Adventures of Dolly, The 40
Adventures of Frank Merriwell, The 276
Adventures With D. W. Griffith 109
Affairs of Anatol, The 7, 191, 192, 198, 450-453, photos 192, 198, 450, 451, 452
Agnew, Francis 66
Agnew, Robert 468
Ainsworth, Phil 413
Aitken, Spottiswoode 353, 356, 359, 382
Alden, Mary 354, 356, 358, 359, 382
Aldwyn, Irene 384
Alexander, Gus photo 76
Alias Mike Moran 419-421 photo 420
All for a Girl 329
Allison, May 185
Alvin Japanese Theater advertisement 319
Always Audacious 180, 191, 440, 441, photos 180, 441
American Film Manufacturing Company 87, 88, 327, 330, 332, 335, 336, 338, 340-343
American Mutoscope and Biograph Company (*see Biograph*)
An Evening's Entertainment 256
An Indian Outcast 329
Anderson, Claire 354, 374
Angelotti, Marion Polk 407
Animal, The 332

Ankewich, Camille 391, 395
Annie Oakley (film) 45
Another Chance 358
Arbuckle, Roscoe Conkling "Fatty" 89, 163, 164, manslaughter charge 186-187, 191, 201, 252, 368, 417
Ardmore, Jane 138
Arling, Charles 380
Arms and the Gringo 100, 358
Armstrong, Paul 98
Artcraft Pictures Corporation 386, 395, 400, 425, 429, 431, 433, 434, 436, 438, 440, 442
Arthur, George K. 475
Around the World in 80 Days 26
Arvidson, Linda, 39, 60
Ashton, Sylvia 328, 429, 445
Astor, Camille 376
At Cripple Creek 35, 326
At Dawn 353
At Scroggins Corner 324
At the Old Cross Roads 14, 35
Avenging Conscience, The 100, 353
Ayres, Agnes 204, 445, 446, 447, 450, 468, 469, photos 445, 447, 469
Baby's Ride 358
Bachelor Apartment 281
Bains, Beulah 442
Baird, Leah 321, 328, 329, photo 321
Baker, George D. 321
Balfour, Sue 326
Ballard, John Frederick 405
Bambrick, Gertrude 335
Barnes, T. Roy 473
Barnett, Chester 344
Barnum, P. T. 43
Barron, Elwyn Alfred 405
Barrows, Henry A. 391, 405

Barry, Eddy photo 76
Barrymore, John 131, 190, 205, 411
Barrymore, Lionel 328, 335
Barthelmess, Richard 180, 190, 280
Bartlett, Frederick Orin 419
Bassett, Russell, photo 84
Bateman, Victor 259
Bayne, Beverly 97
Beal, Frank 88
Beers, Ethel Lynn 335
Beery, Noah 252, 395, 405, 409, 411, 412, 415, 425, 427, photos 412, 427
Beery, Wallace 424
Before the White Man Came 76, 325
Belasco, David 89, 117
Believe Me, Xantippe 405-407, photos 406
Belmont, Joseph 358
Belmore, Lionel 457
Bennett, Charles 440
Bennett, Frank 382
Beranger, Clara 465, 468
Beranger, George 100, 353, 358, 359
Bergère, Ouida 453
Bernard, Dorothy 335
Bernhardt, Sarah, 17, 68, 87, 122, 124
Bernstein, Isidore 93
Best Man Wins, The, photo 84
Big Timber 214, 392, 393, photos 392
Billy the Kid 50
Biograph 39, 40, 59, 60, 61, 78, 88, 89, 98-101, 332, 335, 344
Birth of a Nation, The 7, 8, making of *The Clansman* 101, 104, 105, 106, premier of *The Clansman* 107-108, 111, 116, 132, 138, 140, 172, 195, 359-363, photos 104, 105, 106, 360-363

Bison Film Company (*see Bison Life Motion Pictures*)
Bison Life Motion Pictures 78, 86, 327-330, 332, 334-336, 338, 342, photo 334
Black Friday 276
Blackton, James "Jimmy" Stuart 31, 32, 63, 67, photo 67
Blackton, the Evening World Cartoonist 32
Blackwell, Carlyle Jr., photo 275
Blaisdell, George 98
Blake, Loretta 358
Bledsoe, Benjamin 260
Blinn, Genevieve 455
Blue Flame, The 195
Blue, Monte 382, 450
Blystone, John G. 346, 349, 351, 352
Bodeen, Dewitt 95, 97, 215
Boggs, Frank 78
Bolder, Robert 436
Bolton, Lucille 350, 351
Bomber's Moon 276
Boone, Arabella 26
Booth, Elmer 328
Borah, Senator William Edgar 238-240
Borden, Fred 193
Borzage, Frank 332, 338-340, 342, 343, 346, 352
Bosen, James (*see James Cruze*)
Bosworth, Hobart 386, 395, 400
Bowles, Donald 393
Boyd, William 450, 465, 466, photo 466
Bracey, Sidney 462
Bradbury, William 376
Brady, Alice 417, 473
Brady, Edward 93, 252, 320, 338, 340, 343-350, 391

Brand of Death, The 392
Bray, Helen 393
Breed O' The Mountains 347
Brockwell, Lillian 348, 351, 352
Broken Laws 266, 267
Brook, Clive 267
Brooke, Van Dyke 319, 321, photo 321
Brothers, The 324
Broun, Alexander 448, 449, photo 449
Brower, Otto 433
Brower, Robert 429, 470
Brown, Hope 475
Brown, Karl 109, 122
Brown, Lucille 382
Brown, Mabel 344
Brown, Milton A. 82, 368, 380
Brown, William 366, 382, 425
Browne, Porter Emerson 415
Browning, Robert 59, 348, 349
Browning, Tod 382
Brownlow, Kevin 88
Bruce, Kate 344, 383
Brunton, William 425
Buchanan, Thompson 204
Buck, Nell Roy 453
Bucking Bronco 45
Buckland, Wilfred 424
Buffalo Bill (*see William Frederick Cody*)
Buffalo Bill's Wild West Show 42-44, 142
Buffalo Dance 44
Bunny, John, at Vitagraph 65, on stage 66, 67, 319, 321, 322, 325, photos 65, 321
Burglar on the Roof, The 32
Buried Alive 141, 390
Burns, Edmund 424
Burns, Fred 354-356

Burns, John 390
Burns, Neal, photo 76
Burton, Charles 429
Burton, Charlotte 344
Burton, Clarence 351, 438, 445
Burton, John 391, 393
Bush, Pauline 88-90, 92, 332-338, 342, 386, 390, photos 333, 337
Bushman, Francis X. 97
Butler, Fred 462
Butler, Kathleen 335
Butterworth, Ernest 386, 438, 445
Byron, Nina 411, 413, 417, 418, photo 418
Cabanne, William Christy 100, 101, 328, 335, 353-359, 363-365, 374
Calamity Jane 50

Caldwell, Fred 472
Calhoun, Jean 419
Call to Arms, The (see *In Love and War*)
Cardinal Film Corporation 386
Carewe, Arthur 465
Carewe, Ora 415
Carey, Harry 328, 335, 344
Carey, Olive 384
Carmen (film) 121, 126, 128, 131, 132, 133, 368, 370, 371, photos 128, 371
Carmen (opera) 120, 121, 132
Carpenter, Florence 391
Carpenter, Francis 368
Carpenter, Horace B. 368, 370, 373, 374, 380, 386, 399, 400, photo 373
Carr, Harry 246
Carter, Calvert 409
Casey, Leslie 457
Cassinelli, Dolores 453
Castle, Vernon 137

Centaur Film Company 75
Centennial Summer 280
Chadwick, Cyril 470
Chailee, Joseph S. 326
Chalk Garden, The 280
Champion Film Co. 324
Chandler, Robert 350
Chaney, Lon 332
Chaplin, Charles "Charlie" Spencer 7, 89, 95, 108, 134, 159, 233, 252, photo 95
Chapman, Edythe 370, 373, 380, 419, photo 373
Charm School, The 179, 211, 442-444, photos 211, 443, 444
Chase, Julian 56
Cheat, The 117
Cheatham, Maude 112, 133
Cheriff, Hadj 45
Chorus Lady, The 366, 367, photo 367
Christie, Alfred "Al" Ernest 76, photo 76
Christie, Charles H. 76, photo 76
Christy, Lillian 91, 327, 330, 335, 338
Chumps 67, 321-322, photos 321, 322
City Beautiful, The 100, 357
Civilization 472
Clansman, The (see *The Birth of a Nation*)
Clarence 229, 237, 238, 468-470, photos 229, 469
Clark, Marguerite 131
Clarke, Victor 252
Clary, Charles 386
Cleveland, Stephen Grover 31
Clifford, William 329
Clifton, Elmer 359, 363, 382, 383

Clonblough, G. Butler (*see Gustav Von Seyffertitz*)
Cloud, Dark 354
Cody, William Frederick 42, *Wild West Show* 43, early Edison films 44, 47, 48, Irma Hotel 49, building Shoshone River dam 49-52, death 142, photos 42, 48
Cohan, George M. 417
Coigne, Frank B. 324
Collier, Edmund 17
Compson, Betty 76, 473, photo 76
Condon, Frank 475
Confession, The (play) 14, 72, 73, photo 72
Conklin, William 384, 386, 390
Conway, Jack 81, 326, 472
Coolidge, Dane 402
Cooper, Edna Mae 402
Cooper, James Fennimore 47, 330
Cooper, Miriam 71, 101, 108, 172, 177, 353, 356, 359, 382
Cooper, William F. 330
Corsi, Antonio 431
Cortés, Hernán 397
Cortez, Hernán (*see Cortés, Hernán*)
Cosgrave, Luke 475
Costello, Mae 325
Countess Betty's Mine, The 345, photo 345
Course of True Love, The 329
Courting of the Merry Widow, The 318
Courtwright, Charles 358
Cowboy Guardians, The 328
Coxen, Edward 327, 330, 335, 338, 344
Cracksman Santa Claus, A 96
Cracksman Santa Clause, A 338, 339, photo 339
Cracksman's Reformation 92, 96, 338

Crane, Ogden 425
Craven, The 374
Crawford, Florence 358
Crisp, Donald 100, 335, 353, 354, 356, 358, 359, 402, 403, 405, 406, 407, 408, 409, 410, 412
Cross Purposes 92, 340
Crothers, Rachel 465
Crowell, Josephine 353, 356, 359, 366, 374, 382
Crown of Thorns, A 35
Crucifix of Destiny, The 431
Cruze, James 156, 166, 167, 170, 172, 191, 211, 213, 239, 240, 246, 279, 399, 405, 409, 411, 415-430, 440-444, 457, 458, 462-464, 470, 471, 472, 474, 475, photo 167
Cryer, George E. 259-260
Cudahy, Floria 282
Cudahy, John P. 282
Cumming, Dorothy 455, 456, photo 456
Cummings, Richard 358, 425
Cuneo, Lester 215, 216, 220
Cunningham, Jack 473
Cupid and Incognito 349
Curfew Shall Not Ring Tonight 325
Curley, James 383
Curwood, James Oliver 352
D'Albrook, Sidney 459
Dalton, Dorothy 417, 473
Dancin' Fool, The 190, 434-436, photos 435
Daniel, H. B. 404
Daniels, Bebe 252, 434, 436, 438, 450, 451, 452, 465, 466, 473, photos 451, 452, 466
Daniels, Phyllis 391
Darkfeather, Mona 378
Darling, Ruth 383

Darmond, Grace 168, 169, 170, 171, 425, 426, photo 171, 426
Daughter of a Crook, The 350
Daughter of the Confederacy, A 15
Daughter of the Redskins 330
Davenport, Alice 79, 83, 84, 93, 95, 147, 179, 228, 247, 249, 252, 253, 263, photos 84, 95
Davenport, Dorothy, marriage to Wally 8, 79-86, 88-98, 102, 103, 106, 111, 114, 134, 136, 140, 141, birth of son 144-149, 154-156, 158-160, 163-166, 173-175, 178-180, 182-188, 194-196, 201-203, 209-213, 215-218, 220, 223-228, 231, 232, 237, 241-248, Wally's death 249-255, 257-270, 272-275, 277, 279, 320, 326, 338-340, 343-352, 363, 386, 390-393, 417, 440, photos 80, 81, 84, 85, 94, 106, 145, 146, 154, 185, 202, 216, 217, 254, 255, 260, 261, 265, 267-269, 273, 277, 339, 345
Davenport, E. L. 79
Davenport, Fanny 17, 79
Davenport, Harry 79
Davidson, Max 39, 382
Davies, Marion 473
Davis, Horace, photo 76
Davis, Richard Harding 363-364, 462
Daw, Marjorie 366, 382, 386
Dawn, Hazel 131
Day, Shannon 450
Dayton, James 347
De Briac, Charles 455
De Briac, Raymond 455
de Cordoba, Pedro 368, 374, 375, photo 375
De Grasse, Sam 359, 382

de Mille, William 139-140, 143, 222, 238, 368, 374, 386, 397, 465, 466, 468, 469, 473
De Vaull, William 359
Dead Man's Shoes 338
Dean, Barbara 453
Deane-Tanner, William Cunningham (see William Desmond Taylor)
Decker, Lou 49
Decker, May 50, photo 48
Deerslayer, The 47, 330, 331, photo 331
Del Riccio, Lorenzo 206, 207
DeLeon, Walter 465
DeMille, Cecil B. 114-118, 121, 126-131, 133, 139-143, 149, 151-153, 191, 198, 241, 250, 274, 281, 298, 368, 370-374, 376, 386-389, 395, 397, 398, 400, 401, 450, 453, 469, 473, photos 128, 149, 192, 198, 230, 274
DeMille, Beatrice 400
Dempsey, Jack 242
Den of Thieves, The 352
Desmond, William 160
Devil Stone, The 153, 400, 401, photo 401
Dexter, Elliott 198, 204, 450, 453, 455-457, photos 198, 456
Diamond Cut Diamond 325
Dickey, Paul 465, 468
Dickson, William Kennedy Laurie 44
Dictator, The 213, 215, 229, 233, 462-465, photos 229, 463, 464
Dillon, Edward 356, 382
Dion, Hector 326
Dix, Beulah Marie 391, 395, 400
Dixon, Reverend Thomas F. 101,107, 108, 359
Dodd, Reverend Neal 252

Dominicus, Evelyn 330
Don't Tell Everything 190, 233, 455-457, photos 456
Donnelly Stock Company 32
Double Speed 176, 431-433, photos 432
Down by the Sounding Sea 356
Down the Hill to Creditville 100, 356, photos 357
Dowst, Henry Payson 435, 436
Doyle, Sir Arthur Ignatius Conan 405
Dr. Jekyll and Mr. Hyde 190
Drew, Cora 354
Du Crow, Tote 402
Du Maurier, Daphne 453
Dub, The 158, 417-419, photo 418
Duel in the Sun 280
Dumont, J. M. 440
Dunbar, Helen 457, 470
Dunham, Phil 93, 340, 343, 345-352
Dunn, Ethel 330
Dunn, William R. 323, 326, photo 323
Duse, Eleonora 17
Dwan, Allan 88, 89, 330, 332-336, 338, 341-344
Eagle Eye 354, 355
Eagles, Curly 82
Early Days in the West 328
Eaton, Charles 453
Edeson, Robert 40
Edison, Thomas 27, 31, 32, 44, 45, 47
Edwards, Grace 442
Edwards, Snitz 442, 445, 465, 468
Edwards, Walter 413, 414
Elliott Hicks, Maxine 431
Elmer, William 368, 380, 386, 391, 402, 407, 417, 419

Elmore, Pearl 382
Emerson, John 112-114, 368, 369
Enoch Arden 100, 364-366, photo 365
Epoch Film Corporation 359
Escape, The 98, 102
Essanay Film Manufacturing Company 88, 97
Evangeline 172
Every Inch A Man 86, 327
Every Woman's Problem 195-196
Excuse My Dust 176, 274, 275, 433, 434, photos 434
Exposure, The 354
Eye of a God, The 344
Eye, Eagle 354
Eyton, Charles 197
Fagan, James B. 430
Fahrney, Milton J. 80, 320
Fairbanks, Douglas 159, 252, 417
Fairfax, Marion 366, 409, 421, 425
Fall of Babylon, The 134
Famous Players Film Company 87, 89, 133, merger with Jesse Lasky 134
Famous Players-Lasky Corporation 116, 122, 124, fire 130, 133, merger with Jesse Lasky 134, 180, 181, 366, 368, 370, 374, 376, 379, 380, 382, 384, 386, 390, 391, 392, 393, 395, 399, 402, 405, 407, 409, 411, 413, 415, 417, 419, 421, 422, 424
Famous Players-Lasky-Paramount (*see Famous Players-Lasky Corporation*)
Fanning, Frank 215
Farhney, Milton H. 326
Farley, James 405
Farnum, Dustin 115, 160
Farnum, William 190, 417

Farrar, Geraldine 118, 119, 120, arriving in Hollywood 121, meeting Wally 122, meeting Lou-Tellegen 122, 123-129, 131-133, 138, 139, making *Joan the Woman* 140-142, 151-153, 155, 156, 220, 282, 368, 371, 374-376, 386, 387, 389, 395, 397, 398, 400, 401, 417, photos 123, 127, 128, 371, 375, 387, 398, 401
Farrington, Adele 405, 442
Faversham, William 417
Fawcett, George 383, 453, 454, 473, photo 454
Faye, Julia 397, 450, 465, 466, 473, photo 466
Ferguson, Elsie 204, 206-208, 214, 417, 453, 454, 473, photos 207, 454
Ferguson, William J. 457
Fernley, Jane 326
Field, George 324, 329, 338, 341-344
Fighting Chance, The 182
Fillson, Al 353, 366
Finch, Flora 325
Finley, Ned 319, 344
Finnigan, Frank X. 402
Firefly of France, The 407-409, photos 408
Fires of Conscience 346
Fires of Fate, The 92, 344
Firpo, Roberto 272
First National 159
Fischer, Margarita 327, 329
Fiske, Minnie Maddern 89
Fitzmaurice, George 206-208, 214, 453, 454
Flake, Kolma 176
Flash in the Dark, A 346

Fleming, Robert 376, 379, 380, 382
Flotz, Virginia 429
Flowers, Bess 475
Flying A Company 91, 330
Folies Bergére 115
Foltz, Virginia 425
Fool and a Girl, A 38
Foote, Courtenay 356
For Her Father's Sins 353
For Those Unborn 359
Forbes, James 366
Ford, Harrison 429
Ford, Henry 97
Ford, Ray 325
Forde, Eugenie photo 81
Forde, Victoria 79, 326
Foreign Spy, A 343
Forever 201, 205, 206-208, 210, 214, 215, 453-455, photos 207, 454
Forman, Karl 368
Forman, Tom 376, 384
Four Horsemen of the Apocalypse, The 190
Foxe, Earle 329, 379
Francis, Evelyn 324
Francis, Ray 329
Francisco, Betty 459
Franklin, Edgar (*see Edgar Franklin Sterns*)
Frazee, Benjamin 252
Frederick, Pauline 131, 417
French, George, photo 76
Frohman, Caryl 41
Frohman, Charles 66
Frohman, Daniel 41
Fruit of Evil, The 349
Gabortau, Émile 405
Gaden, William 445
Gage, Howard 354, 358
Gaillard, Robert 319, 320, 323, 327, photo 323

Gallagher, Ray photo 76
Gamble, Fred 346
Gamblers, The 328
Gardner, Helen 324
Gaskill, Charles L. 324, 325
Gaston, Mae 356
Gaye, Howard 358, 359, 382
Geldart, Clarence 384, 386, 390, 391, 393, 395, 405, 407, 417, 421, 422, 429, 436, 440, 448, 457, photo 422
Geldart, Frank 448
Geraghty, Thomas J. 440, 442, 475
Gest, Morris 117
Gettinger, William 347, 349, 351, 352
Ghost Breaker, The 236, 465, 467, 468, photos 467
Gibbons, Cardinal 73
Gibson, Hoot 82, 326
Gibson, James 368
Gillette, William 17
Gilpatrick, Wallace 374
Girl and the Ranger, The, 56, 62, 132
Girl from Arizona, A 62
Girl of the Golden West, The 119
Gish, Dorothy 9, 71, 100, 112-114, 280, 328, 344, 356-358, 368, 369, photos 113, 357, 369
Gish, Lillian 71, 100, 103, 111, 112, 180, 280, 328, 344, 356, 359, 363-366, 382, 417
Gish, Mary 114, 328
Gismonda (play) 17
Glendon, J. Frank 472
Glyn, Elinor 204, 450
Goddard, Charles William 465, 468
Gold Rush Maisie 276
Golden Chance, The 117, 118, 132, 370, 372, 373, photos 118, 372, 373

Golden Fetter, The 390
Golden, Joseph A. 344
Goldfish, Samuel (*see Samuel Goldwyn*)
Goldstein, Max 45
Goldwyn, Samuel 114, 116, 121, 122, 126, 133, 156, 159
Good Little Devil, The 89
Goodwin, Harold 368
Gordon, Dorothy 468
Gordon, Harris 475
Gordon, Julia Swayne 324, 328
Gordon, Phyllis 350
Gowland, Alice 276, photo 276
Gowland, Peter 276
Grant, General Ulysses S. 359
Gratitude of Wanda, The 338
Grauman, Sid 252
Gray, Robert 376
Gray, Stephen 386
Great Train Robbery, The 47
Greater Devotion, The 346
Greater Love, The 344
Green, Alfred 465
Greenstreet, Sydney 66
Greenwood, Winifred 405, 415, 429, 436, 437, photo 437
Grey, Olga 359, 382, 397
Griffith, David Wark, 8, 38, in stock companies 39, first Edison films 39-40, 59-61, 78, 88, 89, 97-109, 111-113, 115, 134, 135, 138, 159, 179, 181, 190, 195, 280, 328, 332, 335, 344, 353, 356, 359, 360, 361, 363-366, 368, 382, 384, 465, photos 61, 135
Griffith, Lawrence (*see David Wark Griffith*)
Griffith, Linda (*see Linda Arvidson*)
Guerilla Menace, The 332

Guest, Morris 119, 120
Guimerá, Angel 374, 376
Guise, Tom 413
Gypsy Romance, A 349
Hackathorne, George 259
Hackett, James K. 38, 89
Hadj Cheriff Arab Knife Juggler 45
Hadley, Reverend 33
Hagard, H. Rider 397
Haines, Rhea 440
Hair Coat 44
Halbardier of the Little Rheinschloss, The (see *You're Fired*)
Hale, Alan 462
Hall, Delores 472
Hall, Winter 405, 407, 417, 419, 450
Halleran, Edith 322, 329, 330
Hamer, Fred Booth 101
Hamilton, Clayton 470
Hamrick, Burwell 400
Handforth, Ruth 382
Handworth, Octavia 344
Hanson, Speed 168
Harding, President Andrew 187
Harland, Kenneth 111
Harms Brothers, The 18
Harris, Elmer 429
Harris, Mildred 364, 383
Harris, Theodosia 340, 343
Harron, Robert "Bobby" Emmett 101, death 179-181, 186, 328, 335, 344, 353, 355, 356, 359, 382, photo 181
Hart, William S. 142, 160, 252, 417
Harvest of Flame, The 337
Harvey, Chief 329
Hatton, Raymond 370, 373, 376, 386, 393, 395, 397-400, 407, 409, 411, 417, 423, 424, 434, 450, photos 373, 398

Hawley, Wanda 422, 424, 428, 429, 431, 432, 450, 451, 470, 471, 473, photos 428, 432, 451, 471
Hawthorne of the U. S. A. 166, 429-431, photos 430
Hay, John 14
Hayakawa, Sessue 417
Hayden, Kathlyn 111
Hayes, Helen 68, photo 68
Hayes, Teddy 242
Hays, William "Will" Harrison, Sr. 187, 197, 199, 228, 230, 240, photo 230
He Comes Up Smiling 411
Hearst, William Randolph 186
Heart of a Cracksman, The 92, 96, 340, 341, photo 341
Heart of the Hills, The 348
Hearts and Horses 343
Heise, William 44
Hell Diggers, The 185, 188, 279, 448-450, photos 185, 449
Henabery, Joseph 358, 359, 382
Henderson, Grace 328
Henry, Catherine 374
Henry, Gale 472
Henry, O. (see *William Sydney Porter*)
Her Awakening 356
Her Innocent Marriage 343
Herbert, Dr. G. S. 242
Herbert, Jack 409, 447, 459
Herman, Charles 326
Hickock, Wild Bill 50
Hidden Treasure, The 330
Hieroglyphic, The 324
Hiers, Walter 465, 467, 468
High Grader, The 358
High Stakes 281
Hill Mailes, Charles 335
Hill, Josephine 472
Hinckley, William 374

His Double Life 280
Commandos Strike at Dawn 280
His Extra Bit 275, 417
His Mother's Son 328, 332
His Only Son 80, 81, 85, 326, photo 85
His Son 320
Hitchcock, Ethan A. 50
Hodges, Walter 27
Hollywood 474, 475, advertisement 474
Holt, Jack 237, 252, 272, 473
Home, Sweet, Home 356
Hoosier Schoolmaster, The 276
Hopi Legend, A 343
Hopkins, Clyde 382
Hopper, E. Mason 380, 381, 390
Horsley, David 75
Horsley, William 75
Hoskins, Charles 324
Hostage, The 395, 396, photos 396
House of Silence, The 405
House with Golden Shutters, The 136
House with Golden Windows, The 382, 383, photo 383
Howe, Herbert 187, 216, 250, 256
Hoxie, Jack 399, 425
Human Hearts 14, 17, 18
Human Wreckage 257-263, 267, 270, photos 258-260
Humphrey, William 327
Hunt, Irene 353, 354, 359
Hunt, Madge 368
Hunted Down 329
Hunting, Gardner 393, 415
Huntley, Fred 402, 429, 450
Huntley, Luray 382
Hurst, Paul 402
Hutchinson, William K. 238
Hyman, E. L. 417

I Never Sang for My Father 280
Icketts, Tom 79
If I Were King 190
Illumination, The 324
Independent Motion Pictures Company (IMP) 86, 326
In Love and War 335
Ince, Ralph 323, 344
Ince, Thomas Harper 257, 260, 266, photo 260
Indian Raiders 327
Indian Romeo and Juliet 322
Ingraham, Lloyd 382
Inslee, Charles 327-330
Intolerance: Love's Struggle Through The Ages 134, 135, 179, 382-384, photo 135
Intruder, The 345
Ivers, Julia Crawford 391
Jackson, Charles Tenney 390
Jacobs, William 382
James, Gladden 344
Jane, "Ukulele" 76
Janecke, Joseph 76, photo 76
Jean and the Calico Doll 68
Jean Intervenes 322
Jean the Vitagraph Dog 322
Jesse L. Lasky Feature Play Company 133
Joan the Woman 139-141, 151, 386-389, photos 387-389
Johns, Bertram 465, 468
Johnson, Emory 419
Johnson, Henry 447
Johnson, Lonnie 24
Johnson, Mary 376
Johnson, Orrin 73
Johnson, Tefft 323, 324
Johnstone, Calder 352
Joke on Yellentown, The 358
Jorgensen, Emilius 386

Joy, Ernest 370, 373, 374, 386, 393, 399, 400, 402, 405, 407, 434, 438, photo 373
Joy, Leatrice 473
Judith of Bethulia 89, 344
Julian, Rupert 348
Kaintuck 325, 347
Kalem Film Company 78, 101
Karr, Darwin 329
Katterjohn, Monte M. 411, 413
Kay Bee Film Company 88-89
Keaton, Buster 163
Keefe, Zena 325, 328
Kelland, Clarence Budington 411
Keller, Edgar 351, 352
Kelly, Dorothy 329
Kelly, John T. 18
Kelsey, Fred A. 100, 353, 354, 358, 374
Kelso, Mayme 402, 468
Kennedy, Clara 423, 431, 435, 436
Kennedy, Madge 417
Kent, Charles 320
Kerrigan, J. Warren 88, 93, 335
Keystone Comedies 89
King of Kings, The 281
King of the Royal Mounted 276
King, Anita 368, 374, 390, 393, 394, photo 394
King, Joe 351, 352, 380, 392, 393, photo 392
King, Karl 318, 320
Kingsley, Grace 82
Kiralfy Brothers 26
Kirkland, David 334, 336, 342, 351, 352
Kirkwood, James 82, 98, 186, 259, 262, 356
Kismet 472
Kiss, The 336
Klein, Charles 328

Knobs of Tennessee, The 14
Knowles, James Sheridan 330
Koch, Hugh B. 386
Koenig, Marie Adrienne (*see Mae Murray*)
Kosloff, Theodore 397, 398, 450, 462, photo 398
Koszarski, Richard 256
Kottler, Terry 249, 279, photo 277
Kummer, Frederick Arnold 384
Kuwa, George 384, 402, 436
Kyne, Peter B. 425
La Belle Marie (play) 25-27, advertisement 25
La Tosca (film) 68
La Tosca (play) 39
Laemmle, Carl 75, 89, 90, 274, photo 75
Lafayette, Ruby 475
Lait, Jack 424
Langdon, Lillian 382
Langtry, Lily 89
Lanning, Frank 393
Lanoe, J. Jiquel 335, 344
Larkin, Dolly 329, 330
Lasky & Rolfe 115
Lasky Feature Show Company 115, merger with Famous Players 134
Lasky Home Guard 143, 144
Lasky, Blanche 115
Lasky, Jesse Louis, Sr. 115-117, 120-122, 126, 128-131, 133, 134, 140-143, 151, 155, 156, 158, 159, 163, 170, 176, 177, 181, 182, 186, 187, 194, 197-199, 204, 206, 214, 215, 223, 228, 233, 237, 246, 282, 376, 379, 380, 385, 393, 395, 436, 438, 442, 446, 450, photos 114, 230
Last Horse 44
Laurel, Kay 425

Law, Rodman 327
Lawrence, W. E. 382
Lawson, Eleanor 475
Lazzarini, Lorenza 436
Leading Lady, The 319, 321, photo 321
Leather Stocking Tales 69, 320
Lee, Alberta 382
Lee, General Robert E. 359
Lee, Jennie 359
Lee, Lila 166, 429, 442, 444, 457, 462-465, 467, 473, photos 166, 444, 463, 464, 467
Lee, Rev. Baker P. 93
Leigh, Frank 448, 450
Leighton, Lillian 386, 391, 395, 400, 434, 457
Leon, Ponce de 119
Leopard's Stripes, The 100-101
LeSaint, Edward J. 390, 393, 394
Less Than Kin 409, 410, 411, photos 410
Lesta, William 423
Lestina, Adolph 328
LeVino, Albert 455, 459
Lewis, Ben 374
Lewis, Ralph 353, 354, 356, 359, 382, 417, 425
Lewis, Vera 382
Li'l Abner 279
Lightning Bolt, The 94, 340
Lincoln, Elmo 104, 344, 359, 383
Linda 273
Little Country Mouse, The 356
Little Lord Fauntleroy 224
Little Red Schoolhouse, The 14
Little, Ann 399, 400, 402, 405, 406-413, 419, 421, 422, 433, 434, photos 399, 408, 410, 412, 413, 422, 434
Littlefield, Lucien 376, 379, 390, 393, 395, 431, 436, 447, 448, 450, 457, 459
Lloyd, Frank 349, 350, 417, photo 350
Lloyd, Harold 252, 472
Lockwood, Harold 79, 81, 417, photo 81
Long, Walter 105, 353, 359, 382, 386, 390, 397. 433, 459, 462, 473, photo 105
Longfellow, Henry W. 253
Loomis, Margaret 440-442, photo 441
Loos, Anita 161, 353, 384, photo 161
Lost House, The 363
Lottery Man, The 172, 174, 428-429, 431, 433, photos 174, 428
Louden, Thomas 459
Lou-Tellegen (*see Tellegen, Lou*)
Love and the Law 327, 330
Love Burglar, The 424, 425
Love Mask, The 379, 380, photos 379
Love Special, The 190, 445, 446, photo 445
Love, Bessie 257, 259, 359, 382, photo 259
Love, Montagu 453
Love's Western Flight 352
Lowery, F. A. 358
Lowery, William 354, 358
Lucas, Wilfred 335
Lusitania 125
Lux Radio Theater 281
Lynton, Christopher 366
Lyons, Eddie photo 76
Lyons, Lurline 348
Lytell, Bert 473
MacAlarney, Robert E. 391
MacDermott, Joseph 335

MacDonald, Bob 279
MacDonald, Donald, photo 81
MacDonald, J. Farrell 465
Machette, Paul 329
Mackley, Arthur 358, 374
Mackley, Mrs. Arthur 382
MacLaren, Mary 459, 461, photo 461
Macpherson, Jeanie 117, 139, 368, 370, 379, 386, 397, 400, 450
Madame Butterfly (opera) 120
Madison, Cleo 92, 340, 341, photo 341
Magee, Patricia 442
Maigne, Charles 390, 393
Mailes, Charles Hill 328, 335
Maison, Edna 348, 349
Maja, Zelma 445, 450
Majestic Film Company 97, 98, 353-359, 363, 364, 366
Making a Living 95
Making Good 326
Man From Funeral Range, The 413-415, photo 413
Man Who Saved the Day, The 390
Man Within, The 351
Man's Duty, A 326, 333
Mann, Hank 89
Manners, Margaret 329
Manon, Marcia 390-391, 395, 429
Mansfield, Richard 368
Mantle, Burns 433
Marburg, Guido 376
Maria Rosa 116, 122, 126, 128, 131, 133, 374, 375, photos 375
Marion, Frances 152, 281
Mark, Alice 399
Marks, Willis 413
Marsh, Betty 364
Marsh, Mae 71, 98, 99, 103, 104, 280, 335, 344, 353, 355, 356, 359, 382, 417, photos 104, 355
Marsh, Marguerite 382
Marshall, Tina 442
Marshall, Tully 143, 383, 386, 390, 400, 401, 402, 413, 415, 429, 431, 433, 434, 436
Martin, Lee 45
Martindel, Edward 465, 468
Masked Avenger, The 215, 275
Mason, Frank 327
Mason, James P. 399
Mason, Lillian 423, 425
Mathieu, Jeff 277
Maurice, Mary 320, 323, 344, photo 323
Maxwell, Perriton 55
Mayall, Herschel 470, 472
Mayne, Eric 259
McAllister, Paul 453
McAvoy, May 468, 469, 473, photo 469
McCan, Martha Nelson 260
McClure, Rev. A. W. 382
McComas, J. L. 472
McCord, Mrs. Lewis 366, 390
McDaniel, George 413
McDermott, Joseph 335, 368
McDowell, Claire 259, 457, 465
McGee, Morris 327
McHugh, Charles 399
McKim, Robert 259
McKinley, William, Jr. 31
McLynn, Gertrude 354
McQuarrie, James 332
McQuarrie, Murdock 332
Meighan, Thomas 204, 473
Melford, George 136, 138, 139, 148, 149, 376, 377, 382-385, 399, 411, 473, photo 136
Menace, The (see *The Powder Flash of Death*)

Menjou, Adolphe 468
Mental Suicide 336
Mercanton, Louis 87
Meredyth, Bess 332, 339, 340, 346, 347, 348, 349
Mérimée, Prosper 368
Mersch, Mary 402
Messick, William 330
Metcalfe, Earl 344
Meyer, Frank 130
Middleton, George 391
Midgely, Fanny 429, 440
Midsummer Night's Dream, A (play) 66
Miller, Alice Duer 442
Miller, Henry Jr. 457
Miller, Patsy Ruth 450
Miller, W. Chrystie 335
Miller, Walter 328, 335
Minter, Mary Miles 173, 214, 473
Mix, Tom 79, 142
Modern Snare, A 342
Modini-Wood, Charles 73, 74
Modini-Wood, Elizabeth 73, 74, 77
Modjeska, Helena 17
Mohawk's Way, A 272
Money Master, The 186
Monogram Pictures 273
Montague, Gladys 349, 350
Montgomery, Frank 330, 378
Moon, Lorna 455
Mooney, Margaret 383
Moonshine Molly 355, photo 355
Moore, Marcia 340
Moore, Owen 356
Moore, Tom 417, 473
Moran, Lee photo 76
Moran, Polly 450
Moreno, Antonio 252, 272, 328
Morey, Harry T. 322, 329, 330, 344
Morgan, Byron 156, 158, 176, 212, 215, 421, 422, 431, 433, 438, 448, 459
Morgan, Joe 159
Morosco Film Corporation 390, 391, 393
Morrison, James 323, 329, photo 323
Mother and the Law, The 134
Mother's Influence, A 354-355
Mother's Love, A 35
Mothers of Men 182
Motion Picture Acting 66
Motion Picture Producers and Distributors of America 187
Mountaineer, The 347
Movies, Mr. Griffith, and Me, The 103, 112, 280
Mullin, Eugene 330
Mumford, Ethel Watts 225, 436
Mummert, Betty Anne, (*see Betty Ann Reid*)
Murray, Mae 137-139, 281, 376-378, 417, photos 139, 377
Mutual Film Corporation 89, 97, 98, 100, 353, 354, 355, 356, 357, 358, 359, 363, 364, 366, 374
Myers, Senator Henry L 238
Mystery of the Yellow Aster Mine, The 332
Nagel, Conrad 252, 465, 466, 473, photo 466
Nagy Anton, photo 76
Naldi, Nita 473
Nan of Music Mountain 148, 149, 153, 399, photos 148, 149, 399
Naylor, Hazel 431
Nazimova, Alla 9, 186, 233
Near to Earth 335
Negri, Pola 252
Neilan, Marshall 90, 332-337, 342, photo 334

Neill, James 338, 340, 348, 376, 382, 386, 391, 397, 400, 409, 415
Neill, Roy William 266
Nestor Film Company 76, 79, 81, 84, 85, 326, 340, 343-352, photos 76, 81, 84
New York Motion Picture Company 343
Nice People 215, 222, 465, 466, photos 222, 466
Niggard, The 354
Night Before Christmas, The 14
Night Life in Hollywood 473, advertisement 473
Night of the Hunter, The 280
Nilsson, Anna Q. 424, 425, 473
Nobles, Dolly 63, 318
Nobles, Milton 63, 318
Nobody's Money 237, 240, 241
Normand, Mabel 89, 214, 335, 417,
North West Mounted Police 276
Northrup, Harry 259, 324, 325
O'Brien, John "Jack" 100, 353, 354
O'Connor, Harry 417
O'Connor, Loyola 383, 424
O'Connor, Mary 366
O'Neill, James 89
Oaker, John 386
Oakley, Annie 43, 44
Oaks, Louis D. 260
Ober, Mrs. Adelaide 322
Odalisque, The 353
Ogle, Charles 399, 402, 403, 405, 407-409, 411, 415, 417, 419, 425, 429, 438, 450, 470, 471, photos 403, 408, 471
Old Heidelberg 112, 368, 369, photos 369
Oliver, Guy 390, 395, 399, 402, 409, 417, 419, 421, 425, 429, 431, 433, 440, 447, 450, 457, 459
On the Firing Lines of Tripoli (see A Red Cross Martyr) 320
One Romantic Night 280
Opperman, Frank 335
Orlamond, Miss 324
Outlaw, The 276
Over the Ledge 353
Owen, Seena 366, 374, 383
Page, Mann 457
Paget, Alfred 364, 365, 383, 393
Palette, Eugene 335
Pallette, Eugene 83, 252, 335, 342, 359, 382, 391
Paramount Pictures Corporation 114, 133, 158, 165, 172, 177, 180, 182, 187, 190, 191, 194, 195, 197, 201, 202, 207, 215, 233, 236, 237, 240, 242, 244, 246, 247, 257, 270, 272, 380, 390, 391, 393, 395, 400, 402, 404, 418, 425, 427, 429, 431, 433, 434, 436, 438, 440, 442, 445, 447, 448, 450, 453, 455, 457, 459-462, 465, 468, 470, 473-475
Parker, William 79, 86, 90, 93, 210, 211, 228, 243, 246
Parsons, Louella 209
Parts His Hair 44
Pasha, Kalla 462, 470
Pasque, Ernest 415
Passing of the Beast 351
Passion Play 71
Path of True Love, The 330
Pathfinder, The 47, 320
Patrick, Jerome 453
Pattallo, George 204
Payday 233
Payne, John Howard 356

Payton, Lawrence 390
Peacock Alley 281
Peddler, The 14, 35
Pegg, Vester 358
Penalty of Silence, The 141, 391
Percy, Eileen 161, photo 161
Pershing, General John H. 143
Peter Ibbetson 201, 205, 206, 210, 215, 453, 454 (*also see Forever*)
Peters, Page 351
Peyton, Lawrence 386
Philanderings of Puddenfoot Pete, The (*see The Hidden Treasure*)
Philbrook, Edward H. 329
Phillips, Carmen 440, 470
Phillips, Edwin R. 325
Phoenix, The (film) 63, 318, 319, advertisement 319
Phoenix, The (play) 17
Pickens, Sam 318, 320
Picket Guard, The 334
Pickford, Jack 356
Pickford, Lottie 413, 414, photo 414
Pickford, Mary 7, 71, 89, 100, 108, 131, 134, 138, 143, 148, 152, 159, 224, 233, 250, 252, 280, 414, 417
Picture of Dorian Gray, The 343
Pillsbury, Helen 442
Pippa Passes 59
Pirate Gold 335
Poe, Edgar Allen 353, 405
Porter, Edwin S. 39, 87
Porter, William Sydney 423
Post, Charles "Buddy" 8, 189, 190, 243, 248, 249, 255, 279
Powder Flash of Death, The 342
Powers Picture Plays 336, 338, 340, 347, 348
Powers, Tom 324, 325
Preminger, Otto 280

Price, Kate 325, 329, 356
Pride of Lonesome, The 342
Prince of the World 14, 32, 35
Printzlau, Olga 405
Prison Without Walls, The 390
Prisoner of Zenda, The 89
Prodigal Night, The 450 (*also see The Affairs of Anatol*)
Pryor, Herbert 423
Pyramid 344
Quack, The 350
Queen Elizabeth 87
Queen of Sheba 472
Queen Victoria 43
Quo Vadis 32, 89, 119
Racing Strain, The 275
Rankin, Carolyn 429
Rappe, Virginia 186
Rattenbury, Harry photo 76
Ravena 329
Raymond, Frances 465
Reader, Ronald 31
Rebecca of Sunnybrook Farm 152
Red Cross Martyr, A 320
Red Kimono, The 267
Redman, Minna 442
Reed, Opie 366
Regeneration 347
Reicher, Frank 366, 367, 379
Reid, Bertha 14, birth of Wallace 15-18, 24, 30, 32, 33, 36, 37, 40, 41, 43, 52-54, 57, 58, 63, 73, 77, 93, 147, 156, 159, 224, 227, 228, 232, 234, 235, 242, 250, 253, 263, 279, photos 30, 235
Reid, Betty Ann 8, 216-218, 223, 231, 244, 245, 249, 251, 277, 279, photos 217, 277
Reid, William "Billy" Wallace, Jr., 8, birth 144, 146, 155, 156, 179, 185, 200-204, 213, 217, 231,

244, 245, 251, 263, 264, 268, 274-277, 417, 433, photos 146, 185, 200, 202, 203, 204, 217, 264, 268, 274, 275, 276
Reid, Brian 274
Reid, Florence 70
Reid, James Halleck "Hal" 6, 12-18, early plays 25-27, 29, 32, 33, 35, 36, 41-43, 47, 52, 53, 56-59, at Selig 62, 63, 66, 72-75, 147, death 178, 320, 322-327, 329, 330, 341-343, 354, 358, 440, photos 12, 13
Reid, Hugh M. 14
Reid, John 14
Reid, Kathe 274
Reid, Lieutenant Colonel James 14
Reid, Mrs. Wallace (*see Dorothy Davenport*)
Reid, William "Wally" Wallace birth 15, theatrical childhood 17-18, in the St Louis Cyclone 18-24, childhood home 27, first stage appearance 29, confirmation 33, at military school 36, college 36-38, at the Irma Hotel 49 50, work on Shoshone River dam 50-52, working at newspapers 54, working on *Motor Magazine* 55, in Vaudeville 56, first film work 62, first role as film actor 63, as silent film mood musician 70, engagement to Elizabeth Modini-Wood 73, arriving in California 78, 1913 leg injury 91, marriage to Dorothy Davenport 93, at Universal 96, working for D. W. Griffith 97, in *The Birth of a Nation* 102, meeting Geraldine Farrar 122, in *The Rotters* play 132, first starring role in feature film132, with The Blue Bungalow Band 133, in *Intolerance* 134, in Lasky Home Guard 143, birth of son 144, train disaster 166, drug rumors 193, in *The Blue Flame* stage play 195, drug tests 198, making *Forever* 205, adopting daughter 216, blindness 226, angering US Congress 238, final film role 240, entering sanitarium 242, death 249
Reliance Film Company 76, 86, 89, 97, 102, 325-328, 354, 356, 358, 374
Rennick, Ruth 429
Rent Free 233, 457, 458, photos 458
Reporter, The 320
Rescued from an Eagle's Nest 39
Retribution 340
Rex Pictures 332, 333, 337, 344, 348
Rhodes, Billie photo 76
Rhodes, Elizabeth 472
Rice, Byron W. 27
Rice, Elmer 457
Rice, W. G. 329
Rich, Vivian 332, 336, 338, 340-343, 395
Richardson, George H. 193
Richardson, Jack 447
Richey, Will M. 417
Ricketts, Tom 327
Ridgely, Cleo 118, 136, 366, 367, 370, 372, 373, 379, 380, 382-386, photos 118, 136, 367, 372, 373, 379, 383, 385
Rimo, Ben 124
Rimrock Jones 153, 155, 156, 402, 403, photos 154, 155, 403
Ritchey, Will M. 419, 433
Road to Ruin, The 273

Roaring Road, The 158, 176, 421, 422, 433, photos 422
Robards, Willis 338
Roberts, Theodore 73, 250, 252, 386, 399, 400, 411, 421, 422-424, 429, 431, 433, 434, 445, 446, 447, 450, 459, 461, 473, photos 399, 422, 434, 447, 461
Robinson, Gertrude 325, 326, 332, 346
Rock, William, photo 67
Rogers, Charles B. 397
Roland, Ruth 93
Rolfe. B. A. 115
Romeo and Juliet 322
Roosevelt, Theodore 14
Rose of Old Mexico 338
Rosen, Philip E. 212, 214, 457, 459, 460, 461
Rosson, Arthur 332, 335, 336, 338
Rosson, Dick 70
Rosson, Richard 325
Royal, Edwin Milton 393
Russell, Annie 66, 383
Sackville, Gordon 84, photo 84
Sadler, Josie 344
Salisbury, Nate 50
Sandford, Stanley 457
Santley, Joseph 275
Santschi, Tom 64, 349, photo 64
Sarno, Hector 335
Sarver, Charles 382
Schnitzler, Arthur 450
Scott, Howard 383
Scott, Leroy 353
Sears, A. D. (*see Allan Sears*)
Sears, Allan 374, 382
Sears, O. O. 363
Second Mrs. Roebuck, The 354
Secret Service Man, The 327
Seepore Rebellion, The 329

Self-Enchanted, The 138
Selfish Woman, The 380, 381, photo 381
Selig Polyscope Company 61, 62, 63, 78, 318, 320, photo 61
Sennett, Mack 89, 472
Sessue Hayakawa 117
Seventh Son, The 323, photo 323
Shakespeare, William 322
Shea, William 321, photo 321
Shepard, Alice (*see Alice Davenport*)
Sheriff for an Hour 374
Shirk, Adam Hull 177
Short, Antrim 348, 349, 350
Short, Gertrude 338, 349, 350, 395, 457
Shortridge, Senator Samuel Morgan 238
Shubert, Jacob Lee 66
Shubert, Samuel S. 66
Sick Abed (film) 436-438, photos 437
Sick Abed (play) 225
Siegmann, George 100, 326, 353, 359, 366, 383
Sierra Jim's Reformation 354
Sills, Milton 473
Sinclair, Bertrand W. 393
Sioux Ghost Dance 44
Siren, The 351
Sisson, Vera 348
Sitting Bull 43
Skeleton, The 349
Slaves of Gold 29
Smalley, Phillips 343, 344, 348
Smith, Albert E. 31, 32, 63, 66, 67, photo 67
Someone and Somebody 415
Song Bird of the North 344
Source, The 411, 412, 413, photos 412

Southern, Eve 465
Spark of Manhood, The 351
Spaulding, George 395
Spearman, Frank H. 400, 445
Spider and Her Web, The 348
Spirit of the Flag 335
Squaw Man, The 115, 116
Squaw Man's Son, The 393, 394, photo 394
St. Denis, Ruth 383
St. Johns, Adela Rogers 52-54, 144, 158, 160, 203, 210, 245, 253
St. Louis Cyclone 18-26, photos 23
Stafford, Harry G. 347, 352
Standing, Jack 325
Stanley, Maxfield 358, 359, 382
Star Nickelodeon 62, photo 62
Starke, Pauline 383
Starlight's Message 378
Starr, Doctor 197
Station Content 374
Stedman, Lincoln 442
Stedman, Myrtle 390-391
Steel, William 329, 347
Steppling, John 436
Sterling, Ford 89
Stern, Jerome 275
Sterne, Elaine 350
Sterns, Edgar Franklin 417
Stevens, Edwin 429, 442, 443
Stevens, Emily 417
Stevens, K. T. 455
Stewart, Anita 320, 344
Stockdale, Carl 383
Storey, Edith 323, 324, 417
Street Singer, The 14
Struggle, The 280
Struss, Karl 450
Sucker Money 273
Sullivan, Edward P. 326
Sunset Boulevard 281, 282

Swager, Barbara 318, 320
Swain, Mack 89
Swanson on Swanson 198
Swanson, Gloria 152, 186, 198, 244, 282, 450, 451, 455-457, 473, photos 198, 451, 456
Sweet, Blanche 71, 98, 99, 100, 335, 344, 353, 354, 356, 359
Taaffe, Alice 424, 425
Tabor, Robert 325
Taft, Charles P. 14
Taft, Helen 347
Taft, William Howard 14, 63
Talmadge, Constance 71, 382
Talmadge, Norma 417
Tapley, Rose 320, 324, 327, 344
Tarkington, Booth 468
Tattooed Arm, The 342
Taylor, Rex 159
Taylor, William Desmond 160, death 214, 391-393
Taylor, Wilton 424, 429
Telephone Girl, The 323
Tellegen, Lou 122, 124, 125, 126, 127, 129, 141, 153, 156, 220, 282, 402, 404, photos 124, 127
Tell-Tale Arm, The 395
Tell-Tale Heart, The 353
Temptation 128, 132, 133
Ten Commandments, The 281
Tenbrook, Harry 329, 330
Tennyson, Alfred Lord 366
Terwilliger, George 356
Tess of the Storm Country 233
Test, The 349, 350, photo 350
Theby, Rosemary 320, 324
Their Masterpiece 335
Thing We Love, The 153, 402, 404, photo 404
This Day and Age 276
Thistle Film Company 84, photo 84

Thomas, A. E. 459, 470
Thomas Edison Motion Picture Patents Company 39, 44, 47
Thomas, Edward 330
Thompson, Fred 68
Thorn, Lizette 329, 330
Thornby, Robert 395, 396
Thorpe, Rose Hartwick 325
Three Brothers, The 374
Tincher, Fay 356
Titanic 87
Tittel, Essie 27
To Have and to Hold 138, 139, 281, 376-378, photos 139, 377
Tol'able David 190
Tomson, Frederick A. 329
Toncray, Kate 368, 442
Too Many Millions 156, 415, 416, photos 416
Too Much Johnson (play) 17
Too Much Speed 447, 448, photos 447
Top Man 280
Traffic in Souls 90
Trespasser, The 282
Triangle Film Corporation 368
Tribal Law, The 327
Trimble, Laurence 69, 320, 322, 329, 330
Trip to Paramountown, A 473
Truss, D. W. 18
Tucker, George Loane 90
Turnbull, Hector 380
Turnbull, Margaret 376, 384, 405, 407
Turner, Captain William Thomas 125
Turner, Florence 320, 322, 329, 330
Turner, Fred 363, 382
Turner, Otis 76, 77, 79, 80, 325, 327

Two Orphans, The 15
Two Reels and a Crank 66
Tyner, Thomas H. 182
Uncle Tom's Cabin 90
United Artists 159
Universal Film Manufacturing Company 75-77, 79, 89, 90, 92, 94-97, 112, 274, 326-330, 332-338, 340, 342-352, 378, 390, photo 76
Unseen Enemy, An 328
Unto the Fourth Generation (play) 40, 41
Urson, Frank 185, 188, 189, 421, 425, 445, 447-449
Valentino, Rudolph 190, 473
Valley of the Giants, The 166, 168, 171, 425-427, photos 171, 426, 427
Van Buren, Mabel 382, 393, 400
Van Trump, Jessalyn 332-334, 336, 338, 339, 342
Via Cabaret 342
Victoria Cross, The 324
Vidor, King 160
Virginius 329
Vitagraph 32, 63, 64, 65, 66, 67, 68, 69, 70, 71, 74, 86, 318-325, 327-330, photos 64, 65, 67, 321, 322, 331
Voice of the Viola, The 347
Von Kleinsmid, Dr. R. B. 260
Von Ritzau, Erik 368
Von Ritzau, Gunther 382
Von Seyffertitz, Gustav 400, 402, 409, 411
Von Stroheim, Eric (*see Erich Von Stroheim*)
Von Stroheim, Erich 368, 382
Von Stroheim, Eric, Jr. (*see Erich Von Stroheim, Jr.*)

Von Stroheim, Erich, Jr. 275, photo 275
Von Trump, Jessalyn 333
Wales, Ethel 465
Wall of Flame, The 141, 386
Wall of Money, The 332, 333, photo 333
Wallace Reid Foundation Sanitarium, photo 269
Wallace Reid His Life Story 278
Walsh, George 382
Walsh, Raoul 172, 354, 356, 359
Waltan, Fred 320
Walters, William 337
Walthall, Henry B. 82, 98, 101-104, 140, 320, 328, 344, 353, 356, 359, photos 104
Walton, Bennie (*see Thomas H. Tyner*)
Walton, Claude (*see Thomas H. Tyner*)
Walton, Fred 318
War 320
Ward, Fannie 117
Wark Producing Corporation 382
Warnack, Henry Christeen 346
Warner Bros. 344
Warner Features (*see Warner Bros.*)
Warrior's Bride, A 141, 386
Washburn, Bryant Jr., 275, photo 275
Way Down East 179, 190
Way of a Woman, The 348
Wayne, Maude 450
Wayne, Richard 415, 424
Ways of Fate, The 332
We Went to College 275, photo 275
Webb, George 384
Weber, Lois 344, 348
Wells, Raymond 368
Welman, Rita 204

West, Billie 353-355
West, Charles 411
Westbrook, Bertha Bell (*see Bertha Reid*)
Westbrook, Bertha Belle (*see Bertha Reid*)
Westbrooke, Virginia 325
Westover, Winifred 383
Whales of August, The 280
What's Your Hurry? 438-440, photos 439
Wheel of Life, The 346
When Jim Returned 336
When Knighthood Was in Flower 40
When Luck Changes 341
When the Light Fades 335
Whispering Smith 400
Whitlock, Lloyd 445
Who So Diggeth a Pit 348
Wife on a Wager, A 352
Wilde, Oscar 344
Wilder, Marshall P. 321, photo 321
Wilkes, Anna Tupper 358
Wilkes, W. E. 413
Williams, Ben Ames 440
Williams, Earle 323, 328, photo 323
Williams, Gus 18
Williams, Kathlyn 392, 393, 402, 404, 468, photos 392, 404
Williams, Percy 415
Willis, F. McGrew 352
Wilson, Fred 386
Wilson, Harold 322
Wilson, Jane E. 358
Wilson, Lois 438, 439, 448-450, 457, 460, photos 439, 449, 460
Wilson, Lucile 346-349
Wilson, Margery 382
Wilson, Thomas Woodrow 87, 107, 125, 142, 144
Wilson, Tom 359, 366, 382

Withers, Mae 14
Withey, Chet 338
Witwer, H. C. 110
Wolbert, William 348, 349, 350, 351, 352
Wolff, Jane 380, 386, 407, 409
Woman Condemned 273
Woman God Forgot, The 151, 152, 395, 398, photos 398
Women and Roses 348
Women and War 336, 337, photo 337
Wonderly, W. Carey 354
Wood, Sam 252, 431, 433-440, 455, 456
Woods, Frank 112
Woods, Joe 193, 272
Woods, Walter 424, 430, 462
Woodward, Henry 399, 405, 407, 422, 424
Working Girl's Wrongs, A 35
World Apart, The 214, 391
World's Champion, The 214, 215, 233, 457, 460, photos 214, 460
Worthington, Charles 93
Wray, John Griffith 258, 259
Wrong Heart, The 141, 386
Wycoff, Alvin 450
Wynn, Ed 137
Yankee from the West, A 366
Yellow Pawn, The 384-385, photo 385
You're Fired 422-424, photo 423
Young Hollywood 275
Young, Jack 438
Young, Rida Johnson 429
Youth and Jealousy 340
Yukon Patrol, The 276
Zany, King 475
Ziegfeld Follies 137, 138
Zukor 45-47, 71, 72, 87, 89, 99, 110, 128-131, 133, 138, 153, 180, 187, 199, 228, 250, 279, photo 46

www.ingramcontent.com/pod-product-compliance
Lightning Source LLC
Chambersburg PA
CBHW051332230426
43668CB00010B/1237